Edmond Biré, John de Villers

The Diary of a Citizen of Paris During 'The Terror'

Vol. I

Edmond Biré, John de Villers

The Diary of a Citizen of Paris During 'The Terror'
Vol. I

ISBN/EAN: 9783337044947

Printed in Europe, USA, Canada, Australia, Japan

Cover: Foto ©ninafisch / pixelio.de

More available books at **www.hansebooks.com**

THE DIARY

OF

A CITIZEN OF PARIS

DURING 'THE TERROR'

BY

EDMOND BIRÉ

TRANSLATED & EDITED BY JOHN DE VILLIERS

WITH TWO PORTRAITS

IN TWO VOLUMES

VOL. I

LONDON : CHATTO & WINDUS
NEW YORK : DODD, MEAD & CO.
1896

PREFACE

This does not pretend to be a history either of the Revolution or even of that period which, though so short, was yet so full of crime and anguish, and which will for ever bear the dread name of the Terror. The most that is attempted in these pages is to present to the world a phase of this lugubrious epoch in the form of a rough and simple sketch. I have read the greater part of the newspapers of the time, and have perused a considerable number of pamphlets; I have paid particular attention to bills and posters, and M. Gustave Bord was good enough to place at my disposal his collection of miscellaneous documents, made with great care and diligence. Living for months together amidst these witnesses of events long past, it almost seemed to me that I had become their contemporary; that, like the ' awakened sleeper ' of poor Cazotte—one of the first victims of the Terror —I, too, walked in the streets of the Paris of '93; that I frequented its public places; that, after a sitting of the Convention, I strolled into a café of the Maison Égalité; that I mingled with the crowd in the squares and the theatres, waiting my turn with the people in front of the bakers'-shops, following them sometimes with a heavy heart and swimming eyes as far as the Place de la Révolution or the barrier of the Trône Renversé, where the tumbrel came jolting along through the midst of the hooting mob, and heads fell to the cry of ' *Vive la République!*

Recognising that the sole means of ridding my mind of these dark visions was to commit them to paper, I did so, and called my notes " The Diary of a Citizen of Paris during the Terror."

I laid them aside for some time after writing them ; then one day I re-read my lines coolly and critically, as I would have read a stranger's work. Deciding to publish them, I thought it not unwise to add some notes and comments, for which I have drawn upon the latest works of historians and critics. I have left nothing undone in order to conscientiously fulfil my duty as an editor, and I have not hesitated to adduce any number of proofs, even at the risk of seeing the text swallowed up by the notes. The latter will at least prove, by their number and extent, that the most scrupulous care has been observed in the compilation of the Diary, that it contains no fiction, and that all the facts, even the most insignificant in appearance, are based upon authentic and contemporary documents.

History, I know, is a Muse, and the most serious and severe of all. But though she should always be treated with respect, can she not occasionally be approached more familiarly ? Are we forbidden to invite her to descend from the heights upon which she loves to hold converse with masters, and would it be derogatory to her dignity to chat for a moment with us in a manner more befitting our weakness ? I, for myself, do not regret having followed her along humbler paths, where I have unearthed many lost details, many generous but forgotten acts, much noble devotion which it is a pleasure to once more bring to light. At the very height of the Terror, whilst the Vendeans (the real and only heroes of '93) were shedding their blood for God and the King, how many honest citizens were there not in Paris—men and women of the people—who laid down their lives to save, or at least to honour, their religious and political opinions ! Historians take little note of them, but as it is only right for the humble to help each other, I have made a point of incorporating their deeds in the following pages.

In his life of Phocion, Plutarch relates how the enemies of that good citizen induced the people not only to order his body to be banished and carried out of Attic territory, but also to forbid any Athenian to bring fire to honour his obsequies. None of his friends dared, therefore, touch his body. A certain Conopion, who earned his living by this kind of work, carried the remains beyond the borders of Eleusis, and there burned them, whilst a woman of Megara carefully gathered up the ashes and buried them at night under her hearth. My ambition goes no farther than that. Like the woman of Megara, whose name Plutarch has not given us, I have piously gathered up the ashes of the vanquished and proscribed, and given them a humble resting-place. I think that I, in my turn, may address to my book the words she spoke to her sheltering hearth : 'I place in your keeping these relics of many good men, that you may guard them faithfully and return them some day to the tombs of their ancestors, when the Athenians shall recognise the wrong they have done them.'

The following lines, with which I may perhaps be permitted to head this work, are contained in the report of M. Camille Doucet, Permanent Secretary to the Académie Française, upon the literary competitions for the year 1889 :

' The second Gobert prize is awarded to M. Edmond Biré for an interesting volume entitled " Paris in 1793."[1] In this history of Paris in 1793 M. Edmond Biré places the narrative in the mouth of an imaginary witness, who gives an account day by day, not only of the events occurring in the capital during that awful year, but also of the impression made by them upon the terror-stricken mind of the public. This daily report possesses all the interest of romance and all the value of real history, not a single fact being advanced without some authority or document to support it. The recital, though of absorbing interest, has a natural and easy flow. The author is not unknown, either as a scholar or as a writer ; by a former work, entitled " The Diary of a Citizen of Paris," and of which the present volume is but a continuation, he had already gained the approbation of the Académie for qualities which that Institution is pleased once more to recognise, and this time to reward.'

[1] Incorporated in the present work.

CONTENTS OF VOL. I.

THE DIARY OF
A CITIZEN OF PARIS

CHAPTER I.

Friday, September 21, 1792.

YESTERDAY morning the walls of the capital bore the following proclamation which had been posted up during the night, and which brought to the cognizance of the Parisians the demise of the Legislative Assembly and the birth of the Convention:

'The National Assembly decrees: That the Archivist shall summon the deputies to meet in the National Convention to-morrow, September 20, at four o'clock in the afternoon, in the hall set apart for them in the national building of the Tuileries (the second apartment of the grand suite at the top of the grand staircase).

'That the Mayor of Paris shall give the necessary orders for a guard to be furnished for the members of the National Convention.

'That this decree shall be posted up to-night.'[1]

In conformity with this decree, the new representatives of the people met yesterday, at four o'clock in the afternoon, at the palace of the Tuileries, in the hall of the Cent-Suisses. The public was not admitted to this first sitting, no arrangements for its accommodation having yet been made. It was

---

[1] 'Archives Nationales,' CI. 382 (Ass. Pol. Législative).

1

half-past five when the sitting was opened, M. Ruhl, the deputy of the Bas-Rhin, the oldest member present, taking the chair. M. Tallien, member for Seine-et-Oise, and M. Penières, member for the Corrèze, performed the duties of secretaries.[1]

After the names had been called over, which showed 371 deputies to be present,[2] the verification of the powers of each member was proceeded with. This was confined to an examination of the election returns, and the proofs of identity of those elected; but when it came to the turn of the deputies of Paris, murmurs of protest and dissent were heard on all sides. Two or three members pointed out that the elections held at the beginning of September had been in the hands of the same men who had organized the massacres; they also protested against the substitution of open voting for the more legal and secret method of voting by ballot.[3] These protests led to no results. The deputies of Paris were admitted equally with all the others. In less than three hours the verification of the powers of the 371 members present was completed. The following resolution was then adopted:

'The citizens appointed by the French nation to form the National Convention, having met to the number of 371, and verified their powers, declare the National Convention duly constituted.'

The first act of the Convention thus constituted was to elect its President and Secretaries. The Constituent and Legislative Assemblies had always proceeded to this operation in the privacy of their offices, and not in a general sitting. The new representatives decided that the President and Secretaries should be elected by an open vote, though it was but a few moments since they had themselves condemned that manner of voting.[4]

---

[1] 'Procès-verbal de la Convention Nationale,' imprimé par son ordre, tome i.

[2] *Ibid.*

[3] The election returns of the departments of the Bouches-du-Rhône, la Corrèze, la Drôme, les Hautes-Pyrénées, l'Hérault, le Lot, l'Oise, and Seine-et-Marne, prove that the adoption of open voting was not limited to Paris. Of the 106 deputies thus elected in violation of the law by these nine departments and Paris, 74 voted for the death of Louis XVI.

[4] 'Mémoires pour servir à l'Histoire de la Convention Nationale,' by Daunou, ch. ii.

Petion obtained 235 votes for the presidency,[1] a few votes being divided between Robespierre and Danton.[2] Condorcet, Brissot, Rabaut Saint-Étienne, Lasource, Vergniaud, and Camus were appointed Secretaries.[3]

A rather important incident marked this election. Just as the Assembly was about to vote, M. Dubois-Crancé, a former member of the Constituent Assembly, and who now sat for the Ardennes, the Var, the Isère, and the Bouches-du-Rhône, asked whether it was right that the first act of the Convention—the election of its President—should be performed with closed doors, and in the absence of the *people of Paris*. His last words were quickly taken up by several deputies, who declared that they were not sent by their departments to court the suffrages of the people of Paris.[4]

The Assembly rose half an hour after midnight,[5] and its second meeting was fixed for ten o'clock next morning at the same place.[6]

————————

The majority of the historians of the Revolution are silent concerning this first sitting of the National Convention held at the Tuileries on September 20. Thiers and Mortimer-Ternaux alone devote a few lines to it. Mignet, Lamartine, Barante, Michelet, and Louis Blanc, ignore it altogether, and seem to think that the Convention met for the first time on September 21, 1792. 'The Republic,' says Louis Blanc (tome vii., p. 223), 'was proclaimed at the first sitting of the Convention. Of the 749 men who met on

[1] 'Procès-verbal de la Convention Nationale,' tome i.

[2] *Révolutions de Paris*, No. 167. 'Robespierre obtained six or seven votes; he was present, but stood apart, mute and motionless. All eyes were turned upon him, but their glances spoke rather of insult than of respect.'—DAUNOU, *op. cit.*

[3] This is the fate which was reserved for the seven members who formed the first officers of the Convention: Petion, outlawed on July 28, 1793, committed suicide in June, 1794, to escape the scaffold; Condorcet, accused on October 3, 1793, arrested at Bourg-al-Reine on March 27, 1794, poisoned himself in prison; Brissot was guillotined on October 31, 1793; Rabaut Saint-Étienne, guillotined on December 5, 1793; Lasource, guillotined on October 31, 1793; Vergniaud, guillotined on October 31, 1793. Camus alone survived the Convention, General Dumouriez having saved his life by delivering him up to the Prince of Saxe-Coburg on April 1, 1793.

[4] *Révolutions de Paris, loc. cit.*

[5] 'Procès-verbal de la Convention Nationale.'

[6] 'Histoire Parlementaire de la Révolution,' by Buchez and Roux, tome xix., p. 9.

September 21, 1792, in that small apartment of the Tuileries in which so many deaths were to be decreed, how few were to return to their homes!' In these four lines there are six mistakes.

The first sitting of the Convention took place, as we have seen, on September 20, and not on September 21.

The Republic was not proclaimed during the sitting of September 21, 1792; it is even a very remarkable fact that not one of all the speakers who called upon the Convention to pronounce the abolition of the Monarchy mentioned the word 'Republic!'

The deputies who met, on September 21, first at the Tuileries, and afterwards in the Riding-School (see our second chapter), numbered 371, and not 749.

The abolition of the Monarchy was decreed in the Riding-School, and not in one of the apartments of the Tuileries.

The apartment of the Tuileries in which the Convention held its first sitting, and in which its members again met on the morning of the 21st, was the hall of the Cent-Suisses, situated in the central pavilion, or Pavillon de l'Horloge. When on May 10, 1793, it definitively took up its abode in the Tuileries, it did not return to its former quarters, but occupied the theatre, situated between the central pavilion and the Pavillon Marsan.

The theatre of the Tuileries, which had been inaugurated in 1671 by Molière's 'Psyché,' and in which Voltaire had been crowned in 1778—in which the Convention sat from May 10, 1793, until October 26, 1795, and in which so many deaths were, indeed, decreed—was by no means a small apartment, for it could hold several thousand spectators.

Michelet is as unfortunate in his account of the opening of the Convention as Louis Blanc. In tome iv., p. 329, he writes: 'Opening of the Convention (September 21, '92),' and he adds: 'On September 21 the Assembly crowds into the small hall of the Tuileries that had served as a theatre. This little Court theatre is to contain a world—a world of infernal storms, the pandemonium of the Convention. The smaller the arena, the more fierce will be the struggles. . . . From the very first day, from the very first moment when they saw each other, these men suffered from their too close proximity. The few feet that separated these deadly enemies permitted neither a hostile word nor look to be lost,' etc. The picture is eloquently drawn, and Michelet creates a great effect with his little Court theatre; he, however, forgets one thing, and this is that the Convention did not enter into occupation of it until eight months later!

CHAPTER II.

Sunday, September 23, 1792.

On Friday,[1] at the same hour as the members of the Convention were assembling for the second time in the hall of the Cent-Suisses, the members of the Legislative Assembly were taking their places on the benches in the Riding-School.[2] An immense crowd filled the galleries, and had it not been for my friend Beaulieu,[3] who is well acquainted with the ushers of the National Assembly, it would certainly have been impossible for me to gain admission. In the hall itself there were, on the contrary, very few deputies present ; since the Tenth of August, the majority of the members of the Right—*constitutionnels, feuillants, feuillantins,*

---

[1] September 21, 1792.

[2] The Riding-School stood on part of the ground now forming the Rue de Rivoli, near the corner of the Rue de Castiglione.

[3] Claude François Beaulieu, journalist and historian, was born at Riom in 1754, and died in Paris in 1827. On June 27, 1789, he founded the paper called *L'Assemblée Nationale,* devoted to the reports of the sittings of the Constituent Assembly, and took part in editing the *Nouvelles de Paris* in 1790, the *Postillon de la Guerre* in 1792, and the *Courrier Français* in 1793. Arrested on the 8th of Brumaire, year II. (October 29, 1793), he was detained first in the Conciergerie, and afterwards in the Luxembourg until the fall of Robespierre. Set at liberty, he again turned to journalism, and was a second time proscribed. On the 18th of Fructidor of the year V. (September 4, 1797), sentence of transportation was passed upon him as editor of the Royalist sheet called *Le Miroir,* but he was fortunate enough to elude the emissaries of the Directory. Besides his 'Diurnal de la Révolution de France pour l'An de Grâce 1797,' Beaulieu published six volumes entitled 'Essais Historiques sur les Causes et les Effets de la Révolution Française' (1801-1803). From 1813 to 1827 he wrote most of the notices for Michaud's *Biographie Universelle* of the men of the Revolution. Few writers were better acquainted with that epoch, and even to-day there is no better work extant on the French Revolution than Beaulieu's 'Essais Historiques.'

modérés, *modérantins* and Fayétistes, all of which names they have successively adopted or received—have ceased to attend the sittings. There were, likewise, many empty places amongst the Montagnards and the Brissotins, but from another cause. Nearly 200 members of the Left have been elected to the Convention,[1] and they were at the Tuileries with their new colleagues.

A little after eleven o'clock twelve Commissioners from the Convention enter the hall of the Riding-School. One of them, M. Grégoire, a former member of the Constituent Assembly, and Bishop of Loir-et-Cher, announces that the National Convention is constituted, and that it is about to take possession of the usual place of the Legislation. This declaration is received with a tempest of cheers from the galleries. The President, M. François de Neufchâteau, at last manages to obtain a hearing, and proclaims that the Legislative Assembly has completed its mission. He vacates his seat, and, followed by his colleagues, proceeds to the Tuileries to meet the new Assembly.

Whilst awaiting the reopening of the sitting, Beaulieu draws my attention to the presence of Bernardin de Saint-Pierre in one of the galleries. The author of the 'Etudes de la Nature' was elected a deputy by the department of Loir-et-Cher, but did not see fit to accept the dignity.[2] Less forgetful than so many others, he still remembers the words addressed to him by Louis XVI. on his appointment as Director of the Jardin des Plantes and the Cabinet d'Histoire Naturelle : 'I have read your works ; they are those of an honest man, and in appointing you I have sought a worthy successor to Buffon.' The writer of the

---

[1] Of the 749 members of the Convention, 77 had formed part of the Constituent, and 192 of the Legislative Assembly. Mortimer-Ternaux (tome iv., p. 457) has given a list of the members of the two Assemblies elected to the Convention. Montgaillard ('Histoire de France depuis la Fin du Règne de Louis XVI.,' tome iii., p. 387) errs in stating that only 75 Conventionalists had sat in the Constituent and 174 in the Legislative Assembly. Jules Claretie also makes a double mistake in his work on 'Camille Desmoulins et les Dantonistes,' where he says (p. 204) : 'There were 45 ex-Constituents and 147 ex-Legislators in the Convention.'

[2] No mention is made in any of the biographies of Bernardin de Saint-Pierre of his election to the National Convention. See in the recent and remarkable work by Gustave Bord on the 'Proclamation de la République' the extract from the election returns in the department of Loir-et-Cher.

'Vœux d'un Solitaire' was certainly not born to sit in this pandemonium by the side of the heroes of June 20, of the Tenth of August, and of September 2. If he cares to busy himself with the interests of mankind, and with those of his country, it is 'at the end of his garden, on a little mossy bank, in the shade of a flowering apple-tree.'

At a quarter-past twelve the members of the National Convention left the hall of the Cent-Suisses, and, crossing the garden, proceeded to the Riding-School. As they entered the hall two by two, the galleries received them with enthusiasm. This was, however, redoubled when the Duc d'Orléans appeared arm-in-arm with Citizen Armonville, a wool-comber, who had on September 4 been elected representative of the Marne, as a reward for his share in the massacres of Rheims. Armonville was adorned with a red cap.[1]

M. Petion then took the chair, and Camus, Condorcet, Vergniaud, Brissot, Rabaud Saint-Étienne and Lasource seated themselves at the clerks' table. When all the other deputies were seated, and the sitting was declared open, the spectators were struck by the small number of members present, more than half the deputies not having yet arrived.

Another fact was also much commented upon.

In the Constituent Assembly the parties known as the Right and the Left sat according to their appellation—the members of the Right to the right, and those of the Left to the left of the President. This was the practice at Versailles,[2] and things remained unchanged when the Assembly was removed to Paris and established in the Riding-School.[3] When the Constituent Assembly was replaced by the Legislative Assembly, the Feuillants and the Constitutionnels, who were about to form the new Right, occupied the seats to the right of the President's chair, the name of the party therefore still remaining in accord with its actual place. Since last January, however, a change has been made. In its sitting of December 27, 1791, the Legislative

[1] 'Mémoires pour servir à l'Histoire de la Convention Nationale,' Daunou, ch. i.

[2] *Moniteur* of 1789, No. 48 ; 'Mémoires de M. de Clermont-Gallerande,' tome i., p. 86.

[3] November 9, 1789.

Assembly determined to rearrange its seats in such a way as to bring the Right to the left, and *vice versâ*.

The *Ami du Roi*, edited by the Abbé Royon, spoke of this change in the following terms in its number of December 30 :

'There being nothing left to upset in the monarchy, our legislators have taken it into their heads to turn their own Assembly topsy-turvy. The President's chair will take the place of the tribune, and the tribune will occupy the space formerly given up to the most illustrious throne in the world and to the clerks' table. It is hoped that this change may help to break down the barrier between the Right and the Left. . . . But, whatever is done, there will always be a Right and a Left in the Assembly, and the good will always manage to separate themselves from the bad.'

The *Journal de Paris* gave the following details :

'The hall of the National Assembly is about to be transformed ; one of the principal changes is that the tribune will be placed at the extremity of the left side, and the President's chair almost half-way up the right side. This will have the effect of making the hall seem shorter, and though neither the President nor the Speaker will retain their former places, their relative position will be unaltered, as they will still face each other across the hall. We trust that this change, which brings members into a closer physical proximity, may soon cause but one opinion to prevail, and inspire the majority, or, rather, the whole of the Assembly, divided only upon the means of success, with the desire of firmly establishing the Constitution and liberty !'

The change referred to by the *Ami du Roi* and the *Journal de Paris* was already an accomplished fact by the first days of 1792, and in its number of January 6 the *Patriote Français* stated that the Patriots would henceforth sit on the right of the President. 'It is idle to think that the change in the hall of the National Assembly will end the division between the Patriots and the Moderates. The division is, and will be, as lasting as the Constitution, as society, as humanity, and the party opposed to the people will always be despised and spat upon, wherever it may sit. We can, therefore, only laugh at the little trick that has been played upon the Patriots by placing the President's chair where the tribune used to be. The Patriots are thus become the Right ; but what matters it ? The Right will now be honourable.' In its number of January 7, the *Ami du Roi*, too, said : ' By the change made in the Assembly, the Right has become the Left, and the Left the Right.'

From that moment, and until the end of the Legislative Assembly, the members of the Mountain[1] and the deputies of the Brissot party[2] therefore sat on the right of the President, whilst the Feuillants sat on his left. Nevertheless the Brissotins and the Montagnards still continued to be called the members of the Left, while the Constitutionnels and the Feuillants still kept the name of the Right. On Friday last no deputy could be found to take a seat on the President's left, that is, on the benches formerly occupied by the Royalist Constitutionnels ; all went over to the right, where the Patriots of the Legislative Assembly were sitting. As, however, the same side would not hold them all, and as, moreover, the members from Bordeaux and their friends were not at all anxious to sit with Marat and the members for Paris, who had taken their seats near the Mountain, at the right extremity of the hall, the centre benches were gradually filled ; a few members even went so far as to seat themselves in despair on the left of the President's chair,[3] occupying the places once filled by the Girardins, the Beugnots, the Ramonds, the Dumas, the Quatremères, and the Jaucourts.

After the first moment of confusion has passed, the spectators in the galleries begin to look out for the more celebrated among the members. Beaulieu is not backward in pointing them out to me. He has attended nearly every sitting of the Constituent and Legislative Assemblies ; he knows everybody, and all that is going on, and one of my principal reasons for keeping this diary is that he has undertaken to furnish me with the particulars for it. He has promised to keep me well posted up in all the news, and in what goes on behind the scenes. I will now pass in review with him the most noteworthy of our new masters.

With his tall stature, his noble mien and his beautiful white

[1] A name applied to the extreme Democratic Party, from the circumstance of their occupying the highest seats in the hall.

[2] The appellation of Girondins was unknown at the time of the Legislative Assembly, and only came into vogue in January, 1793. See my book on the 'Légende des Girondins,' p. 33, etc.

[3] 'Physionomie de la Convention Nationale,' by J. A. Dulaure, deputy, in *Le Thermomètre du Jour*, January 1, 1793.

hair, Petion looks every inch a chairman. Unfortunately his features, pleasing enough at the first glance, are dull and without expression upon closer examination. Although they are by no means harsh, there is something in them that repels confidence, while his receding brow indicates the mediocrity of his intellect. His hair is curled with an affectation unbecoming in a statesman, and recently gave rise to the following just observation in the *Ami du Peuple:* 'Some of our sages, surprised at always seeing you with your hair so neatly curled in these troublous times, beg me to remind you of the value of time, especially to a magistrate, all of whose moments belong to the people.'[1]

The Secretaries are scrutinized as closely as the President, especially two, Brissot and Vergniaud. The latter is not beautiful; he has a big nose, thick lips, bushy eyebrows, and a pale face thickly pock-marked. But his forehead is broad and high, his black eyes sparkle with intelligence, and his glance, when he is not lost in thought, is very searching. His hair is very thick, and is powdered and frizzed like Mirabeau's.[2]

Brissot, who has long ago discarded both powder and tail, wears his hair long and flat. He is below the medium height, but it is easy to distinguish an energetic soul in this small body. His pale face and his grave and melancholy air form a striking contrast to the ruddy features and lively air of his colleague Camus.[3]

Among the members who took their seats on the centre benches may be seen M. La Revellière-Lépeaux, an old member of the Constituent Assembly, and the Abbé Fauchet, formerly a member of the Legislative Assembly and Bishop of Calvados. Small in stature and hunch-backed, M. La Revellière-Lépeaux forms a grotesque figure with his thin legs, greasy hair, and his cold, washed-out face. Beaulieu compares him to a cork

---

[1] 'Marat, the Friend of the People, to Maitre Jérôme Petion': *L'Ami du Peuple*, September 21, 1792. For Petion's portrait, see Mercier, 'Le Nouveau Paris,' xxxvi.; 'Mémoires' of Brissot, iii. 198; Bertrand de Moleville, 'Mémoires,' i. 231, 'Mémoires' of the Comte Lavallette, i. 67; 'Bibliothèque Nationale Cabinet des Estampes.'

[2] 'Notice sur Vergniaud,' by François Alluaud, his nephew.

[3] 'Souvenirs sur Mirabeau,' by Etienne Dumont.

stuck upon two pins.[1] The Abbé Fauchet, on the contrary, is one of the handsomest men in the Assembly; his face beams with kindness and good nature; he has laid aside his clerical costume for a suit of dark brown.[2] Not far from the Bishop of Calvados, Louvet, the editor of the *Sentinelle*, is carrying on a conversation with Gorsas, the author of the 'Courrier des Départements.' Citizen Louvet,[3] with his blue eyes, fair hair, and delicate features, the sweet soft expression of his face and his slim and elegant figure, forms a complete contrast to Gorsas, who is broad-shouldered, has an immense nose, black hair and beard, black eyes, and thick bushy eyebrows.[4]

The members for Paris nearly all sit in the Mountain, to the right of the President. Danton, with his pock-marked face, terrible in its ugliness, and his piercing eyes, reminds one of the elder Mirabeau, the great orator of the Constituent Assembly.[5] Near him sits Camille Desmoulins, his colleague in the Ministère de la Justice. Camille's joy is so great that he can scarcely contain himself; his bilious face is quite lit up. His smile was never more sardonic, nor were his black eyes ever more brilliant; as he proudly raises his broad and well-shaped brow, his long black hair falls back and almost touches his shoulders. Alas! my poor Camille, your 465 electors may have turned you into a deputy, but in spite of their votes you are, and will remain, a stammerer.[6] M. Robert, another of the men employed by Danton after the Tenth of August, is as eager as Camille to show his intense satisfaction, a feeling shared by his mistress, Mdlle. de Kéralio, who is seated in the front row of our gallery. M. Robert often turns towards us his fat face shining with pleasure and health.[7]

On these same benches now occupied by the assassins of

---

[1] 'Les Brigands Demasqués,' by Danican; Lavallette's 'Mémoires': 'Testament et Mort de La Revellière-Lépeaux, Chef des Filous en Troupe' (name given by the people to the theophilanthropists).

[2] 'Vergniaud,' by Ch. Vatel, ii. 329.

[3] Preface to Louvet's 'Mémoires'; D'Allonville, 'Mémoires Secrets,' iii. 302.

[4] *Courrier de Paris*, January 24, 1791.

[5] Beaulieu, 'Biographie Universelle,' article 'Danton.'

[6] 'Souvenirs de la Terreur,' by G. Duval, i. 51; 'Camille Desmoulins,' by J. Claretie, p. 134.

[7] Mme. Roland, 'Mémoires,' Dauban edition, p. 327.

September, and seated near such men as Panis and Sergent, I am grieved to see David, the painter of Socrates, and Marie Joseph Chénier, the author of 'Charles IX.,' both of whom I used to meet in the brilliant *salon* of the Trudaines in the Place Louis XV., now closed by the Revolution.[1] Chénier seems to be more gloomy than usual; a deep melancholy spreads itself like a veil over his pronounced features and puckered brow; his countenance is decidedly more tragic than his plays.[2] Dressed with care and excellent taste, and with his brown locks slightly frizzed, David still wears a society air quite out of keeping with the unkempt appearance of many of his colleagues. His glance is severe, and his face is almost completely disfigured by a swelling in one of his cheeks.[3] He seems to be on most affectionate terms with an ugly, vulgar-looking little man, whose features he is no doubt ambitious to transmit to posterity, for the little man is no other than the famous Drouet, the Postmaster of Sainte-Menehould, now deputy for the Marne.[4]

Some members of the 'Jacobins' and the 'Cordeliers' who are seated near Beaulieu and myself point with legitimate pride to their favourite orators, Billaud-Varenne, Legendre, and Collot-d'Herbois, who have passed direct from these clubs to the National Convention. To hear them, this ex-comedian, with his curled coal-black hair, is more eloquent than Vergniaud himself. They cannot praise too highly the power of his voice and the beauty of his delivery. 'You will see,' they cry, 'that this good Collot has no equal!' They are no less enthusiastic concerning the oratorical powers of Citizen Chabot, the ex-Capucine of Rodez. Their glances rest lovingly upon his greasy head, and his dress awakens their most tender feelings. Like a true *sans-culotte*,

---

[1] Concerning the Trudaines, see Lacretelle, 'Dix Années d'Épreuves pendant la Révolution,' and the introduction to the 'Œuvres en Prose d'André Chénier,' by L. Becq de Fouquières. Of the two brothers Trudaine, one, Trudaine de la Sablière, lived in the Rue des Francs-Bourgeois; the other, Trudaine de Montigny, occupied one of the mansions under the colonnade of the Place Louis XV. Both were guillotined on the 8th of Thermidor, year II., a day after their friend André Chénier.

[2] 'Mes Récapitulations,' by Bouilly, tome ii., p. 260.

[3] 'Louis David, son École et son Temps,' by E. J. Delécluze, p. 29.

[4] Montlozier, 'Mémoires,' ii. 151.

Chabot leaves his neck and chest uncovered, wears a jacket instead of a coat, and dispenses with all nether garments except a pair of knee-breeches of common material.[1] But our Jacobins are by no means exclusive ; while approving the severe garb of Chabot, they also admire the correct and elegant costume of Robespierre, with his frills and cuffs. Robespierre is of medium height, and looks rather delicate. His long chestnut hair is thrown back from a somewhat projecting brow; his nose is straight, and carried with a slight upward tendency. His blue eyes are rather deeply set, and his lips are long, pale, and closely pressed together.[2]

Right at the summit of the Mountain, higher than Danton and Robespierre, sits the Friend of the People, the hideous Marat. I was able to examine him closely. He has a large bony face, a flat nose, thin lips, eyes of grayish-yellow, a livid withered complexion, black beard, and brown hair.[3] Every muscle of his body is constantly being moved by a nervous twitching that makes it difficult for him to keep his seat. Affecting an air of slovenliness,[4] he wears a dirty overcoat, a pair of leathern breeches, shoes without stockings, and a handkerchief tied about his head.[5] Such is the Friend of the People, the man before whom all honest people tremble, before whom all villains bow. Has the Revolution upset the Monarchy only to substitute Marat's dirty handkerchief for the royal crown of the Bourbons ?

Meanwhile all confusion, noise, and private conversation has ceased. The sitting has commenced, and several members are already on their legs. The first to ascend the tribune is Mathieu, deputy for the Oise. Ducos, deputy for the Gironde ; Manuel, deputy for Paris ; Simond, deputy for the Bas-Rhin, and Chabot follow him in close succession. 'Representatives of the people,' cries the last-named member, 'I ask

---

[1] Beaulieu, 'Biographie Universelle,' article 'Chabot.'

[2] 'Vie Secrète de Maximilien Robespierre'; Ch. Nodier, 'Souvenirs de la Révolution et de l'Empire'; 'La Jeunesse de Robespierre,' by M. Paris.

[3] 'Portrait de Marat,' by Fabre d'Églantine, representative of the people. Paris, year II., at Maradan's ; 8vo.

[4] Fabre d'Églantine, op. cit.

[5] 'Histoire des Montagnards,' by Alphonse Esquiros, ii., p. 195.

you never to forget that it is the *sans-culottes* who have sent you here.' The word *sans-culottes*, well emphasized by Chabot, is heard without a murmur by the Assembly, and received enthusiastically by the galleries.

A warm welcome is also accorded, a few minutes later, to Couthon, deputy for the Puy-de-Dôme. Couthon has both legs paralyzed, and is obliged to be carried into the tribune by two of his colleagues. The infirmity from which he suffers, the delicacy of his features, his sweet but impassioned glances, and the persuasive accents of his voice, are calculated to gain him interest and sympathy.[1] But take care. Under this pitiful appearance, behind these winning manners, there lies concealed an unconquerable ambition, envenomed by the recollection of his incurable and horrible infirmity.[2] Beaulieu, who watched and studied him closely during the time of the Legislative Assembly, said to me on leaving the hall : ' Be on your guard against weaklings and cripples !' ' I have no fear,' said Couthon, ' that the Monarchy will ever be mentioned again. It is fit only for slaves, and the French would be unworthy of the liberty they have gained were they to think of preserving a form of government marked by fourteen centuries of crime.'

Collot-d'Herbois puts the question in a more categorical fashion. ' The abolition of the Monarchy,' he cries, ' is a matter that you cannot put off till to-morrow, that you cannot put off till to-night, that you cannot put off one moment without betraying the wishes of the nation.' In vain does Quinette, deputy for the Aisne, maintain that the question should be adjourned until the Constitution itself is under discussion. Grégoire, still wearing his clerical garb, rushes to the tribune. ' There never was a dynasty,' says the Bishop of Loir-et-Cher, ' that was not a devouring race, living on human flesh. I demand that a solemn law be passed abolishing the Monarchy.' Basire, deputy

---

[1] ' Les Conventionnels d'Auvergne,' by M. Bondet, p. 110.

[2] ' It appears that during the autumn of 1787 or 1788 Couthon spent a whole night in a very damp place whilst waiting for an opportunity to make his way into the house where his lady-love lived. A few months later he was attacked by acute pains, which, in spite of every remedy and treatment, culminated in September, 1791, in the entire paralysis of his nether limbs.'—Extract from the ' Notes inédites' of M. de Barante. See also ' Les Conventionnels d'Auvergne,' by M. Bondet.

for the Côte-d'Or, points out what a terrible example it would be for the people if it saw an Assembly, charged with the safety of its highest interests, arriving at conclusions in a moment of enthusiasm; he demands that the question be discussed. 'What need is there for discussion?' replies M. Grégoire. 'Kings are morally what monsters are physically. Courts are the workshops of crime, and the lairs of tyrants. History is the martyrology of nations. We are all equally convinced of this truth. What need is there for discussion? Let us vote, and leave till afterwards the drafting of a resolution worthy of the solemnity of the occasion.' M. Ducos, one of the youngest members of the Convention, rises, and says: 'The preamble of your resolution will be the story of the crimes of Louis XVI., a story with which the French people is only too familiar. There is no need for explanation after the light shed by the dawn of the Tenth of August.'

'Vote! Vote!' is the cry that now comes from all sides. The debate is closed, and a deep silence ensues. M. Grégoire's resolution is then put to the vote in the following terms:

'*The National Convention decrees that the Monarchy is abolished in France.*'

It is carried amid shouts of 'Vive la nation! Vive la liberté!'

Of all the members of the Convention, the first to rise in favour of the decree was a deputy seated at the second corner to the right of the President; it is d'Orléans—Joseph Égalité![1]

The sitting terminated at four o'clock. Superstitious people have remarked that the Monarchy, overturned on Friday, the Tenth of August, was abolished on Friday, September 21.

The minute read at the opening of the sitting by M. Camus, one of the Secretaries, gave the number of deputies present as 371.[2] The number of absentees must, therefore, have been

[1] 'Mémoires Historiques et Politiques du Règne de Louis XVI.,' by Soulavie, vi., p. 476.

[2] *Révolutions de Paris*, No. 168. Mortimer-Ternaux (tome iv., p. 64) thinks that the number given—371—is too high, and quotes the following fact in support of his opinion: 'The notes left by M. Fockedey, a deputy of the Nord, show that he did not arrive in Paris until September 24, and that the Committee of Inspection on that day handed him a card bearing the number 304. It is highly probable that the number of members whose election had been verified by an official return was intentionally substituted for that of the members actually present.'

378, since the deputies elected to the Convention form a total of 749. Thus was this decree abolishing a Monarchy of fourteen centuries passed in a few minutes, without report or debate, by the deputies present merely rising from their seats, and in an Assembly that was still lacking more than half its members.

The decree of the Convention, immediately transmitted to the forty-eight sections, was proclaimed with a flourish of trumpets at all the cross-roads the same evening. At nightfall bands of *sans-culottes* patrolled the streets, calling upon the inhabitants to light up the fronts of their houses. The greater part of the citizens complied with this demand, and until two o'clock in the morning, the city, illuminated as on a day of victory, re-echoed with threats of death against the King, the Queen, and the aristocrats.[1]

It is a remarkable fact that though the Convention, in its sitting of September 21, declared the Monarchy abolished, it did not formally decree the establishment of the Republic. It was not till the morrow, and in an indirect way, that the Republic was legally recognised. At the commencement of the sitting of September 22, the Convention, on the motion of Billaud-Varenne, decreed that 'all public acts were to be dated from the first year of the Republic.' The seal of State was to bear the following words: 'République de France.' The national seal would represent a female figure seated upon a bundle of arms, and holding in her hand a pike surmounted by the cap of Liberty.[2]

Beaulieu pointed out to me this morning that this decree, passed amidst great confusion and when the sitting was scarcely opened, was not to be found either in the report of the *Moniteur* or in that of most of the other papers. 'The Monarchy,' he added, 'was abolished amidst a good deal of noise, but the Republic has not been proclaimed. Its warmest friends seem to have blushed for it upon its introduction into the world. It had to be smuggled in, as if it were contraband.' 'That is true,' I replied, 'but it is also a fact that France became a Republic on the day that the Legislative Assembly shouted,

---

[1] *Révolutions de Paris*, No. 167.
[2] *Ibid.*, No. 168.

" *No more kings!*" and all its members swore eternal hatred to
the Monarchy.   That day was September 4, and for seventy-two
hours Paris had already been given up to cut-throats.   On the
2nd massacres had been going on at the Abbaye, at the Carmes,
at the Force, at the Châtelet, and at the Conciergerie; on the
3rd at the Bernardins, at Saint-Firmin, and at Bicêtre.   On the
4th they continued, during the whole day, at the Abbaye, the
Force, and at Bicêtre.   On the morning of that self-same day,
too, thirty-five women were murdered in the Salpêtrière.
Whilst these things were happening, the Legislative Assembly
was peacefully holding a sitting, at ten in the morning, in the
Riding - School.   Citizen Chabot, one of the Commissaries
charged by the Assembly to superintend the sections, to speak
to the people, and to re-establish tranquillity, mounted the
tribune, and declared that the sole means of restoring order was
to give the people the satisfaction which they demanded and which
was their due.   An authoritative proclamation should be issued
that the deputies held all Kings in abhorrence.   "Declare," he
said, "that you are convinced, by fatal experience, of the vices
of monarchs and monarchy, and that you will eternally detest
them!"   And the whole Assembly shouted: "Yes; we swear it!
There shall be no more Kings!"   Henry Larivière, deputy for
Calvados, added: "We swear by all that we hold most sacred
that no monarch shall ever sully the shrine of Liberty with our
consent.   I ask that M. Chabot be invited to draw up the form
of this oath."[1]   Guadet, one of the most prominent members
for Bordeaux, then rose and said: "The Commission Extraordinaire has anticipated the wishes of the last speaker and of
the Assembly.   In its sitting of last night it drew up an
address, which contains the oath that you have just taken."   He
proceeded to read this "Address to the French," which was
unanimously adopted, and which finished with these words:
" *Your representatives have sworn to struggle with all their
might against monarchs and monarchy.*"   The real date of the
abolition of the monarchy is therefore September 4.   The
Republic was born on that day, at the very hour when the
streets of Paris were flowing with blood, and it was baptized on

[1] *Moniteur* of September 6, 1792.

the 22nd by Billaud-Varenne, the man who on September 2 got upon a scaffold in the courtyard of the Abbaye and addressed his *workmen* in these words: "My friends, my good friends, I shall take care that you are paid the wages that were agreed upon. Be as noble, as great, and as generous as the profession which you follow ; let all things on this great day be worthy of the people whose sovereignty is committed to your care."[1] That is the man who baptized the Republic. Its sponsors were Chabot, an unfrocked monk, Collot-d'Herbois, an actor hissed from the stage, Grégoire, an apostate priest, and Ducos, one of those young men easily caught by fine phrases and high-sounding words.'

'You forget,' rejoined Beaulieu, 'that amongst the good fairies who were present at the baptism of the young Republic, and who promised it their assistance, there was also the paralytic Couthon.'

That less than half the members of the Convention were present when the motion abolishing the Monarchy was adopted is undoubtedly a very striking fact, and yet neither Thiers, Mignet, Lamartine, nor Michelet has taken the trouble to mention it. Louis Blanc (tome vii., p. 223) even asserts, in the face of the official reports, that the 749 members of the Convention were present at the sitting of September 21.

Thiers, Mignet, Lamartine, and Michelet have also omitted to note that at this sitting the Convention forgot to proclaim the establishment of the Republic. Here again Louis Blanc does not hesitate to place himself in contradiction with facts, and writes on p. 233: 'The Assembly votes (sitting of September 21), and the Republic is proclaimed amid loud cheers, which, taken up by all the spectators, are prolonged for several minutes.' Barante ('Histoire de la Convention Nationale,' tome i., p. 333), is careful not to fall into the same error. He states that Billaud-Varenne having proposed 'that all public acts should in future be dated from the year I. of the French Republic, and that the State seal should bear the fasces surmounted by the cap of Liberty, the Assembly, amid noise that drowned the speaker's voice, passed this decree which finds no place in the *Moniteur's* report.' He is, however, wrong

---

[1] Letter written by the Abbé Sicard to one of his friends on the dangers he underwent on September 2 and 3, 1792.

in saying that it was passed at the end of the sitting of the 21st; this was really done at the opening of the sitting of the 22nd.

Although Ternaux is the most exact of all the historians of the Revolution—a fact which we shall often have occasion to prove—he makes a slip when he tells us (tome iv., p. 66) that 'the former members of the Legislative Assembly who fought under the banner of Brissot, Vergniaud, and the other chiefs of the Gironde, no longer occupied their old places on the left, but took their seats on the right, where only a few days before the last defenders of the Constitution of 1791—the Jaucourts, the Girardins, Mathieu Dumas, and the Beugnots—had sat.' From the narrative of the deputy Dulaure, who was an eye-witness of the facts, it is very clear that matters did not take place in the sitting of September 21 as reported above, and that the friends of Brissot and Vergniaud showed very little haste in occupying the benches on the right. The deductions which Mortimer-Ternaux had drawn—' They wish to mark a change of policy by this change of place '—from a fact which is now proved to be untrue are therefore valueless.   Dulaure's narrative, published under the eyes of the participators in the facts he relates, is too curious and too little known to be omitted here : ' When the Convention,' he says, ' held its first sittings, there was not a single member willing to sit on that side (that which the Feuillants of the Legislative Assembly had occupied); but as it was impossible for all the members to sit on one side, some were obliged to cross over to the other.   Soon this repugnance entirely ceased, and members sat on either side indiscriminately.   This state of things was changed when Robespierre was denounced as an aspirant to the dictatorship ; when Marat was charged with the same crime, and with exciting the people against the Convention ; when the departmental force was spoken of, and when the Rolandists and Robespierrots began to be more distinctly mentioned.   Everyone, according to his temper or his opinion, took his seat on the side where such temper or opinion was most favoured and least opposed, it being very uncomfortable to sit by the side of men who do not share one's ideas and views.   Thus, all the Maratist members moved imperceptibly towards the Mountain, whilst those called Brissotins, and those who were of no party at all, went over to the opposite side, or remained in their accustomed seats.'—' Physionomie de la Convention Nationale,' by J. A. Dulaure, deputy.

CHAPTER III.

JACQUES CAZOTTE.

Wednesday, September 26, 1792.

On August 17 the Legislative Assembly ordered the establishment of a criminal tribunal to try the crimes committed on the Tenth of August and other crimes relating to or connected with them.

Is it necessary to say that by ' the crimes committed on the Tenth of August ' the Assembly did not mean the armed revolt and the overthrow of the Constitution; nor the murders of Suleau, of Clermont-Tonnerre, of the Commandant Carle, and of some hundred other victims; nor the heads chopped off and borne aloft on pikes ;[1] nor the scenes of cannibalism that took place in the Tuileries after *the people's victory*—that poor devil of a scullion, stuffed down into a copper, and left to stew over a blazing fire,[2] and those unfortunate wretches who were cut to pieces and thrown upon the lighted braziers in the courtyards of the palace ?[3] Those who committed these acts are the heroes of the Tenth of August. Besides, is it not well known that since July 14, 1789, murder is quite legitimate, provided it be for the good of the Revolution? The criminals, those for whom the Legislative Assembly has established this extraordinary tribunal, are the victims and the vanquished—the men who tried to prevent the fall of the throne and wished to remain faithful to law and duty.

The tribunal of August 17, divided into two sections, which sit uninterruptedly, is composed as follows :

1. Seven directors of juries, to draw up and arrange cases ;
2. Two Presidents, six Judges, and eight assistants ;

---

[1] 'François Suleau,' by Auguste Vitu.
[2] 'Le Nouveau Paris,' by Sébastien Mercier, cb. xxxiv.   [3] *Ibid.*

3. Two national Commissaries and two public prosecutors ;

4. Four recorders and eight clerks ;

5. One hundred and ninety-two jurymen.

The two national Commissaries are the only officials whose appointment has been left to the executive power. The jurymen have been chosen directly by the forty-eight sections of Paris, each of which elected four, whilst the Presidents and Judges have been appointed by an electoral body composed of an elector from each section.[1]

The accused is allowed only twelve hours to examine the evidence to be brought against him, and three hours to prepare his defence.[2] He is not examined before being brought into court, and the right of appeal is denied him.[3]

This decree, which delivers up the victims of the Tenth of August to juries chosen by the sections of Paris, that is, to the men who took part in that bloody day, and are, therefore, both judges and parties in the cause, which deprives the accused of the means of preparing his defence, and which, after having brought him before a tribunal of his enemies, takes away even the last resource of an appeal—this odious, unheard-of decree, was passed *unanimously !*[4] It is more especially the work of the Brissotins and of the members of the Gironde, who since the Tenth of August have enjoyed almost absolute power in the Assembly, on account of the ever-diminishing number of constitutional Royalists and the still undeveloped strength of the Mountain. It was passed, too, on the report of the Special Commission of Twenty-one, on which sat Brissot, Guadet, Gensonné, Vergniaud, Lasource, and Condorcet. It was Brissot who undertook to prove the advantages of suppressing appeals in the following terms :

' There remained a last method of expediting sentences without the violation of any principles, and one that had already been adopted by the National Assembly in the trials at Mons and Tournay. There the number of accused and the necessity for a speedy despatch had forced it to take that step, and here

---

[1] Fouquier-Tinville already makes his appearance in this tribunal, not as a public prosecutor, but as one of the directors of juries.

[2] Ch. Berriat Saint-Prix, ' La Justice Révolutionnaire à Paris,' p. 8.

[3] Decree of August 17, 1792, article 3.

[4] ' Histoire Parlementaire,' tome xvii., p. 96.

the same motives come into play. It was, therefore, permissible for the Assembly to employ the same means as before, and in suppressing the right of the accused to appeal to a higher court it has done so.'

In the name of the Special Commission Brissot added these words, which will remain among the most abominable that the Revolution has condemned us to hear :

'*Nothing has, therefore, been left undone to promote either dispatch or* JUSTICE.'[1]

The tribunal organized on August 17 was opened at five o'clock on the afternoon of the 18th,[2] in the Hall of Saint Louis, in the Palace of Justice.[3] I have just witnessed the trial there of the venerable M. Cazotte, a good man and a well-known writer.

The day before yesterday he was brought before the second section, presided over by M. Laveaux. The sight of his long silver locks, the look of candour and virtue that shone upon his face, but more especially the presence beside him of the heroic girl who had already once saved his life, wrung pity even from the wretches who form the usual audience of the court-room, and who generally greet the entry of the prisoners with laughter and ribaldry.

After having replied to the questions of the President concerning his name, profession, and age—the latter he gave as seventy-four—M. Cazotte placed upon the table a protest against the jurisdiction of the court, arguing that, since he had been tried and acquitted by the sovereign people and the municipal

[1] 'Histoire Parlementaire,' tome xvii., p. 88.

[2] M. Berriat Saint-Prix, who has written some conscientious and remarkable accounts of revolutionary justice in Paris and the departments, is wrong in saying that 'the first sitting of the tribunal was held on August 25.' Installed on the 18th, the tribunal held its first real sitting on the 20th. The first case was that of Collenot d'Angremont ; it ended in a sentence of death, and D'Angremont was executed at ten o'clock on the evening of the 21st.

[3] One of the two sections of the Revolutionary Tribunal established on March 10, 1793, sat in the same Hall of Saint Louis, then called Hall of Liberty, the other section occupying the former seat of Parliament, dubbed Hall of Equality. The Halls of Liberty and Equality were both burned by the Commune in 1871, though the First Chamber of the civil tribunal of the Seine is now established upon the site of the old Hall of Equality. Before the fire of 1871 the Hall of Liberty or of Saint Louis was used as a Court of Appeal.

officers, no one could again try him upon the same facts without impairing the sovereignty of that same people.

His objection was overruled, and the charge, drawn up by Fouquier-Tinville, was then read.   M. Cazotte, who has been living at Pierry, near Épernay, for the past thirty-two years, kept up a very brisk correspondence from October, 1790, to July, 1792, with his friend M. Ponteau, secretary to M. de Laporte, intendant of the Civil List.   These confidential letters, written by his daughter's hand, and containing the unveiled expression of his Royalist sentiments, were seized after the Tenth of August. Fouquier has manufactured a vast conspiracy out of them, and made the author of the 'Diable Amoureux' the chief of the conspirators.

Upon the demand of M. Réal,[1] the Public Prosecutor, the letters were read, the President frequently putting questions, which were all answered by the accused with remarkable coolness and serenity.

The weakness of M. Cazotte's voice having called forth some remarks from the jury and the Public Prosecutor, the tribunal ordered a new seat to be arranged, to which the prisoner was conducted, after an adjournment of a quarter of an hour.   I can almost see him now, seated near the Judges, and opposite the jury, with his daughter on his right and M. Julienne, his defender, on his left.   I can again hear his replies, so clear, so exact, so noble, and so true, in which were sometimes heard the simplicity of an idealist, but in which there always rang the accents of an honest man.   The following are a few examples :[2]

[1] Pierre François Réal soon after changed his post of Public Prosecutor at the tribunal of August 17 for that of Assistant Solicitor to the Commune of Paris, and thus became the colleague of Hébert, editor of the *Père Duchesne*. After having, on January 10, 1795 (21st of Nivôse, year III.), presented a petition to the Convention in the name of the Corn-market section, ending with a demand for *a democratic Republic or death*—after having been appointed Historiographer to the Republic by the Directory, he became a Councillor of State under Bonaparte, and was, until 1814, the real head of the imperial police.   During the Hundred Days he performed the duties of Prefect of Police.   The former colleague of Fouquier-Tinville, Chaumette, and Hébert, the man who had demanded sentence of death against Cazotte 'for having conspired against his country,' died as a Count of the Empire on March 7, 1834.

[2] For details of the trial of Jacques Cazotte, Nos. 16, 17, and 18 of the 'Bulletin du Tribunal Criminal du 17 Août' may be consulted, as well as

When asked to what sect he belongs, whether it is not that of the *enlightened* (*illuminés*), he replies: 'I do not know whether I am on my trial for being an idealist, but my belief is that the counter-revolution can only be brought about by prayer.'

Again, he is asked to explain these words which occur in one of his letters : 'Since all the churches are closed either by order or by sacrilege, turn your houses into oratories.' 'You know very well,' adds the President, 'that the constitutional churches are not closed.' He replies that he went to Mass and confessed to the constitutional Vicar. The President hereupon professing surprise that he should have gone to hear the Mass of a priest in whom he did not believe, he answers that, being Mayor of Pierry, and one of the oldest men in the place, he did so to set a good example. Besides, was not Judas, too, one of Christ's disciples, and did he not perform miracles with the rest of the Apostles ?

The next words that he was asked to explain were *fanaticism and robbery*. 'By fanaticism I mean extreme excitement ; it reigns in all parties—in that of Liberty as well as in others. Fanaticism in Liberty is when every human consideration is left behind.'

Referring to the plans contained in one of his letters, the President observed that they aimed at bringing the nation once more under the yoke of absolute obedience to the King. 'Such was not my intention,' replied Cazotte, 'since absolute obedience is due to God alone.'

To this question, 'How do you explain this passage : " Let Louis XVI. be careful not to yield to one of his weaknesses— clemency " ?' he replied : 'There were, of course, many criminals in the nation. I demanded that they should be punished, especially the authors of the Avignon massacres.'

The fifth letter read, written some time after the King's flight to Varennes, contained this phrase : 'I was in favour of the flight,

the very curious work published under the following title in the year VI. 'Cazotte's Secret Correspondence with Laporte and Ponteau, Intendant and Secretary of the Civil List, from 1790 to 1792, containing interesting details concerning the journey of the late King to Varennes,' preceded by a historical sketch of the life and works of that celebrated man, together with his trial and sentence.

but never to the frontiers.' Asked for the meaning of these words, he replied as follows : ' I wrote that letter about the time of the King's flight ; I was always desirous, I do not deny it, that the King should leave a city in which his authority was disregarded and his person kept prisoner. I have likewise always desired that the National Assembly should leave Paris and sit in some other city, no matter which, provided it was mistress of its deliberations, which it was not in the capital, as the decrees passed by it testify.'

As he spoke these words, M. Cazotte raised his voice somewhat, and the strong conviction that animated him did not fail to make a deep impression upon his hearers.

Another letter, of more recent date, ran : ' Mon ami, we have received five letters from Coblentz, Trèves and Brussels, one of them being from a commanding officer and a man of real merit.' Having been asked to give the name of this officer, he replied very firmly : ' In my present position I shall not be such a coward as to turn informer, even should my silence cost me my life.'

Night fell, and the President asked the accused whether he was not tired. ' The tribunal,' he added, ' is ready to grant you any time you may desire for taking rest or food.' ' Mon Dieu ! Monsieur le Président,' answered M. Cazotte, ' I am deeply grateful to the court for its consideration, but I feel quite ready to go on with my examination, thanks to the fever which is sustaining me. Besides, the sooner my trial is over, the sooner I, as well as my judges and the gentlemen of the jury, will be rid of it.'

The examination then recommenced, and went on right through the night, the unhappy man's courage and presence of mind never deserting him for a moment.

This strange conspirator had written in a letter, dated May 14, 1793 : ' My house is a house of prayer. Thus, whilst three-fourths of the churches are closed by Divine right and the rest by secular force, God establishes temples in human hearts where He is truly and faithfully served . . . I have already told you that there are eight of us in the whole of France who, absolutely unknown to each other, like Moses, unceasingly uplift our eyes, our voice and our arms to Heaven.'

'What does this mean?' asked M. Laveaux. 'I was told in a vision,' replied the accused, 'that there were eight of us in France who raised our hands to Heaven. In support of what I say, I may remind you of what is written in the Scriptures— that the young shall have dreams, and the old visions.'

Another letter was then read in which one of the prisoner's relatives was mentioned. The President having asked him to give this relative's name, he replied : 'I should be very sorry to drag my family into the same position as I am in myself.'

The incriminating letters were thirty-two in number, and most of them seven or eight pages long. Conspirators are not gener- ally so explicit. Their perusal and the interrogatory to which it gave rise occupied twenty-three hours. The light of day was just breaking through the windows of the court when the Public Prosecutor commenced his speech. M. Réal was obliged to pay a tribute to the virtues of the man whom he was accusing. 'Why,' he said, addressing the prisoner, 'why must I call you guilty after seventy-four years of a virtuous life? . . . The life that Jacques Cazotte led at Pierry was one of patriarchal simplicity. Beloved by the inhabitants who had grown up around him, he applied himself to making them happy ; why need he have conspired against the liberty of his country?' The Public Prosecutor concluded by saying that the participation of Jacques Cazotte in plots formed against the liberty of the sovereign people had been fully proved.

During this speech, of more than an hour's duration, Cazotte kept his eyes constantly fixed upon the Public Prosecutor, his face betraying not the slightest emotion. His daughter, on the contrary, seemed fully alive to all the points made by M. Réal, and could not restrain her tears when he drew his terrible con- clusions. Her father thereupon bent over her and whispered a few words in her ear that seemed to quiet her.

M. Julienne, the official defender, then replied to M. Réal. I had not heard him speak before. He is a young man of very great talent, and possesses a marvellous flow of eloquence ; his only fault being that of excessive impetuosity.[1] His language

[1] 'Souvenirs de M. Berryer, Doyen des Avocats de Paris, de 1774 à 1838,' tome i., p. 319.

is fiery, highly coloured, and brilliantly imaginative. His defence
of M. Cazotte was marked by great power and depth of feeling,
and his speech, which lasted only half an hour, drew tears from
all present.[1]

M. Cazotte was as cool and impassive during the speech of his
own lawyer as he had been during that of his accuser. His
daughter seemed to gain more courage. Upon her pale face,
and in her tearful eyes, I thought I saw a faint look of hope.

The President then summed up, and the jury retired to
consider their verdict, the trial up to this point having lasted
twenty-seven hours. Meanwhile Mdlle. Cazotte was led out of
the court and conducted to a room in the Conciergerie.

The jury soon returned, and after hearing their verdict the
Judge passed sentence of death upon the prisoner. Upon hearing
his doom the old man half turned—no doubt in order to be
quite sure that his daughter was not present—and his face,
clouded for a moment, resumed its wonted serenity.

The President then addressed the condemned man in the
following strange words: 'Sad sport of old age! Unhappy
victim of the prejudices of a life passed in slavery! You, whose
heart was not large enough to feel the value of a sacred liberty,
but who have proved by your tranquillity here that you know
how to sacrifice even your life to support your opinions, hearken
to the last words of your Judges! May they bring to your
soul the precious balm of consolation! May they not only
cause you to pity the fate of those whose duty it is to condemn
you, but inspire you with stoicism in your last moments, and
fill you with that respect which the law imposes upon us! . . . .
Come, summon up all your courage and strength; look death
fearlessly in the face, and remember that it has no right to
terrify a man like yourself.'

This speech did not seem to make the least impression upon
M. Cazotte. Only at the words 'Look death fearlessly in
the face' he shook his head and raised his eyes to heaven with
a composed and serene air.

M. Laveaux continued speaking for some time. He praised
the humanity of the law which sends old age and innocence

[1] 'Procès de Jacques Cazotte,' p. cxxv.

to the scaffold. 'Have no fear!' he cried. 'Though the law is severe against those who transgress it, the sword soon falls from its hands when judgment is once pronounced. . . . Justice now sheds tears over those white hairs which she has respected until sentence has fallen upon you ; may that spectacle bring you to repentance ! . . .' I have not the courage to reproduce the whole of this watery and high-flown harangue, which was listened to by the audience in astonishment.[1]

The trial at length comes to an end, and M. Cazotte is led away to the condemned cell. 'I am only sorry for my family,' he said to those about him. The executioner having come to cut his hair, he requested him to cut it as close as possible, and to give it to his daughter. He then spent an hour with the priest. At the opening of the trial, the day before yesterday, he said to M. Julienne : 'I am ready for death, and went to confession three days ago.'

Before leaving the Conciergerie, he asked for pen and ink, and wrote these words : 'Do not weep for me, my wife and children, and do not forget me, but remember never to offend God.'

[1] 'Procès de Jacques Cazotte,' p. cxxviii. Jean Charles Thiébault Laveaux was born at Troyes in 1749, and died in Paris in 1827. Prior to the Terror he had been professor of literature at Stuttgart, professor of the French language and literature at the University of Berlin, and editor of the *Courrier de Strasbourg*. In 1793 he became editor of the *Journal de la Montagne*, Chef de Bureau Militaire du Département de la Seine under the Consulate, and Chef de Division and Inspector-General of Prisons and Hospitals under the Empire, posts which he held until the second return of the Bourbons, in 1815. A distinguished lexicographer, he is the author of a 'Dictionnaire de la Langue Française' and of a 'Dictionnaire Raisonné des Difficultés Grammaticales.' Besides these two standard works, he published sixty-six other volumes and six pamphlets. And yet this indefatigable compiler, who has put his name to seventy volumes, could not get that name correctly given by the historians who speak of him in connection with the tribunal of August 17, and many of whom, perhaps, had his 'Dictionnaire' in their library. Buchez and Roux ('Histoire Parlementaire,' xvii., p. 211), Louis Blanc (vii., p. 100), Granier de Cassagnac (' Histoire des Girondins,' ii., p. 233), Hamel ('Histoire de Robespierre,' ii., p. 385), Wallon ('Histoire du Tribunal Révolutionnaire de Paris,' i., p. 34) all write 'Lavaux.' Berriat Saint-Prix ('La Justice Révolutionnaire à Paris,' p. 11), and Mortimer-Ternaux ('Histoire de la Terreur,' iii., p. 40) write ' Lavau.' Charles Monselet ('Histoire Anecdotique du Tribunal Révolutionnaire,' p. 233) is the only writer who gives the correct name of the President of the Criminal Tribunal of August 17.

On his way to the place of execution, Cazotte kept his gaze constantly fixed on high. It was seven o'clock at night when the tumbril reached the Place du Carrousel, and on perceiving the scaffold erected there he smiled. Before giving himself up to the executioner, he turned towards the crowd, and amid the silence that suddenly fell upon it he cried: 'I die as I have lived—true to God and my King!'[1]

*   *   *   *   *

By her supplications Mdlle. Cazotte had managed to save her father's life during the massacres at the Abbaye, but the tribunal of August 17 was less merciful than that of Maillard. Heroic Sombreuil, may your father be more fortunate than Jacques Cazotte![2]

[1] 'Notice sur Jacques Cazotte,' by Bergasse. See also 'Œuvres de Cazotte,' 1817, tome i., containing the 'Correspondance' and 'Procès.'

[2] M. de Sombreuil had also been saved by his daughter and spared by the *workers* of September; he was condemned by the Revolutionary Tribunal, and executed on the 29th of Prairial, year II. (June 17, 1794). Michelet relates the episode of Mdlle. Cazotte at the Abbaye in the following peculiar way: 'Cazotte, the seer of visions and writer of comic operas, was none the less an aristocrat, and there were a good many written proofs against him and his sons. The chances of saving him were very slight. Maillard granted the young lady the favour of being present at the trial and execution, and of having free access everywhere. The brave girl took advantage of this permission to *captivate* the murderers, and she charmed them so effectually that, when her father appeared, he found no one willing to kill him.'—'Histoire de la Révolution,' tome iv., p. 161.

CHAPTER IV.

Friday, September 28, 1792.

WHEN the members of the Convention substituted a Republic for a Monarchy—when they implanted in the soil of France, from which Monarchy had sprung like a natural product, in harmony with the genius of the French nation, with its good qualities and its faults, its greatnesses and its weaknesses—when they implanted in that soil, I say, a new form of government, having no roots or precedents in the past, did they fully grasp the gravity of the act they were committing? Did they quite understand that their enterprise, in order not to be criminal, must be successful—must succeed, not partially or temporarily, but completely and for ever? Yesterday—under Louis XVI. as under Louis XIV.—France was still at the head of European nations. This uncontested position it owed to the monarchical principle, to that happy concord which made us all—nobles, priests, citizens, artisans, and peasants—all Royalists. Some of us might have had grievances against the others, and at home we might have had many a question to thresh out amongst ourselves; but abroad, before strangers, we had all only one heart, one faith, and one King. If a people have no unity they cannot possibly have greatness. Now, it is this very unity, the best and greatest of all our belongings, that the Convention destroyed, without discussion or deliberation, on the very first day of its existence. By the establishment of the Republic there are now two nations in France; there are, alas! two Frances. The authors of this lamentable division can only obtain pardon by their own disappearance and self-effacement.

By their wisdom, their ability, and their virtues they must make us forget the Monarchy ; they must attract all minds and hearts towards themselves, so that under the Republic, as formerly under the Monarchy, France may again be one in heart, one in soul, one in faith.   But if they do not obtain that result, if their triumph be limited to sowing the seeds of discord and hatred in the heart of the nation, to merely postponing instead of preventing the re-establishment of the Monarchy, and to giving up their country to alternations of anarchy and despotism—if such are to be the consequences of the proclamation of the Republic—then may they be accursed who have thus irreparably broken the old unity of France !!1

September 29.

I have just read over again the page I wrote yesterday while a prey to feelings of intense anguish.   I should like to be able to efface it, or to believe that the future will belie my words— that the members of the Convention, honest, generous and moderate, will succeed in inspiring the whole nation with love for the Republic, and leave France happy, reconciled, and united. But how can I entertain such hopes when I look at this Assembly and let my mind dwell for a moment upon the elements of which it is composed ?

Seventy-seven of its members formed part of the Constituent Assembly, but great care was taken, in making a choice amongst the eleven hundred members of the Constituent,2 to include none who, whilst pledging themselves to the Revolution, refused at the last moment to countenance anarchy, nor any who, like Barnave, Thouret, Chapelier and Bailly, thought something due to the claims of order, as well as to those of Liberty.   Vadier, Prieur, Lofficial, Goupilleau, Voulland, Rewbell, Dubois-Crancé, Thibault, and sixty others quite as little known, are the old Constituents whom the electors have sent to the Convention ;

---

1 'On September 21 France was proclaimed a *Republic one and indivisible*, in spite of the oracle Mirabeau, who declared that it was geographically monarchical.'—PELTIER, ' Dernier Tableau,' ii., p. 393.
2 The exact number was 1,118, made up of 291 members of the clergy, 270 members of the nobility, and 557 of the Third Estate.   Of the latter, 272 were barristers ('Mémoires de Mirabeau,' edited by Lucas de Montigny, tome vi., p. 36).

possessing no talents, they make a show of most exaggerated opinions, and that suffices. Robespierre, Buzot and Merlin owe their election, not to the talent they formerly displayed, but solely to the violence of their principles and language.

In the case, too, of the 192 members of the Legislative re-elected to the Convention the facts are exactly the same. They all sat on the Left, and all were the organizers or abettors of that war against Monarchy and religion which resulted in the Tenth of August and September 2.

Are the new members of the Convention men to inspire us with greater confidence? Assuredly not. The Constituent Assembly contained 272 barristers;[1] barristers and lawyers formed more than half the Legislative Assembly, and in the Convention they are again in a majority. What assemblies become in the hands of lawyers is fully proved by the history of the past four years. Let us take two of the most honest of these men. Here is Barnave, who comes to Versailles from the Dauphiné. At Grenoble and Vizille he followed in the footsteps of Mounier, but he has no sooner taken his seat in the States-General than he separates himself from his master and friend. Mounier in astonishment asks him the reason of this rupture. 'M. Mounier, you have made your reputation—I have mine to make.'[2] That was his reply. Now let us hear M. Emmery, member for the bailiwick of Metz. In an interview that he had one day with M. de Bouillé, the latter spoke as follows: 'I am neither an aristocrat nor a democrat; I am a Royalist pure and simple. I conform to your detestable Constitution, because my Sovereign has accepted it, but if he ever refuses to continue his allegiance, I would instantly withdraw mine too.' 'You are frank,' replied M. Emmery; 'had I been born a noble, I would think and act like you; but a man like myself, destined never to be aught but a lawyer, must naturally desire a revolution.'[3]

---

[1] 'It may be said that the success of the Revolution is due to the order of barristers.'—BAILLY, 'Mémoires,' i. 53. 'It is well known,' says Marmontel ('Mémoires,' tome ii., p. 243), 'what interest the body of barristers had to change reform into revolution, the Monarchy into a Republic. What it wished to set up was a perpetual aristocracy.'

[2] 'Mémoires' of M. de Montlosier, tome i.

[3] 'Mémoires' of the Marquis de Bouillé, tome i., p. 202.

And yet, in times of Revolution, the journalists are even more dangerous than the lawyers. The mob has no courtiers more servile, no flatterers more hateful than they, and of all the journalists who every morning instil anger, envy and hatred into the hearts of the people, I see only one, the miserable Hébert, who has no seat in the Convention. Many of them have even been returned for several departments.

Carra, the editor of the *Annales Patriotiques*, was elected in six : Saône-et-Loire, Loir-et-Cher, l'Eure, l'Orne, la Charente and la Somme.

Condorcet, the editor of the *Chronique du Mois*, in five : l'Aisne, la Sarthe, le Loiret, l'Eure and la Gironde.[1]

Thomas Paine, one of Condorcet's literary colleagues, in four : l'Aisne, l'Oise, le Puy-de-Dôme, and le Pas-de-Calais.

Brissot, editor of the *Patriote Français*, in three : le Loiret, l'Eure, and l'Eure-et-Loir.

Robespierre, editor of the *Défenseur de la Constitution*, was elected in Paris and in the Pas-de-Calais ; Gorsas, editor of the *Courrier des Départements*, in the Orne and in Seine-et-Oise ; Mercier, editor of the *Annales Patriotiques*, in Seine-et-Oise and Loir-et-Cher ; Anacharsis Cloots, who is not content with being the Orator of Mankind, and who writes almost everywhere, was elected in the Oise and in Saône-et-Loire ; Barère, editor of the *Point du Jour*, also had the honour of a double election : in the Hautes-Pyrénées and in Seine-et-Oise.

Paris sent, with Robespierre, Marat, the editor of the *Ami du Peuple* ; Camille Desmoulins, editor of the *Révolutions de France et de Brabant* ; Robert, editor of the *Mercure National* ;[2] Fabre

---

[1] According to Mortimer-Ternaux, tome iv., p. 57, Condorcet was elected for only four departments—l'Aisne, l'Eure, la Sarthe, and la Loire. But in this he makes a triple error. Condorcet was returned for five departments, not for four. He was returned for le Loiret, and not for la Loire ; in 1792 no such department as la Loire existed. This is not the only error made by Mortimer-Ternaux in his list of multiple returns to the Convention. He mentions Sieyès as having been elected only for the Orne and the Sarthe, whilst that member enjoyed a triple return for the Orne, Sarthe, and la Gironde. He omits Mercier, returned for Seine-et-Oise and Loir-et-Cher, and Albitte, returned for l'Eure and the Seine-Inférieure. (For the elections to the Convention, see the 'Proclamation de la République,' by G. Bord.)

[2] 'Mémoires de Mme. Roland,' p. 327.

d'Eglantine, editor of the *Révolutions de Paris*;[1] Collot-d'Herbois and Dussaulx, editors of the *Chronique du Mois*.[2]

The department of Seine-et-Oise elected, besides Mercier, Gorsas, and Barère, Guy-Kersaint, editor of the *Chronique du Mois*, Tallien, editor of the *Ami des Citoyens*, and Audouin, founder of the *Journal Universel*.

Dulaure, editor of the *Thermomètre du Jour*, was returned for the Puy-de-Dôme; Lequinio, editor of the *Journal des Laboureurs*, for the Morbihan; Lanthenas, editor of the *Chronique du Mois* and of the *Patriote Français*, for the Rhône-et-Loire; Rabaut Saint-Étienne, editor of the *Moniteur* and of the *Feuille Villageoise*, for the Aube; Garran de Coulon, editor of the *Chronique du Mois*, and Louvet, editor of the *Sentinelle*, for the Loiret; Charles Villette, editor of the *Chronique de Paris*, for the Oise; and the Abbé Fauchet, editor of the *Bouche-de-Fer*, for Calvados.

Is that all? No; we have still Boileau,[3] Bancal des Issarts,[4] and Robert Lindet, of whom Camille Desmoulins once said, as he reviewed his colleagues: 'Each of us has his share. . . There is Brissot the diplomat, Robert Lindet the democrat, Noël the academician.'

There are about thirty of them altogether, and I must certainly have omitted more than one—the Abbé Grégoire, for instance, who in May, 1791, took charge of Gorsas' paper while the latter was ill.[5]

To enumerate the services rendered to their country by all these journalists would certainly be an interesting task, but one which would occupy a good many volumes. I will simply say a few words concerning Carra, the editor of the *Annales Patriotiques*, and a member of the Brissot party. Speaking at

---

[1] Peltier, 'Dernier Tableau de Paris,' tome i., p. 197.

[2] The *Chronique du Mois* (November, 1791, to July, 1793) appeared under the auspices of fourteen editors—Condorcet, Mercier, Guy-Kersaint, J. P. Brissot, Garran de Coulon, Dussaulx, Lanthenas, Collot d'Herbois, Auger, Oswald, Broussonnet, Bidermann, Bonneville, and Clavière. The first eight were returned to the Convention.

[3] Deputy for l'Yonne. He wrote in the *Feuille Villageoise*.

[4] Deputy for the Puy-de-Dôme and one of the editors of the *Chronique du Mois*. In 1835 were published the 'Lettres Autographes de Mme. Roland adressées à Bancal des Issarts.'

[5] See *Journal de la Cour et de la Ville*, May 25, 1791.

the Jacobin Club on January 4 of the present year, he put forward the following idea, already mooted by him in his paper: 'That if Louis XVI. should a second time run away to join the refugees, or if his Ministers were suspected of treason in the proposed war, it would be necessary to place AN ENGLISH PRINCE upon the Constitutional throne of France.'[1]

There is another fact, not a whit less startling than the last, standing to the credit of the editor of the *Annales Patriotiques*; he was sentenced to two years' imprisonment by the tribunal of Mâcon for robbery with violence. On February 21 the *Spectateur et Modérateur*[2] published an article by Chas[3] entitled, 'Carra accused, arrested, and imprisoned for Robbery and Violence upon Dame Reboul, Widow of Sieur Tisserand, of the town of Mâcon.' A full account of the matter appeared in Cerisier's *Gazette Universelle*.[4]

What a fine profession that of a Patriot is! Here is a man who wished to bring his country under the sceptre of a foreign Prince—a man who has been branded by justice. Six departments contend for the honour of sending him to sit among the representatives of the nation! And first among these departments figures the one in which he was condemned as a thief!

[1] See André Chénier's article on the 'Parti Jacobin,' which appeared in the sixty-sixth supplement of the *Journal de Paris*, on May 11, 1792.

[2] No. 83, pp. 334-336. Amongst the contributors to the *Spectateur* was M. de Fontanes, who defended with both talent and moderation the cause of the Monarchy and of true liberty, his conduct even gaining him the honour of being insulted by Camille Desmoulins.

[3] Chas, born at Nîmes about 1750, took part in editing several Royalist journals from 1789 to 1792. He is the author of a drama in three acts, entitled the 'Death of Robespierre,' which he published after the 18th of Brumaire, and which is preceded by a poem on 'Anarchy,' sent to the Académie Française some time before the Tenth of August. 'In this play,' he says, 'I wrote a tirade against those who abandon their country; but since I persuaded the President d'Ormesson to remain in France, I have erased it with tears of blood.' Chas died in Paris about 1830, completely forgotten, although since 1784 he had never allowed a year to pass without publishing a book, or at least a pamphlet.

[4] *Gazette Universelle*, or *Newspaper of Every Country and Every Day* (December 1, 1789, to the Tenth of August, 1792), 5 vols., in 8vo. Carra tried to defend himself in the *Annales Patriotiques*, but, obliged to acknowledge the fact of having undergone two years' imprisonment, he confined himself to protestations of his innocence. See 'Œuvres de François de Pange,' edited by L. Becq de Fouquières, p. 203.

CHAPTER V.

Saturday, September 29, 1792.

WE have a Republic—I grant it—but have we any Republicans; not Republicans got up for the occasion, but Republicans from conviction; not Republicans of yesterday, but Republicans of long standing?

The Monarchy was abolished on the motion of Collot-d'Herbois, seconded by Grégoire, and in what terms is well known.

It is not so very long since Collot-d'Herbois was a Royalist, and a very ardent one. He wrote a play entitled 'Retour de Nostradamus'[1] in honour of Monsieur, the King's brother, and hailed the birth of the Dauphin[2] by some very commonplace verses which he himself declaimed in the theatre at Rouen.

In February, 1791, he again alluded to our good Louis XVI. in a comedy called the 'Port-feuilles.' The following words conclude and form the moral of the piece: 'My son is on duty at the Tuileries. . . . We must go and join him. We cannot finish our day in a better manner. We shall see our good King, embrace our friends, and assure our own happiness by making our dear relatives happy.'[3]

---

[1] In a pamphlet issued by Brissot on October 24, 1792, bearing the title 'A Word to all the Republicans of France upon the Jacobin Club of Paris,' we read: 'I was loudly anathematizing both Kings and Monarchy whilst these fervent Republicans of yesterday were still grovelling before princes, whom they called "bright sons of glory." See the plays written and performed by Collot-d'Herbois, such as the "Retour de Nostradamus en Provence," in honour of the *ci-devant Monsieur*.'

[2] This was the **eldest son of** Louis XVI., born October 22, 1781, died June 4, 1789.

[3] 'Les Porte-feuilles,' a comedy in two acts and in prose, by J. M. Collot-d'Herbois, performed at the Théâtre de Monsieur, Rue Feydeau, February 10, 1791.

At the sitting of the National Assembly of August 28, 1789, M. Mounier, in the name of the Committee of Constitution, read the draft of a decree containing the following articles:

Article 1.—The Government of France is a Monarchical Government.

Article 5. — The crown is indivisible, and descends from branch to branch, from male to male, by order of primogeniture.

Article 6.—The person of the King is inviolable and sacred.

Upon this draft the Abbé Grégoire was the first to speak. Was he about to protest against these principles? No; he supported, and even amplified, them. 'He points out that nothing has been said concerning the minority of a King, but that it is undoubtedly the wish of the Assembly to determine the duration of such minority.'[1] A few weeks before that, on July 14, whilst the walls of the Bastille were falling, the Abbé had given utterance to the following words, so full of deep Monarchical sentiment: 'When France awakens—when after two centuries the family is once more united under the eyes of a beloved King, when a Prince issue of our Kings takes his place amongst us . . . then reason proclaims its empire. It shines forth on all sides; it will consecrate the respective rights of a nation that worships its Monarch, and of a Monarch who finds his best support in the love of his people. . . . It is true, alas! that our King is surrounded and deceived by his enemies and ours, and whoever deceives the King, says Massillon, is as guilty as if he wished to dethrone him. It is our duty, gentlemen, to rise in his defence, and to help him restore the temple of our country.'[2]

As the President of the National Convention, M. Petion proclaimed the abolition of the Monarchy—M. Petion, whose Royalist sentiments the *Moniteur* has many a time laid before the world. In the report of the sitting of August 27, 1789, I read, for instance, that 'M. Petion is opposed to the hasty discussion of the articles relating to the Monarchy. He says that amongst these articles there are some—such as the preser-

<hr>

[1] 'Archives Parlementaires,' from 1787 to 1860, edited by Mavidal-Laurent, and Clavel, tome viii., p. 504.

[2] *Ibid.*, tome viii., p. 232.

vation of the Monarchy and the male succession to the throne —evidently essential to the peace of the French nation ; but that there are other articles which appear to him to be less evidently essential, and he asks that the examination of these be referred to the Committees.'[1]

The Secretaries of the Convention—MM. Camus, Rabaut Saint-Étienne, Lasource, Vergniaud, Condorcet, and Brissot— are, like the President, Republicans of recent date.

During the same sitting of August 27, 1789, in which M. Petion proclaimed the evident utility of the preservation of the Monarchy, M. Camus moved that they should immediately proceed to the discussion of those self-same articles, concerning which, in his opinion, no difficulties could arise.[2]

M. Rabaut Saint-Étienne is the author of a motion in five clauses, submitted to the National Assembly at its sitting of August 12, 1789, under the title of ' Principles of all Constitution.' In Article 4 we find, *The person of the King is inviolable and sacred.*[3]

In the Legislative Assembly M. Lasource was one of the most advanced members of the Brissot faction. On April 18, 1792, the King wrote to inform the President that his son[4] being now seven years old, he had appointed M. de Fleurieu his governor. M. Lasource spoke on the question. It was a fine opportunity for a Republican to make a profession of anti-Monarchical faith, but he seemed to have no desire to take up that stand. On the contrary, he fully admitted the principle of hereditary Monarchy, and merely asked that the heir-presumptive to the throne should receive an education in keeping with the wishes of the Assembly and those of the French people.[5]

'"The law and the King" will henceforth be the rallying cry of all good citizens.' These were the words of M. Vergniaud, in a circular drawn up by him and sent by the Society of Friends of the Constitution in Bordeaux to all municipalities in the department of the Gironde, on May 17, 1790. ' Let us thank

---

[1] ' Archives Parlementaires,' tome viii., p. 232.
[2] *Ibid.*   [3] *Ibid.*, p. 407.
[4] Louis Charles of France and of Bourbon, the second son of Louis XVI., was born at Versailles on Easter Sunday, March 27, 1785.
[5] *Moniteur* of 1792, No. 110.

Heaven,' he wrote, ' for having given us a chief who has recognised these great truths. . . . Let us bless Louis XVI. for having recognised that the power of Kings emanates from the will of the people. . . . Let us bless him for having recognised that his grandest title is that of Citizen-King.'[1]

Was the Marquis of Condorcet a Republican when he wrote in his preface to ' L'Homme aux Quarante Écus ': ' Those who were the first to say that the right of property in its fullest extent—that of making a perfectly free use of one's industry and possessions—was a more natural and much more important right for ninety-nine men out of a hundred than that of forming a ten-millionth part of the legislative power; those who added that the preservation of security and of personal liberty has less connection with the freedom of the Constitution than is generally believed . . . . all those who have uttered these truths have been of use to Society in teaching it that happiness is closer at hand than is thought, and that it is not by overturning the world, but by enlightening it, that we may hope to find happiness and freedom ' ? Was he a Republican when, in his edition of Voltaire's ' Dictionnaire Philosophique,' he added the following significant note to the article ' Patrie ': ' Political existence is of three kinds only—monarchy, aristocracy, and anarchy ' ? Was he a Republican when he accepted from the King the post of Treasurer, with a salary of 20,000 francs? Was he a Republican when he allowed himself to be enrolled a member of the Society of 1789, with Bailly, Beaumetz, Chapelier, Démeunier, Dupont de Nemours, Girardin, Jaucourt, Pastoret, Ramond, Rulhière, and André Chénier, and when he contributed to the journal of that society ?[2]

J. P. Brissot makes a great boast of the purity and longstanding of his Republicanism, but his claims in this respect, though oft repeated, will scarcely bear a moment's examination. In an address *on the means of modifying the rigour of the penal*

---

[1] ' Le Barreau de Bordeaux,' by Henri Chauvot, p. 118.

[2] ' Rules of the Society of 1789, and List of Members,' Paris, 1790. The number of members is 416.   The journal of the society appeared every Saturday ; the first number is dated June 5, 1790 ; the last, September 15 of the same year.   There are eight articles by Condorcet ; the other contributors were Grouvelle, Kersaint, André Chénier, François de Pange, Dupont de Nemours, etc.

laws, which was awarded a prize by the Académie of Châlons-sur-Marne, in 1780, he praises the beneficence of Louis XVI., who was then his *august monarch ;* he asks that ' the hand of education should indelibly engrave upon our hearts these words dictated by Nature : Man, love thine equals. *Subject, cherish thy Sovereign.*' He desires no mercy for those who commit the *abominable crime* of attacking the Monarchy. But here his own words become too interesting to be omitted. ' First in this category of crimes,' wrote Brissot, ' must be placed those which either tend directly to the subversion of the existing form of government in France, or which attack *the sacred person of our Kings ;* in the first degree they are called crimes of high treason, in the second of sedition, rebellion, etc. Our history gives a number of instances, even in the most remote times, of trials for *these abominable crimes. . . .* High treason is undoubtedly the most unpardonable of such offences. There is no other of which the consequences are more fatal to a State ; and if the true measure of punishment is the harm which an offence does to Society, no torture should be spared these delinquents. To them alone, *and especially to regicides,* no mercy must be shown ; for them alone cruelty is permitted, and even commanded by humanity. *Can we regret that the executioner's art exhausted its resources on such creatures as Châtel, Ravaillac, and Damien, monsters sent from hell to plunge our nation into grief ?* My pen refuses to calculate the punishment due to such crimes. I should be afraid of failing in my duty either to Society or to Nature. I shudder to find in history the name of a crime of which the thought alone horrifies me, and which will undoubtedly never appear again. Oh, my country, may your annals henceforth be free from the stain of such outrages ! Yet if some madman should . . . Fear not ; I raise my voice only in the defence of humanity ! Let that monster be mercilessly torn from his fellows and delivered up to the most terrible forms of human justice, so that the story of his sufferings may live to deter such wretches as might be tempted to imitate him. If there is one country on earth where the life of the people and the excellence of the Government make these awful crimes least to be feared, that country is undoubtedly the happy one in which we dwell.

Renowned for the gentleness of its disposition, the French nation is still better known for the unchangeable love it bears its Kings, and for the equanimity with which it wears the slender chains of a temperate monarchy.'

Let us now turn to Brissot's ' Theory of Criminal Law,' and see how the Republican there speaks of the King : " When Heaven bestows a blessing upon earth in the form of such a Prince, it seems as if he were the sun coming to disperse the black clouds that lie upon the horizon. The impure ministers of secret debauch disappear before his imposing glance ; the wit ceases his immoral quips and cranks ; the outraged wife resumes her rights ; the husband no longer shirks his responsibilities ; and innocence and candour reappear in that Court from which the empoisoned air of licentiousness had banished them. This picture is not mere fancy. I have the original before me, and in my heart. All my readers will say : It is he ! But were he to read these lines, he would be the last to see the likeness— genius does good without knowing it.'[1]

' What matters it,' says Brissot, ' what I may have done or written before 1789 ?' Ah ! my good sir, that matters a good deal. But be it so ; we shall not go back beyond that date. In 1790 Brissot is still a member of the Society of 1789 ;[2] he was therefore still a Royalist. On July 10, 1791—after the flight to Varennes—he states in a speech at the Jacobin Club that there are only two solutions possible : either Louis XVI. reigning under the supervision of an elected Council, or Louis XVI. reigning with the aid of his Council of Ministers, as in the past. ' The latter combination,' he went on to say, ' is what the pure Royalists ask for ; the Patriots accept the former. That, gentlemen, is the whole of the mystery ; that is the key to this ridiculous accusation of Republicanism.'[3] If, therefore, he was not a *pure* Royalist, he was at least still a Royalist in 1791. But in 1792 ? On July 25 of that year—less than two months before the abolition of the Monarchy—Brissot delivered a great speech, in which he attempted to pulverize the Republicans.

---

[1] ' Théorie des Lois Criminelles,' by Brissot de Warville, tome i., p. 58.
[2] ' List of Members of the Society of 1789.' Paris, 1790.
[3] Camille Desmoulins, *Révolutions de France*, tome vii., p. 30.

' If there exist,' he cried, ' men who are plotting to build up a Republic on the ruins of the Constitution, the sword of justice must fall upon them as it fell upon the partisans of the two Chambers, and upon the counter-revolutionaries of Coblentz.'[1]

I might stop here. If the members who were chiefly instrumental in abolishing the Monarchy—if the President and the Secretaries, who were elected to their office almost unanimously, are not thorough and well grounded in their convictions, is it not plain that their colleagues must be, like them, mere casual Republicans ? But let us continue our researches in this field, for they seem to me deficient neither in interest nor in instruction.

[1] *Moniteur*, July 27, 1792.   The motion for Brissot's speech to be printed was carried by a large majority.

CHAPTER VI.

Sunday, September 30, 1792.

SINCE neither Brissot, nor Vergniaud, nor Condorcet are aught but mushroom Republicans, we may safely conclude that the rest of the members of the Brissot party are no better. Let us take five of the most ardent workers of the party—Gensonné, Dufriche - Valazé, Bishop Fauchet, Barbaroux the Marseillais, and Gorsas the journalist.

On November 20, 1790, the town of Bordeaux proceeded to the installation of the first district tribunal. In his capacity of Procureur de la Commune, Gensonné had to administer the oath to the new Judges. In the speech he made on that occasion, I find this passage : ' What marks of gratitude, gentlemen, do we not owe that virtuous Monarch who, loyally supporting the representatives of the nation, attaches his happiness and glory to the success of their labours ; who, recognising the rights of the nation, deserves to be called the restorer of French liberty !'[1]

In 1784 M. Dufriche-Valazé published a treatise on the penal laws, and dedicated it in humble and respectful terms to Monsieur, brother of the King.

Bishop Fauchet bore but a very short time ago the title of Prédicateur du Roi. This is how the *Révolutions de Paris* spoke of the sermon which he preached in the metropolitan church of Paris on November 1, 1791 : ' What was our astonishment to hear the member for Calvados preach in Paris as they still preach in Rome, preach in 1791 as they preached in 1400 ! Bishop Fauchet does not style himself Prédicateur du Roi for nothing.'

[1] 'Le Barreau de Bordeaux,' by Henri Chauvot, p. 179.

When Barbaroux came to Paris from Marseilles in June, 1788, it was not to upset the throne, but to solicit a post, or at least a room in the School of Mines; and as, to attain his object, he required the assistance of M. de Lambert, Comptroller of Finances, and of Baron de Breteuil, Minister of the Royal Household, he neglected no opportunities of gaining their protection.[1] With what zeal did he then extol their virtues! How enthusiastically did he speak of the Court, and of M. de Breteuil's nephew in particular, who received him at all hours, and who allowed him to write every day: 'Monsieur, I am the friend of the nephew of the Minister!'

Gorsas, who now makes such a show of his Republicanism, writing on January 7, 1791, says: 'My respect for the virtues of our august Sovereign is well known. Those who read my *Courrier*, which has now reached its twentieth volume, know that I have never spoken with aught but veneration of that cherished Monarch.'[2] And on March 18 he wrote: 'The King's recovery has brought joy to the hearts of all true patriots. Yesterday every house was illuminated, and on Sunday a *Te Deum* will be sung in the episcopal and metropolitan church to celebrate this happy convalescence. In the evening there will again be illuminations.'[3]

A few days before the Tenth of August—that is, about two months ago—he inveighed most strongly against the Republic. In an article of July 25 he said: 'We have already long since given our opinion on a Republican France, and after a few arguments that seemed to us well grounded, we quoted the fable of the Frogs. We recall these facts to prove how far we are from defending Republicanism.'

[1] 'Mémoires inédits de Petion' and 'Mémoires de Buzot et de Barbaroux,' edit. Dauban, 1886, pp. 286 and 290. 'Lettres inédites de Barbaroux': 'I may flatter myself that I have gained the Minister's favour, and this favour takes deeper root every day. Notwithstanding this, matters cannot be hastened, and you have a false idea of the Court if you think that it is sufficient to have protection in order to get what one wants. To begin with, suitors must possess real merit, and it is only after having proved this that one can gain the Minister's favour. . . . If the Minister's nephew receives me whenever I like to call, if he pays visits expressly to procure me some useful connections, if he permits me to write to him every day without any ceremony, can I doubt that I have managed to please him?'—Letter of August 10, 1788.

[2] *Le Courrier de Paris*, tome xx., p. 105.   [3] *Ibid.*, tome xxii., p. 284.

We must evidently give up the idea of finding a true Republican in the Brissot party; perhaps we shall come across one on the benches of the Mountain.

Let us commence with Robespierre—*ab Jove principium*. An ardent Royalist in 1789, on the eve of the States-General, he addressed Louis XVI. in the following terms: 'Oh! what a glorious day, sire, will that be when these principles which are engraved on your Majesty's heart, and proclaimed by those august lips, shall receive the inviolable sanction of the first nation of Europe! To lead men to happiness by paths of virtue—to make fast anew the immortal chain that should bind man to God and to his fellows by destroying those oppressive and tyrannical things that engender fear, distrust, pride, selfishness, hatred, greed and all other vices—such, sire, is the glorious undertaking to which you have been called.'

On the day of the King's flight to Varennes (June 20, 1791), several politicians met at Petion's house, and one of them happened to mention the word 'Republic!' 'Republic! Republic!' exclaims Robespierre, with a grin; 'what's a Republic?'[1]

In the *Address of Maximilien Robespierre to the French*, published in the following month of August, I note this passage: 'As for the Sovereign, I by no means share the fear with which the title of King inspires nearly all free nations. Provided that the people be put into his place, and that free scope be given to that patriotism which the nature of our revolution has produced, I would fear neither a Monarchy, nor even the hereditary transmission of Monarchical functions.' And further: 'Our enemies had already been careful to spread about that we were the leaders of a pretended Republican party, though it was well known that we had never opposed either the existence, or even the hereditary transmission, of the Monarchy.'

A Royalist in 1791, Robespierre was still one in 1792. At the beginning of that year a political club in the Jura addressed a letter to the Society of Friends of the Constitution in Paris asking for the establishment of a Republic. Dulaure, now member for the Puy-de-Dôme, was deputed to reply to this

[1] 'Mémoires' of Mme. Roland, p. 255.

communication. The draft he submitted was not sufficiently Royalist to please Robespierre and the other members of the committee who were under his influence, and Dulaure—who himself tells the story—was obliged to retouch his own letter three times in order to *monarchize* his reply.[1]

On May 17, 1792, the first number of Robespierre's paper, *The Defender of the Constitution*, made its appearance. The first article, entitled 'An Explanation of my Principles,' contains this declaration : 'It is the Constitution that I wish to defend—the Constitution as it exists. From the moment when the Acte Constitutionnel was concluded and approved by general consent, I have always confined myself to a demand for its faithful execution.' In another number Robespierre said : 'The Legislative Assembly has no right to meddle with the Constitution which it has sworn to maintain ; any change would now only alarm the friends of Liberty.' 'I prefer,' he wrote further, 'a popular representative Assembly with free and respected citizens *under a King*, to an enslaved people under the rod of an aristocratic senate and of a dictator. I like Cromwell no better than Charles I., and I can no more bear the yoke of the Decemvirs than that of the Tarquins.'[2] Thus, on the very eve of the Tenth of August, Robespierre defended the Constitution of 1791, *as it existed*, that Constitution which ran: '*The Government is Monarchical. The Crown is indivisible, and descends by hereditary right, and in order of primogeniture, to males of the reigning dynasty. The person of the King is inviolable and sacred.*[3]

After Robespierre, Danton ; after the Jacobin, the 'Gray Friar.' On February 4, 1790, after Louis XVI. had appeared

---

[1] 'Observations à mes Commettants,' J. A. Dulaure.

[2] The *Défenseur de la Constitution* appeared every Thursday, and consisted of from forty-eight to sixty-four pages. The twelfth and last number, which appeared a few days after the Tenth of August, concluded with the following announcement : 'The present state of affairs and the approaching opening of the Convention render the title of our publication somewhat unsuitable. . . . We shall henceforth continue the paper under a name more in keeping with the conjuncture in which we are.' The new publication appeared from the end of September, 1792, until March 15, 1793, under the title of *Letters from Maximilien Robespierre to his Constituents*.

[3] Constitution of 1791, clause iii., article 4 ; chapter ii., articles 1 and 2.

in the National Assembly and sworn allegiance to the Constitution, a member of the Commune of Paris proposed to send a deputation to the King offering him the homage of the city. Danton, who then sat in the General Assembly of the Commune, gave his vote in favour of this royal demonstration. He likewise supported another motion, proposing that all the members of the Commune should renew their oath of allegiance to the nation, to the laws, and to the King, and should swear to maintain with all their might the Constitution as settled by the National Assembly, and accepted by the Monarch. Thinking that this even was not sufficient, he proposed that the whole of the public in the galleries, men and women, should also be allowed to take this oath—a proposal, says the *Moniteur*,[1] that was received with loud applause.

In January of the present year, on the day of his installation as deputy for the Procureur de la Commune, he delivered a speech in which we find the following energetic profession of Monarchical faith :

' I have been appointed to guard the Constitution, and to see that the laws sworn to by the nation are carried out. I will keep my oath, fulfil my duties, and maintain the Constitution with all my might. . . . My predecessor[2] has told you that the King, by calling him to the Ministry, has given a fresh proof of his attachment to the Constitution ; the people, by electing me to this post, have shown an attachment to that Constitution at least as great as the King's, and have therefore well seconded the royal wishes. May it be that I and my predecessor have spoken two eternal truths ! . . . A constitutional Monarchy may possibly endure longer than a despotic one has done. . . . I repeat that, whatever may have been my individual opinion at the time of the revision of the Constitution, I would, now that this Constitution has been solemnly adopted, demand the death of the first man who raised a sacrilegious hand against it, were he my brother, my friend, my own son ! Such are my sentiments.'[3]

General Lafayette, whose conduct, in more than one matter, has been open to severe criticism, but whose honesty is above suspicion, declares that Danton, in his presence, admitted

---

[1] *Moniteur*, No. 37 of 1790.

[2] Cahier de Gerville, appointed Minister of the Interior November 28, 1791.

[3] 'Révolutions de Paris,' No. 134, p. 229 ; and No. 138, p. 415.

having received money from the Court, and that, in trying to defend himself, he used the words: 'General, I am more Royalist than you.'[1]

Danton's two secretaries in the Ministry of Justice, Fabre d'Églantine and Camille Desmoulins, are, like their chief, Republicans of recent date.

In his first piece, 'Les Gens de Lettres, ou le Poète de Province à Paris,' performed at the Théâtre Italien[2] on September 21, 1787, Fabre had written only four good verses, and those verses are Royalist in tone. It is not much more than a year since there was performed at the same theatre a comedy from his pen entitled 'Le Convalescent de Qualité,' in which he preaches respect and love towards the King.[3]

---

[1] The following is the exact text of the important note left on this subject by General Lafayette, and inserted in the third volume of his 'Mémoires,' p. 85: 'Danton sold himself on condition that he should receive 100,000 francs as a compensation for the suppression of his post as *avocat au conseil* instead of the 10,000 francs originally fixed. The King's present was therefore 90,000 francs. Lafayette had met Danton at M. de Montmorin's on the very evening the bargain was concluded. . . Danton was ready to sell himself to all parties. At the time when he was proposing incendiary motions at the Jacobins, he was their spy at Court, where, however, he gave regular accounts of what was going on at the club. Later he received a good deal of money. On the Friday before the Tenth of August he was given 50,000 crowns. The Court, thinking him safe, regarded the preparations for that day with equanimity, and Mme. Elisabeth said: 'We have no fear—we may rely on Danton.' Lafayette knew of the first payment, but not of the others. Danton himself spoke of it before him at the Hôtel de Ville, and, seeking to justify himself, said: 'General, I am more Royalist than you.''' See also 'Mémoires de Lafayette,' tome iii., p. 376. Concerning Danton's venality, see the testimony of Bertrand de Moleville, 'Mémoires,' tome i., p. 354, and 'Histoire de la Révolution de France,' tome x., p. 249; Mirabeau, letter of March 19, 1791, in his 'Correspondance avec le Comte de la Marck,' tome iii., p. 82; Brissot, 'Mémoires,' tome iv., p. 193; Garat, 'Mémoires,' tome xviii., and p. 447 of the 'Histoire Parlementaire'; Roederer, 'Œuvres inédites,' tome iii. Louis Blanc has thoroughly gone into (tome x., p. 409) this question of Danton's venality, and he has no hesitation in answering it with a bold affirmative.

[2] In 1787 the Théâtre Italien occupied the Salle Favart. Built on the site of the Choiseul mansion, this *salle* was opened on April 28, 1783, for the performance of comedies and operettas. Notwithstanding its name, the pieces and the actors were French.

[3] The *Feuille du Jour* for January 30, 1791, says: 'On Friday (January 28), the "Convalescent de Qualité" was performed for the first time at the Théâtre Italien. . . . The audience encored the verses referring to the King, and the enthusiasm showed how dear the Sovereign is to his people.' The 'Révolutions de Paris,' No. 82, criticised the piece in the

Camille Desmoulins boasts of having been a Republican ever since he left college. But on July 18, 1789, he wrote in *La France Libre :* ' Louis XVI. set off again amid the roar of cannon and of the 30,000 voices that called down the blessings of Heaven upon his sacred head. The King triumphs, and the nation triumphs, the happiness of the people being the victory of a good King.' Two years later, in July, 1791, he declared that the imputation of Republican ideas to him and his friends was a ridiculous and a wicked calumny.[1]

Let us go higher, and ascend to the very summit of the Mountain. Here sits Saint-Just, a new-comer, who has taken his place by the side of Robespierre ; here sits Sergent, one of the members of the famous Vigilance Committee ; and here sits Marat.

In 1786 M. Florelle de Saint-Just solicited the honour of being admitted into the guards of the Comte d'Artois whilst awaiting permission to enter the King's body-guard. If his petition was not granted, it was because he was arrested by his mother's request, and detained for six months for having carried away from home at night some family plate and jewellery, which he sold to a receiver.[2]

following terms : ' In the scene between the Marquis and the Doctor there are some fine sentiments expressed in fine verse, but there are also some passages which the Royalist Club itself would not disavow. . . . These passages were most applauded, and the sycophantry of the old *régime* which the poet has been weak enough to put into his work had to be repeated. The eulogy upon the King alone occupies almost as much space as the whole history of the Revolution. The author has not stopped there ; he has falsified the facts in order to leave no shadows upon the highly-coloured portrait of the Monarch.'

[1] *Révolutions de France et de Brabant,* tome vii., p. 301. In May, 1793, Camille Desmoulins wrote in his ' Histoire des Brissotins ' : ' On July 12, 1789, there were perhaps no more than ten Republicans in Paris.' And he added in a note : ' Those few Republicans were for the most part young men, who, having fed on Cicero in college, were mad after liberty.'

[2] See the complete set of papers relating to this affair, found in the ' Archives Nationales ' and in the ' Archives de la Préfecture de Police,' by MM. Campardon and Vatel, and published by the latter in his work on ' Charlotte Corday et les Girondins,' tome i., p. 141, etc. In the ' Examination of Saint-Just,' on October 6, 1786, we find : ' Asked what he intended to do, after having spent the said money, he answered that he expected to be admitted into the guards of the Comte d'Artois until he was tall enough to enter the King's body-guard.'

4

Sergent, the man of June 20, of the Tenth of August, and of September 2, was a copper-plate engraver at the beginning of the Revolution, and he has more than once helped to illustrate Royalist sentiments. When he was appointed a municipal officer in February, 1792, the *Révolutions de Paris* could not help asking : 'Have we not decorated with a sash M. Sergent, an artist who not so very long ago published an engraving representing Louis XII., Henri IV., and Louis XVI., with the following sum in a triangle below the three busts, " XII. and IV. make XVI.," which is as much as to say that Louis XVI. alone is as good as Louis XII. and Henri IV. put together. When the Prince Royal is taught arithmetic, it will be by this ingenious plate that he will learn how to add up. Under the old *régime* the artist would have been rewarded with the black cord, but we trust that he has other claims to the tricolour sash.'[1]

Marat—*tu quoque, Brute*—was no Republican before the Revolution, when he dedicated his translation of Newton's 'Optics' to the King, when he published his writings in honour of Monsieur, Comte de Provence,[2] and when he pompously wrote his title of Médecin des Gardes du Corps de Monseigneur le Comte d'Artois[3] upon his ' Recherches sur la Lumière ' and his ' Recherches sur l'Électricité.' Has he become one since the Revolution ? By no means. On p. 17 of his ' Plan of Constitution,' published in 1790, I read : 'In a great State the form of government must be Monarchical ; it is the only one befitting France. The extent of the kingdom, its position and the multiplicity of its relations, necessitate this, and policy would

---

[1] *Révolutions de Paris*, No. 136, February 18, 1792.

[2] Prudhomme, ' Histoire des Révolutions,' tome i., p. 296.

[3] In ' Charlotte Corday et les Girondins,' Vatel publishes Marat's commission, which runs as follows : ' To-day, June 24, 1777, Monseigneur the Comte d'Artois being at Versailles, and having received a report upon the good character, talents, and experience in the art of medicine of Sieur Jean Paul Marat, doctor of medicine of several faculties in England, Monseigneur, desiring to grant him a mark of his favour, bestows upon him the post of physician in his guards, and desires that the said Sieur Marat shall enjoy the honours, prerogatives, and advantages accruing therefrom, and style himself accordingly in all public and private acts.' (Secrétariat de Mgr. le Comte d'Artois. Provisions et Brévets, pièce 213. ' Archives Nationales,' série O, 1955, 1956.) Marat continued to receive the salary attaching to this post (2,000 francs) until April 23, 1786.

have to yield to so many powerful reasons even if the disposition of the people permitted a change of *régime*.' And on p. 43 : 'The King can only be approached through his Ministers ; his person is sacred.'

He is not less explicit in the *Ami du Peuple*. On February 17, 1791, he wrote : ' I do not know whether the counter-Revolutionaries will force us to change the form of government, but I am convinced that a very limited Monarchy is that which suits us best to-day. . . . As for Louis XVI., I believe he has only the faults of his education. . . . Taking him altogether, just as he is, he is the King we want. We ought to thank Heaven for him, and pray for his long life, taking every care to keep him amongst us !'[1]

On April 20, 1791, he reproaches Condorcet ' with impudently calumniating the Jacobin Club, and with perfidiously accusing it of wishing to destroy the Monarchy.'[2] On June 13 following, he attacks those who violate the oath they took at the time of the Federation, since 'to defend the Constitution is the same as to be faithful to the nation, the law, and the King.'[3] Finally, in July last, he sends Barbaroux a pamphlet to be circulated amongst the Marseillais as soon as they arrive. This was nothing less than an invitation to them to fall upon the Legislative body. According to Marat, it was necessary to protect the Royal Family even at the cost of exterminating an Assembly in which anti-Revolutionary sentiments were evidently predominant.[4]

But let us not be discouraged ; we will not leave the benches of the Mountain yet. Not far from Marat sits Marie Joseph Chénier, bearing no traces of embarrassment at finding himself in such strange company. Does Chénier remember that in the dedicatory epistle of his ' Charles IX.' he wrote : ' Oh, Louis XVI. ! King of justice and of mercy ! you are indeed fitted to be the leader of the French' ?

On the same benches as Chénier and Marat, a little below Robespierre, I see several of their colleagues in the Constituent

---

[1] *L'Ami du Peuple*, No. 374.   [2] *Ibid.*, No. 431.   [3] *Ibid.*, No. 488.
[4] Barbaroux, ' Mémoires,' p. 61.   See also a remarkable study of Marat by Granier de Cassagnac in his ' Histoire des Causes de la Révolution,' tome iii., pp. 415-441.

Assembly—Anthoine (of Metz), Vadier, Voulland, and Merlin (of Douai).

In September, 1789, Anthoine wrote to the editor of the *Journal de Paris :*

'You accuse the National Assembly of having neither love for the person of the King, nor the most elementary notions of politics. The three propositions were: *The inviolability of the King's person, the indivisibility of the throne,* and *the hereditary transmission of the crown. These three propositions were carried unanimously, and by acclamation. . . .* That, sir, is the exact truth, and it is the more necessary to point it out since your incorrect report might lend credit to the calumnies already too widely spread by the enemies of the nation. They have dared to say in the Assembly that the safety of the King's person was in danger, and that attempts were being made to deprive the Dauphin of the succession to the throne. Let France know at once that the majority of the Assembly is as ready to maintain the rights of the throne as those of the nation's liberty.'[1]

Whilst speaking in the Constituent Assembly on July 16, 1791, Vadier made the following declaration: 'I detest the Republican system, and I would willingly lay down my life to efface the decrees that have been passed.'[2]

Voulland, in 1791, was the secretary of the Feuillants, an essentially Royalist club !'[3]

Merlin used to sign all his articles in the *Répertoire de Jurisprudence :* 'Merlin, Secretary to the King, House and Crown of France.' On September 28, 1789, he gave 1,000 francs as a patriotic contribution, to be deducted from his salary as Secretary to the King, at the same time announcing his intention of giving more, as soon as he was reinstated in his office.[4] He evidently expected to remain a Royal Secretary. On July 3, 1791, he wrote to the *Journal des Hommes Libres :* 'Heaven preserve me from adopting your ideas concerning the Monarchy. If I wished to plunge France into a frightful civil war and give her up to her most cruel enemies, I would take up the same line as you. A people so numerous and so unequal in riches as the French cannot be turned into a Republic. I challenge

---

[1] *Révolutions de Paris*, No. 11.   [2] *Moniteur* of 1791, No. 198.
[3] Camille Desmoulins, 'Notes sur le Rapport de Saint-Just.'
[4] *Moniteur* for 1789, No. 63.

you to give me an instance of any great Republic that existed for any appreciable time and without continual storms. We have a Constitution; let us keep it.'[1]

Shall I continue this edifying journey round the Riding-School? Shall I ask Lepeletier de Saint-Fargeau, Salle, La Revellière-Lépeaux, Barère and the Abbé Sièyes, all of whom sat in the Constituent Assembly, for their certificate of Republicanism?

Elected by the nobility of Paris to represent them in the States-General, Lepeletier de Saint-Fargeau was at first an ardent defender of the Monarchy. On August 24, 1789—the day of Saint Louis—he proposed that the following address should be sent to the King:

'Sire, the Sovereign whose revered name your Majesty bears, and whose virtues religion celebrates to-day, was, like yourself, the friend of his people.

'Like you, Sire, he desired the liberty of the French. He protected it by laws which adorn our annals, but he could do nothing to revive it.

'That glory, reserved for your Majesty, will give you an immortal right to the gratitude and tender veneration of the French.

'Thus will for ever be united the names of two Kings who, with centuries between them, vie in performing the most signal acts of justice in favour of their people.

'Sire, the National Assembly has suspended its labours for a few moments in order to fulfil a duty that it holds dear, and one which is not beyond the scope of its mission, since, in assuring its King of the love and fidelity of the French, it is promoting the best interests of the nation and gratifying its most ardent desire.'

M. Salle, member for the Meurthe, whose *rôle* in the Constituent Assembly was not an inglorious one, made the following declaration on August 31, 1791: ''The hereditary succession to the throne is, in my opinion, the wisest law we have. And,' he added, 'nothing shall ever shake me in this opinion.'[2]

On the preceding July 15, in the course of the grand debate that followed the return from Varennes, he had stoutly defended the principle of the King's inviolability, and in his speech on

---

[1] 'Mémoires' of General Lafayette, tome iii., p. 383.
[2] 'Opinion de M. Salle, Député, sur les Conventions Nationales,' published in Paris, August 31, 1791.

that occasion there occurs this passage : 'Some speak of turning
out the Monarchy and of putting in its place an Executive
Council elected by the eighty-three departments. . . . I declare
that I would rather lay down my life than allow the supreme
power, in any form whatever, to be placed in the hands of more
than one.'[1]

Foremost among those who applauded this language must
have been M. de la Revellière-Lépeaux. Was he not one of the
Constituent deputies most assiduous in their attendance at the
Club des Feuillants ?[2] Did he not, on May 18, 1791, make the
following anti-Republican profession of faith in the National
Assembly ? 'In a country of such extent, the bonds of government should be more tightened than at Glaris or at Appenzell,
otherwise the State would be given up to the horrors of anarchy,
and so fall into the hands of a few tricksters. I, who have most
decidedly no liking for Courts, am therefore ready to declare that
the day when France shall cease to have a King she will exchange
her liberty and her peace for the terrible despotism of eternal
factions.'[3]

Barère made himself famous by his eulogies of Louis XII.,
of Cardinal d'Amboise and of Séguier, all imbued with the
purest Monarchical sentiments.[4] His paper, the *Point du Jour*,[5]
testifies that he had not yet lost these sentiments when he took
his seat on the benches of the Constituent Assembly. As a

---

[1] Speech of M. Salle, member for the Meurthe, upon the events of
June 21, 1791, delivered in the Assembly on July 15, printed by order of
the National Assembly, and sent to the departments.

[2] Beaulieu, 'Essais Historiques,' tome iii., p. 48.

[3] *Moniteur* of May 20, 1791.

[4] 'Éloges de Montesquieu, de J. J. Rousseau, de Louis XII., de
d'Amboise et de Séguier,' by Barère de Vieuzac, 1789. In the 'Éloge de
Louis XII.,' p. 32, I find : 'That day clearly proved the truth of the great
axiom, that *a good King is the image of the Divinity on earth*'; and on
p. 45 : 'Such was this Monarch who occupies a place in our annals
between Charles V. and Henri IV. Such was the Prince whose wise laws
have been praised by Councils, Senates, and National Assemblies, and
whose memory will be blessed in all ages. We cannot dwell without
emotion upon this epoch of our history, when the nation was so happy.
We cannot utter the name of FATHER OF HIS PEOPLE without a holy
veneration   good Kings inspire a kind of idolatry.'

[5] *Le Point du Jour* was exclusively devoted to a report of the proceedings of the National Assembly. The first number appeared on June 19,
1789 ; the last on October 2, 1791

proof of this I will quote the following lines written by him after the sitting of July 15, 1789:

'The whole Assembly rushed out after his Majesty,[1] and, without having had time to concert any plan of action, every member was seized with the same idea of escorting him from the Assembly to the palace. The Sovereign was so touched by this mark of affection that he decided to perform the journey on foot. The head of the nation, surrounded by the three orders of its representatives—united by a common love for their common chief—passed through the midst of an immense multitude, which, by its vociferous shouts of joy, by its oft-repeated expressions of love, and by its eagerness to catch a glimpse of its idol, seemed to have gone mad with delight. . . . This spectacle was followed by another equally beautiful and no less touching—that of the Queen standing on the balcony of the palace and holding in her arms the Dauphin, whom she repeatedly kissed and presented to the people. . . . The King, not forgetting amidst these popular rejoicings that they were blessings from heaven, hastened to the chapel to render thanks to God for having permitted him to retain the love of his people in spite of terror and calamity. He received a fresh proof of affection in the shouts of joy that greeted him on entering the chapel, and which, even in the house of God, seemed but a fitting tribute to one who had proved himself *a touching image of the Divinity*—a comforter of woe.'[2]

In the following month of September, when Louis XVI. sacrificed his gold and silver plate and sent it to the Mint, Barère's Royalist fervour again burst forth. 'The King,' he wrote, 'in his contempt for all useless pomp, has sent all his plate and all the Queen's jewellery to the Mint. Louis XIV. certainly did the same thing, but it was to defray the expenses of a ruinous war; Louis XVI. employs these means to secure the basis of that liberty which is to regenerate the nations of Europe.'[3] The Assembly having begged the King to forego the making of this sacrifice, Louis XVI. replied: 'I am deeply touched by the feelings that animate the Assembly, but I persist in my resolve, rendered necessary by the scarcity of money. Neither the Queen nor myself attach any importance to this

---

[1] On July 15 the King had gone to the Assembly without any guards, and accompanied only by his two brothers.

[2] *Le Point du Jour.* See also No. 196. [3] *Ibid.*, tome ii., 74.

sacrifice.' Barère, in his paper, made the following comment upon this reply : ' When justice and probity occupy the throne, all the other virtues accompany them.'[1]

Two years later, on May 26, 1791, Barère, in submitting his report concerning the palaces that should be dedicated to the King's use, concluded with these words : ' Such are the generous gifts that a great people bestows upon virtue !'[2]

Finally, this same Barère was a member of the Société de 1789, and President of the Club des Feuillants.[3]

To-day the former editor of the *Point du Jour* (the *Dawn*) is uncertain from which side the sun will rise, and meanwhile sits midway between the Robespierre and the Brissot parties. His colleague, the Abbé Sièyes, who, like him, was a member of the Société de 1789,[4] keeps him company. Ah ! if the Abbé only had as much courage as talent, what a fine essay he could write on the following subject : ' What is the Republic ?' But he will be very careful not to do so, and were it in his power, there is no doubt that he would efface from the *Moniteur* of 1791 that famous letter signed ' Emmanuel Sièyes,' in which he says :

' A rumour is being circulated that I am taking advantage of our position to go over to Republicanism. It is said that I am trying to convert people to that system. Up to the present I have never been charged with the pliancy of my principles, nor with too easily changing my opinions. Men of good faith, and it is to such alone that I appeal, have only three means of judging another's sentiments—by his deeds, words, and writings. I submit to my countrymen these three kinds of proofs. They are not hidden ; they date from before the Revolution, and I am sure that I have never belied myself. . . .

[1] *Le Point du Jour*, tome ii., p. 74.
[2] *L'Ami du Roi*, May 28, 1791.
[3] 'Rules of the Société de 1789 and List of Members'; Camille Desmoulins, 'Notes sur le Rapport de Saint-Just.' Barère, in his ' Mémoires,' written a long time after these events, makes no secret of the fact that he was in no way a Republican : ' On June 21, 1791, it was my opinion, as it still is after the divers phases of the Revolution, that a Republic is no more fitted for the French than the English Government is for the Turks, and I took sides with the majority in the National Assembly, who wished and expected to gain nothing more from the march of events than a Monarchical or Constitutional Monarchy.'—Tome i., p. 321.
[4] Ten members of the Convention belonged to the Société de 1789. They were Barère, Brissot, Chénier, Collot d'Herbois Condorcet, David, Kersaint, Sièyes, Treilhard, and Villette.

It is from no weak force of habit, nor from any superstitious sentiment of Royalism, that I prefer the Monarchy. *I prefer it because it
has been proved to me that a citizen enjoys more liberty under a Monarchy
than under a Republic.* Any other motives would be childish. The best
form of government is, in my opinion, that under which, not one,
and not only a few, but all peaceably enjoy the greatest possible
liberty. If I perceive this quality in the Monarchical State, it is
clear that I must desire it above every other. That is the whole secret
of my principles, and my full confession of faith. I shall soon, perhaps, have time to go further into this question. . . . I hope to
prove, not that the Monarchy is preferable in these or those circumstances, but that *under all circumstances it gives the subject more freedom than a Republic.*[1]

Once more I ask where I shall find a Republican among all
these men who so loudly proclaim their Republicanism? In
the Mountain, on the Right and on the Left, in the parties led
by Robespierre and by Brissot, amid the ex-Constituents and the
old members of the Legislative—whichever way I turn, I see
only so-called Republicans, who but yesterday were Royalists.

'Do not waste your time in looking any longer,' said my
friend Mercier to me this morning; he is the author of the
'Tableau de Paris,' and now a deputy for Seine-et-Oise. 'Near
me, for instance, sit some of the most fiery members of the
Legislative Assembly — Lequinio, Couthon, Robert Lindet,
Hérault Séchelles and Lacroix (from Eure-et-Loir). In July,
1790, Lequinio wrote in his " École des Laboureurs": " We
have a good King who would like to see us all happy, and who
fully deserves our love and gratitude. . . . Our good King,
greatly troubled, himself came down to the National Assembly.
You can imagine with what joy and love our good King was
received." He never calls the King anything but "our good
Louis Seize." Couthon, in 1790, was the first presiding Judge of
the district court of Clermont-Ferrand. Having to administer
the oath to the recently-appointed Royal Commissaries, he made
an excellent Monarchical speech. Before 1789, Robert Lindet
held the commission of Procureur du Roi at Bernay. When he
was elected Mayor of that town in 1790, his address to the

[1] *Moniteur* of July 6, 1791. See also a very long 'Note Explicative' on
July 16, in which Sièyes develops the ideas contained in his letter of
the 6th.

King was couched in terms of the deepest devotion. " We have," he said, " sworn unalterable attachment to your sacred person, and have staked our destinies and those of the Empire upon the inviolability of our oath. In our love for you, the names of King, father and country are synonymous. We shall bring up our children in these sentiments of love and respect which are not only commanded us by law, but inspired by Nature and gratitude."[1]

' Hérault Séchelles is the cousin of the Duchesse de Polignac. Received at Court, he was presumably not too much of a Republican when he was appointed Avocat-Général by the King, and received from the hands of the Queen a sash that she had embroidered herself. In 1791 Lacroix was one of the forty-two judges of the Court of Appeal. After the flight of Louis XVI. to Varennes, Gensonné, one of the members of the Court, proposed to leave out from the oath the words containing an engagement of fidelity to the King. Lacroix strenuously opposed this proposal, which he characterized as factious and Republican. The motion was negatived, and on the next occasion when the oath, in its usual formula, was administered to a new Judge, Gensonné put in no appearance. Hereupon Lacroix, in the ardour of his Royalist zeal, had his colleague fined for his absence.'[2]

' Have you read,' I then asked Mercier, ' the speech in which Citizen Charles, another deputy for Eure-et-Loir, thanked his constituents for having sent him to the Convention? The man who used such language must undoubtedly be, and always have been, a good Republican. Besides, you know that no sooner had he arrived in Paris than he took his seat on the very summit of the Mountain.' ' Are you then unaware,' rejoined Mercier, ' that Citizen Charles, after having entered the Church, made a name in 1785 by a work entitled " Timante ; or, A Faithful Portrait of most of the Writers of the Eighteenth Century," which led M. de Conzié, Archbishop of Tours, to appoint him

---

[1] 'Notices Historiques sur la Révolution dans le Département de l'Eure,' by L. Boivin-Champeaux, p. 160.

[2] Gensonné's ' Mémoire inédit,' written during his detention in the Conciergerie, and published by M. Chauvot in the ' Barreau de Bordeaux de 1775 à 1815.'

Canon of his cathedral ; that, after the Revolution, he, together with his brother, established a paper called the *Correspondant*, full of Monarchical principles, and that he was also upon the staff of the *Ami du Roi?* I verily believe,' said Mercier, on taking leave of me, ' that, of all the members of the Convention, I am the only one who was a Republican before '89.'

On reaching home, I turned to one of the works of my friend Mercier, and there I found the most judicious and conclusive arguments—in favour of the Republic? No ; in favour of the Monarchy.

' The throne being legal, its authority is well based and respected. The base of the throne strengthens that of the State ; ambition may tear away a few shreds of authority, but never the whole of it. A Monarchical throne has, moreover, a lasting majesty of its own. Look at Republics, which have a constant need of dictators.

' The best form of government is that of a free Monarchy, in which the Sovereign unites in his person both the legislative and executive powers, and, while aided in the work of administration by intermediary bodies, is debarred from making any changes in the fundamental laws.

' The power of the Sovereign, tempered by good laws, is best fitted to effect the happiness of a nation ; this is because, in a Monarchy, the person who governs can easily unite his wishes, and bring his will into play with direct force.'[1]

To sum up, this Convention, in which everyone now makes such a show of Republicanism, contains seventy-seven members who formed part of the Constituent Assembly, and all of whom, Robespierre included, loudly acclaimed in September, 1789, the fundamental laws of the Monarchy—*the inviolability of the King's person, the indivisibility of the throne, and the hereditary transmission of the Crown.*[2] It contains 192 members who formed part of the Legislative Assembly, and all of whom,

---

[1] ' L'An 2440,' by S. Mercier, tome ii., pp. 52 and 56.

[2] ' Archives Parlementaires,' tome viii., p. 643 : Sitting of September 15, 1789 : ' One of the Secretaries read the text of the three articles which have been passed by acclamation. It runs as follows : " The National Assembly has unanimously recognised as the basis of the French Monarchy that the person of the King is inviolable and sacred ; that the throne is indivisible ; that the Crown descends by hereditary right and in order of primogeniture to males of the reigning dynasty, to the perpetual and absolute exclusion of females and their descendants." '

Brissot included, swore, in July last, that *they held the Republic in abhorrence*.[1]   As for the new members, I should hardly think that any of them pretend to be ahead of Marat, Danton and Camille Desmoulins, and we have seen the quality of the Republicanism of these three *Grey Friars*.   Surely no provincial deputy would dare call himself a Republican of longer standing than the Jacobins of Paris, who were still Royalists in 1791 and 1792.   On January 25, 1791, a deputy having uttered the word *Republicans* at the club in the Rue Saint-Honoré, shouts of *We are no Republicans!* came from all parts of the hall, and the speaker was obliged to withdraw the expression.   In the month of June last, Billaud-Varenne was nearly expelled from the club for having dared to question the necessity for a Monarchy.[2]

And the nation itself is still less Republican than its representatives.   I require no other proof than the demonstration that took place in the Legislative Assembly less than two months before the Tenth of August, on the reading of Lafayette's letter, written from the camp at Maubeuge on June 16, 1792. Siding most strongly with the Monarchy against the factionists, the General asked the Assembly to support the following principles : 'That the royal power remain intact, since it is guaranteed by the Constitution ; that it be independent, since that independence is one of the factors of our liberty ; that the King be revered, since he is invested with the majesty of the nation.'   Seventy-five departments spontaneously declared their adhesion to the principles contained in Lafayette's letter.

The truth is that, though we have a Republic, we have no true Republicans—Republicans from conviction and principle ; how, then, can we look forward to the continuance of a Republic in a country possessing neither Republican men nor Republican traditions ?   It is madness to expect that a form of govern-

---

[1] These are the very words of Bishop Lamourette's resolution, passed by acclamation, amid indescribable enthusiasm, at the sitting of July 6, 1792 (*Moniteur* of July 8, No. 290).   Vergniaud styled the vote of July 6 the Decree against the Republic (Notes prepared by Vergniaud for his defence, and edited by Vatel ; 'Vergniaud,' tome ii., p. 297).

[2] 'In 1791 the Jacobins were still Royalists.'—MICHELET, 'Histoire de la Révolution,' tome ii., p. 419.   'In June, 1792, the Jacobin Club is still quite Royalist.'—QUINET, 'La Révolution,' tome i., p. 342.

ment opposed to all established ideas and customs will be able to give us order, peace, justice and liberty !

October 1, 1792.

Eureka ! I have at length discovered, on the benches of the Convention, two real Republicans, Thomas Paine and Anacharsis Cloots—an English Quaker and a Prussian Baron—both naturalized a few moments, or, to be absolutely correct, twenty-seven days before they endowed France with a Republic ![1]

The preceding pages clearly show that the Republic, at the moment of its establishment, had no roots at all in France. To the facts and proofs already adduced, and which are all anterior to September 21, 1792, let us add the significant avowals that escaped some of the principal Revolutionaries after that date.

Brissot, in his manifesto ' À Tous les Republicains de France,' says that in 1791 *there were only three Republicans, Buzot, Petion, and himself !* This estimate is still rather high, since Brissot and Petion, as we have shown above, were Royalists in 1791. As for Buzot, he declares in his ' Mémoires ' that France is not Republican. After having stated that, ' According to many well - informed men, the government that suited France best was that established by the Constituent Assembly '—that is, a Constitutional Monarchy ; after having spoken of the men who, ' possessed of an intimate knowledge of the nature and principles of government, were persuaded that a Republic was unsuited to the genius of the French people,' he adds : ' We cannot disguise the fact that the majority of the French were sighing for the Monarchy and the Constitution of 1791. It was in Paris that the discontent was most general, and least afraid of showing itself. There were only a few men with noble souls and high ideals who really dreamt of firmly establishing such an institution as a Republic in a country naturally frivolous and inconstant. The rest, with the exception of a herd of wretches having neither brains nor means, who belched forth insults against Royalty, as they will in six months do against the Republic—the rest desired nothing but the Constitution of 1791,

---

[1] It was at the sitting of August 26, 1792, that the Legislative Assembly, on the motion of Guadet, conferred the title of French citizens upon Thomas Paine, Anacharsis Cloots, and sixteen other foreigners. Imprisoned on January 1, 1794, Thomas Paine did not recover his liberty until after the 9th of Thermidor. His death, on June 8, 1809, resulted from his passion for drink. Arrested on the same day as Thomas Paine, Anacharsis Cloots was guillotined on March 24, 1794.

and spoke of real Republicans as one speaks of very honest fools.
Can we believe that the events of June 2, 1793, and the misery,
persecution, and outrages which they occasioned, have caused the
majority of Frenchmen to change their opinion? No; but in the
towns people pretend to be *sans-culottes*, because they are guillotined if
they are not; in the country, too, people comply with the most unjust demands, out of fear of the guillotine. The guillotine is the
almighty argument—it is the grand motor of the French Government. . . . But if we examine things more closely, if we enter the
homes of the people and sound their hearts, if they dare to un-
bosom themselves to us, we shall hear of hatred against that government which fear imposes upon them; we shall see how all their
hopes and wishes tend towards the Constitution of 1791.'—'Aux
Amis de la Vérité,' by F. N. L. Buzot, pp. 32-34. Gensonné
(*Chronique de Paris*, February, 1793) admits that in July, 1792,
the majority of the nation was in favour of retaining the Constitution of 1791, and consequently the Monarchy. Petion ('Discours
de Jérôme Petion sur l'Accusation Intentée contre Maximilien
Robespierre,' November, 1792) declares that at the time of the rising
of the Tenth of August, 'there were not five men in France who
wanted a Republic.' Durand de Maillane, another member of the
Convention, states, in his 'Mémoires,' that before the Tenth of
August the Girondins were by no means Republicans. He says
(p. 45): 'It is clear from all these proofs that until the Tenth
of August, or, rather, until the forced resolutions that prepared it,
the Petion party never dreamt of a Republic. The Girondins
themselves, who were so strongly opposed to General Lafayette and
his partisans, were grieved to find themselves under the painful
necessity of abjuring the Monarchy.' Garat, who was a Minister of
the Republic from October 3, 1792, to August 15, 1793, is no less
emphatic in his 'Mémoires Historiques sur la Vie de M. Suard,'
tome ii., p. 331 : 'It has been said that the deputies of the Gironde
came from Bordeaux expressly to transform the Monarchy into a
Republic. The writer of these "Mémoires" knows for a positive
fact that five or six days before the night of the Tenth of August
the two most powerful men in that party had but a faint suspicion
of the existence of a few Republican ideas in the Legislature, and
that this suspicion, which then came to them for the first time, made
them tremble with indignation and anger, like honest men who are
being dragged into a crime against their will.' Governor Morris,
Minister Plenipotentiary of the United States in France from 1792
to 1794, a most judicious and well-informed observer, wrote from
Paris to his friend Thomas Jefferson on October 23, 1792: 'The
majority of the Convention defends itself from the reproach of

Republicanism ; it maintains that the party called Brissotins had no desire of overturning the Monarchy, but simply wished to share the loaves and fishes with their friends ; that the affair of the Tenth of August took place not only without the support, but in spite of the efforts of the deputies.'—' Mémorial de Gouverneur Morris,' tome ii., p. 215. An unpublished letter of Lafayette's (in possession of M. Gustave Bord), written by him to young Dietrich on September 21, 1800, contains the following passage 'As for the Girondists, we now know that they did not then desire the Republic, but only change of Ministers, and that even after the Tenth of August they proposed to put the young Prince on the throne with a Regent.' In a work published in January, 1793, J. L. Soulavie was able to say without fear of contradiction : ' Three thousand workmen effected the Revolution of the Tenth of August, 1792, in spite of a whole kingdom of Royalists, in spite of the majority of the Parisians, and in spite of the majority of the National Assembly, which had been unwilling to vote for the removal of either a perfidious King or of the General who abetted him."—' Mémoires du Maréchal Duc de Richelieu,' tome ix., p. 384. Let us close these quotations with another passage from the same writer, whose good faith is above suspicion, he having been appointed in 1793 resident Minister of the French Republic in Geneva : ' The party called Feuillants wished to govern France constitutionally under Louis XVI. The Girondists desired a Regency during the minority of the King's son, in order to control and baffle the Queen, whose schemes of a counter-Revolution imperilled not only the political existence, but the very lives of the Girondists. Neither Robespierre nor Marat had any ideas of a Republic. Danton, Marat, and the ' Grey Friars ' were attached in September, 1792, to D'Orléans. At the meetings of the central committee, formed before the Tenth of August for the purpose of expediting the King's overthrow, the motion brought forward by Xavier Audouin for establishing a Republic in place of the Monarchy was rejected by all present, and even by Collot-d'Herbois. . . . This committee and a meeting of the deputies of Paris also decided that the petition demanding the King's abdication should be in accordance with Constitutional forms. In the interval between the Tenth of August and September 22, Petion continually opposed all ideas and suggestions referring to a Republic. The Legislative Body had recently uttered anathemas, and the Jacobins had constantly risen up against the scheme of a Republic. . . . On the very day of the declaration of the Republic, three-quarters of an hour after the close of the sitting of the Convention, Condorcet and a few Girondists met in the dining-room of the Valois Club, in the Palais Royal. All seemed in a state of consternation, and hardly dared look each other in the face.   Condorcet, breaking the silence, said to the company : "It has always been my real opinion that the French Republic would be a grand thing." '—'Mémoires Historiques et Politiques du Règne de Louis XVI.,' by J. L. Soulavie, tome vi., p. 449, etc.

From all this evidence, it may safely be concluded that France was still Royalist in 1792, and that the very men who proclaimed their Republican opinions so loudly were at heart no Republicans.   We have thought it useful to prove this for two reasons.   Firstly, because this fact has generally been neglected or distorted by the historians of the Revolution ; secondly, because it explains most of the events that are to follow, and because there is no need to seek elsewhere the origin and cause of the persecution, outrages, and crimes into which the Republic of September 22 was led.

CHAPTER VII.

THE TUILERIES.

Monday, October 1, 1792.

ON the 8th of last month the Section of the Sans-Culottes[1] sent a deputation to the Conseil-Général de la Commune to draw attention to the advantages the nation would reap from the sale of the old convent des Feuillants. The spokesman expressed his surprise at seeing the representatives of the sovereign people crowded together in a small riding-school whilst Kings had always dwelt in palaces, and he proposed to present a petition to the National Assembly inviting it to choose in the Tuileries proper accommodation for holding its sittings.

The petition was immediately presented to the Assembly in the name of the Conseil-Général by M. Petion, the Mayor, who asked the Legislature to decide that the Convention should sit 'in the old *salle* of the Théâtre-Français, in the Palace of the Tuileries.' The matter was referred to the Special Commission of Twenty-one and to the Committee of Public Instruction. So great was the favour with which our deputies received the idea of locating the Legislative Body in the palace, which but yesterday was the abode of Royalty, that in less than a week plans, reports, and resolutions were all passed, and as early as September 14 M. Roland, the Minister of the Interior, was authorized to put them into execution with as little delay as possible. The work was entrusted to M. Vignon, the architect, who promised that it should be completed before December 1.

[1] This section, which from 1790 to the Tenth of August, 1792, was called the Section du Jardin-des-Plantes, met in the church of Saint-Nicolas-du-Chardonnet.

I was very anxious to visit the Tuileries once more before the palace was overturned and used for entirely different purposes, and it may not be out of place to give a description of it here as it still is, and as it was on the day when the grandson of Louis XIV. and the daughter of Maria Theresa left it for the Temple Tower.

I was accompanied by François Nepveu, one of M. Vignon's pupils.

We entered the gardens by the Pont-Tournant,[1] or swing-bridge, and immediately came upon the charred ruins of the barracks formerly inhabited by the Swiss Guard. The disgusting evidences of the shameful orgy with which the heroes of the Tenth of August had celebrated their victory had been removed. For more than a fortnight the remains of the broken bottles lay strewn about the gardens in such immense quantities[2] that it almost seemed as if the paths had been intentionally paved with pounded glass.

We enter the principal avenue, and recall to mind the terrible scenes enacted here. After having left the palace by the King's orders, the Swiss Guards made for this avenue, and, upon reaching it, divided themselves into two columns. The first kept under cover of the trees, and made its way towards the Riding-School, whilst the second proceeded towards the Pont-Tournant. This column, though exposed to the bullets that came whistling from behind the trees, succeeded in reaching the Place Louis XV., but only to find it occupied by some battalions of National Guards, who received the unhappy Swiss with a heavy volley. Attacked on both sides, the column, which had till then remained unshaken, was dispersed, some of the brave men who formed it rushing across the Pont-Tournant to the foot of Louis XV.'s statue, where they nearly all met their death. Those who remained in the gardens made off in all directions, but not a single one escaped. They were massacred under the trees, in the ornamental waters, on the terraces, in the Dauphin's garden, in the Orangerie, and at the foot of the marble statues.

[1] The Pont-Tournant crossed the moat which then separated the Tuileries from the Place Louis XV.

[2] Mercier, 'Le Nouveau Paris,' ch. cxlviii.

A common grave dug near one of the chestnut-trees received their bodies.[1] Such are the reminiscences awakened by the sight of trees slashed with sword and bayonet, statues bearing the marks of bullets, basins whose waters are still tinted with the blood of the victims. We reach the terrace, and before us, through the railings of the palace, we can see in the Place du Carrousel the guillotine erected upon the pedestal formerly adorned by the statue of Louis XV.[2]

From the guillotine my eyes wander to the word 'REPUBLIC,' which shines in letters of gold upon the front of the Tuileries, and where it is undoubtedly in its proper place. Is it not, indeed, the one idea naturally suggested by these mutilated statues, these blood-stained walls, and these blackened stones? *Lapides clamabunt!*

From the dome of the palace floats a tricolour flag bearing the words: '*The Mayor of Paris was nearly murdered here on the night between the* 9th *and* 10th.' With downcast eyes we pass this lying standard, and enter the palace by the Pavillon du Milieu.

The grand staircase, the stone balustrade of which is ornamented with allegorical and armorial devices, mostly smashed with pikes and axes, leads to the Salle des Cent-Suisses, and thence to the suite of apartments forming the south wing.

The Salle des Cent-Suisses is a very lofty hall situated over the vestibule, and was used by the Convention for its first sitting on September 20. On leaving it, we enter the Salle des Gardes. This is an immense apartment sometimes called Galerie de Diane, on account of the paintings by Nicolas Loir with which it is adorned. It was in this room that 200 noblemen, who had hurried to the Tuileries at the first rumour of danger on the morning of the Tenth of August, saluted the assembled Royal Family with a cry of devotion. They wore no uniforms, and

---

[1] This is the tree known as the *marronnier* of March 20, and which might more appropriately be called the *marronnier* of the Tenth of August.

[2] The following is an order of the Commune of Paris, dated August 23, 1792 : 'The Conseil-Général decrees that the guillotine shall remain standing in the Place de la Réunion (formerly Place du Carrousel) until further orders, the cutlass to be removed by the headsman after every execution.'

carried their weapons concealed beneath their coats. 'Long live the King of our fathers!' cried the young men. 'Long live our children's King!' replied the old. And both young and old lift up on high the Dauphin, for whom they are about to die; it is the last farewell of the old French nobility to that dynasty which has created France. But the Galerie de Diane is connected with the memory of a still more touching scene. In June, 1791, after the King's return from Varennes, the most rigorous precautions were taken by Lafayette to prevent a second escape. The celebration of Mass in the chapel was forbidden, on the ground that the latter was too far from the royal apartments, and a simple wooden altar, adorned with a few vases of flowers, and surmounted by an ebony crucifix, was set up in a corner of the gallery. Here Mass was celebrated every Sunday by the Abbé d'Avaux, the Dauphin's tutor.

After the Salle des Gardes comes the King's ante-room, or Salle de l'Œil-de-Bœuf (the Bull's-eye). Over the fireplace there used to be a fine painting by Mignard, representing Louis XIV. on horseback being crowned by Minerva; but Mignard's masterpiece was torn to shreds by the heroes of the Tenth of August. In this room Louis XVI. witnessed the march past of the Revolution on June 20. For four hours he unflinchingly bore with astonishing serenity and courage the insults of an infuriated mob armed with pikes, scythes, pitchforks, saws, bludgeons, guns, and pistols, and displaying the most hideous trophies and threatening devices. Some bore a guillotine with the inscription: '*For the Tyrant*'; others a gibbet from which hung the effigy of a woman with these words: '*For Antoinette*'; others, again, bore huge strips of bleeding flesh, labelled: '*From the Aristocrats*,' but all marched past shouting, '*Down with Véto! To hell with Véto!*' and yelling out the most atrocious insults and threats of death.[1] The King had with him only a few friends, three of his Ministers, MM. de Beaulieu, de Lajard, and Terrier de Montciel, Marshal de Mouchy, one or two Knights of Saint Louis, and five or six National Guards. He was seated on a high bench in the recess

---

[1] 'Mémoires' of Ferrières, tome iii., p. 109; 'Mémoires' of Mme. Campan, p. 331; 'Essais Historiques,' by Beaulieu, tome iii., p. 369.

of one of the windows that looked out upon the principal courtyard. Mme. Elisabeth, who could not be prevailed upon to
leave her brother, was in the next recess, and was mistaken by
the rioters for the Queen, for the 'Austrian woman.' 'Do not
deceive them,' she said to the friends who were standing round
her.[1] A bayonet almost touched her breast; she turned it
aside with her hand, saying in a sweet voice: 'Take care, sir;
you might hurt someone, and I am sure you would be sorry to
do that.'

The Salle de l'Œil-de-Bœuf leads to the larger of the King's
rooms called the State Bedroom.[2] This, again, communicates
with the Grand Cabinet, or Council Chamber, so called because
it was here that the Council of Regency met during the minority
of Louis XV. On June 20, when the mob broke into the
palace, the Queen came hastening from the Dauphin's room to
share her husband's danger, but was stopped in the State Bedroom by M. d'Aubier, one of her most faithful servants. 'Let
me pass!' she cries; 'my place is with the King. I will join
him, and perish, if necessary, in defending him.' M. de
Rougeville,[3] a Knight of Saint Louis and officer in the National
Guards, joins M. d'Aubier in his efforts, and in the meantime

---

[1] 'Mémoires' of Mme. Campan, p. 330.

[2] Louis Blanc (vi. 381) is wrong in giving the State Bedroom as the
scene of the last-mentioned episode. See the procès-verbal drawn up by
the Juge de Paix of the Section of the Tuileries concerning the events of
June 20.

[3] The Tenth of August found the Chevalier de Rougeville once more
at his post of honour and devotion in the Tuileries. Thrown into prison,
he escaped on the eve of the September massacres. Again arrested, he
managed to baffle the vigilance of his gaolers on June 1, 1793. In
September he succeeded in getting into the Conciergerie, in the hope of
saving the Queen, and of handing her a carnation containing a note.
(For this attempt and its consequences, see 'Marie Antoinette à la
Conciergerie,' by Émile Carpardon.) In 1795 he was arrested a third
time, and kept a prisoner in the Temple for two years. During the
Empire he was for a long time under police supervision at Rheims. When
the Allies entered France, he publicly declared himself for the Bourbons.
Brought before a council of war in 1814, he was condemned to death.
The Chevalier de Rougeville was born at Arras in 1760. The son of a
farmer of taxes, who had left him a considerable fortune, he had served
with the flower of the French nobility under Lafayette in the American
War of Independence, by the side of that heroic Comte de Fersen who
was also to become one of the most faithful defenders of Louis XVI. and
Marie Antoinette.

other courtiers come to their aid. Marie Antoinette is surrounded, and is at length made to understand that it would be
impossible to get through the serried ranks of the assailants;
that, if not murdered, she would be suffocated before reaching
the King; that her efforts would be fatal to him whom she
wished to save, since he would naturally break through the mob
to reach her.[1] She thereupon allows herself to be led back into
the Dauphin's room, takes the boy in her arms, and, supported
by Mme. Royale, traverses the corridor that leads from the
Dauphin's room to that of the King. Attended by Mmes. de
Tourzel, de Tarente, de la Roche-Aymon, and de Maillé, and
surrounded by a band of brave grenadiers, she stations herself
in the recess of a window in the Council Chamber, with a large
table before her. After having marched past the King and
crossed the State Bedroom, where they indulge in a thousand
ribald jests, the mob passes before the Queen. A young woman
stops and pours forth a volley of curses. 'Have I done you
any harm?' asks Marie Antoinette. 'No,' replies the girl; 'but
you are ruining the nation.' 'You have been deceived,' says
the Queen. 'I am the wife of the King of France and the
mother of the Dauphin. I am a Frenchwoman now, and shall
never see my native home again. Henceforth I shall be happy
or unhappy only in France, and I was *so* happy when you loved
me!' The girl begins to weep: 'Ah, madame, forgive me! I
did not know you; I see that you are good.'[2]

The King's private apartments, consisting of a bedroom and
a study, were situated to the right of the State Bedroom and
the Council Chamber, and looked out upon the gardens.[3]

---

[1] 'Exact and Detailed Narrative of what passed at the Palace of the
Tuileries on Wednesday, June 20, 1792.' Paris, 1792.

[2] 'Mémoires' of Mme. Campan, p. 331.

[3] In the King's bedroom, and at the side of his bed, was a door opening on to a wainscoted passage, three feet wide, that led to the Dauphin's
room. It was in this passage that Louis XVI., having decided to leave
Paris in March, 1791, had a small hiding-place made for the papers he did
not want to take with him. This place of concealment, afterwards known
as the *iron cupboard*, was a plain, rough hole, about two feet deep and
fifteen inches wide, dug in the wall about four feet from the floor. The
hole was covered with an iron door about a foot and a half square, and
concealed by a panel of the wainscoting ('Biographie Universelle,' article
'Gamain,' by Eckard). The *iron cupboard* was not discovered until
November 20, 1792.

The Dauphin occupied the ground-floor under the King's rooms, the apartments of Mme. Royale being on the floor above. On breaking into the Dauphin's study, the rioters seem to have been somewhat quieted at the sight of a child's books, maps, and writing materials.

Behind the Council Chamber is another state room and the billiard-room—the latter contiguous to the Pavillon de Flore. The King's private apartments were also connected with that pavilion by a wide gallery, called the Galerie des Carraches, or des Ambassadeurs.[1] Under this gallery were the Queen's *grands appartements*, consisting of six rooms, almost on a level with the terrace. The Queen's *petits appartements* were over the Galerie des Carraches. Marie Antoinette's rooms were the only ones that the insurgents of June 20 did not enter.

It was not so on the Tenth of August. After the King had left the Tuileries to proceed to the Assembly, the Ladies-in-waiting entered the Queen's apartments on the ground-floor, and, hearing the sound of shots, drew the blinds and lit all the candles. The insurgents, on breaking open the door, were dazzled by the myriads of lights reflected in the mirrors of the *salon*, and drew back in astonishment. The more courageous of the ladies took advantage of this respite to parley with the foremost of the invaders, and obtained permission to leave the palace in safety.

The Pavillon de Flore, situated on the quay, opposite the Pont-Royal, was inhabited by Mme. Elisabeth. It was there that the Dauphin had spent the night between October 6 and 7, 1789, when Louis XVI. was brought back from Versailles to Paris. The room on the ground-floor which looks out upon the Cour des Princes had at first been set apart for the King's sister, but it was found to be too exposed to the gaze of the curious.

It was under the windows of this room that an immense

---

[1] It was in this gallery that Louis XIV. used to receive the Ambassadors, hence its name. The other name was given it, not because it contained paintings by the Carraches, but because Colbert had filled it with reproductions of the principal subjects in the Farnese Gallery, painted by Annibal and Augustin Carrache ('Curiosités de Paris, 1771,' tome i., p. 118).

crowd gathered on the morning of October 7, 1789, shouting
'*Long live the King! Long live the Queen!*' and demanding
the appearance of the Royal Family. The Queen appeared first.
She was wearing a large hat that shaded part of her face, and
being requested to remove it, she did so. For several days the
mob filled the Cour des Princes, and became so importunate that
some of the market-women jumped into Mme. Elisabeth's room.
The Princess thereupon begged the King to have her lodged
elsewhere, and was given the firstfloor of the pavilion, the
Dauphin being removed to one of the rooms in the King's own
suite.[1]

A handsome staircase, called the Escalier des Princes, leads
from the courtyard of that name to the Pavillon de Flore.
Another branch of the same staircase leads to an iron gate
giving access to the gardens, and called the Queen's Gate.

We had visited every part of the palace inhabited by the
Royal Family, and at every step we had found horrible traces
left by the rioters in their bloody passage through the magnificent apartments. Mirrors smashed and tapestries torn down ;
chimney-pieces dismantled and walls laid bare ; furniture,
clocks, works of art, all thrown pell-mell out of window on that
Tenth of August. The walls and floors are all stained with
gore, the victims' blood having even reached the priceless
paintings that adorn most of the rooms.

From the Pavillon de Flore we went down into the Cour des
Princes, the first of the four courts that enclose the palace on
the side of the Carrousel. The second court, the Cour Royale,
is opposite the central pavilion. It was there that the two
guns belonging to the battalion on duty at the palace were
stationed after October 6, 1789. The third court, called Cour
des Suisses, or Cour des Écuries, contained the barracks in which
the Swiss Guards were lodged. The fourth court, called the
Cour de Marsan, from the name of the pavilion in its northern
corner, lies between the palace and the Brionne mansion.

Some small buildings, principally built of wood, shut off the
rest of the palace from the Place du Carrousel. These were
burnt on the Tenth of August, and the conflagration very
nearly spread to the Pavillon Marsan and the Pavillon de Flore.

[1] 'Mémoires' of Mme. de Tourzel, tome i., p. 27.

The Commune, though charged by the Legislative Body with the care of extinguishing the fire, made no effort to do so. The President of the Assembly was himself obliged to intervene, and to give orders which were exceedingly difficult to execute, since Santerre's men persisted in firing on the firemen. The ruins were cleared away, and a wooden hoarding now separates the Tuileries from the Place du Carrousel. Above the door of this temporary partition is the following inscription: '*The Monarchy was abolished on the Tenth of August; it will never rise again.*'

The façade of the Tuileries has suffered a good deal more on this side than on that of the gardens. The Patriots have taken care to have the words '*Tenth of August*' inscribed over every mark left on the stone by the cannon-balls directed against the palace.

Entering the buildings once more by the central pavilion, we rapidly traversed the second half of the palace, extending from the grand staircase to the Pavillon Marsan, and consisting of the chapel, the theatre, and the suite occupied by the King's aunts.

The door of the chapel opens out upon the first landing of the grand staircase. On Sunday, August 5, whilst vespers were being read before the King and Queen, the choristers chanted the following verse of the *Magnificat*, in loud and threatening tones: '*Deposuit potentes de sede, et exaltavit humiles.*' The Royalists replied by the chant of, '*Domine salvum fac Regem,*' adding three times '*et Reginam!*'[1] Five days after the choristers were satisfied. The King was deposed, and in the chapel the bodies of seven Swiss soldiers were ranged upon the altar. The pavement was streaming with blood, and strips of flesh and men's brains were trodden under foot.[2]

Behind the chapel is the theatre. This was generally called the Salle des Machines, on account of the ballets which were performed here before Louis XIV. and his Court; after the burning of the Opera-house in 1763, the actors took refuge in this *salle*, and from 1770 to 1783 it accommodated the

---

[1] *Révolutions de Paris*, No. 101; 'Mémoires' of Mme. Campan, p. 345; Castil-Blaze, 'Académie Impériale de Musique,' tome ii., p. 7.

[2] 'Montgaillard,' tome iii., p. 152.

Comédiens Français. Whilst the latter were at the Tuileries, the spectators entered the theatre by the Cour des Suisses. It was there that Lekain appeared as Vendôme, Tancred and Orosmane for the last time, and that Mdlle. Clairon, also for the last time, played the part of Medea. Voltaire was crowned there on March 30, 1778. The theatre has three tiers of boxes, and is capable of holding several thousand spectators. The Convention will hold its sittings there as soon as the works undertaken by M. Vignon are completed.

While we were there, Mercier, the deputy, also came to visit the Salle des Machines. As usual, he was rather strangely dressed in a shabby gray coat, a long vest studded with tarnished spangles and coloured beads, frills of a week's wear, and an eyeglass.[1] He went out with us, and we walked about in the gardens for some time whilst he told us about the Tenth of August. 'I was here,' he said, 'and will tell you what I saw. Heads came flying out of the windows, and bleeding corpses were thrown from the topmost galleries. In the kitchens everyone, from the head-cooks to the scullery-aids, had been killed. A poor devil of a scullion was stuffed into a boiler and left to stew there over the blazing fire. More than one improvised furnace, too, had been prepared by the conflagration in the courts. The bodies of the Swiss Guards were roasted over them, and women stood there calmly gazing upon the smoking entrails of the victims. The heat was overwhelming, and there was not the slightest breeze to disturb the clouds of flies that swarmed around this field of carnage, settling upon the gaping wounds of the dead and dying men. In the vestibule, at the foot of the grand staircase, men and women were dancing in streams of blood and wine, while on the terrace a miserable wretch was playing the fiddle amidst a heap of bodies still warm.[2] Were you present at the sitting of the Assembly? No? But you read the account in the *Moniteur*. You were moved, no doubt, by the story of those honest insurgents who appeared at the bar laden with the valuables found in the Tuileries—of that brave fellow carrying a box of the Queen's jewels, of those *sans-culottes* depositing in the Convention a

---

[1] Charles Nodier, 'Souvenirs de la Révolution et de l'Empire.'
[2] Mercier, 'Le Nouveau Paris,' ch. xxxiv.

chest full of plate. You no doubt admired those half-clothed citizens bringing in, unopened, bags full of gold and silver coin, the plate from the chapel and the royal table, a hat filled with louis, bank-notes, and the rest.[1] You read all that, did you not? Well, this is what *I* saw. Whilst the leaders of the insurrection were having the large silver candlesticks of the chapel, the silver plate, and a bag containing a hundred louis, carried in great pomp to the Assembly, their men were forcing the cabinets of the King and Queen, of Mme. Elisabeth, of Mme. de Lamballe, and of the Court ladies, carrying off bank-notes, gold and silver, watches, jewellery, diamonds and other precious stones. They took dresses, linen, plate, wines, candles, books — anything, in fact, they could lay their hands on. Nothing worth having escaped the practised eye or the industry of these honest people—they even tore the gold braid from the royal liveries and stuffed it into their pockets, smashing the most costly china vases for the sake of the gold or silver fastenings.'[2]

'Then it is not true,' inquired Nepveu, 'that, according to the *Révolutions de Paris*, the slightest theft was punished as soon as it was perceived? Prudhomme even said in his journal, if I remember rightly, that a thief had lost his life in the palace, being killed by those who caught him in the act.'[3]

'Yes,' replied Mercier, 'that is one of the ghastly jokes of that memorable day : thieves, with their pockets full of gold, hung up other thieves to the balustrade of the grand staircase.'[4]

We had now reached the Pont-Tournant. Before leaving the gardens, we turned once more to take a last look at the Tuileries. It was a beautiful day, and the autumn sun cast its golden veil over the gardens and the palace ; its rays, promoters of life and joy, lovingly caressed the walls mutilated by smoke and shot, and, playing through the branches of the half-stripped trees, lit up with harmless flames the great windows of the façade ; whilst on the other side of the palace, in the Place du Carrousel, we could see, bathed in the same light, the beams of the guillotine.

[1] *Révolutions de Paris*, No. 161 ; the *Journal Logographique*, supplement to tome xxvi.

[2] Mercier, *loc. cit.* [3] *Révolutions de Paris*, No. 161. [4] Mercier, *loc. cit.*

CHAPTER VIII.

THE OFFERING TO LIBERTY.

Wednesday, October 3, 1792.

A PIECE of great good news has brought a momentary truce to our terror and anguish : the Duke of Brunswick has given up the idea of marching on Paris, and the Austro-Prussian Army is on its way back to the frontier. From the Convention, where the Minister of War read a letter from Dumouriez, dated from Sainte-Menehould on October 1, and announcing the retreat of the enemy, the news spread with lightning speed through every quarter of Paris. This morning the Patriotic newspapers attempt to get up a reaction against the enthusiasm it excited. Knowing well enough that their Republic has not the slightest stability, that it has no more hold upon French soil than an airy tent, they fear the victories of our Generals even more than those of our enemies. They understand, too, that their factitious Government, having neither past nor future, will fall, like the walls of Jericho, at the first trumpet-blast of a fortunate soldier. They therefore lose no opportunity of throwing discredit upon the Generals who have saved the country, turning the exploits of Dumouriez and Beurnonville to ridicule, and exercising their wit at the expense of the Achilles and Ajax of France.[1] In a few days' time these wretched sheets, which deserve the epithet

---

[1] ' Brave Beurnonville, who has been christened the Ajax of France. . .' —Letter from Dumouriez, dated October 1, 1792. Hereupon the *Révolutions de Paris*, No. 169, wrote : ' Let us take care that Dumouriez does not call Beurnonville the Ajax of France only to get himself called our Achilles. The lying chronicler of the time says that without Achilles Troy would not have been taken. But here we have the legislator Carra already making an Agamemnon of him, and a Diomedes of General Duval. No doubt Carra will be the Homer who will sing their exploits.'

of Austrian more than the unfortunate Marie Antoinette, will
no doubt have got over the common-sense of the people, but
in the meantime the Parisians are simple enough to rejoice at
the success of our armies. Yesterday evening the joy was
universal. On all sides, both in private and in public, the good
people of Paris gave themselves up entirely and unreservedly
to the glad feelings that filled their hearts, and I, for my part,
shall never forget the demonstrations that I witnessed at the
Opera-house.

Since the beginning of the Revolution, the former Académie
Royale de Musique had performed no piece to do honour to the
new order of things. In vain did our other theatres set it an
example, which for a long time the opera seemed little disposed
to follow. At length the management was moved to try its
hand at political pieces, and everyone must admit that its first
attempt was a master-stroke.

The bills for yesterday evening announced ' Corisandre,'[1] and
' The Offering to Liberty, a Religious Scene based upon the
Song of the Marseillais.' The success of ' Corisandre,' which
was never very great, has long been exhausted. In the Religious
Scene, which was to be performed for the first time, the public
did not seem to expect anything very extraordinary, for the
theatre, although well attended, was far from being full.[2] The
three acts of ' Corisandre' were listened to coolly enough, but
as soon as the curtain again rose the feelings of the audience
underwent a sudden change, and everyone present, struck by
the grandeur of the scene, and excited by the news just received
from the Army of the North, was seized with an enthusiasm that
went on increasing until the end.

Liberty, represented by Mdlle. Maillard, was standing on the
top of a rock that occupied the middle of the stage, and at the
foot of which a crowd of mounted and unmounted warriors,

---

[1] ' Corisandre,' an opera in three acts, words by Linières and Lebailly,
music by Langlé, was performed for the first time on March 8, 1791.
Langlé, born at Monaco in 1741, was a teacher of music in Paris, whither
he had come in 1768. His wife was the sister of M. Sue, the well-known
physician, father of Eugène Sue, the novelist.

[2] The receipts at the first performance amounted to 4,223 francs ; at
the second they rose to 5,200 francs.

accompanied by women and children, came flocking together at the sound of the trumpet. The variety and brilliancy of the costumes, the power of the orchestra, the spectacle of these masses blended in artistic and harmonious disorder, the warriors on their well-trained chargers, and the creature of radiant beauty enthroned in the midst of this busy and striking scene—all these were calculated to blind the eye and exalt the imagination. The effect was irresistible and tremendous. The warriors prepare themselves for battle, or rather for victory, which the women and children already celebrate by their songs :

*' Allons, enfants de la patrie,
Le jour de gloire est arrivé !'*

The glorious 'Hymne des Marseillais' is commenced and continued to the end, for the ' Offering to Liberty ' is nothing more than that hymn put into action. As the song proceeds, the most picturesque groups are formed, corresponding to the sentiments expressed in the lines, the arrangement reflecting the greatest credit upon the talent of P. Gardel, the author of the ballets of ' Télémaque ' and ' Psyché.' The most charming dancers of the opera, led by Mme. Gardel, rightly called the Venus de Medicis of dancing, temper with their grace the violence of the celebrated refrain :

*' Aux armes, citoyens ! Formez vos bataillons !
Marchez ! . . . Qu'un sang impur abreuve nos sillons !'*

But now comes the last verse—' *Amour sacré de la patrie !'*

It is sung slowly and softly, like a prayer, by the women alone, the contrast between these religious accents and the warlike shouts of the preceding lines being very striking. At the words

' Liberté, liberté chérie,'

all the actors kneel before the figure of Liberty on the rock. Even the horses, ranged in battle-order to the right and left, bend their heads and slowly kneel, whilst their riders salute with their arms and standards.

A long silence ensues after this verse, suddenly broken, not by the expected refrain, but by the blast of trumpets calling

the defenders of the country to battle. The tocsin is heard,
the drums beat the *générale*, and the cannon thunders in the
distance ; the horses rear and champ their bits, eager for the
fray ; the actors rise and brandish their arms, whilst an immense
throng bearing axes, pikes, and torches invades the stage.
Then all in unison attack the grand refrain : ' *Aux armes,
citoyens !*

Never have I witnessed a scene of greater dramatic intensity.

I have heard the song of the Marseillais yelled out by the
most abandoned wretches on earth on the Tenth of August
and September 2. Its verses, stained with blood, are henceforth hateful to all honest men. But I must confess that last
night I could not refrain from admiring the wonderful effect
with which the composer Gossec has reproduced it. Of this
song he has made a grand, an almost sublime, poem, and it is
to be hoped that those Patriotic journalists who but yesterday
accused poor Gossec of professing political principles less trust-
worthy than his musical talents will deign to approve his ' Offering,' and will no longer reproach him with having belonged
to the Royalist club of the Sainte-Chapelle, and with having
signed the petition against the acts of June 20.

Of all the political pieces performed during the Revolution, the
' Offering of Liberty ' is perhaps the most remarkable, and that
which had the greatest effect upon the public. No mention is, however, made of it either in Jauffret's ' Théâtre Révolutionnaire ' or in
Théodore Muret's ' Histoire par le Théâtre.' Henri Welschinger
(' Le Théâtre de la Révolution,' p. 298) gives it only four lines, and
wrongly gives October 20, 1792, as the date of its first performance.
It has been said above that the last verse of the ' Marseillaise ' is
that which begins : ' *Amour sacré de la patrie.*'

That was true on October 2, 1792 ; but twelve days later, on
October 14, the *fête* of Liberty was celebrated. In the Garde
Nationale of Paris were two battalions of children. One of these
battalions took part in the *fête*, and in its honour was added the
verse with which the hymn now ends :

> ' *Nous entrerons dans la carrière,*
> *Quand nos aînés n'y seront plus.*'

CHAPTER IX

OATHS OF ALLEGIANCE.

Thursday, October 4, 1792.

It is just a year ago to-day since the following scene was enacted in the hall now occupied by the Convention.

M. Pastoret is in the Presidential chair, and the Secretaries are MM. Cérutti, François de Neufchâteau, Garran de Coulon, Condorcet, and Guyton-Morveau. The business is the taking of the oath of allegiance to the Constitution. M. Michon-Dumarais, deputy for Rhône-et-Loire, moves that the original Acte Constitutionnel itself, now deposited in the Archives, shall be brought to the Assembly and placed on the tribune, and that every member, as he takes the oath, shall lay his hand upon the sacred document. This motion is received with applause and passed. It is also decided that a deputation, composed of the twelve oldest members of the Legislature, shall go in solemn procession to the Archives, where the Acte Constitutionnel shall be delivered to them. The twelve Commissioners, for once proud of their age, assemble in the centre of the hall, and march out with M. Ducastel, the Vice-President, at their head.

What reception is to be accorded them when they return, holding in their hands the Book of the Law? Rouyer, member for the Hérault, suggests that the whole Assembly shall rise as the deputation enters. Another member moves that the oath which they are about to take shall be written in large letters above the President's chair, so that every speaker shall constantly be reminded of the duties he has undertaken. Lecoz, a Constitutional Bishop, desires that the taking of the oath shall be announced to the people by the firing of cannon. Jean

Debry, member for the Aisne, moves that, since the Assembly has decided that its oldest members should bring in the Acte Constitutionnel, the youngest members should be allowed to receive it.

At length there is no more speaking, and for some minutes the deepest silence reigns in the hall. The whole Assembly, and even the galleries, seem plunged in a kind of religious reverie, as at the approach of a Divine manifestation. Suddenly an usher at the door cries: 'Gentlemen, I beg to announce the Acte Constitutionnel.' All the members as well as the spectators immediately rise. Preceded by ushers, and escorted by a detachment of National Guards, the Vice-President and the twelve elders advance in procession; in their midst Camus, the Archivist, devoutly pressing to his breast the thrice sacred document. To see him, one would think he was Moses descending from Sinai with the tablets of the law, the shining glory that is said to have covered the face of the great legislator being well replaced by the beetroot colour of the Archivist's features.[1]

On reaching the foot of the tribune, one of the elders, in a voice broken with age and emotion, cries: 'Countrymen! fellow-citizens! behold the pledge of peace prepared by the Legislature! Upon this token of the people's will we are about to swear to live as free men or to die, to defend the Constitution at the price of . . .' The last words of the old orator are drowned by the cheers that welcome the appearance of M. Camus and the Acte Constitutionnel in the tribune.

The law relating to the organization of the Legislative Body simply stipulating that each member shall ascend the tribune and say, '*I swear it*,' the Assembly declares this to be insufficient, and directs that all the words of the oath shall be repeated by each member. A deputy pointing out that no deliberation can take place whilst the King is present, it is decided that this shall also be the case whilst the Acte Constitutionnel is in the Assembly. Another deputy moves that all the armed men shall withdraw. 'The Acte Constitutionnel,' he adds, 'is in no danger

---

[1] 'Mirabeau used to jestingly call the rigid Camus *the Red Flag*, in allusion to the red flag of the martial law. His face was highly inflamed, and his nose was the colour of blood.'—ÉTIENNE DUMONT, 'Souvenirs sur Mirabeau,' ch. xv.

6

in the Assembly; it has no need of defenders here.' The National Guards and *gendarmes* withdraw, and the ceremony begins.

The President leaves his chair, and is the first to ascend the tribune. Laying his hand upon the new Gospel, which is still in the keeping of M. Camus, he utters the following formula: '*I swear to maintain with all my might the Constitution of the kingdom as decreed by the Constituent National Assembly in the years* 1789, 1790, *and* 1791, *to propose or to consent to nothing in the course of legislature which might impair it, and to be in all things true to the Nation, the Law, and the King.*'

Each deputy, as his name is called by one of the Secretaries, then ascends the tribune, and, placing his right hand on the Acte Constitutionnel, pronounces the same formula in full.

The ceremony lasted two hours, and during the whole of that time the Archivist, with head erect, one hand on his breast and the other on the precious document, did not for a single moment abandon the sacred charge entrusted to him.

He at length left the tribune, and again took his place in the midst of the Commissioners, who, in solemn procession, escorted the Acte Constitutionnel back to the Archives.

On their return to the Assembly one of them made the following speech: 'You will no doubt be glad to hear that the Commissioners have discharged the duty with which they were entrusted, and that the precious document has been put away with such precautions as preclude all danger. But, gentlemen, that is not exactly what I rose to say, for these precautions, after what has taken place, appear superfluous. After the oath that we have taken, the Acte Constitutionnel has found a place not only in the hearts of those present, but in the hearts of all Frenchmen.'[1]

In attending the sitting of the Convention to-day, October 4,

[1] For the whole of this scene, very imperfectly reported by the *Moniteur*, see the *Ami du Roi*, October 6, 1791 : the *Révolutions de Paris*, No. 117 ; the 'Histoire de la Révolution de France,' by Two Friends of Liberty, tome vi., p. 337 ; the 'Essais Historiques,' by Beaulieu, tome iii., p. 42 ; the *Journal des Débats et des Décrets*, first National Legislative Assembly, No. 4 ; *Journal Logographique*, first Legislature, by M. le Hodey, tome i., pp. 35, etc. ; 'Mémoires' of Hua, a member of the Legislative Assembly, p. 75.

1791, how could I help being reminded of that scene which took place just a year ago? In this Assembly which has just abolished the Monarchy, and which keeps the King a prisoner in the Temple, I recognised those same deputies who but a year ago swore so solemnly to be true to the King and to the Monarchical power. In the places of honour I saw Condorcet, Brissot, Vergniaud, and Lasource, men who had taken an oath before God and their fellow-citizens ' to maintain with all their might the Constitution of the kingdom, to propose or to consent to nothing in the course of legislature which might impair it, and to be in all things true to the Nation, the Law, and the King.' And beside them, filling also an official post, I saw the hero of October 4, 1791, the austere guardian of the Constitution, Camus himself—the Archivist Camus!

CHAPTER X.

Thursday, October 18, 1792.

GENERAL DUMOURIEZ has been in Paris since the 11th. On the 12th he appeared at the bar of the Convention, and showed himself at the Opera. Escorted by Citizen Santerre, he proceeded to the Section of the Lombards on the 13th. On the 14th, which was Sunday, he was present at a meeting of the Jacobin Club, Danton being in the chair.[1] Truly a strange man this Dumouriez, one who both patronizes and frightens the Jacobins, who has something of an adventurer and of a genius in him, and whom everyone both admires and mistrusts; a man whose abilities have done more for France than an army, and who could justly boast, amid the plaudits of the Convention and the galleries, that his soldiers, more fortunate than the Spartans at Thermopylæ, had stopped the Prussians in the passes of the Argonne forest. I had not yet seen him when, on Tuesday last, Tassin, the banker,[2] invited me to accompany him to a *fête* to be given at Madame Talma's in honour of the General. I gladly accepted the invitation.

At ten o'clock I was at Tassin's house in the Rue Vivienne, where I found Roucher,[3] who is a frequent visitor at Mme.

---

[1] *Journal des Débats . . . de la Société des Jacobins*, No. 263.

[2] Louis Daniel Tassin, a banker, a member for the Third Estate of the city of Paris in the States-General, and an officer of the battalion of the Filles-Saint-Thomas, of which his brother, Tassin de l'Estang, was Commandant en Premier. Both brothers, who were conspicuous by their bravery on the Tenth of August, were brought before the Revolutionary Tribunal and guillotined on the same day, May 2, 1794.

[3] Roucher, the poet, the friend of André Chénier, and his companion to the scaffold.

Talma's. When we reached the Rue Chantereine,[1] the *fête* was
at its best, and quite dazzled me by its brilliancy, for it was such
a long time since I had seen anything of the kind. Here were
men and women not only decked out in *gala* costume, but their
faces actually wreathed in smiles of joy and welcome! Tassin
and Roucher presented me to the hostess, who was probably the
only woman in her *salon* who wore no diamonds, the exquisite
simplicity of her dress admirably harmonizing with the grace
and delicacy of her charms.[2] We next made our way towards
the group surrounding the General. He is of slight build, but
his countenance, with its sparkling black eyes, is very striking.[3]
There is nothing to equal his warmth, his military ardour, his
smart and witty speech. I have rarely come across a more
seductive talker. He would be perfectly irresistible, were there
not something sardonic in his smile, and something in his glance
bordering upon impudence and repelling those whom his wit
attracts. Whether he made the same impression upon others I
do not know, but in any case he was the lion of the evening—I
was almost about to say the King, forgetting, alas! that this
title now recalls anything but ideas of triumph and happiness.
Around him was a crowd of all the most eminent men in politics,
art or literature now in Paris. The leaders of the Brissot party
were there to a man. I recognised Brissot, Vergniaud, Fonfrède,
Gorsas, Ducos, Kersaint and Louvet.[4] Men of letters, dramatists
and poets—all had eagerly accepted Mme. Talma's invitation.

[1] Now the Rue de la Victoire. Built by Le Doux for the Marquis de
Condorcet, the mansion in the Rue Chantereine had been bought by
Julie Carreau, of the Opera, who became Talma's first wife in 1791. It
was occupied by Bonaparte on his return from the expedition to Egypt,
and it was from this house that the conqueror of the Pyramids rode with
his staff to strike the blow of the 18th of Brumaire. The building was
pulled down a few years ago. Mme. Talma was also the owner of the
house in which Mirabeau died, in the Chaussée-d'Antin ('Mémoires de
Mirabeau,' tome vii., p. 350).

[2] Concerning Julie Talma and the part she played in the Revolution,
see Peltier, *Ambigu*, May 8, 1805 ; Arnault, 'Souvenirs d'un Sexagénaire,'
tome ii., p. 132, etc. ; Louise Fusil, 'Souvenirs d'une Actrice,' tome i.,
ch. xx. ; Bouilly, 'Mes Récapitulations' ; Tissot, 'Souvenirs Historiques
sur la Vie et la Mort de Talma.'

[3] 'Mémoires sur Dumouriez,' by Ledieu ; Michaud, *Biographie
Universelle.*

[4] Vergniaud's examination on the 26th of the first month of the
year II. of the Republic ('Vergniaud,' by Ch. Vatel, tome ii., p. 242).

La Harpe was exchanging epigrams with Chamfort. Ducis was talking with young Legouvé, the author of ' La Mort d'Abel'; as Roucher was acquainted with them both, we were enabled to take part in their conversation. Ducis, who is a very tall man, robust, and slightly rustic in appearance, formed a striking contrast to Legouvé, who is pale, delicate and slim. In seeing them side by side, one was reminded of La Fontaine's fable of 'The Oak and the Reed.'[1] They were speaking of the approaching production of Ducis' new tragedy of ' Othello.'[2] Talma is to undertake the *rôle* of Othello, and Mdlle. Desgarcins is to be the Desdemona. ' You shall see my fifth act,' said Ducis, in his blunt, unaffected way. ' It may be bad, but I shall be surprised if Talma and Mdlle. Desgarcins do not make it go excellently. The face of Talma in his fury, his wild gait and his gestures of utter abandonment, are all strictly true to nature. And Mdlle. Desgarcins ! What a wealth of intelligence and sensibility !'[3] ' You will have a deal of trouble,' said Legouvé laughingly, ' to make me love your hero. You know that I always take the women's part, and it is no use talking to me of a man who takes advantage of the slumbers of the woman he loves to smother her with a pillow.' ' I know, my young friend, that the ladies have in you an ardent and sincere defender, and far be it from me to reproach you with it. With regard to that wretched pillow, I can set your mind at rest, for I have not introduced it. To be more in accordance with the traditions of our stage, I have made Othello stab Desdemona.'

Joseph Chénier, who was leaning against the wall talking to Dugazon, the actor, saluted me rather coldly, and appeared surprised to see me at Talma's. ' You know,' said Roucher, ' that Chénier is the most welcome guest here. To him Talma owes the two parts that have made his reputation, and Mme. Talma in her gratitude has given her twin sons the names of Charles IX. and Henri VIII.'[4]

Tassin then led me into the principal gallery, brilliantly lighted and adorned with Gallic helmets, Greek daggers, Indian

[1] Bouilly, ' Mes Récapitulations.'
[2] The first performance of ' Othello' took place on November 26, 1792, at the Théâtre de la République, Rue de Richelieu.
[3] *Révolutions de Paris*, No. 177   [4] Bouilly, ' Mes Récapitulations.'

arrows and Turkish yatagans.   Here the learned Millin was
carrying on a discussion with Langlès, the Orientalist.   Leaving
these erudite adversaries to continue their bloodless battle, we
made our way through *salons* filled with the perfume of the
choicest flowers, and re-echoing with the merry prattle of the
most charming women.   There were two of the latter who attracted universal attention—Mdlle. Candeille, pale and languish-
ing as a creole, and by the side of the majestic Mme. Vestris
stood Mdlle. Desgarcins, with her sweet beauty and winning grace.

The hum of conversation and the silvery ripples of laughter
ceased as if by magic when Mdlle. Candeille sat down to the
piano.[1] For some moments her light but sure touch sped swiftly
over the ivory keys; then her voice rang out, and whilst she sang
I experienced a strange sensation.   I seemed to be escaping from
a horrible nightmare.   The innumerable crimes and horrors that
we had witnessed for the past three years—October 6, June 20,
the Tenth of August, and September 2—Danton, Robespierre
and Marat—all seemed to vanish like the visions of night at the
approach of morning.   I breathed again.   Paris—my dear old
Paris—had not ceased to be a city of honest men, the abode of
light-hearted merriment and joy. . . .

A confused noise at first, growing gradually louder and louder,
and an oft-repeated name—Marat!—recalled me to reality.
Marat! It was indeed he.   He wore a *carmagnole*, or short
jacket, and around his neck was negligently wound a dirty
handkerchief.   His head was enveloped in a piece of red cotton
from the folds of which escaped a few locks of greasy hair.[2] He
was accompanied by two members of the Convention—Bentabole
and Maribon-Montaut, both friends of his.[3] With an impudent
smile on his face he walks straight up to Dumouriez, who greets
him coolly and disdainfully with these words: ' Ah!   Are you
the man they call Marat?'[4] 'General,' replies Marat, 'we have
come, in the name of the Society of Friends of Equality and
Liberty, to ask you for an account of the measures taken against

[1] 'Souvenirs d'une Actrice,' by Louise Fusil, tome i., ch. xx.
[2] *Ibid.*
[3] *Le Courrier des Départements,* November 7, 1792.   Bentabole was
member for the Bas-Rhin, Maribon-Montaut for Gers.
[4] 'Mémoires' of General Dumouriez, liv. iv., ch. i.

the battalions of Mauconseil and the Republic.'[1] 'I have placed all the papers in the hands of the Minister of War.' 'I have been to the Ministry, and have not been able to get hold of a single document.' 'I have laid my report before the Convention, and I must refer you to that.' 'Oh! you shall not get out of it in this way; the Vigilance Committee has no documents on the matter, and simply demands that the battalions shall be protected.' 'I am sure that I have sent the documents.' 'Then tell me where they are.' 'I think that I deserve to be believed.' 'If you deserved entire confidence, we should not have done what we are now doing. There is something behind all this. Who can be persuaded that 1,200 men gave themselves up to excesses of this kind without any motives? It is said that the murdered men were French refugees.' 'Well! what if they were refugees?' 'Refugees are traitors to their country, and the measures you took against the battalions were of unpardonable violence.' 'You are too sharp, M. Marat, for me to enter into a discussion with you.'[2] 'Ah! you little expected to see me here this evening,

---

[1] 'On October 3, 1792, four Prussian soldiers arrived at Ville-sur-Retourne (department of the Ardennes), and, laying down their arms, asked to be received into the French Army. Taken to Rethel, three of them were placed in the 10th Dragoons; the fourth, being a surgeon, was left to await the orders of General Chazot. Two battalions of Parisian volunteers, known as those of Mauconseil and the Republic, were then stationed at Rethel. The Patriot Palloy, who was in command of that of the Republic, had the four Prussian deserters seized during the night, and in addition to ill-treating them, said: "I have promised to send the heads of four refugees to Paris. I shall send yours, preserved in leaden boxes filled with spirits." In the morning Chazot gave orders for marching upon the enemy, who had made his appearance two miles from the town. The Parisian volunteers refused to march, dragged the four deserters from their quarters, and, after having murdered them, danced the *carmagnole* around their bodies. On hearing of this murder, Dumouriez ordered all arms, cannon, equipment, and standards to be taken from the Republican battalion, in order to compel it to give up the murderers. The rest of the battalion was to be dismissed, and ordered to report itself at its proper section in Paris. The Mauconseil battalion, being less guilty, was to remain until further orders in somewhat close quarters outside Mézières. Such were the measures which Marat demanded an account from Dumouriez. On December 18, 1792, the Convention, upon the motion of Marat, decreed that the sixty volunteers arrested by order of the Commander-in-Chief should be set at liberty, and that the two battalions should be reincorporated in the ranks of the army.'—MORTIMER-TERNAUX, 'Histoire de la Terreur,' tome iv., p. 563, note upon the four deserters murdered at Rethel.

[2] Marat's account at the Jacobin Club on October 17; *Journal des Débats . . . de la Société de Jacobins*, No. 285.

in a house of this kind and in the midst of this troop of counter-Revolutionaries, aristocrats and concubines.'[1]

At this Talma stepped forward. 'Citizen Marat,' he cried, 'by what right do you come here to insult our wives and sisters?' 'Am I, then,' added Dumouriez, 'not to be allowed to rest from the fatigues of war in the midst of my friends without hearing them outraged by indecent epithets?' With these words the General turned his back upon Marat and walked away to another room. M. de Rohan-Chabot and M. Moreton, his Aides-de-camp, and several other officers, together with Gorsas, Talma and many of the guests, surrounded the Friend of the People, who beat a retreat whilst uttering the most fearful threats.[2]

Everyone was in a state of consternation. Gorsas, indeed, tried to make merry over it, but his wit fell flat and found no echo. 'Ah!' he cried, 'what a fine scene it was! Can anything funnier be imagined than the appearance of this figure out of the Apocalypse, flanked by two jades leaner than the steed of the visionary of Patmos?'[3]

Dugazon was a little happier with his joke. Taking a censer filled with perfume, he purified all the places through which Marat had passed.[4] This pleasantry brought back to the assembly a little of its former gaiety, and things resumed their course. Mdlle. Candeille was persuaded to take her seat at the piano once more, and after she had sung some of Garat's romances, Lefèvre played us some airs on the flute.[5]

The next day the newspaper boys were shouting in the streets : 'Discovery of a great plot by Marat, the Friend of the People ! Great meeting of aristocrats and counter - Revolutionaries at Talma's !'[6]

This scene, I admit, made a deep impression upon me. I cannot help thinking that Vergniaud's Republic will share the same fate as Talma's evening party. Now that they have over-thrown the Monarchy, Vergniaud and his friends dream of

[1] Louise Fusil, 'Souvenirs,' tome i., ch. xx.   [2] *Ibid.*

[3] *Courrier des Départements*, October 17, 1792.

[4] *Le Courrier de l'Égalité*, No. 78.

[5] Louise Fusil, 'Souvenirs,' tome i., ch. xx.   [6] *Ibid.*

turning Paris into a modern Athens, where eloquence and art
shall be held in honour, where God shall have no altars, but
where Beauty shall have her shrines and her worshippers.   Let
them beware !   An uninvited guest may break into their
Republic, like Marat broke into the *salons* in the Rue
Chantereine.   And it is probable that then the disturber will
go further, and throw out of window those *bourgeois* who think
themselves Republicans, but who are in his eyes only aristocrats
and counter-Revolutionaries !

Dumouriez, in his ' Mémoires ' (liv. iv., ch. i.), speaks of the preceding scene without mentioning where it took place.   Barrière
and Berville, in their edition of the ' Mémoires ' published in 1823,
gave Mdlle. Candeille's *salon* as the scene of the interview between
Marat and the General.   This indication has led astray Thiers,
Lamartine, and Michelet.

' Marat,' says Thiers (tome iii., p. 66), ' proceeds to the different
theatres, and at last hears that Dumouriez is at a *fête* given by the
artistes at Mdlle. Candeille's house.   In spite of the dirty state he is
in, Marat has no hesitation in presenting himself there.'   And
Thiers refers his readers to Marat's version of the affair, which he
reproduces in his Appendix (note iii., p. 381) under this heading,
' An Account of the Visit paid by Marat to Dumouriez at Mdlle.
Candeille's house, taken from the *Journal de la République Française*,
and written by Marat himself in the number of October 17, 1792.'
Had Thiers only taken the trouble to read that extract, he would
have found the following statement in the very first line : ' We
learnt that Dumouriez was to sup at Talma's house, in the Rue
Chantereine.   The line of carriages and the brilliant illuminations
indicated the temple in which the son of Thalia was entertaining a
child of Mars.'

' Marat and his two colleagues,' says Lamartine, in his ' Histoire
des Girondins ' (liv. xxxi.), ' fell upon Dumouriez in the midst of a
triumphal feast that Mme. Simons-Candeille, the friend of Vergniaud
and the Girondins, was giving in honour of the victor of Valmy.'
Lamartine, at least, is not so negligent as to put under his readers'
eyes the article in which Marat himself speaks of *Talma's house*.   It
is true that to the mistake of his predecessor he adds another,
though a slight one.   In 1792 Mdlle. Candeille was not yet
Mme. Simons.   It was not till 1798, six years later, that she married
M. Simons, the head of a large carriage manufactory in Brussels.

Michelet has devoted several pages to the *fête* given to Dumouriez, and he has written of it with his usual inaccuracy. In tome iv. of his 'Histoire de la Révolution,' p. 392, he says : 'Vergniaud did not share the aversion of the Girondists for Danton. The woman he loved, the good and beautiful Mdlle. Candeille, made an heroic attempt to cement the two parties. It was on the occasion of a *fête* given in honour of Dumouriez, at which both Danton and Vergniaud were present. . . . The big, broad figure with the yellow face entered escorted by two long Jacobins, both taller than he by a head. Marat also had intended to produce a big effect.'

Danton was *not* present at the *fête* given to Dumouriez. The extremely circumstantial account given by Louise Fusil, and that of Marat himself, leave no˚ doubt on this point. The *heroic attempt* made by *the good and beautiful Mdlle. Candeille* to bring Danton and Vergniaud together therefore only existed in Michelet's imagination.

As to the love of Vergniaud for Mdlle. Candeille, to which Michelet again refers in tome v., p. 44, and in which he is supported by Lamartine (liv. xviii.) and Louis Blanc (tome vii., p. 271), it matters very little to history whether his statement be correct or not. But it would, perhaps, be as well, in view of new editions, to state that in 1817 the *Biographie des Hommes Vivants*, edited by Michaud, having drawn attention to this rumour, Julie Candeille, then Mme. Simons, successfully refuted it in a pamphlet entitled ' Reply of Mme. Simons-Candeille to an Article in the *Biographie* of June 17, 1817.' On p. 4 she says : 'I can scarcely call M. Vergniaud's features to mind, and I have never spoken to him.' This direct affirmation, published at a time when a great many of Vergniaud's contemporaries were still living, was not contested. Michaud apologized for the allusion, and in another article that appeared a few years later in the *Biographie Universelle* (tome lx.) there is no mention of the pretended amours of the Girondist orator and the *good and beautiful Mdlle. Candeille*.

CHAPTER XI.

Saturday, October 20, 1792.

THE Girondists are giving themselves airs and making fine speeches in the Assembly. Because they have not only the best posts, but also the best speakers, because Guadet sits in the Presidential chair,[1] and Vergniaud delivers Ciceronian orations, the poor men think themselves the masters of the Revolution. They do not see that they possess only the outward show of power, and that it is in reality the Commune that governs—that Commune in which sit the organizers of the September massacres. Nothing has been done during the past two months but what has been desired or ordained by that body. Yesterday it imposed its wishes upon the Legislative Assembly ; to-day it dictates laws to the National Convention, and the Convention bows in submission. In fact, every event that has taken place since the Tenth of August, and particularly those relating to the captivity of the Royal Family, show clearly enough that the influence of the Commune is at work in all directions.

On the Tenth of August it was the Commune that sent a deputation to the Legislative Assembly to demand the arrest of Louis XVI. A few moments later the Assembly, on the motion of Vergniaud, passed a decree suspending the King from his duties as head of the executive power, and ordered fitting accommodation to be provided for him and his family at the Luxembourg.

The Luxembourg is a palace, and the Commune therefore sets its face against the proposal. The Legislative Assembly rescinds

---

[1] Guadet was elected President on October 19.

its former order, and fixes upon the Chancellerie in the Place Vendôme. Fresh refusal on the part of the Commune, which proposes the Temple Tower. The Legislature gives way once more, and on August 13, at five in the afternoon, the Royal Family is removed from the Tuileries to the Temple.

The Legislative Assembly was not only content to slavishly obey the orders of the Commune in this matter, but allowed the men who form that body to subject the captives to the most infamous treatment and the most brutal outrages. Upon this point the Convention has cared as little for its own dignity and the honour of the nation as its predecessor. ' It was the duty of the Convention to have an exact account of what went on in the Temple, and to impose upon the custodians of Louis XVI. a sense of decency, and the respect due to misfortune.' These are the words of Prudhomme himself, in No. 170 of his *Révolutions de Paris*, and he admits that this duty the Convention either would not or could not discharge.

The Conseil Général de la Commune has entrusted the municipal officers on duty at the Temple with full powers.[1] These men, who are allowed to treat those who were the King and Queen of France in any way they choose, are creatures steeped in crime ; their names are Simon, Jacques Bernard, and Hébert. But not a single protest against their doings is raised in the Assembly. The members from Bordeaux, generally so eloquent, are dumb ; even Vergniaud is silent in the face of *Père Duchesne* ! They held their peace, these men, during the massacres of September, while the Abbaye, the Force, and the Carmes were turned into human shambles. Again they hold their peace while a murder, not less horrible and cowardly, is being slowly perpetrated in the Temple prison !

I must again quote from Prudhomme. Already on the morrow of the Tenth of August, he asked that a scaffold should be erected for *Louis Nero*. A few days ago he wrote : ' Louis XVI., behold your life ! See how execrable it is ! Here is

[1] The Conseil-Général de la Commune was composed of the 144 members of the municipality, elected by the 48 sections. The municipal officers, 48 in number, were elected by the sections from the members of the Conseil-Général ; they formed the Conseil Municipal of Paris, whilst still remaining members of the Conseil-Général.

the terrible list of the crimes committed by you since 1789. Seeing this, can anyone desire to prolong your wicked days? No! . . . Countrymen, if you wish to be free, have no pity for the tyrant who oppresses you.'[1]

The number of the *Révolutions* which appeared this morning begins with a long article headed ' The Trial of Louis XVI.,' the opening words of which are as follows : ' In our last article we conclusively proved that the *ci-devant* Louis XVI. deserved to die ; we also proved by the history and example of all nations that he ought to be tried and executed ; to-day we are about to prove that what was formerly the Constitution has neither the right nor the power to stop us in our course. The crimes of Louis XVI. are admitted ; it is only traitors like himself who can entertain doubts about them, and these crimes demand to be avenged. . . . The whole Republic is full of them, and it is time that the arm of the law, too long held back, should at last strike a blow, and let the traitor expiate his guilt before the eyes of the world.'

Now, it is from this paper, which has been so conspicuous in demanding the head of Louis XVI., that I shall take the picture of Louis XVI. in prison. It is that very paper which will show us the Monarch calm and serene, full of dignity and courage— the most unfortunate of men, and yet greater than his mis- fortunes.

In this morning's number, at the end of the article on the King's trial, we read :

' How does Louis XVI. pass his time in prison ? He either sleeps or reads his breviary. The events that go on around him, and of which he is fully cognizant (for, unknown to his wife, he reads the evening papers regularly), do not have the slightest effect upon his impassive soul. . . . One would think him the most stoical philosopher, were it not well known that he has grown into a most stupid—that is to say, a most devout man. . . .

' Louis XVI. has a room to himself in the Tower ;[2] he had two or

[1] *Révolutions de Paris,* No. 169.

[2] The Tower, situated in the enclosure of the Temple, was a square keep more than a hundred and fifty feet high, and flanked by four turrets. Adjoining it was a smaller building, oblong in shape, and also surmounted by two turrets; this was called the *Small Tower,* and did not communicate with the keep, generally called the *Big Tower,* or simply the

three thousand books brought there a short time since, and allowed no one but himself to arrange them. It appears that the only thing which troubles the *ci-devant* King in his imprisonment is a feeling of boredom. He occupies the second floor, with Cléry, his valet. . . . Médicis-Antoinette sees her husband three times a day, and for an hour each time. In the morning the municipal officer on duty comes to tell her that breakfast is ready ; dinner is served at two, and supper at eight. The Queen and all the family join the King at these meals, and leave immediately they are over, no whispering nor talking by signs being permitted. The blinds are arranged in such a way that the prisoners can only see the sky, and communication with anyone below is impossible. Louis Capet scarcely ever goes down into the garden ; he keeps his room, and very seldom talks to the municipal officer who has charge of him.

' Médicis-Antoinette's health does not appear to have suffered much, but her hair is turning prematurely gray. . . .

' The warders, who wear red caps, are not embarrassed by the presence of Royalty, and make as much noise as they can in opening and closing the doors, which are provided with strong bolts. In order to reach the room occupied by Louis XVI., there are three doors to be opened, one of which is of iron. The Austrian Médicis seems to make very light of all this ; the King's sister adopts the same course, whilst the children appear not to notice it.

' Big Elisabeth has not yet assumed that modest bearing befitting misfortune. Having neither an almoner nor chaplain, she, like her brother, is most assiduous in reading her breviary. A short time ago she bought a small parcel of books for about fifteen or twenty *corsets*,[1] nearly all of them being on devotional subjects. One would like to see in her a little more of that Christian humility of which she must find so many examples in the course of her pious reading. Her niece copies her in every particular. . . . But these faults do not authorize the sentinels on duty in the Tower to behave as

---

Tower. It was in the Small Tower that Louis XVI. and his family were first incarcerated—the Queen, Mme. Royale, and the Dauphin on the second floor ; the King and Mme. Élisabeth on the third. On September 29, 1792, the Conseil-Général ordered that 'Louis and Antoinette should be separated ; that each prisoner should have a separate cell ; that Citizen Hébert should be added to the five Commissioners already appointed.' The same evening Louis XVI. was taken to the *Big Tower*, whilst Mme. Élisabeth, Marie Antoinette and her children were not removed thither until October 26. At the date of the present chapter—October 20 —the *Révolutions de Paris* was therefore correct in saying that ' Louis XVI. had a room to himself in the (*Big*) Tower.'

[1] The *corset* was a note for five francs (Peltier, 'Histoire de la Révolution du 10 Août,' tome i., p. 133).

though they were in their guard-house. They sing at the top of their voices night and day, and dance the *carmagnole* with such zest that very little of their horse-play is lost upon the captive family.'[1]

What can be added to such a description? In spite of the big talk and the insulting epithets, the truth will out, compelling this implacable enemy to admit the greatness of these truly royal and Christian souls.

The history of the captivity of the Royal Family in the Temple is admirably given in De Beauchesne's book, ' Louis XVI.: his Life, Agony, and Death'; but the publication *in extenso* of the ' Register of the Deliberations of the Commissioners of the Commune on Duty in the Temple ' and the ' Minutes of the Commune ' relating to the royal prisoners is still much to be desired. There Louis XVI. appears more noble and dignified than in the narratives even of Cléry. Never did greater virtues force a more striking testimony of admiration from more merciless foes. So great was the effect produced by the reports of the Temple Commissioners that Hébert, on December 28, 1792, moved in the Commune that ' the Commissioners on duty in the Temple should be instructed to keep out of their reports any detail that might lead to the commiseration of the prisoners,' a motion which was immediately adopted. What certain Revolutionary writers, Michelet amongst others, call the *Temple legend* is based not only upon the narratives of Cléry and Hue, but also upon the reports of these Commissioners, some of whom were the leaders of the Commune. What, then, must be thought of these statements of Michelet?—' Who are the narrators of what passed in the Temple? There is not one Jacobin, not one of the Mountain nor of the Commune, amongst them. The only witnesses responsible for the details of the King's stay in the Temple are his valets, Hue and Cléry ' (tome v., p. 145). And Michelet boldly adds : ' We have also the *pretended* memoirs of *Madame d'Angoulême, written in the Temple Tower*, where she could not have written, having had neither ink nor paper. Those who came to liberate her were moved to see that she had been reduced to pencilling on the walls.' The pretended memoirs of the Duchesse d'Angoulême (to whom, we think, Michelet might well have given her real title, were it only in memory of the days when he was professor of history to Mademoiselle, the daughter of the Duc de Berry) are a narrative of admirable simplicity and of indisputable and undisputed authenticity—for here

---

[1] *Révolutions de Paris*, No. 171.

the pure and simple denial of Michelet is of no account. They were published for the first time, under the Restoration, by the Imprimerie Royale ; another edition was brought out by M. Barrière in his collection of ' Mémoires sur la Révolution,' whilst the Duchesse d'Angoulême was still alive, and by Alfred Nettement, in his ' Vie de Marie-Thérèse de France.' They therefore appeared with the full consent of the Princess, and she would certainly not have lent herself to a fraud of this kind, to a lie that would have cast a reflection upon her royal parents. Louis Blanc, who can have no reasons for concealing his true opinion, does not harbour the slightest doubt about the authenticity of these memoirs, and frequently quotes from them. Sainte-Beuve, who was never known to sin from excess of Royalism, and whose sharp scent was not to be taken in by apocryphal documents, writes, in tome v. of his ' Causeries de Lundi' : 'The Duchesse d'Angoulême has told the story of her captivity and of the events that took place in the Temple from the time when she entered it until the day of her brother's death, and she has done so in simple, unaffected language, well befitting a sensitive soul that relates in all sincerity those real and unutterable sorrows that are beyond description. She keeps herself in the background as much as possible, and stops at the death of her brother, the last of the four victims sacrificed.' With regard to the statement that Mme. Royale possessed neither ink nor paper, and was reduced to the necessity of scribbling on the walls of her prison, this, again, is some of Michelet's misleading information. There is no doubt that for a long time the daughter of Louis XVI. could only scribble on the walls of her room. Rovère, the Conventionalist, tells us that after the departure of Mme. Royale he found the following words pencilled on the walls by the orphan in the Temple : *Oh, my Father, look down on me from heaven !* And again : *Oh, my God, pardon those who killed my parents !* After the death of Louis XVII. (June 9, 1795), the press agitated loudly in favour of Mme. Royale. The city of Orleans sent a deputation to the Convention to demand her liberation, and, in view of the general feeling of the public, it was decided to lessen the rigour of the Princess's captivity. On June 20, 1795, the Committee of General Security ordered a female companion to be given her, and Mme. Bocquet de Chanterenne was chosen for this post. On August 2 the royal prisoner was further allowed to have books, paper, pencils, pens and ink. Thenceforth she spent her mornings in writing, and her afternoons in reading, embroidering, or drawing. In September Mme. and Mdlle. de Tourzel and Baroness de Mackau, formerly assistant-governess to the *Children of France*, obtained permission to visit her twice a week ; they arrived at the Temple about mid-day, and left at about seven or eight at night.   It is therefore clear that after August 2, 1795, the daughter of Louis XVI. was able to write in the Temple Tower, and was not obliged to scribble on the walls ; by affirming the contrary, Michelet—*mirabile dictu !*—has slandered the Republic !

Since writing the above note, the publication we so much desired has been undertaken by the Société d'Histoire Contemporaine, and bears the following title, ' Captivité et Derniers Moments de Louis XVI.   Being original narratives and official documents collected and edited by the Marquis de Beaucourt.'   The Marquis Costa de Beauregard has also published the ' Memoirs written by Marie-Thérèse-Charlotte of France, upon the Captivity of the Royal Family from the Tenth of August, 1792, until the Death of her Brother, on June 9, 1795,' according to the original manuscript in the possession of the Duchesse de Madrid.

CHAPTER XII.

A RELIC.

Sunday, October 21, 1792.

THE walls are everywhere covered with abominable and infamous posters, and all day long filthy papers and pamphlets are being sold in the streets. Pamphlets, papers, and posters all preach murder, and hold assassins up to admiration, whilst hurling insults and threats at all that is honourable or worthy of respect. It seems, indeed, as if hell had been let loose in Paris. But Paris always has been a city of contrasts; virtue rubs shoulders with crime, and if crime is nowhere more abject, virtue is nowhere more heroic. By the side of the prison to which the informers drag their victims, there is the door which opens to afford refuge to the outlaw. In a small street that re-echoes with the shouts of the hawkers of *Père Duchesne* there is a humble dwelling in which an old priest, upon whose head a price has been set, is reciting Mass before a few poor women. We have returned to the days of Nero and Diocletian; persecuted believers take refuge in the Catacombs, and the old cry of ' *Death to Christians !*' is heard in the Paris of Marat and Danton as it was once heard in Rome under the Cæsars, whilst here as there the fury of the executioners is equalled only by the sublime heroism of the martyrs. Already people seize upon the objects that belonged to murdered priests of the Carmes and Saint-Firmin, and regard them as relics. One of these is in my possession; it is a small piece of paper, printed on both sides, and reads as follows :

A prayer to the Most Holy Virgin, which the pious are asked to recite every day for the King.

Divine Mother of my Saviour, who in the Temple of Jerusalem didst offer to God the Father Jesus Christ, His Son and thine, I now offer thee our well-beloved King Louis XVI. He is the heir of Clovis, of Saint Clotilde, and of Charlemagne; the son of the pious Blanche de Castile, of Saint Louis, of Louis XIII., of the virtuous Marie de Pologne, and of Prince Louis the Dauphin. Will these names, so dear to our religion, not be to thee what the names of Abraham, Isaac, and Jacob were to the God of Israel?

Consider, Most Pure of Mothers, Maid of Mercy, that this good Prince has never stained his soul with any of the vices that thou hast most detested; that he has been neither a bloodthirsty man nor the tyrant of his people. Almighty Virgin, channel of all blessings and virtues, it is through thee that his soul is pure, that he loves justice and righteousness, and that his good heart has ever refused to permit the shedding of a single drop of blood to save his own life.

Queen of Heaven and of the Catholic Church, Queen of our Kings and of France, protect this beloved Ruler. Receive him as thou didst receive at the foot of the Cross the chaste and well-beloved disciple of meekness and charity, and prove to him that thou art his Mother.

Oh, Mary, if thou art for him, who will be against him? Reign thou over his person, his heart, and his actions. Prolong his days, and make them happy. Augment unceasingly his Christian and his royal virtues. Sanctify his trials and his sacrifices, and grant him a crown more radiant and lasting than the most resplendent of earthly diadems.

Mother of God, thou who knowest the innermost recesses of the heart, and the sincerity of my wishes, intercede with Jesus for the son of Saint Louis and for his people. Has He ever refused thee aught?[1]

This prayer is stained with blood in three places. It was found in the breviary of the Abbé Gros, massacred at Saint-Firmin on September 3.[2]

---

[1] This prayer is to be found in the *Révolutions de Paris*, No. 165.

[2] The Abbé Joseph Marie Gros had been one of the representatives of the clergy of the city of Paris in the States-General. Deprived of his cure for having refused to take the oath, he went to live in the Rue de la Vieille-Estrapade, and was arrested there on August 17, 1792. Imprisoned in the seminary of Saint-Firmin, in the Rue Saint-Victor, he was massacred there with seventy-five other priests, his head being carried in triumph through the streets. He left a will, bequeathing all his property to the poor of his parish. Foremost amongst his assassins were Gossiaume, a soapmaker, who had more than once been assisted by him, and Dumoutier, a locksmith, who, on September 3, killed fourteen priests with his own hand. ('Les Martyrs de la Foi,' by the Abbé Guillon, tome iii., p. 237.)

CHAPTER XIII.

Wednesday, October 24, 1792.

On the motion of M. Guadet, one of the principal members of the Gironde, the Convention on October 9 determined the mode of procedure to be adopted with regard to refugees who are taken armed. It was decided that, as soon as it had been proved to a court-martial composed of five persons that the prisoners before them were French refugees, taken armed, they were to be immediately shot.

On Friday, the 19th, thirteen of these unfortunate men were brought to Paris. They had scarcely arrived, when they were taken before the Conseil-Général of the Commune to give their names, and then marched from the Hôtel de Ville to the Conciergerie between two files of soldiers, and amidst the cries of an infuriated mob clamouring for their instant death.

On the morrow, immediately the sitting of the Convention was opened, Jean Debry, member for the department of the Aisne, moved that five Commissioners should at once be appointed from the Paris division, commanded by General Berruyer, to decide the fate of the thirteen prisoners. M. Monestier moved an amendment, providing that in the court-martial there should be at least one non-commissioned officer and one private. The motion, so amended, was then adopted.

Meanwhile, crowds had been gathering in the courts of the Palais de Justice, and agitators were inciting the people to hasten the execution of the prisoners, amongst whom there was said to be the Prince de Lambesc. The Commune having published the motion passed by the Convention, the ferment was a trifle stilled.

On Sunday, the 21st, the Minister of War informed the Convention that the five Commissioners appointed were General Berruyer, and an officer named Desplanche ; Claude Sableau, a gunner ; Antoine and Marly, gendarmes.

This Commission sat with open doors in the Palais de Justice on Monday, the 22nd. The prisoners were brought in, all still wearing the uniform in which they had been arrested. Neither the Prince de Lambesc nor any person of note was amongst them. With the exception of a former Councillor in the Parliament of Bordeaux, forty-five years old, and one of the King's body-guards, they were all very young men, whose ages ranged from nineteen to twenty-nine.

The first to be examined replied that his name was Dammartin Fontenoy, that he was twenty-five years old, and a native of Metz. When the Revolution broke out, he had already been living in Germany for two years. ' Did you not hear that there had been a Revolution in France ?' asked the President. ' I thought there had been four,' replied the accused, in a somewhat weak voice. 'Speak louder,' said General Berruyer ; 'you are here before the Republic, *for the people of Paris form the whole of the Republic !* The Commissioners then retired to the Council Chamber, and, returning in a few moments, each of them successively declared that the prisoner deserved death. General Berruyer hereupon pronounced the sentence, which the condemned man heard without betraying the slightest emotion.

The second prisoner, M. Dumesnil, a native of Nancy, formerly a captain in Esterhazy's regiment of hussars, deposed that he had served as a volunteer in Berchiny's regiment, but that he had sought every means of escaping to France ; that on September 23 he had, of his own free will, made his way into the French lines, and given himself up to a cavalry officer. His words could not be disputed, and it is a remarkable fact that no information was volunteered by the authorities as to the manner in which the prisoners had been arrested. M. Dumesnil was also condemned to death, and heard his sentence with great coolness.

Louis Mirambel, the third prisoner, aged nineteen, shared the same fate. He had been in the body-guard of Monsieur, the King's brother. 'So so,' exclaimed General Berruyer, 'you

guarded Monsieur! It would have been better had you brought
him with you.'

The next to receive sentence were Jean Béon, aged twenty,
and Maurice Santon, aged twenty-one.

Honoré Godefroy had served in the King's body-guard, and
Charles Godefroy, his brother, was a naval lieutenant. Although
it was proved that the former had left his corps three days
before the time of his arrest, and that Charles had surrendered
voluntarily, both were summarily condemned.

Gauthier de la Touche, formerly a councillor in the Parliament of Guyenne, was arrested at Brière, where he said he had
been for five days waiting for some opportunity to get back to
France. In his pocket-book was found a card bearing a heart
surmounted by a crown of thorns, and pierced by several arrows,
with this inscription: '*Cor Jesu, miserere nobis.*' He was
naturally treated with no more indulgence than his comrades
in misfortune.

More guilty still was M. Bernage de Saint-Hillier, of the
King's body-guard, amongst whose papers a document was found
bearing the words: '*Account paid by the Triple Alliance.*'
Saint-Hillier was evidently one of the leaders of the counter-
Revolution, one of the principal agents of the Duke of Brunswick, of Frederick William, and of the Emperor Francis.
'What have you to say to this?' asked General Berruyer,
flourishing the terrible document. 'The Triple Alliance—
is that clear enough?' 'The explanation is a very simple one,'
replied Saint-Hillier. 'On October 6, 1789, I was lying in the
hospital at Versailles, when I received warning of the danger
that was threatening. I escaped over the roofs with two of my
comrades. After hiding for two days, we determined to return
to Paris. The others had no money with them, and I was left
to pay all the expenses on the road, as well as during our stay
in the capital. My comrades, however, obliged me to keep an
exact account of what I laid out, and that is the origin of the
document before you; the heading is a mere joke. We are all
young, Monsieur le Président, and have not yet lost that gaiety
so natural to youth, and we christened our friendship *the Triple
Alliance.*'

Saint-Hillier had spoken with soldierly frankness, whilst a smile of confidence and good-fellowship accompanied his words, and when Berruyer passed sentence of death upon him, the smile was still upon his lips.

The four remaining prisoners were poor devils of servants, who swore that they had only followed their masters in the hope of being paid the wages due to them. They were acquitted.

The execution took place yesterday morning in the Place de Grève, opposite the principal entrance of the Hôtel de Ville. All the condemned displayed the same courage and assurance on the scaffold as they had shown before the tribunal. Young Mirambel, a mere boy, died with the heroism of an old soldier. Gauthier de la Touche, with eyes raised to heaven, seemed to be repeating: '*Cor Jesu, miserere nobis.*' Saint-Hillier was grave and sad, but when he heard the mob shouting: '*Vive la République!*' his smile came back to him, and in a loud, clear voice that was heard all over the square he cried: '*Vive le Roi!*'[1]

[1] 'Report of the Court-Martial,' published in No. 172 of the *Révolutions de Paris.* The same number contains an illustration of the execution of the nine refugees.

CHAPTER XIV.

Friday, October 26, 1792.

THE Convention had scarcely been called into existence, when, on the motion of M. Buzot, a special committee of six members was appointed 'to draw up a scheme for placing at the disposal of the National Convention an armed force drawn from the eighty-three departments.' As chairman of this committee, Buzot laid his scheme before the Convention on October 8. The chief points of this scheme are as follows: For every member returned by each department, two mounted and four unmounted men are to be sent to the capital, thus providing a national guard of 4,470 men. The men themselves are to be chosen by the Conseils-Généraux of the departments, and the choice of a commander is to be left to the National Assembly.

Although no date has yet been fixed for the discussion of Buzot's scheme, it has been most violently attacked by all who regard as an incontestable axiom those celebrated words of General Berruyer: '*The people of Paris form the whole of the Republic.*' A week ago the delegates of the forty-eight sections, appearing at the bar of the Convention, plainly intimated to the deputies that they would have to reject 'this hateful and dangerous scheme.'[1] I have no doubt that it really will be rejected, and yet a very large majority of the Assembly considers it a useful, and even necessary, measure. But what of that? The Convention, as I have already had occasion to state more than once, has only the semblance of power. The real sovereignty rests with the mob of Paris, with that factious

[1] Sitting of October 19, 1792.

minority which makes up by impudence what it lacks in numbers, and which is represented by the Commune and the sections.

In order to fully understand what is going on, it is necessary to have some idea of the origin and organization both of the sections and of the Commune.

I will speak of the sections first, for they are the origin of the Commune.

Before 1789 Paris was divided into twenty-one districts.

The royal proclamation of April 23, 1789, convoking the three estates of the city of Paris, divided the capital into sixty *arrondissements*, a division that existed until June 27, 1790.

On that date the Constituent Assembly substituted forty-eight sections for the sixty districts. It was the right or duty of all the active citizens[1] in each section to meet in common assembly, and appoint one elector of the second degree for every hundred citizens present or absent. It was the idea of the legislator of 1790 that the sections were to have no other mission than that of electing representatives and of superintending purely local matters. Their sittings were not to be public, nor were they to be permanent. They could not meet without being specially convoked by the municipal body. It therefore seemed as if every precaution had been taken to keep the sections within reasonable limits, and to prevent them from meddling with matters beyond their sphere. But if it be true, as Bossuet has said, that human wisdom is always short-sighted, it is especially true of the wisdom of the Constituent Assembly. After having laid down in Clause I. of this Act the provisions just mentioned, it inserts in Clause IV. an article providing that the municipal body shall be compelled to convoke the forty-eight sections upon the demand of eight only, and, in order to facilitate the exercise of these civic rights, another article established in each section a permanent committee of sixteen members, which was to meet at least once a week.

One must have been blind not to foresee that these permanent

---

[1] Active citizens were those who, being Frenchmen, had attained the age of twenty-five, and paid a direct contribution equal to three days' wages.

committees would aspire to power, that they would demand a convocation of the section as often as possible, and that, in a city so full of revolutionary passions, it would always be easy for agitators to find eight sections willing to move the municipal body to call the others together.

And this is exactly what happened. For the past two years the sections have formed the most powerful element of agitation and disturbance. It is from them that most of the measures subversive of the Constitution have sprung, and by them that nearly all the revolutionary demonstrations and riots have been organized.

By the decree of May 18, 1791, all constituted bodies are forbidden to present addresses or collective petitions.[1] But the sections are not legally-constituted bodies, and, taking advantage of the law's disregard of them, they have presented addresses and collected petitions to the National Assembly in order to influence its deliberations and impose their will upon it.

Thanks to the creation of the permanent committees of sixteen, communication—at first intermittent, but afterwards continuous—was soon established between these committees, and, as a result, between the sections themselves. By this means they were able to combine their action and render it irresistible.

In the month of July last, whilst preparations were being made for the Tenth of August, a central office for the more rapid interchange of communications between the forty-eight sections of Paris was established in the Hôtel de Ville, by order of the municipality. Forty-eight Commissioners were to call here at least once a day, in order to give notice of the resolutions passed in their own sections, and to take cognizance of what had been done in the others. This order was dated July 17.

The leaders of the Jacobin party had at last succeeded in centralizing the efforts of the sections, and in giving them that power which springs from unity of direction. This was an important result, but to complete it there was still wanting that

---

[1] 'The right of petition belongs to every individual, and cannot be delegated. It cannot, therefore, be exercised by electoral, administrative, or municipal bodies, nor by the sections of the communes, nor by societies of citizens.'

publicity and permanence which had hitherto been denied the
meetings of the sections.

As a matter of fact, long before the Tenth of August, many
of them had held their sittings in public, and had thrown open
their doors to all citizens without distinction. Galleries, too,
had been erected, and those sections which still refused to admit
the general public were surrounded whenever they met by the
lowest class of agitators, who blocked up the doorways and
hooted such men as were known for their moderation. When,
on August 5, Collot-d'Herbois, Marie-Joseph Chénier, and two
other Commissioners of sections, admitted to the bar of the
Legislative Assembly, demanded that the sections should
deliberate in open meeting, Collot-d'Herbois adduced, as an
unanswerable argument in favour of public sittings, the dis-
orderly scenes to be witnessed outside those sections which still
remained faithful to the law.

The meetings of all the sections are now public, and they
are, moreover, permanent. The law of permanence was passed
by the Legislative Assembly on July 25, on the motion of
M. Thuriot; an announcement in the *Moniteur* of August 6
reads as follows :

> ' The assemblies of the forty-eight sections are permanent.
>> ' Petion, Mayor,
>> ' Royer, Secretary.'[1]

The publicity and permanence of these assemblies have placed
them in the power of the worst demagogues, even in those
sections where such characters are not in the majority. When,
for instance, any section is not *up to the mark*, when the citizens
forming it are suspected of moderation, citizens belonging to
other districts invade the galleries of the offending section,
fraternize with the Jacobin minority, interrupt the speakers,
take part in the discussion, and carry the vote. More dangerous
still are the consequences of the permanence of the section
meetings. The halls in which the sittings are held being open

---

[1] This Royer, Secretary to the Corporation of Paris, is the same who,
having become famous by the name of Royer-Collard, said to M. Odilon-
Barrot, 'Sir, I knew you forty years ago; you then called yourself
Petion.'

night and day, any agitators can seize the moment, when peaceable citizens have gone home, to put up a secretary and a president of their own, and to pass amongst themselves any motions they please. A resolution negatived at nine o'clock at night is sometimes passed at two in the morning. This snatch vote, frequently emanating from an infinitesimal majority, is cleverly made the most of on the morrow, carried from section to section, transmitted to the Commune, and sometimes laid before the National Convention as an expression of the people's will.

I have indicated the origin of the Parisian sections, and have shown the nature and the extent of their action. It is impossible to trace that action to the events themselves, for that would mean writing a history of the Revolution from the end of 1790. I will simply give here the names of the forty-eight sections as existing on the Tenth of August, 1792, the places where they met, and the number both of active citizens and of electors of the second degree in each. I will then briefly indicate the changes that have since taken place.

When Paris was divided into sixty districts, each of these districts bore the name of the church in which the first meetings had been held in 1789. They were thus called district of the Filles-Saint-Thomas, district of Saint-Roch, district of the Grey Friars, etc.

The Constituent Assembly, when it substituted forty-eight sections for the sixty districts, had no desire to perpetuate the names borne by the latter, recalling as they did religious ideas. It was at first proposed to call each section by the name of some celebrated man whose ashes lay interred there. But this suggestion was abandoned, and the names were taken from public buildings, monuments, squares or streets. The Filles-Saint-Thomas became the Bibliothèque; Saint-Roch made way for the Palais Royal; the Grey Friars for the Théâtre Français, etc.

LIST OF THE FORTY-EIGHT SECTIONS ON THE TENTH OF AUGUST, 1792.

NAMES OF THE SECTIONS.	NUMBER OF ACTIVE CITIZENS.	NUMBER OF ELECTORS OF THE SECOND DEGREE.	PLACE OF MEETING.
1. Tuileries	1,700	17	Church of the Feuillants.
2. Champs-Elysées	900	9	Chapel of Saint-Nicolas.
3. Le Roule	1,300	13	Church of the Capucins Saint-Honoré.
4. Palais Royal	2,400	24	Church of Saint-Roch.
5. Place Vendôme	1,200	12	Church of the Capucines.
6. The Bibliothèque	1,500	15	Church of the Filles-Saint-Thomas.
7. Mirabeau[1]	900	9	Former barracks of the Gardes Françaises, at the corner of the Boulevard and the Chaussée d'Antin.
8. The Louvre	2,000	20	Church of Saint-Germain-l'Auxerrois.
9. The Oratoire	1,900	19	Church of the Oratoire.
10. The Corn-market	1,900	19	Church of Saint-Honoré.
11. The Post-Office	1,800	18	Church of Saint-Eustache.
12. Place Louis XIV.	1,400	14	Church of the Petits-Pères.
13. Fontaine-Montmorency	1,100	11	Church of Saint-Joseph.
14. Bonne-Nouvelle	1,600	16	Church of Bonne-Nouvelle.
15. Ponceau	2,300	23	Church of the Trinity, Rue Bourg l'Abbé.
16. Mauconseil	1,700	17	Church of Saint-Jacques-l'Hôpital.
17. Marché-des-Innocents	1,100	11	Church of Sainte-Opportune.
18. Lombards	2,500	25	Church of Saint-Jacques-la-Boucherie.
19. Arcis	1,800	18	Church of Saint-Jean-en-Grève.
20. Faubourg-Montmartre	700	7	Church of Saint Joseph.
21. Poissonière	800	8	Church of Saint-Lazare.

[1] This section was called by the name of La Grange-Batelière from 1790 until August 2, 1792, when it took the name of Mirabeau. At the sitting of December 11, 1792, 'one of the Secretaries (of the Convention) read a resolution passed by the former Section Mirabeau, which, no longer wishing to bear the name of a man who betrayed his country, and desirous of giving the citizens of the eighty-fourth department a proof of its attachment, has changed its name to that of *Mont Blanc*.'

LIST OF THE FORTY-EIGHT SECTIONS ON THE TENTH OF AUGUST, 1792
(continued).

NAMES OF THE SECTIONS.	NUMBER OF ACTIVE CITIZENS.	NUMBER OF ELECTORS OF THE SECOND DEGREE.	PLACE OF MEETING.
22. Bondy	1,400	14	Church of the Récollets.
23. Temple	1,700	17	Church of the Pères-Nazareth.
24. Popincourt	1,300	13	Church of Trainel.
25. Rue de Montreuil ...	1,500	15	Church of Sainte-Marguérite.
26. Quinze-Vingts	2,000	20	Church of the Enfants-Trouvés.
27. Gravilliers	3,300	33	Church of Saint-Martin-des-Champs.
28. Faubourg-Saint-Denis	1,300	13	Church of Saint-Laurent.
29. Rue Beaubourg ...	2,300	23	Church of Saint-Mery.
30. Enfants Rouges ...	1,800	18	Church of the Enfants Rouges.
31. Roi-de-Sicile	1,800	18	Church of the Petit Saint-Antoine.
32. Hôtel-de-Ville	1,700	17	Church of Saint-Gervais.
33. Place Royale	1,900	19	Church of the Minimes.
34. Arsenal	1,400	14	Church of Saint-Louis-la-Culture.
35. Ile-Saint-Louis ...	1,100	11	Church of Saint-Louis-en-l'Ile.
36. Notre-Dame	1,700	17	Hall of the old Chapter-house.
37. Henri IV.	900	9	Church of the Sainte-Chapelle-Basse.
38. Invalides	1,100	11	Church of the Invalides.
39. Fontaine-de-Grenelle ...	2,100	21	Church of the Jacobins-Saint-Dominique.
40. Quatre-Nations ...	3,900	39	Church of Saint-Germain-des-Près.
41. Théâtre-Français ...	2,600	26	Church of Saint-André-des-Arts.
42. Croix Rouge	1,600	16	Church of the Prémontrés.
43. Luxembourg	2,100	21	Church of the Barefooted Carmelites.
44. Thermes-de-Julien ...	2,000	20	Church of the Maturins.
45. Sainte-Geneviève ...	2,800	28	Church of the College of Navarre.
46. Observatoire	1,700	17	Church of the Val-de-Grâce.
47. Jardin des Plantes ...	2,200	22	Church of Saint-Nicolas-du-Chardonnet.
48. Gobelins	1,200	12	Church of Saint-Marcel.
Total	82,900	829	

Many of these sections have changed their names since the Tenth of August. The following is a full list :

OLD NAMES.	NEW NAMES.
3. Section du Roule.	Section de la République.
4. „ du Palais Royal.	„ de la Butte-des-Moulins.
5. „ de la Place Vendôme.	„ des Piques.
6. „ de la Bibliothèque.	„ de Quatre-Vingt-Douze.
9. „ de l'Oratoire.	„ des Gardes Françaises.
11. „ des Postes.	„ du Contrat Social.
12. „ de la Place Louis XIV.	„ du Mail.
13. „ de la Fontaine-Mont-morency.	„ de Molière-et-Lafontaine.
15. „ du Ponceau.	„ des Amis de la Patrie.
16. „ Mauconseil.	„ Bonconseil.
17. „ du Marché-des-Inno-cents.	„ des Halles.
28. „ du Faubourg-Saint-Denis.	„ du Faubourg-du-Nord.
29. „ de la Rue Beaubourg.	„ de la Réunion.
30. „ des Infants Rouges.	„ du Marais.
31. „ du Roi-de-Sicèle.	„ des Droits de l'Homme.
32. „ de l'Hôtel-de-Ville.	„ de la Maison-Commune.
33. „ de la Place Royale.	„ de la Place-des-Fédérés.
35. „ de l'Ile-Saint-Louis.	„ de la Fraternité.
36. „ de Notre-Dame.	„ de la Cité.
37. „ de Henri IV.	„ du Pont-Neuf.
41. „ du Théâtre-Français.	„ de Marseille.
44. „ des Thermes-de-Julien.	„ de Beaurepaire.
45. „ de Sainte-Geneviève.	„ du Panthéon-Français.
47. „ du Jardin des Plantes.	„ des Sans-Culottes.
48. „ des Gobelins.	„ du Finistère.

Another change, more important than these changes of name, was made in the constitution of the sections on August 11. On that day the Legislative Assembly abolished the distinction made by the Constituent between active and non-active citizens, deciding that admission to the meetings of the sections was to be granted to 'every Frenchman over twenty-one years of age, living on his income or on the product of his labour, and not being a servant.'

This decree doubled the number of voters in the sections of Paris, and brought it up to about 192,000.[1] The demagogic

[1] Before the decree of August 11, 1792, the number of voters in the department of Paris was 96,700. There was an elector of the second degree for every 100 active citizens, and a list of these electors is to be found in the 'Almanach Royal' for 1792. It comprises 829 electors for the forty-eight sections of Paris, and 138 for the sixteen rural cantons

element, already so powerful in the sections, when these contained only active citizens, has now complete sway. Peaceable citizens infected with moderation, men who formed part of the old National Guard, subscribers to the petition of the Twenty Thousand or that of the Eight Thousand—all stand aloof and leave the course free to plotters and Revolutionaries, to the blood-stained men of September.

There are few sections which have not in their ranks, and even at their head, men who are reproaches to humanity, and whom Paris—the Paris of the Revolution—acclaims and recognises as its leaders. The Section Bonne-Nouvelle has *le père* Duchesne and Citizen Hébert; the Section of the Quinze-Vingts has Huguenin, Rossignol and Santerre;[1] the Mauconseil section has Lulier;[2] the Montreuil section has Jean Claude Bernard, formerly vicar of the church of Sainte-Marguerite, and now a member of the Conseil Général of the Commune;[3] the Section of the

---

of the department—967 in all. In his 'Histoire des Girondins et des Massacres de Septembre' (tome i., p. 289), Granier de Cassagnac has committed a serious error : 'In November, 1791,' he says, 'the new Mayor of Paris was elected. La Fayette's friends put him forward as a candidate, and on November 17, the day of the election, he came to Paris *incognito;* but his defeat was overwhelming, as he only obtained 3,000 votes. Petion, the successful candidate, obtained only 9,000, for, in spite of the exhortations of the political clubs and of the press, the people of Paris were so little anxious to exercise the electoral rights that had been granted them, that out of 200,000 voters, only 12,000 went to the poll.' The voters of the sixteen rural cantons had no voice in the election of the Mayor of Paris, and the voters of the forty-eight sections were, as has been shown, not more than 82,900 in number—there is an enormous difference between this and 200,000 ! Mistakes seldom go alone, and in the lines quoted above we find one or two others. The most important is that Petion did not obtain 9,000 votes, but only 6,708. There were only 10,632 votes recorded altogether, and not 12,000, the numbers being distributed as follows : Petion, 6,708 ; La Fayette, 3,123 : Dandré, 77. The others went to Robespierre, Fréteau, Camus, and others.

[1] Huguenin was the leader of the rioters on June 20, and President of the Insurrectional Commune of the Tenth of August. Rossignol, one of the victors of the Bastile, presided over the massacres in the Force on September 2 and 3.

[2] Public Prosecutor to the Tribunal of August 17. Arraigned together with Danton, he was acquitted ; but the Revolutionary Tribunal ordered him to be detained until the declaration of peace. He was imprisoned in Sainte-Pélagie, where he committed suicide on May 5, 1794. Historians spell his name 'Lhuillier,' but I have before me a large number of autographs signed by him 'Lulier.'

[3] One of the two Commissioners charged to take Louis XVI. to the scaffold. He was guillotined, with Robespierre, on the 10th of Thermidor, year II.

Fontaine-de-Grenelle has Xavier Audouin, formerly vicar of Saint-Thomas-d'Aquin, founder of the *Journal Universel*, and a member of the Convention ; the Section of Gravilliers has Leonard Bourdon ; the Section of the Bibliothèque has Collot-d'Herbois ; and the Section des Piques has Robespierre.

But the most illustrious of all, that before which all other sections pale, is the Section of the Théâtre-Français, which has lately adopted the name of Marseilles in order to honour the memory of those Marseillais who took up their abode near the place of its meetings.   The Section of Marseilles, which has alone sent thirteen deputies to the National Convention,[1] has Danton, Chaumette, Camille Desmoulins, Fréron, Fabre d'Églantine, Billaud-Varenne ; Vincent and Ronsin ; the printers Brune and Momoro ; Duplain, the bookseller, and Sergent, the engraver, subscribers to the address sent on September 3 to all the municipalities, inviting them to imitate Paris and massacre all suspects ; Fournier, called the American, who presided over the massacre of the prisoners in Orleans, and above all—*Immanis pecoris custos, immanior ipse*—Marat, the Friend of the People !

[1] Danton, Manuel, Billaud-Varenne, Camille Desmoulins, Marat, Sergent, Robert, Fréron, Fabre d'Églantine, Boucher Saint-Saveur, members for Paris ; Dulaure, member for the Puy-de-Dôme ; Pons de Verdun, member for the Meuse, and Garran de Coulon, member for the Loiret, all dwelt in the section of the Théâtre-Français.   Out of these thirteen deputies, eleven were electors, and this fact led the Procureur de la Commune ' to authorize the section of the Théâtre-Français to appoint eleven electors in the place of those who had been sent to the Convention.'—' Inventaire de Autographes et des Documents Historiques composant la Collection de Benjamin Fillon.'   Series 3 and 4, No. 532.

CHAPTER XV.

Monday, October 29, 1792.

ONE day last week the two Trudaines, François de Pange, Tassin and I were dining at the house of our friend Roucher, in the Rue des Noyers. Thanks to our host, the conversation had for a long time been entirely confined to literary topics—a rare thing in these times. De Pange,[1] who with his delicate wit, excellent taste, and sound judgment, is not only an authority in the world of letters and of science, but is himself an astronomer and musician, a journalist, mathematician and even poet—De Pange, happy to forget for a moment the troubles that sit so heavy upon us all, was good enough to treat us to an ingenious and witty parallel between the Abbé Delille and André Chénier. He quoted several passages from a splendid play by André— 'l'Aveugle'—in which the life of the ancients is drawn with truly Homeric breadth and inspiration. He then took a few examples from Delille's translation of the 'Georgics,' and with remarkable clearness showed us the faults and the weak spots in the worthy Abbé's work. Here Roucher interrupted him. 'There is no one,' he said, 'who admires Chénier's talent more than I do, and like De Pange, I am convinced that when the public is better acquainted with his works, it will give him a place amongst the first poets of France. But at the same time we must be just to the Abbé Delille, and not lightly pass over that grace and harmony, that indescribable charm of manner, which, even in its French garb, has succeeded in pleasing im-

---

[1] See the remarkable notice upon him with which Becq de Fouquières has prefaced the edition of his prose works.

partial classical critics.'[1]   And here the author of the 'Mois'
dwelt upon the talent of the translator of the 'Georgics' with
a warmth that was quite contagious, crowning his praises of the
poet with a eulogy of the professor and the man.   'I am his
neighbour,' he added, 'and it used to be a real treat for me to
hear his lectures at the Collège Royal.[2]   I would invite you to
come and hear them were it not, alas! that this pleasure, like so
many others, is a thing of the past.   Delille is no longer professor of poetry; the Revolution has given him a rest.   His
chair has been taken by Citizen Pâris, formerly a member of
the Oratoire, who has written some odes on air-balloons, elec-
tricity and Rousseau, and who is, besides, a municipal officer.
In the morning he lectures at the College that once was Royal,
and in the evening he harangues our section in the church of the
Collège de Navarre.'[3]

The Abbé Delille had brought us to Citizen Pâris; Citizen
Pâris precipitated us into politics.   The Pantheon section is
one of the most Revolutionary in the capital.   This is the
section which on October 20 resolved to elect a mayor, in disregard of the law, by open and audible voting, and declared
that if its president and secretary were summoned to the bar of
the National Convention, the whole of the section would accompany them in arms.[4]

Charles Trudaine having expressed a wish to be present at a
meeting of this section, we went in a body at about eight o'clock.
The Collège de Navarre,[5] in the chapel of which the meetings
are held, is situated in the Rue de la Montagne Sainte-Geneviève,
in close proximity to the Rue des Noyers.   The statues of Philip
the Fair and Jeanne de Navarre, his wife, who founded the college
in 1304, adorn the gateway; the head of Philip the Fair has
been broken, and his queen has lost both her hands.   The chapel,
which is at the bottom of the first court-yard, was quite full

---

[1] 'Consolations de ma Captivité, ou Correspondance de Roucher.'
[2] The Collège Royal is now the Collège de France.   Delille was professor of poetry, and had rooms in the college itself, in the Place de
Cambrai.
[3] 'Mémoires de l'Abbé Morellet,' ch. xxiii.
[4] 'Tableaux de la Révolution Française,' by Adolphe Schmidt, tome i.,
p. 99.
[5] Closed in 1790.

when we arrived, and the meeting seemed a very uproarious one. Citizen Hû was in the rostrum.

Citizen Hû, a wholesale grocer of the Rue de la Tournelle and a Justice of the Peace for the Pantheon section, is a rather important personage, who took a leading part in the September massacres.   On the third of that month he appeared, in the name of the Vigilance Committee, before the general assembly of the Sans-Culottes section.   Having presented his credentials, he explained that he was charged with the arrest of some traitors, and that he had come to obtain the assistance of the guard stationed at Saint-Firmin to help him in fulfilling his mission. He added that he could confide his secret orders to the President only, promising to communicate them to the assembly as soon as their execution had commenced.   After a conference with the President, twelve National Guards were added to the force already under him.   The doors of the assembly were then closed, so that no one should leave the hall until Citizen Hû's mission had been completed.[1]   That mission was simply the massacre of the priests imprisoned in the seminary of Saint-Firmin.

One can easily understand that after such public services, the Justice of the Peace[2] has great influence over the members of his section, and that his proposals are received with marked favour. He concluded his speech by moving that all citizens should be obliged to appear before the captains of their section and declare in writing whether they accepted the Republic or not.   Those who answered in the negative, or those who did not come at all, would be treated as traitors to their country.   These proposals were adopted.[3]

Citizen Pâris then succeeded Citizen Hû in the tribune.   He

---

[1] ' Registre des Délibérations de l'Assemblée Générale de la Section des Sans-Culottes ' ; ' Procès-verbal ' of September 2 and 3, 1792.

[2] It is a monstrous fact, and such as can only be found in the history of the Revolution, that the help given in the butchery of the seventy-nine victims was the chief reason for conferring upon Hû the dignity of a Justice of the Peace.   And this is by no means an exceptional case.   On September 2, Citizen Joachim Ceyrat, President of the Luxembourg section, proposed ' to purge the prisons by putting all the prisoners to death ' (Mortimer-Ternaux, ' Histoire de la Terreur,' tome iii., pp. 218 and 479).   The motion was carried, and some time afterwards Joachim Ceyrat was appointed Justice of the Peace for the same section.

[3] Schmidt, *op. cit.*

is a cold-blooded man, though not without some natural wit. The theme of his discourse was the duty of obeying the law, except in such cases where the law ran counter to public opinion. He tried to show that all the events of the past four years have strikingly proved the necessity of acting in accordance with this theory, and that every one of the great days of the Revolution, from July 14 to the Tenth of August, was based upon the principle that the will of the people is above the law. The arguments that he brought forward were continually interrupted by cheers and cries of ' *Vive la République !*' and on resuming his seat, the walls of the old chapel rang with thunders of applause.[1]

When silence was again restored, a third orator, Citizen Gobert, undertook the difficult task of speaking after Citizen Pâris. 'Citizens,' he cried, 'you are the sovereign people. The Constitution trespassed upon the rights of the people, and has therefore been swept away ; the laws that it passed have no longer any weight. There must be no other laws than those sanctioned by the people. The people have not yet sanctioned the decrees of the National Assembly, and the sections have therefore the right to do as they please, and to vote openly at all elections in defiance of any interference.'[2] This terrible logician goes even farther than Citizen Pâris. According to Pâris, there are some laws which should be obeyed, provided they do not run counter to public opinion. According to Gobert, there are no laws at all.

Citizen Hû, the Justice of the Peace ; Citizen Garnier, his clerk ; and Citizen Oudeau, his usher, all seemed mightily pleased with these utterances. Roucher also pointed out to us the other leaders of the section—Belliot, Fosseyeux, Lalande, Tencé, Laserre and Croutelle, all men of straw, living from hand to mouth, whose airs of importance would seem ridiculous did we not remember that they and their like are masters of the forty-

---

[1] Schmidt, *op. cit.* Citizen Pâris remained a member of the Commune until the 9th of Thermidor, year II. Proscribed by the Convention as an accomplice of Robespierre, he was sent to execution by the Revolutionary Tribunal on the 11th of Thermidor.

[2] Schmidt, p. 100.

eight sections of Paris, and that these sections rule the National Convention and France.

I left the hall in despair, meditating upon the fact that it was in the Collège de Navarre that Bossuet had studied philosophy and theology, and delivered his first discourse before the victor of Rocroi.[1] In that same chapel in which Citizens Fosseyeux and Croutelle now preach hatred of the rich and contempt of the law, Bossuet preached many a sermon upon devotion to the Virgin Mary.   On June 27, 1663, he pronounced a funeral oration over Nicolas Cornet, Grand-Master of Navarre, one of the most eminent men of his century, who was buried, according to his express wish, in the most obscure corner of the chapel, near the door.   On reaching home I wished to purge my mind of the immoral speeches I had heard, and taking down a volume of the 'Oraisons Funèbres,' I read the following pages, which contain so true and forcible a description of present events that they are perhaps some of the most remarkable that ever came from Bossuet's pen :

'O people born in the bosom of the Church, see whither these reformers would lead you with their theories.   Though the first efforts of these turbulent spirits are but a feeble flutter, there is something more dangerous and violent at the bottom of their hearts —a concealed disgust of all authority, and a longing to go on creating endless reforms. . . .   When any power is desirous of arrogating the rights and authority of the Church, nothing can restrain its violence, and Heaven, to punish such sacrilege in a people, abandons it to its mad intemperance, the fury born of its senseless disputes and self-constituted religion becoming the most dangerous of its diseases. We must therefore not be astonished to see such nations lose all respect for the majesty of the law, nor to find them breaking out into factious and stubborn rebellion.   Religion is weakened by reform, and loses some of that power which alone is capable of controlling nations.   There is in every people a spirit of restlessness that shows itself as soon as this salutary check is removed, and when once they are allowed to become masters of their religion they can have no respect for aught else.   Hence we have ideas, hitherto

---

[1] The Collège de Navarre also numbers amongst its students Chancelier Gerson and Cardinal Richelieu.   In the year XIII. the École Polytechnique was transferred here.—'Les Anciennes Maisons de Paris sous Napoléon III.,' by Lefeuve, tome v., p. 71.

unknown, which aim at the abolition of the Monarchy and the imposition of equality upon men—a seditious chimera, born of treason and sacrilege, and one which proves that thoughts must naturally revert to crime and rebellion when once the authority of religion is overthrown.   But why seek for proofs of a fact that is made so manifest in the Scriptures themselves? The Lord Himself threatens to forsake and to abandon to civil war those nations which alter the religion He has established.   Listen to His words as spoken by the mouth of Zachariah, His prophet: *" Anima eorum variavit in me ; et dixi : Non pascam vos : quod moritur, moriatur ; et quod succiditur, succidatur ; et reliqui devorent unusquisque carnem proximi sui."* [1]

O real and truly fulfilled prophecy !

[1] Bossuet, ' Oraison Funèbre de la Reine de la Grande-Bretagne,' delivered November 16, 1669.

CHAPTER XVI.

Wednesday, October 31, 1792.

IT is the aim of the Revolution to metamorphose not only all things, but even their names. To establish a Republic in a country which has existed for fourteen centuries with a Monarchy and by a Monarchy, a clean sweep must be made of the past, and every trace of it removed. France must become a nation without ancestors, a people without a history ; a pitiless hand must be laid upon the statues of our heroes, and upon anything that might conjure up old recollections. And that is why our streets, our squares and our gardens, are losing those names which were old acquaintances, old friends to the citizens of Paris—*popular* names, in the best sense of the word, names now tabooed by the pretended friends of the people. The city of Sainte-Geneviève and of Saint Louis, of Philippe-Auguste and of Louis XIV., must be turned into a new city, dating from July 14 and the Tenth of August—an impious attempt, mortifying, I am sure, to all who love their old Paris ; a foolish attempt, too, for though they may pull down a statue or a church, they cannot efface history, nor tear from the soil and the heart of the nation the deeds and the memory of its great men.

It may be interesting to take note of a few of these changes of names, for I do not think that they will last very long.

The Place du Carrousel is called Place de la Réunion ; the Place Vendôme, Place des Piques; the Place des Victoires, Place de la Victoire-Nationale ; the Place Dauphine, Place de Thionville ; the Place Henri IV., the Parc d'Artillerie ; the

Place de Sorbonne, Place de Beaurepaire ; the Place de Grève, Place de la Maison Commune ; the Place Royale, Place des Fedérés.

The Hotel de Ville is now called the Maison Commune, and the Palace of the Tuileries the Palais National. The Palais Royal, which in June, 1791, after the flight to Varennes, had already changed its name to Palais d'Orléans, has now become the Palais d'Égalité (a scarcely compatible compound). Even the fountain in the Passage de Valois has been rechristened with the name of Égalité. The Quai d'Orléans, which extends from the Pont de la Tournelle to the lower end of the Ile-Saint-Louis, is now the Quai de l'Égalité ; the Rue de Condé, the Rue de Bourbon-Villeneuve, and the Passage de la Reine de Hongrie, all being dubbed with the same name.

The members of the Commune do not appear to hold liberty in such honour as equality. The former has had to content itself with lending its name to the Rue des Fossés Monsieur le Prince, to the Quai des Balcons, and to the Rue Honoré Chevalier. The Rue Saint-Louis-en-l'Ile has become the Rue de la Fraternité; the Rue Saint-Louis-en-la-Cité, the Rue Révolutionnaire. The latter name has also been given to the old Rue Princesse, leading from the Rue du Four Saint-Germain to the Rue Guisarde, which has itself become Rue des Sans-Culottes. The Rue de Bourbon has made way for the Rue de Lille, the Rue de Bourbon le Chateau for the Rue de la Chaumière, the Rue du Petit Bourbon for the Rue du Petit Muséum. The Palais Bourbon, the Place Louis XV. and the Rue Royale, have respectively become the Palais, the Place, and the Rue de la Révolution.

On September 21 the name of the Rue Sainte-Anne, in which the revolutionizing philosopher Helvétius was born, was changed to Rue Helvétius by virtue of an order of the Conseil Général de la Commune. Whilst the other saints are awaiting the fate of Saint Anne, the Carrefour de la Croix Rouge has become the Carrefour du Bonnet Rouge, the too religious appellation of the Rue de l'Observance being altered to that of the Rue de Marseille.[1]

[1] 'The section of the Théâtre-Français has just changed its name to that of Marseilles, in honour of the brave Marseillais who live in the immediate neighbourhood.'—*Patriote Français* of August 14, 1792.

On October 18 M. Manuel proposed that the Rue de Sorbonne should cease to bear a name recalling a vain and crafty body, hostile to philosophy and humanity. The proposal was adopted, not, however, without some protests, and the Rue de Sorbonne became the Rue Catinat. Prudhomme, in his *Révolutions de Paris*, is of opinion that the new appellations should serve as a contrast or corrective to the old ones. He therefore proposes to give the name of Rue de la Vérité to that Rue de Sorbonne 'which led to those schools where falsehood was so long taught with truly priestly brazenness.'

Another proposal of Manuel's was to call eighty-three of the principal streets by the names of the departments. This motion was also favourably received.

The Mirabeau section did not wait for the orders of the Conseil Général de la Commune, but placed the following resolution on the minutes of its proceedings of October 6 : 'Acting in conformity with a motion passed on September 30, the Assembly has unanimously agreed that the names of certain streets shall be changed as follows

OLD NAMES.	NEW NAMES.
Grange-Batelière et Neuve-Grange-Batelière.	Scévola.
Pinon.	des Gracques.
le Pelletier.	Manlius.
d'Artois.	Cérutti.
de Provence.	Franklin.
Taitbout.	Brutus.
le Cul-de-sac Taitbout.	l'Impasse Brutus.
Duhoussay.	de l'Égalité.
Chantereine.	de la Liberté.
Saint-George et Neuve-Saint-George.	Guillaume Tell.
Chauchat.	des Phocéens.
Saint-Lazare.	des Belges.
des Trois-Frères.	Caton.
de la Rochefoucauld.	Fabius.
de Laval-Montmorency.	Décius.
Nouette.	Socrate.
Royale.	de la République.
des Martyrs.	Régulus.

I am not displeased with these names on the whole. I will even admit that some of them are quite to my taste, especially that which it is intended to give to the Cul-de-sac Taitbout, and which might be applied to the whole of the Republic. As a matter of fact, is not the Republic, indeed, an *impasse Brutus* ?[1] I also wish to point out that all these names are either Greek, Roman, American, or Swiss, not a single one being French. Is not this apparently trivial fact in reality of great significance ? Would it not serve to show—if proofs, indeed, were required to support so evident a truth—that the Republic is a foreign importation, the artificial fabric of a few rhetoricians, and of many evildoers ; that it is in keeping with nothing in our past, and that, in a word, it is not French ? Of all these names the least foreign to France is that of Cérutti, who was born in Turin, but who died in Paris in the street which is to bear his name. This ex-Jesuit, who has the honour of a place between Manlius and Cato, was the editor of the *Feuille Villageoise*, the author of a good many patriotic pamphlets, and a writer of bad verse.

Like Loustallot, the editor of the *Révolutions de Paris*, whose name has been given to the Rue des Fossés Saint-Victor, Cérutti, too, will have his memory kept green. But before long Loustallot, Cérutti, and even Mirabeau, whose name now adorns the corner of the Rue de la Chaussée d'Antin, may share the same fate as La Fayette. He, too, had given his name to the former Rue de Calonne. But alas ! the Rue La Fayette has already made way for the Rue du Contrat Social.

After our streets, our towns will have their turn.

The citizens of Bar le Duc have already changed the name of their town to Bar sur l'Ornin.

On October 25 M. Lehardy, member for the Morbihan, proposed in the Convention that the town of Port Louis should thenceforth be called Port de l'Égalité. It was decided that the Committee of Legislation be charged with the duty of changing the names of all places that smacked of the old *régime*.[2]

Now, Messieurs du Comité, to work ! Efface with one stroke of the pen fourteen centuries of our history.

---

[1] *Impasse*=blind alley.   [2] *Moniteur* of October 27, 1792.

CHAPTER XVII.

Saturday, November 3, 1792.

UNDER my windows the newsboys are crying out *The Charge against Maximilien Robespierre!* This is the philippic pronounced by Louvet at the sitting of October 29 against the Vigilance Committee of the Commune, against Marat, against the deputies of Paris, and against Robespierre in particular. Between the Robespierre and the Brissot parties the struggle waxes keener than ever. It is carried on everywhere and in every way, both on the floor of the Convention and in the rooms of the Jacobin Club, in the newspapers, in the streets, and even on the walls, where the two parties engage in a combat of posting.

Many honest people who take no heed of what may happen to-morrow, nor care to remember the events of yesterday, are grateful to the Brissotins for coping with the Maratists, and for heaping curses upon Robespierre and his satellites. They do not pause to consider that if the Brissotins are now doing all they can to stop the course of the Revolution, it is because they are in power; that if they are attempting to upset the Commune, it is to prevent the Commune from upsetting them; that if they attack Robespierre, it is because Robespierre has sworn to destroy them. Such people have the simplicity to think the party composed of honest men, friends of law and order, and even willing to compromise itself to save the innocent. They forget that Brissot and his friends have trodden under foot the Constitution they swore to maintain; that they have incited insurrection as often as it served their purpose; that they had no mercy upon Louis XVI. and his defenders, and that their ambition has never shrunk from any cowardice or crime.

I must admit that personally I cannot so easily forget the events of yesterday, nor so many hateful deeds for which France will long have to suffer—deeds which neither dramatic harangues nor speeches containing more rhetoric than courage can ever efface. If the Girondists desire to be looked upon as honest citizens, let them commence by asking forgiveness of God and men. Until they do that, it is our duty to remember.[1]

[1] Concerning the tactics of the Girondists in the Legislative Assembly on the Tenth of August and during the massacres of September, see our 'Légende des Girondins,' ch. ii., iii., and iv.

CHAPTER XVIII

Monday, November 5, 1792.

SINCE the opening of the Convention, and since the day on which we became a Republic, the public agitation and disturbance has continually increased ; disorder and terror reign supreme.

Walk through the streets, stop in the public squares, read th news-sheets and the placards that adorn the walls, attend the sectional assemblies, enter the clubs of the Cordeliers and the Jacobins, penetrate even into the National Convention—on al. sides you will find shouts of death, rumours of rebellion, threats of murder.

On October 29 Roland, the Minister of the Interior, laid before the Convention a report on the state of Paris. 'The principles of rebellion and bloodshed'—so runs this official document— 'are openly professed and applauded in every assembly ; murmurs are even heard against the Convention itself. I can no longer doubt that partisans of the old *régime* and enemies of the people, hiding their madness or their villainy under a mask of patriotism, have conceived a plan of a complete revolt, hoping to rise once more to power by the aid of bloodshed, atrocities, and gold.'[1] The worthy Roland is well aware that the villains he denounces are anything but partisans of the old *régime*, and rank, on the contrary, amidst the staunchest defenders of the Republic. But to recognise and to proclaim this fact, to

[1] 'Report of the Minister of the Interior on the Condition of Paris,' read to the Convention on October 29, 1792.—' Histoire Parlementaire,' tome xx., p. 103, etc.

boldly attack those patriots who would sweep away him and his friends, more energy and honesty were required than may reasonably be looked for in the poor man who praised the zeal and patriotism displayed by Fournier the American, the author of the 'Massacre of the Prisoners of Orleans.'[1]

On November 3, a few days after his report to the Convention, Roland wrote the following letter to the Conseil Général de la Commune :

'*Paris, November 3,* Year I.

' I cannot refrain, citizens, from praising your zeal and exhorting you to exercise the greatest vigilance. On all sides I hear rumours of plots, and plans of murder and outrage, but I am willing to believe that by your care all mischief will be prevented, and that the people of Paris, whose peace and safety are in your keeping, will maintain in the eyes of France and the nations that reputation for bravery and prudence which has at all times distinguished them.'[2]

This certificate of bravery and prudence awarded to the Parisians exactly two months after the massacre of September is, to say the least, peculiar. But let that pass. What is still more remarkable is the Minister's confession that he hears on all sides rumours of plots, and plans of murder and outrage.

Meanwhile, the prisons emptied on September 2 are being daily refilled with fresh suspects. The arrests made by order of the Vigilance Committee of the Commune between October 10 and November 1 amounted to 1,032. The total number of prisoners at the beginning of the month was 1,375. We learn under what conditions these arrests were made from Roland's report read at the sitting on October 29. The Minister there draws attention to ' the arbitrary acts which have caused the prisons to fill so soon after the terrible executions that had emptied them '; and he adds: ' I have furnished the National Assembly with proofs of these arbitrary acts by laying upon their table between five and six hundred warrants, some of which are signed by one subordinate official only ; the majority

---

[1] Letter from Roland, Minister of the Interior, to the President of the National Convention, dated October 6, 1792.

[2] *Moniteur* of November 5, 1792.

bear the signatures of two or three members of the Vigilance Committee, whilst many give either no reasons at all for the arrest, or simply allege suspicions of treason.'[1]

On the day before these words were read out, delegates from the criminal courts of Paris had visited the Convention, and M. Target, President of one of the courts, and spokesman for the deputation, expressed himself in the following terms, after having briefly stated the chief points of the criminal law : ' Citizens, such is the law, and these are the facts : the prisons were emptied seven weeks ago by a bloody catastrophe, and they are already refilled. The motives for the arrest of so many citizens are unknown ; the prison registers have been badly kept, and no complaint has been made to the courts by the police officers. The Commune therefore reduces the courts to inactivity, and hence it comes that the citizens of a Republic are more oppressed than they were under a despot.'[2]

Prisons overflowing with victims, rebellion in the public streets, anarchy everywhere, commerce suspended, work stopped, workshops deserted, misery and starvation in every home—such is the Paris which the Revolution has given us. Hear the avowal of the most ardent Republicans—Robespierre declaring in the Jacobin Club on October 29 that 100,000 Frenchmen are on the eve of starvation ;[3] Marat writing in his paper : ' The trade of Paris is absolutely ruined, and more than 100,000 of its inhabitants who were in comfortable circumstances before the fall of the Bastille are now in penury.'[4] Starvation stares us in the face, but though the people of Paris are without bread, they shall have their shows. The trial of Louis XVI. begins to-morrow.

---

[1] *Moniteur*, No. 302.   [2] *Ibid.*, No. 303.
[3] Letters from Maximilien Robespierre, member of the National Convention, to his constituents.
[4] 'Journal de la République Française,' by Marat, *l'Ami du Peuple*, No. 15, Tuesday, October 9, 1792.

CHAPTER XIX.

Thursday, November 8, 1792.

THE trial of Louis XVI. has commenced. M. Dufriche-Valazé, member for the department of the Orne, and one of the principal members of the Brissot party, rose in the Convention on Tuesday, and, on behalf of the Special Commission of Twenty-four,[1] read his "Report on the Crimes of the Late King, Proofs of which were found in the Papers seized by the Vigilance Committee of the Commune of Paris." The report concluded with a demand that Louis XVI. be condemned to death as a punishment for his manifest crimes.

This fact will ever remain one of the most shameful monuments of popular passion and one of the basest deeds ever perpetrated by revolutionary fury.

In the name of the Commission of Twenty-four, in the name of the Girondist party, and amidst the applause of Robespierre's followers, Dufriche-Valazé exclaimed: 'Of what was this monster not capable? You shall see him at bay before the whole of humanity! I will charge him with having bought up all the provisions of this city!'[2]

---

[1] The Special Commission of Twenty-four had been appointed on October 1, 1792, to examine the papers seized by the Vigilance Committee of the Commune of Paris, and especially, as far as concerned Louis XVI., the papers found with Laporte and Septeuil, the one Intendant, and the other Treasurer of the Civil List. It was composed of Bailleul, Bailly, Barbaroux, Bernier, Birotteau, Boutroüe, Cavaignac, Danbermesnil, Delahaye, Delbrel, Derozey, Drouet, Dufriche-Valazé, Froger, Laurenceot, Laurent, Lehardy, Lejeune, Lesage, Pelletier, Petit-Jean, Phillippeaux, Poulain-Grandpré, and Vernier.

[2] In the trial of Louis XVI., the Girondist Dufriche-Valazé was not behindhand in keeping this promise. During the King's examination, on December 11, he was charged with the duty of reading the documents

History will despise these mean and lying accusations, and
posterity, basing its judgment of Louis XVI. on facts, will say :
' Never was there a Sovereign animated with more generous intentions or more liberal ideas ; never was there a man more sincere
in his desire to do good, or more eager to carry out that desire.'

' Seated on the throne to which it has pleased God to raise us, we
trust that in His mercy He may guide our youth and lead us to the
means by which our people may be made happy, for that is our only
desire. . . . We must do our best to relieve our people as far as
possible of the weight of taxation. . . . There is expenditure
personal to ourselves, and some relating to our Court ; in both these
matters we can more promptly follow the impulse of our own heart,
and we are already attempting to bring these sums within reasonable limits. Such sacrifices will not be felt by us as long as they
are made in the interests of our subjects ; their happiness will be
our glory, and the benefits they reap will be the sweetest reward
for all our care and labour.'[1]

Such were the words, and such was the programme, with which
Louis XVI. inaugurated his reign ; his acts have ever been in
harmony with this language, worthy the utterance of a King, a
Frenchman, and a Christian.

His first act of authority was a deed of kindness. At the
beginning of each reign it is usual for the King to receive a
fine of *confirmation* for the offices and privileges previously
granted, whilst also levying an accession tax upon municipalities
and individuals. On May 30, 1774, Louis issued an edict
granting remission of all taxes due to him by reason of his
accession to the throne.

seized, and acquitted himself of his task with an air of contempt and
inhumanity that disgusted even the most furious demagogues. (See
Révolutions de Paris, No. 179 ; the *Courrier des Départements*, December 14, 1792 ; Barère's ' Mémoires.') On January 26, 1793, five days after
the execution of Louis XVI., Dufriche-Valazé wrote to his constituents
a letter from which I take this passage : ' My friends, since October 1
last, the day on which I was appointed a member of the Commission
of Twenty-four, all my time has been given to the examination and
verification of the documents that proved the guilt of Louis Capet.
I arranged these myself, and made them prove as much as possible against
the culprit we had to try. I was the first to denounce him, and all the
strength that Heaven gave me I put forth in these matters.'—' Archives
Nationales,' A. F. II., 45 (Committee of Public Safety).

[1] Preamble of the Edict of May 30, 1774. Louis XVI. mounted the
throne on May 10, 1774, being then twenty years of age.

Nor was this all. All soldiers whose pensions were in arrear were paid in full out of the King's privy purse.[1]

Resolved to retain only as much pomp as was absolutely necessary to the dignity of the throne and the nation, he did not hesitate to reduce his military household in conformity with his ideas of order and economy. An Edict of December 15, 1775, disbanded the sixth brigade in each company of his body-guard, and abolished a number of unnecessary posts. Three additional Orders of the same date disbanded the regiment of Mounted Grenadiers, and the two regiments of Musketeers of the Guard, and reduced in number the two regiments of Gendarmes and of Light Cavalry of the Guard.

Greater still were the reforms made by Louis XVI. in the Royal Household. On December 22, 1776, he liquidated all debts, and decided that in future the estimates for the following year should be laid before him in December.

On the same day he made an order concerning pensions and other money grants. 'The King,' so ran this Order, 'upon a close examination of the Royal Treasury, has been pained to find it much exhausted by excessive liberality, and has felt the necessity of obviating this state of things in future. . . . Whilst taking into consideration the justice of every demand, he has determined to limit the grants made, and to bring these expenses within reasonable bounds. . . . He desires to dispel the mystery that often covers the extent of a demand by giving publicity to all grants, and thus discouraging unjustifiable solicitations. All persons who shall in future demand money grants will, at the same time, have to make a return of whatever emoluments they may already enjoy.'

By his Edict of July, 1779, the King abolished the offices of sixteen different Treasurers of departments, and created in their stead a single office of Paymaster-General for the expenses of the whole Royal Household. From January to August he abolished no less than 420 offices connected with his Household. The amount paid to the Court musicians before 1782 was 500,000 francs per year. By the Edict of May, 1782, this was

[1] Seguièr's speech before the King on November 12, 1774 (Isambert, tome i., p. 82).

reduced to 257,400 francs. An Order of August 9, 1787, effected fresh economy in the Household expenses, and promised that every effort would be made to cut these down as much as possible. Article 8 of the same Order showed that every department of the Queen's Household had been considerably reduced : so many unnecessary posts had been abolished that, notwithstanding the payment of substantial sums in commutation of salaries, there resulted a net benefit to the Treasury of more than 900,000 francs.

These reductions did not fail to give rise to much discontent at Court. But this Louis XVI. was brave enough to defy, animated as he was by the desire to diminish taxation and to relieve the people.

Having from the moment when he first ascended the throne given special attention to the food-supply of the kingdom, Louis soon established absolute freedom of trade in corn throughout the land. Such was the object of the Order in Council of September 13, and of the Letters Patent of November 2, 1774.

Another Order in Council of April 24, 1775, promised bounties upon the importation of corn from abroad, and forbade any interference with the transit of corn from one province to another.

But there was another question which Louis XVI. thought of even greater importance than that of food-supply. He proposed to abolish for ever servitude, both real and personal, and to enfranchise both individuals and property. He carried out his idea without allowing himself to be deterred by the opposition he met with, and, what was perhaps more difficult still, without violating ancient rights.

The statute-labour for the construction and maintenance of the highways gave rise to numerous complaints. The Edict of February 17, 1776, ordered its abolition, and prescribed in its stead a contribution payable by all owners of real property. Equitable as this measure was, it nevertheless called forth very serious resistance, especially on the parts of the Parliaments,[1]

[1] The *Parlements* were bodies charged with the administration of justice under the old *régime*. They held sittings in the principal towns of the kingdom, and, in addition to their judicial duties, assumed political powers of immense importance.

and Louis XVI. was obliged to summon a Diet on March 12, 1776, for the express purpose of registering the said Edict. The resistance continuing, the King was forced ' to provisionally re-establish the ancient custom observed for the maintenance of the highways.'[1] But Louis, convinced of the justice of this reform, was not discouraged. On November 6, 1786, he made his Council issue an Order for the temporary commutation of the statute-labour by payment of money. On June 27, 1787, he again returned to the subject, statute-labour being this time definitely abolished throughout the kingdom and replaced by money payments.

Remains of servitudes still existed in some of the provinces by virtue of the law of mortmain, while certain vassals were attached to the soil by the name of serfs. The latter were incapable of making any testamentary disposal of their property, and, except in certain cases, could not even leave their children the results of their labour, neither were they free to dispose of their persons or to leave the manor, under pain of losing all right to the property which they held. Although these last traces of servitude existed only in a very few places, Louis XVI. was fully alive to their injustice, and the Edict of August, 1779, shows how sincere a partisan he was of real liberty and equality :

' We should have liked to abolish without distinction these vestiges of a rigorous feudalism, but our finances will not allow us to buy up the rights of the lords of the manors. Though restrained by the regard we shall always have for the laws of property, which we consider the safest foundation of peace and order, we have seen with satisfaction that, whilst respecting these principles, we could still effect some of the good we had in view by abolishing servitude not only on all lands held by us, but also on all domains held from us and our predecessors. We have therefore invited all such holders as considered themselves wronged by this condition to give up the holdings they at present occupy, and to claim from us the sums paid by them or their ancestors.

' We desire, moreover, that in cases where land is acquired by, or returns to, the Crown, all serfs shall have their liberty the instant we enter upon possession of a new domain or manor ; and to

---

[1] Proclamation of August 11, 1776.

encourage as far as lies in our power all holders of fiefs to follow our example, and considering these enfranchisements less as an alienation than as a return to what is naturally right, we have exempted this sort of act from the formalities and the taxes to which the old severity of the feudal law had subjected them.

'Though the principles that we entertain hinder us from abolishing the right of servitude in its entirety, it is our opinion that in the exercise of this right there was an excess which we could not allow to go on any longer; this excessive right even the tribunals have hesitated to countenance, and the principles of social justice can no longer tolerate its existence. It will therefore delight us to see that our example, and that love of humanity peculiar to the French nation, will bring to pass in our reign the abolition of the rights of mortmain and servitude; this will give us the satisfaction of witnessing the complete enfranchisement of our subjects, who, in whatever rank it has pleased Providence to place them, are the objects of our care, and have equal rights to our protection and love.'

By the suppression of statute-labour Louis XVI. had freed the hands of the agriculturists; similar attempts were made by him to restore commerce and industry to their natural liberty. The Edict of February, 1776, decreed the suppression of guilds and companies in arts, trades, and commerce. Its first article ran as follows:

'It shall be free to all persons, of any quality or rank, even to aliens, to embrace and to exercise in the whole of our kingdom, and especially in our good city of Paris, whatever branch or branches of art, trade, or commerce they prefer; to which end we hereby abolish and suppress all bodies and companies of merchants and artisans, as well as every kind of guild, and abrogate all privileges, statutes, and charters given to such bodies. . . .'

Like the Edict for the suppression of statute-labour, the decree for the abolition of guilds met with so much resistance on the part of the Parliaments that it was necessary to hold a fresh Diet on March 12, 1776, and in the month of August a second Edict modifying the first was issued with the following preamble:

'Persevering in our efforts to destroy the abuses which existed prior to the issue of our Edict of February last in the companies and guilds of arts and trades, we have thought it necessary, whilst again creating one company of merchants and a few guilds of arts

and trades, to give entire freedom to certain branches of trade
which should not be subject to any restrictions whatever, to unite
all professions that are at all similar, and to lay down such rules for
the government of the said companies and guilds as shall provide
for the maintenance of discipline and the exercise of authority
between master and man without entrenching upon any of the
advantages arising from the free exercise of such art, trade, or
commerce. . . . The professions, which will be open to all persons
to exercise, will continue to be a resource for the poorest of our
subjects. The dues payable upon entry into the said companies
and guilds, very much reduced, and proportionate to the class and
utility of the commerce or industry, will no longer form an obstacle
to admission. Girls and women will no longer be excluded.
Several trades may be carried on together where possible. . . .
Whilst thus suppressing what experience has shown to be bad,
whilst laying down new regulations for a more wise and equitable
administration, whilst abolishing, by a legitimate exercise of our
authority, practices which had given birth to infinite abuses and
excesses, we shall preserve in these ancient institutions all those
advantages tending to good order and public tranquillity.'

There is a liberty more precious than that of commerce and
industry — liberty of conscience. In January, 1784, Louis
decided that the Jews should be liberated from the poll-tax
and other taxes to which they were subjected. The Edict of
November, 1787, concerning non-Catholics, Protestants, Jews,
etc., authorized them to have their births, marriages, and deaths
properly registered, so that, like all other French subjects, they
might enjoy full civil rights. By his reply to the remonstrances
addressed to him by a Parliament on January 18, 1788, Louis
showed the importance which he attached to this law and to its
immediate execution: 'I give orders to my Attorney-General
to lay this Edict before the Parliament on Tuesday ; I desire
that it shall be registered immediately. You '—turning to the
first President—' will report this to me on Wednesday.'

The carrying out of reforms in the administration of the law
was a duty that Louis XVI. discharged in a manner befitting
an heir of Saint Louis.

During the first days of his reign an Order in Council, dated
August 18, 1775, forbade the interception of letters even for the
purposes of justice :

'His Majesty, taking into consideration that these letters have been obtained (for the Superior Council of the Island of Saint Domingo) only by intercepting them on the vessel to which they had been entrusted, and that such odious means leave no other course open but that of maintaining silence and sending the intercepted letters to the person to whom they belong—His Majesty, taking further into consideration that intercepted letters can never become matter for deliberation, that every principle of right relegates private correspondence to that circle of sacred things into which neither tribunals nor individuals have the right to pry, and that the Superior Council had therefore no right to take note of the information laid before it, orders, in the interests of public peace and for the security of citizens and trade, the prosecution of the authors and accomplices of the said interception. . . .'

On December 12, 1775, a royal Order abolished the death sentence against deserters, and laid down new penalties proportionate to the motives and circumstances of desertion.

In spite of the Parliaments and the opinion of a large number of lawyers, Louis abolished the cross-examination of prisoners by proclamation, dated August 24, 1780: 'The ancient codes had always imposed this cross-examination upon those charged with a crime punishable by death when circumstantial evidence was strong against the accused, but no absolute proofs of his guilt existed. . . . We think it our duty to abrogate this custom.'

On May 8, 1788, the King held a Diet to register four Edicts introducing still further reforms into the administration of justice.[1]

Moved by the sad lot of the prisoners, and by the state of the prisons in some of the principal towns of the kingdom, Louis XVI., in the early years of his reign, had paid for many improvements out of his own pocket. A royal proclamation of August 30, 1780, decreed the establishment of new prisons for debtors. 'Filled with a desire to relieve the unfortunate' —so runs the preamble—'and to hold out a helping hand to those who owe their misfortunes to their folly, we have long been pained by the state of the prisons in most of the towns in

---

[1] 'De l'Amélioration de la Loi Criminelle,' by M. Bonneville de Marsangy, tome i., p. 513.

our kingdom, and in spite of the war we have contributed out of our own pocket towards their reconstruction. . . . We shall not lose sight of them when peace furnishes us with fresh means, but having received more precise information of the sad state of the prisons in our capital, we have thought it impossible to defer the question of their reform. . . .' Appreciable reforms were indeed introduced, and the author of a curious little book entitled 'Paris en Miniature,' published in Amsterdam in 1784, wrote : 'The kindness of Louis XVI. makes the prisons almost pleasant. We find them spacious, clean, and healthy.'

If Louis was so taken up with the lot of the prisoners, how much more did the fate of the sick poor move him! If the state of the prisons interested him, how could that of the hospitals fail to do so in a much greater degree!

At the time of his accession the hospitals of Lyons, Marseilles, Bordeaux, Brest, and many other towns, were admirably organized.[1] Such was not the case in the capital. Louis, wishing to have an exact idea of the abuses that required reform, went disguised to the Hôtel-Dieu, and paid particular attention to what he saw there. In many instances he found four patients in one bed, and he left the building resolved to remedy some of the evils he had witnessed.[2] In 1772 a large portion of the Hôtel-Dieu had been destroyed by fire.[3] Louis XVI. desired to replace it by four large hospitals, built on more spacious and salubrious sites, and he issued an appeal for subscriptions towards this good work. The idea failed in consequence of the opposition of the hospital authorities, who hastened to reconstruct the ruined buildings on the same site. Louis, however, obtained for each patient the privilege of a separate bed, and even this concession was mainly due to his generosity. But this was not enough for the King ; the question of the hospitals was always in his mind, and fresh plans and estimates were drawn up by his own hand. In 1786 a commission, formed of members of the Académie des Sciences, was charged with the examination of a new scheme. The report of this commission concludes with the following *résumé* :

[1] 'Les Réformes sous Louis XVI.,' by Ernest Sémichon, p. 125.
[2] 'Louis XV. et ses Vertus,' by l'Abbé Proyart, tome i., pp. 89, 90.
[3] 'Essai Historique sur l'Hôtel-Dieu,' by Roudonneau de la Motte.

'The Hôtel-Dieu, as at present situated, is too small to accommodate the number of patients which Paris, with its vast population, sends. . . . The new hospital, planned by M. Poyet, has great advantages over the present one ; but we believe that the building would be too large, and have the disadvantage of bringing too many patients to the same spot. We propose to split up this vast plan, and to build four hospitals, each to hold 1,200 patients, the buildings to be constructed in long parallel galleries. In case there should be a desire to economize the expenses, we are of opinion that the hospitals of Saint Louis and Sainte Anne might be utilized for two of the new institutions, and that the two others would be well placed, one on the site of the Célestins and the other near the École Militaire.

'We must bring to the notice of the Academy the interesting information, which we have from M. de Breteuil himself,[1] that, though the King has not yet decided upon anything in this matter, he has long weighed in his heart the interests of the sick poor. He is convinced that a large hospital is a great calamity, and in his sovereign kindness he has conceived the idea of substituting for it several smaller ones. If the poor are once made to know this, they will not forget it. When lying in separate beds in these hospitals, they will remember that they owe it as much to the kindness of the man as to the generosity of the Monarch.'

This report was signed by Lasonne, D'Aubenton, Tenon, Bailly, Lavoisier, La Place, Coulomb, and Darcet, as well as by the Marquis de Condorcet, now a member of the Convention, and one of the judges of Louis XVI.

On June 22, 1787, the Council finally decided to build four new hospitals in Paris—Saint Louis, Sainte Anne, Sainte Périne at Chaillot, and one at La Roquette.

The solicitude of the King did not stop here. Having been informed that every year more than two thousand infants were brought from all parts of the country to the Foundling Hospital in Paris, that they were brought by public carriers, who were a long time on the way, and had other business to attend to, so that nearly nine-tenths of these children died before the age of three, Louis XVI. remedied this state of things on January 10, 1779. All carriers, messengers, and other persons, were forbidden, under a penalty of 1,000 francs, to take charge of

---

[1] Minister of the King's Household.

new-born or deserted infants, except for the purpose of handing them over to nurses, or taking them to the nearest foundling hospital. The King declared that in case this measure should increase the expenses of any provincial hospital to such an extent as to bring them in excess of the revenue, he would make good the amount out of his own pocket until means had been found for supplying the deficit permanently.

The Abbé de l'Épée, in establishing the admirable institution which he set up for the instruction of the deaf and dumb, had a most devoted fellow-worker in Louis XVI., who made him many grants of property (certain portions of the monasteries of Paris), and who also found the necessary funds for the mainten-ance of indigent deaf-mutes.

A list of the measures due to the King's kindness of heart and pity for sufferers would be interminable. He was one of the first to take a share in the work of helping the poor in their own homes ; by Letters Patent of December 9, 1777, he also set up in Paris the pawn-broking establishment known as the Mont-de-Piété, under the direction of the administrators of hospitals.

He himself determined how the bread for the troops was to be made, and took care that the orders given for the well-being of the soldiers were properly carried out.[1]

Parmentier, in his efforts to promulgate the cultivation of the potato in France, was hedged in by prejudices which seemed insurmountable, until the King came to his aid, and ordered potatoes to be served upon the royal table, so that they might the sooner reach the tables of the poor. When the discovery and introduction of vaccination met with almost universal opposi-tion, Louis XVI. did not hesitate to have himself inoculated, together with his brothers and Madame la Comtesse d'Artois, thinking this public example one he owed the safety of his subjects.[2]

But all these acts, and others too numerous to mention, which had gained him the glorious title of *Louis the Good*, are perhaps

[1] 'Administration Militaire,' vol. 3,696, pièce 54. Letter from the Comte de Saint-Germain, Minister of War, to the Comte de Broglie, Lieutenant-Général, at Metz.

[2] 'Louis XVI., Marie Antoinette et Mme. Élisabeth,' by F. Feuillet de Conches, tome i., p. 41.

less meritorious than those by which he himself laid aside a part of his authority in order to ensure, as he believed, the happiness of his people.

On July 12, 1778, he established a Provincial Assembly in the department of Berry. The Provincial Assembly of the Haute Guyenne was next organized, according to an Order in Council dated July 11, 1779.

By virtue of an order of June 1, 1787, Provincial Assemblies met in the following twenty-one chief towns : Bourges, Montauban, Châlons, Amiens, Soissons, Paris, Orléans, Tours, Maine, Riom, Moulins, Nevers, Valenciennes, Rouen, Alençon, Caen, Nancy, Metz, Strasbourg, Perpignan, and Auch.

In Bordeaux, La Rochelle, Besançon and Grenoble, Provincial Assemblies, although convoked by the King, were not held on account of the opposition of the local Parliaments.

In six provinces, the old assemblies called Estates were again convoked, as in the past, at Montpellier, Dijon, Rennes, Lille, Pau and Aix. Invitations to the Provincial Assemblies were issued to the Clergy, the Nobility, and the members of the Third Estate, the latter numbering as many votes as the two other orders put together. These assemblies were invested with considerable powers.[1] They were charged with the collection and partition of the taxes, both for the Treasury and for roads,

[1] See 'Les Assemblées Provinciales sous Louis XVI.,' by M. Léonce de Lavergne. The author of this book, a liberal-minded man, and in no way suspected of weakness for the old *régime*, does not hesitate to say that 'what Louis XVI. has done ought to have been sufficient to ensure him universal gratitude,' and that 'his reign was the best epoch in our history.' 'I am sure,' he writes, 'that no one is more passionately attached than I am to the ideas of justice, equality, and liberty, which they say the French Revolution has inaugurated ; but it seems to me fully proved that France made more progress in the application of these ideas during the fifteen years between the accession of Louis XVI. and August, 1789, than during the twenty-five years from 1789 to 1815. . France has never enjoyed greater liberty than in 1788 and 1789 ; instead of developing political freedom, the Revolution has only choked it. Equality has gained a little more in appearance, but not in reality. Let us remember that three-quarters of a century have passed since 1789, and let us measure in our thoughts the progress that would have been made during that period if the impulse animating the better classes had been allowed to pursue its course uninterruptedly. The greatest evil of the Revolution was not so much the wholesale bloodshed as the sowing of such elements of hatred and revenge as still hinder a reconciliation in the common interest. No one has gained by the Revolution, but everyone has lost.'

public works, indemnities, aids, repairs to churches, and all other expenses. 'We will,' said the King, 'that the said expenditure, be it common to the said provinces, or be it peculiar to certain districts and communes, be, according to its nature, passed, approved, and administered by the said Provincial Assemblies, or by the Commissions subordinate to them.' M. Lamoignon de Malesherbes, the Keeper of the Seals, in a speech which he delivered upon the law relating to Provincial Assemblies, declared that they were to impose all taxes without exception, and to distribute the amount collected.

Is there any necessity to recall the fact that Louis XVI. did not stop at the creation of Provincial Assemblies, important as that step was; that on August 8, 1788, he decided to convoke the States-General, and that on June 23, 1789, a royal proclamation was read to the deputies of the three Estates, of which the following are the principal clauses?

'No new tax shall be imposed, nor any old one prolonged beyond the term fixed by law, without the consent of the representatives of the nation; no loan shall be raised without the consent of the States-General; the estimates of revenue and expenditure shall be published annually; tallies shall be abolished, and the tax replaced by another based upon equitable principles, without distinction of birth, rank, or position; the right of *francfief* shall be abolished as soon as income and expenditure are equally balanced; statute-labour shall be completely abolished, and for ever; the abolition of the right of mortmain, for which the King has set an example, will be extended to the whole of France; when the promises made by the Clergy and Nobility to renounce their pecuniary privileges shall have been confirmed in their assemblies, it is the intention of the King to sanction these reforms, so that in the payment of taxes there may exist no privilege or distinction whatever; the States-General will deliberate upon the scheme proposed by the King to place the officers of Customs upon the frontiers in order that both home and foreign produce may circulate with perfect freedom within the limits of the kingdom; the unhappy results of the tax on salt will be carefully examined, and in any case means will have to be proposed to alter the method of its collection; a regular conscription will be substituted for the present manner of drawing for the militia; the King, desirous of assuring the personal liberty of all citizens in a sound and durable manner, invites the States-General to lay before him a scheme for abolishing the orders known

as *lettres de cachet*, without endangering the public safety. The
States-General will report to the King upon the most expedient
means of reconciling the liberty of the Press with the respect due
to religion, morals, and the honour of the State.   In the different
provinces of the kingdom there will be established Provincial Estates
composed as follows : Two-tenths of members of the Clergy, three-
tenths of members of the Nobility, and five-tenths of members
of the Third Estate.'

After the reading of this proclamation Louis XVI. added
with perfect justice : ' Up to the present it is I who have done
everything for the happiness of my people, and it is, perhaps,
seldom that the sole ambition of a Sovereign is to get his subjects to agree to accept his favours.'[1]

We are far from having enumerated all the favours of
Louis XVI., or from having mentioned all his reforms.   There
is one, however, that cannot be passed over, and that should
not be forgotten, either by the writers who are now judging
Louis XVI. in the newspapers, or by those who are about to
try him in the Convention.   It was the King who proclaimed
the principle of ownership in letters, and who formally recognised
that the right of authors to their works should be perpetual.
It was upon his initiative, and owing to his persistence, that the
following Order in Council of August 30, 1777, was passed :
' Every author who shall in his name obtain the privilege of a
work shall have the sole right of selling it, and shall enjoy such
privilege for himself and his heirs in perpetuity.'[2]

Such is the man, such is the Prince, whom an infuriated mob
to-day calls *Louis the Tyrant*, and whom the most despotic
assembly that ever existed is preparing to arraign at its bar !
Let him come !   Let him be dragged from the Temple Tower
to the Riding-School by General Santerre, escorted by the pike-
bearers of the *faubourgs*, insulted by the mob, and deafened by
the refrain of the *Marseillaise*.

By the side of this procession there is another which will

---

[1] 'Archives Parlementaires de 1787 à 1860,' by J. Mavidal, Laurent,
and Clavel, tome viii., p. 146.
[2] See in the ' Portraits Intimes du Dix-huitième Siècle,' by Edmond
and Jules de Goncourt, a letter from Louis XVI., dated September 6,
1775.

escort Louis XVI. before his judges, and will strew palms and wreaths before the accused. The abolition of statute-labour and of mortmain ; the extinction of servitude throughout the royal domains ; the bestowal of civil rights upon Protestants and Jews ; the suppression of the cross-examination of prisoners ; the reform of our criminal procedure ; the amelioration of prisons and hospitals ; the institution of Provincial Assemblies ; the convocation of the States-General ; the improvement of our navy, and the reconquest of our colonies ; so much mercy, so many sacrifices, and that halo of martyrdom with which, according to Bossuet, misfortune adorns virtue—such are the witnesses who will support Louis XVI. at the bar of the Convention, such is the escort that will accompany him to the scaffold, if mount it he must, and such is the testimony that will plead for him with posterity !

CHAPTER XX.

Thursday, November 22, 1792.

At its sitting on the 7th of this month, the Convention received the report laid before it in the name of the Committee of Legislation by M. Mailhe, member for the Haute-Garonne, and which embodied the following recommendations :

1. Louis XVI. is to be arraigned. 2. He must be tried by the National Convention. 3. Three Commissioners chosen by the Assembly will be charged with the collection of all documents, information, and proofs relating to the crimes imputed to Louis XVI. 4. The Commissioners will draw up the indictment. 5. If this indictment be agreed to, it will be printed and communicated to Louis XVI. and to such defenders as he may appoint. 6. The originals of the documents, should Louis XVI. demand to see them, will be taken to the Temple, and brought back to the Archives Nationales by twelve Commissioners of the Assembly, who shall not give them up, nor allow them to go out of their sight. 7. The National Convention shall fix the day upon which Louis XVI. is to appear at its bar. 8. Louis XVI. shall present his defence either in person or by counsel, verbally or in writing. 9. The National Convention shall give its verdict by an open vote.[1]

The discussion, which was opened on the 13th, continued until the 15th, and no vote has yet been taken. Whilst this great debate holds France and the whole of Europe in suspense, the Minister of the Interior and his wife, Citoyenne Roland, are sufficiently light-hearted to busy themselves with—titles of nobility.

[1] 'Histoire Parlementaire,' tome xx., p. 297.

The following is a circular which Mme. Roland has just addressed in her husband's name[1] to the administrators of the departments :

'Paris, *November* 20, 1792.

'The most absurd of all distinctions, that which pretended that some men are born above others, no longer exists, but its ridiculous traces are still found in certain places. In many provincial libraries there exist genealogical and other similar works calculated to perpetuate pride of birth and the remembrance of the old slavery of reason. The decree which prescribed the burning of all titles of nobility did not actually mention genealogical and heraldic books, but there can be no doubt that in the reign of equality the Republican administrations must extend the proscription of the law to all such objects. I therefore charge you to have them collected in all the national libraries, and to give the necessary orders for them to be destroyed in the same way as titles of nobility.

'The Minister of the Interior,

'ROLAND.'[2]

Citizen Roland did not always profess such severe contempt for distinctions of nobility. His eldest brother, a Canon of the collegiate church of Villefranche,[3] possessed a small field called la Plâtière, situated two miles from the town. The future Minister of the Republic hit upon the idea of adding to his name that of his brother's field, and in 1784 he applied for letters of nobility, while Mme. Roland came to Paris expressly to support her husband's request.[4] It is a pity that she was not

---

[1] In her 'Mémoires,' p. 357, Mme. Roland says 'Whenever a circular, a letter of instructions, or an important public document had to be written, I took up my pen, which I had more time than my husband to wield, and delighted in drawing up those compositions, which gave me more pleasure than if I had really been known to be their author.'

[2] 'Tableaux de la Révolution Française,' by Adolphe Schmidt, tome i., p. 102.

[3] Dominique Roland, Canon of the collegiate church of Villefranche, Beaujolais, was guillotined at Lyons on December 22, 1793, aged seventy-one years ('Les Martyrs de la Foi pendant la Révolution Française,' tome iv., p. 507). The author, who had known the two brothers, testifies that the one was as good a priest as the other was irreligious.

[4] 'Roland has been reproached with having applied for letters of nobility. . . . That was in the commencement of 1784, and I know of no man who at that time and in his position would have thought it imprudent to do the same. I came to Paris.'—MME. ROLAND, 'Mémoires,' p. 200.

successful, for in that case the merit of the circular would have been much greater. But who knows? M. and Mme. Roland, had they been ennobled, might perhaps have placed at the service of the Royalist cause that truly extraordinary ardour which they have displayed in the cause of the Revolution.

How many fierce partisans of equality are there to-day who, before 1789, wrapped themselves up in names and titles of nobility to which they had no right, and shamelessly kept up, like the worthy Roland, the most absurd of all distinctions !

Danton, the son of Jacques Danton, *procureur* of the bailiwick of Arcis-sur-Aube, and of Jeanne-Madeleine Camut,[1] signed himself *d'Anton*. Upon the minutes of the General Assembly of the Grey Friars section we read under date of January 19, 1790 :

'The Assembly having proceeded to the election of the said guardians of Liberty, its choice fell upon MM. d'Anton, Saintin, Chestel, and Lablée.

'(Signed)   PARÉ, President,

FABRE D'EGLANTINE, Vice-President,

D'ANTON, Secretary.'[2]

Though Robespierre's father and grandfather both signed their name in one word, the member for Arras illegally adorned himself with the particle. On the minutes of the celebrated meeting in the Tennis Court he signed *de Robespierre*, with a considerable space between the name and the particle.[3] In the month of June, 1790, Camille Desmoulins having attributed to him a rather smart *mot* concerning the Dauphin, he hastened to protest against the want of reserve with which he was charged, and signs his letter *de Robespierre*.[4]

---

[1] See in the *Critique Française* of March 15, 1861, a biographical fragment on Danton by M. de Saint-Albin.

[2] 'Charlotte de Corday et les Girondins,' by Ch. Vatel, tome ii., p. 245 ; 'Inventaire des Autographes composant la Collection de M. Benjamin Fillon,' séries iii. and iv., p. 57.

[3] Ch. Vatel, *loc. cit.*

[4] Letter of June 7, 1790. 'Œuvres de C. Desmoulins,' tome ii., p. 72. C. Hamel, in his 'Histoire de Robespierre,' tome i., p. 10, proves that certain biographers are wrong in assigning a noble origin to the family of his hero. 'Robespierre was not,' he says, 'like Mirabeau, a deserter from the nobility. His father and his grandfather signed "Derobespierre," as may be seen in the entry of his birth.'

Petion had followed the example of his friend Robespierre, whose *alter ego* he then was. He called himself *Petion de Villeneuve*, and in this name he signed the minutes of the proceedings in the Tennis Court, without having any right to a title of nobility.

Brissot, the son of an inn-keeper of Chartres, impudently called himself *Monsieur de Warville*, or even the *Chevalier de Warville*. He always signed Brissot de Warville.[1]

A long list could be made of the other members of the Convention, Girondists or Montagnards, who protested against privileges and nobility whilst trying to pass themselves off as nobles—Louvet de Couvray, Collot-d'Herbois, Barère, who had added to his name the title of Baron de Vieuzac,[2] Fabre d'Eglantine, and Thuriot de la Rozière. Let but the Monarchy be restored, and we shall see these austere democrats, who are now burning the titles of nobility, snatch them from the ashes and worship what they once destroyed.[3]

---

[1] 'It was considered the proper thing to have a territorial name with a handle; he therefore took the name of Chevalier de Warville, and, to be more interesting, and enjoy more consideration in society, he did not hesitate to put a *de* after his family name.'—' Vie Privée et Politique de Brissot.' In her 'Mémoires,' Mme. de Genlis never called him anything but M. de Warville, because that was the name he gave himself in society. See also ' Mémoires de Brissot,' ch. iii. Ouarville is a village about four miles from Chartres, where Brissot's father possessed some land.

[2] 'Histoire de la Révolution,' by B. de Moleville, tome x., p. 459.

[3] This was, indeed, the case under the Empire, when Napoleon, wishing to create Dukes and Princes, Barons and Counts, took them from the crowd of Conventionalists. There were then Prince Cambacérès, Duke Fouché, Counts Sieyès, Grégoire, Treilhard, Garron de Coulon, Berlier, Dubois-Dubais, Chasset, Merlin, Cochon, Thibaudeau, Doulcet de Pontécoulant, and Barons Alquier, Debry, Guyton-Morveau, Quinette, Jean-Bon-Saint-André, Isnard, etc.

CHAPTER XXI.

Monday, November 26, 1792.

'To abolish the Monarchy in France, you must first suppress religion.' These are the words of Mirabeau, and they are very true. France is the work of Kings and of Bishops; it was born and has grown up under this double influence. The Monarchical idea and the Christian idea have been so closely interwoven that it has become impossible to separate them. Such an attempt must be given up in the face of the certainty that France will not cease to be Royalist as long as it is Christian. Our statesmen, to do them justice, fully recognise this fact, and are acting accordingly; but I doubt whether their efforts will be successful.

On August 25 last the Conseil-Général de la Commune issued a decree ordering 'crucifixes, lecterns, and all objects made of fusible metal used in churches to be melted down for engines of war; not more than two bells to be left in each parish, and all the silver in the sacristies and upon the altars to be sent to the Mint.' That was on the eve of the September massacres. Though Paris was terror-stricken, a portion of the population was not afraid to show its opposition to the measures decreed by the Conseil-Général. Crowds formed around the churches to prevent them from being plundered. Manuel, the *procureur* of the Commune, was obliged to issue the following proclamation : 'The highest form of religion is obedience to the law. . . . The people's want has necessitated the confiscation of the superfluous bells—of those bells which disturbed the sleep of the poor in order to flatter the pride of the rich even in their graves.' The phrase was a high-sounding one, but it produced no effect, and it was necessary to resort to more decisive arguments. The Commune ordered General Santerre to employ force, if necessary, and authorized the sections to eject from the churches any persons inclined to oppose the removal of the bells.[1]

A few days ago the *Patriote Français* published a letter from Charles Villette, a Girondist member of the Convention, who held up to the indignation of the *brothers and friends* the fidelity of the people to their old beliefs.

'Brothers and friends,' wrote the *ci-devant Marquis*, the present owner of Voltaire's heart, which he devoutly keeps in a marble vase, 'let me hold up to your indignation the fools and rogues who have had a fine and freshly-painted crucifix, ten feet high, set up on the Pont de Sèvres. . . . Let me denounce the fools and rogues who parade their god in the Rue Montmartre, and who with much gravity bless the soldiers of the body-guard. . . . Brothers and friends, do not tolerate this tomfoolery any longer.'

What must Charles Villette have thought of the sight that Paris presented yesterday and to-day, of the scenes that took place but a couple of yards from Voltaire's monument in that city which witnessed the deeds of the Tenth of August and of the Second of September?

The *fête* of Geneviève, the patron saint of Paris, falls on November 26. The honest folk of whom the Conseil-Général de la Commune is formed, as well as the enlightened philosophers who edit the public news-sheets, were probably unaware of this fact. In consequence of this happy ignorance, the Commune took no measures to prevent the celebration of the *fête*, nor did the journalists write any articles to insult the memory of the saint. It was the people—the real people—who took upon themselves to remind France that Geneviève had saved the capital, that she had wrought miracles, and that they, the people, had faith in her and faith in the God who inspired her, as in later times He inspired Jeanne d'Arc when the country was in danger.

---

[1] Minutes of the Proceedings of the Conseil-Général de la Commune de Paris, August 29, 1792.

From six o'clock yesterday evening crowds of believers began to flock from all quarters of Paris and from the country to the church of Sainte-Geneviève-du-Mont, where the bones of the saint are deposited. Nearly every member of the huge congregation had brought an offering, and the throng was so great that more than a thousand persons were unable to obtain admission, and, in spite of the intensely cold weather, spent the night outside the church. At midnight a solemn Mass was celebrated; the saintly relics were taken from the altar upon which they reposed, and during the whole of to-day thousands of people have knelt before the coffin of the saint in fervent prayer, touching it with handkerchiefs, shirts, and shrouds.[1]

On leaving the church I heard a *sans-culotte* addressing a crowd at the corner of the Rue des Sept-Voies, and shouting: 'It is our fault; we ought to have thrown the bones into the river, and taken the coffin to the Mint!' Have no fear, brave *sans-culotte*; that will be done one of these days—very soon, perhaps. But even when the coffin is in the Mint, and the bones are in the river, the *fête* of Sainte-Geneviève will still be celebrated in Paris as long as there shall be one Christian soul— as long as one poor *ouvrière*, faithful to the memory of the humble shepherdess of Nanterre, shall kneel before the image of the saint fastened by two pins to her whitewashed attic wall.

[1] *Révolutions de Paris*, tome xv., p. 85.

CHAPTER XXII.

'CASTOR AND POLLUX.'

'Castor and Pollux' is to be played at the Académie Nationale de Musique this evening. Beaulieu and Lacretelle[1] have asked me to go with them, but I have not the courage to do so. The last time that I saw Rameau's opera was on September 20, 1791. The King and Queen, the Prince Royal and Mme. Elisabeth, were present at that performance, all the details of which are engraved upon my memory. It would have been too painful to see this piece played again at the same theatre and by the same actors, but under such totally different circumstances. Here, at least, with none but my books about me, with no other witnesses but the portraits of those dear to me, I can in sweet sadness conjure up once more all the episodes of that never-to-be-forgotten night of September 20, 1791.

On Monday, the 19th, there had been a special and free performance[2] of 'Castor and Pollux' given in honour of the establishment of the Constitution.[3] On Tuesday, the 20th,

---

[1] Charles Lacretelle, called the Younger, was born at Metz on September 3, 1766, and died at Mâcon on March 26, 1855. A friend and collaborator of Beaulieu, he wrote during the Revolution in several Royalist papers, was outlawed on October 5, 1795, arrested on September 4, 1797, and imprisoned for two years. A Professor to the Faculty of Letters of Paris, and a member of the Académie, as well as his brother, Pierre Louis Lacretelle, called the Elder, he left, beside a large number of historical works, of which the most remarkable is his 'Histoire de la Révolution Française' (1821-1826), a very interesting volume of souvenirs, entitled 'Dix Années d'Épreuves pendant la Révolution.'

[2] As a rule, the Opera was only open on Tuesdays, Fridays, and Sundays, and in winter on Thursdays. This order was changed in 1817, when it was opened on Mondays, Wednesdays, and Fridays.

[3] The Constitution had been completed on September 3, 1791, and accepted by the King on the 13th.

although the bills did not bear the words *by order* as usual on such occasions, it was known that the King and the Royal Family would be present at the performance that evening. When the King and Queen, the Prince Royal and Mme. Elisabeth, left the Tuileries at half-past five, the streets and the boulevards were lined with an immense crowd eager to see them, and to rend the air with cries of ' *Vive le Roi! Vive la Reine!*'

As the King entered the royal box, the whole audience rose and broke out into prolonged applause. Instead of the overture to ' Castor and Pollux,' the orchestra struck up the air from ' Lucile ': *Where are you better than in the bosom of your family ?*[1] and the audience applauded once more. The piece commenced. Of all French operas, ' Castor and Pollux ' is the richest in scenery and costume, as well as in the variety and brilliancy of its ballets. The scenes of Hell, the Elysian Fields, and Olympia, with their funereal pomp and their games, succeed each other in harmonious blending without appearing out of place. The management, in placing this piece upon the stage after an interval of several years, had spared no expense in making the scenery worthy of the poet's work and the beauty of the music. Gentil-Bernard's lines, though not equalling those of Quinault, have earned for their author a high place among dramatic poets. Bernard has embodied in his work with rare ability all the effects and embellishments to which lyric drama lends itself ; he has, moreover, as M. de la Harpe justly points out, managed to give his piece a dramatic basis and an interest rarely seen on the lyric stage, and has thus been able to dispense with that atmosphere of effeminacy inseparable from opera. Love is not absent from ' Castor and Pollux,' but it is subservient to the glorified friendship which permeates the whole piece and holds the interest of the audience. Rameau, who composed the music, was no less inspired than the author of the lines, and it is universally admitted that here he excelled himself.

At the revival in question, the rendering of ' Castor and

[1] ' Lucile,' a musical comedy in one act, words by Marmontel, music by Grétry, was performed for the first time in 1769.

Pollux' was fully worthy of the work. The *rôle* of Pollux was undertaken by Laÿs, whose voice is of wide compass and great power; the music could not have been sung better.[1]   Mme. Chéron played the part of Télaïre.   This actress is small and thin, but her full fresh voice and her intelligent acting make her hearers overlook these physical shortcomings.   Serious illness had for a long time kept Gardel from the stage, but he re-appeared in the ballet of 'Castor and Pollux' to enjoy a greater success than ever.

In fact, on that evening all the actors seemed to have pledged themselves to do their very best, and never had an opera been performed with more warmth and animation.   The enthusiasm of the actors soon spread to the audience, and round the theatre ran a kind of electric current that went from the boxes to the pit, and from the pit to the stage, kindling in all hearts and all eyes one flame and one feeling.   As soon as the opening lines of the first scene celebrating the beauty of Télaïre were recited, all spectators turned towards the royal box, and by their applause paid a compliment to the grace and beauty of the Queen.

It was more especially the fourth act that gave rise to the most touching and significant demonstrations.   Led by Mercury, Pollux wishes to make his way into Hell, but Monsters and Demons bar his way.   In this scene the magnificence of the decorations, the beauty of the dances, and the charm of the music, all combined to excite astonishment and admiration. The Demons continue their dances to the refrain of '*Let us break our chains.*'   This line was vehemently applauded by the audience, amidst shouts of '*Vive le Roi!*'   Had Louis XVI. not broken the chains of his people?   Was he not the *Restorer of French liberty?*   The scene now changes, and shows us the Elysian Fields.   The Happy Shades come to meet Castor, while giving utterance in song to the following wish:

'May you be as happy as ourselves!'

The enthusiastic audience emphasized these words with their

<hr />

[1] 'L'Espion des Coulisses,' p. 6, and 'Revue des Comédiens,' by M——, an old actor, and by the author of the 'Lorgnette des Spectacles,' tome ii., p. 144.

applause, when a Shade, advancing to the footlights, calls down fresh blessings upon the occupants of the royal box.

In the following scene Pollux, still led by Mercury, at last finds his brother again, and, addressing him, says :

> 'The whole universe awaits thy return ;
> Reign on over thy faithful people.'

At these words, admirably sung by Laÿs, the enthusiasm knew no bounds. All eyes and hands were directed towards the royal box, and the theatre re-echoed with an immense shout of ' *Vive la Reine !*' An encore was demanded on all sides, and the actor was obliged to repeat the famous verses.

Enthusiasm now gave way to delirium. To the shouts of applause and the cries of the audience was added the noise made by the orchestra, who frantically showered blows upon their instruments in their excitement. Actors, musicians, and audience, with eyes fixed upon the King, turned the last lines, not only into an invitation, but an oath of fidelity, whilst these words escaped from the mouth of the Queen : ' *The dear people ! Their only wish is to love us !*'[1]

The departure as well as the entry of the Royal Family was the signal for the most striking and unanimous display of the joy their presence had occasioned. The King and Queen returned to the Tuileries escorted by a throng every whit as enthusiastic as that through which they had passed a few hours before.[2]

Such was the night of September 20, 1791, the last that Louis XVI. and Marie Antoinette spent at the opera.[3]

---

[1] *Révolutions de Paris*, No. 115.

[2] *Mercure de France*, October 1, 1791. The title of this paper then ran : ' *Mercure de France*, dedicated to the King ; the literary portion edited by MM. Marmontel, De la Harpe, and Chamfort, all members of the Académie, and by MM. Ginguené, Framery, and Berquin.' M. Mallet du Pan had sole charge of the historical and political portion.

[3] Welschinger's ' Théâtre de la Révolution' makes no mention of this performance of ' Castor and Pollux.'

CHAPTER XXIII.

THE GILLES AFFAIR.

Thursday, December 13, 1792.

FROM amongst the papers and pamphlets with which my table is covered, Beaulieu had taken up Dufriche-Valazé's 'Report on the Crimes of the *Ci-devant* King,' and was idly turning over the leaves of this odious and cowardly libel, in which rhetoric and misrepresentation find mutual support. 'I see,' he suddenly cried, 'that you have placed a note of interrogation opposite this passage,' and he read :

'The man Gilles, whom we have not been able to find, was charged with the organization of a body of sixty men, and during the months of May and June last he received for that body a sum of 72,000 francs, according to the two receipts we have found. What is the meaning of this mysterious band when we have our own soldiers? In this matter we invoke against Louis Capet that Constitution under the shadow of which he is always ready to shelter himself. That Constitution gives the Legislative Body (clause iii., chapter iii., article 1) the right to determine annually the number of men and vessels of which the army and navy shall be composed. The Legislature, however, was ignorant of the existence of these troops. They were paid for out of the Civil List, but their existence is a crime, and proves that hostile plans are being nurtured. It has now been proved that men were secretly enrolled to assist the *ci-devant* King, and though the written proofs refer to no more than sixty men, that is no reason for supposing this number to have been the maximum. I argue as follows : The secret enlistment of sixty men only would have been a totally useless act, and not worth the trouble of incurring the rigorous penalty laid down by the Code. The existence of these sixty men is, therefore, a proof that there were a good many more. The production of Gilles' receipts forms the first link in the chain.'[1] . . .

[1] 'Rapport de Dufriche-Valazé,' pp. 23, etc. |

'You were no doubt inquisitive,' said Beaulieu, 'to know something of this M. Gilles, the terrible organizer of mysterious bands destined to overthrow the Constitution? And on Tuesday last[1] you were more than ever puzzled when Barère said to the King: "In Paris you secretly formed for your own use troops which were to aid you in your plans for a counter-Revolution. D'Angremont and Gilles were two of your agents, paid out of the Civil List. The receipts given by Gilles for sums with which to raise a company of sixty men will be placed before you. What answer have you to this?" The King replied: "I have no knowledge of the plans imputed to me."[2]

'I am in a position to furnish you with most reliable information concerning this matter, having been closely mixed up in it myself.

'M. Gilles is an active, intelligent, and devoted Royalist, and was one of the very small number of members of the Club des Feuillants not terrified by the insolence of the Jacobins. He considered it to be the duty of all honest men to make a stand against the enterprises of disloyal citizens, and to do their best to unmask their plots. In the beginning of 1792 the Minister de Lessart proposed to make him the editor of a Constitutional

---

[1] On Tuesday, December 11, 1792, Louis XVI. had appeared before the Convention, then presided over by Barère. His examination lasted over five hours. The calm dignity and presence of mind with which he replied to all the questions put to him wrung cries of admiration from his most deadly foes, and even from Marat himself. The latter, writing in the *Journal de la République Française* of December 13, 1792, says: 'He, who had never heard any name but that of Majesty in his ears, heard himself addressed as Louis a hundred times without betraying the least ill-humour, and when they kept him standing all the time, he, before whom no man had ever dared to sit, showed not the least impatience. Had he been innocent, how great this humility would have made him appear in our eyes!' The *Révolutions de Paris* (No. 179) spoke of the King's attitude during his examination as follows: 'The President of the Convention asked the *ci-devant* King most irrelevant questions, some of which take up entire pages. . . . Louis spoke with royal brevity (*brevitate imperatoria*), whilst the Conventionalists employed a style lacking both force and dignity.' Durand de Maillane, a member of the Convention, describes the sitting of December 11 in the following terms: 'Louis XVI. was brought to our bar. . . . He replied to every charge made against him. Some of his answers moved me to tears, while the clearness and precision of his language called forth my admiration. The great calm he preserved could only be born of great piety and virtue.'

[2] Minutes of the Proceedings of the National Convention on December 11, 1792.

paper which the Government thought of starting. He accepted the offer, and the first number appeared on April 26. It was called the *Postillon de la Guerre*, and waged war unrelentingly upon the Jacobins, denouncing all their intrigues, and laying bare all their movements with such unfailing precision and promptness as no other paper could attain. This was because M. Gilles had at his disposal sixty men, paid out of the Civil List, who hunted up news in the different quarters of Paris, attended the meetings of the Jacobins and Grey Friars, and mixed with the crowds in the streets and in the cafés. Sometimes they even had personal encounters with the enemies of the Constitution—hence the name of *Constitution* given by them to the heavy sticks which they generally carried. Every morning they either sent or brought to M. Gilles reports of what they had seen and heard. These were immediately utilized by the sub-editors in writing their articles. I was myself on the staff of the paper at that time, and can certify that, far from being a band of conspirators, we had no other object than that of fighting the worst enemies of the Constitution—the Jacobins—of preaching respect of the law, of defending the King and the authorities that existed before the Tenth of August. This is to what the great conspiracy discovered by M. Dufriche-Valazé reduces itself—to a subsidy given by a Minister to a Constitutional paper, to agents charged with enlightening the public mind.[1]

'M. Gilles left France after the Tenth of August. He is now in London. Mme. Gilles is in Paris, and by her request I have written an account of the matter, and have sent it to the deputies. Will there be found one amongst them with sufficient courage to ascend the tribune and to hold up to the contempt of honest men the gross ineptitude and miserable lies of this Valazé?'[2]

[1] Beaulieu, 'Essais Historiques,' tome iii., p. 214; tome iv., p. 217; Bertrand de Moleville, 'Mémoires Secrets,' tome iii., p. 70, etc.

[2] 'Memoir to the National Convention, by Citoyenne Lauchard, wife of Jean Baptiste Gilles, containing important information concerning one of the principal charges brought against Louis Capet.'

CHAPTER XXIV.

Sunday, December 16, 1792.

THE Convention yesterday decreed that Louis XVI. should appear at the bar for the last time on Wednesday, December 26. It also decided, on the motion of Laurent Lecointre, that the accused should be permitted to see his family. This motion had scarcely been passed before it gave rise to violent dissensions. After a long and stormy debate, the Assembly, partly rescinding its decision, authorized Louis to see his children, but only on condition that the latter should not be allowed to communicate with their mother or aunt until after judgment had been passed upon the King.[1] I was present at the sitting. As my glance passed along the benches, I carefully studied the faces of the occupants. I was particularly struck by the excitement displayed by Vadier, one of my old acquaintances in the Constituent Assembly, who was now seated on the benches of the Mountain surrounded by a score of other shrieking fanatics. It was also by a curious chance that I noticed M. Chabroud in one of the galleries; he, too, had been a member of the Constituent Assembly, and is now one of the Judges in the Court of Appeal. I had scarcely recognised him, when a strange reminiscence occurred to me. I recollected that the *Sabbats-Jacobites* had published about eighteen months ago a short play, the principal personages in which were MM. Petion, Danton, Robespierre, Vadier and Chabroud. The play was called 'The Regicides,' and the scenes and some of the verses came back to me. In

---

[1] Rather than deprive his children of their mother's care, Louis XVI. decided to forego the pleasure of embracing them.

vain did I try to drown my importunate memories ; it was impossible to get rid of them.   On returning home I took down
the *Sabbats-Jacobites*[1] and re-read ' The Regicides,' finding in
it a strangely precise prediction of the crimes now being
committed.

'The Regicides' was written and published at the beginning
of July, 1791.   At that moment the fury of the Revolutionaries against Louis XVI. and the Royal Family was at its
height.   Camille Desmoulins, Fréron, Prudhomme, Carra, and
Gorsas, were vomiting forth the grossest insults and the most
horrible threats against the King and Queen.   The *Orator of*
the People demanded that Marie Antoinette, like Frédégonde,
should be dragged through the streets of Paris tied to the tail
of a stallion.[2]   The *Révolutions de Paris* declared that she
deserved the fate of Brunehaut, and that ' Antoinette already
ranked among the number of notorious miscreants.'[3]   The club
of the Cordeliers passed the following resolution : ' The free-
born Frenchmen who form the Society of the Rights of Man
make known to their fellow-citizens that this society contains as
many tyrannicides as members, all of whom have individually
sworn to assassinate any tyrant who shall dare to attack our
frontiers or our liberty in any way whatever.'[4]

Such acts and such publications throw sufficient light upon
the plans of their authors.   And yet how many people refused
to see the abyss to which they were being led !   Marchant, a
Royalist writer, thought it would be a good thing to enlighten
them.   This he attempted to do in ' The Regicides,' by showing
what would become of the King, the Queen, all honest folk, and
even France itself, if ever the Jacobins came into power.   The
honest folk shrugged their shoulders, and charged him with
drawing a picture of impossible calamities.   And yet all that
he predicted has been realized from beginning to end.   Seldom

[1] Tome ii., p. 257, etc.   *Les Sabbats-Jacobites*, by Marchant, 1791 and
1792.   The seventy-five numbers of this paper form three volumes.
Marchant also edited *Les Grand Sabbats*, as a continuation of *Les Sabbats-
Jacobites*, and *La Jacobinéide*, an *heroi-comi-cirique* poem.   Marchant was
one of the most spiritual writers of the Royalist press.
[2] The *Orateur du Peuple*, by Fréron the Younger, tome vii.
[3] *Révolutions de Paris*, No. 102.   [4] *Ibid.*

has the future been *read* in a more astonishing fashion. The following quotations will serve as a fair sample of the whole.

The scene is laid in one of the rooms of the Jacobin Club, where Petion, Robespierre, Vadier, Danton and Chabroud have met.

Petion explains the object of their meeting in the following terms :

> ' Illustrious quellers of the power of Kings,
> Whose hands are shaping realms into republics,[1]
> Where law can do so little—crime so much.'

He demonstrates what the Jacobins have done, the progress they have made, and the results they have obtained :

> ' Sirs, you have heard what we've as yet accomplished ;
> Hear now what still remains for us to do.'

Louis is a prisoner in his palace, but no one doubts that he will soon seek to reconquer his liberty. In that case, would not the plotters have an excellent pretext for robbing him of his sceptre and his crown ?

> ' DANTON.
>
> Louis is guilty and deserves to suffer ;
> But, that his death may have some show of justice,
> He needs must be arraigned by my Committee—
> There I will pass his sentence. You perchance
> May deem he'll try to quell and overawe me ;
> Fear not—I need not hear him to condemn him.'[2]

Vadier[3] claims the honour of trying the King, while Danton maintains that he has a better right to this than the member for Pamiers ; the discussion becomes heated, and develops into a quarrel.

---

[1] At the sitting of the Convention of September 21, 1792, Petion being President, the Monarchy was abolished, and the kingdom changed into a Republic.

[2] 'We will not try Louis XVI.; we will kill him,' Danton's words in November, 1792 ('Histoire Générale et Impartiale des Erreurs, des Fautes et des Crimes commis pendant la Révolution Française,' by Prudhomme, tome v., p. 120).

[3] 'In July, 1791, I was the only one who had the courage to propose a National Convention for trying this runaway and perjured King. . . . I even dared to demand, in the name of the outraged nation, the head of this crowned villain.'—'Opinion du Citoyen Vadier concernant Louis XVI.,' November, 1792. At the King's trial Vadier voted for death, against the appeal to the people, and against the respite.

' PETION.

Nay, sirs, no temper. 'Tis not hard
For me to satisfy you both in this.[1]
You can condemn the King—and you his consort.'

Chabroud is averse to these extreme measures, and draws upon
himself the following taunt from Vadier :

' 'Tis well.   Sir Whitewasher, I understand you.[2]
You would be pleased, I fancy, to restore him,
That you may make all Bourbon white again
In hopes of gaining full and ample guerdon
From Louis.'

At last Robespierre speaks :

' All Frenchmen must be Kings—save Louis only ;
Louis must suffer—innocent or guilty.

PETION.

What is your will, in brief ?

ROBESPIERRE.

The King's destruction—[3]
Then, that his wife goes with him to his doom ;
Next, that their children never shall be more[4]

---

[1] Concerning the vile and odious, but considerable, part played by
Petion in the trial of Louis XVI., see our 'Légende des Girondins,'
ch. v.

[2] Charles Chabroud, a member of the Third Estate of the Dauphiné in
the States-General, was one of the principal members of the Left.   In
his report concerning the events of October 5 and 6, 1789, he omitted all
the facts relating to the Duc d'Orléans, which gained him the sobriquet
in the Royalist press of Chabroud, the Whitewasher.   He had no seat in
the National Convention, and was appointed to the Tribunal de Cassation,
where he remained until 1797.   Under the Empire he held a post in
the same tribunal, in the Conseil d'État, and in the Conseil des Prises.
He was born at Vienne (Isère), and died on February 1, 1816.

[3] 'There can be no trial ; Louis is not accused , you are not his judges ;
you are, and can only be, statesmen and representatives of the nation.
You have not to pass sentence upon a man, but a measure of public
safety. Louis was the King, and a Republic is now established. The question before you is decided by these simple words. Louis can therefore
not be tried, being already condemned. . . . The trials held by nations
are not like those of judicial courts—their sentences are hurled like
thunderbolts ; they do not condemn Kings ; they plunge them back
into space.   This kind of justice is as good as that of tribunals.'—
Robespierre's speech at the sitting of December 3, 1792.

[4] 'Louis must die, in order that the country may live. As for his wife
and all the persons involved in this affair, you will send them to the
tribunals. His son must be kept in the Temple until peace and liberty are
firmly established.'—Loc. cit.

Than simple citizens—and our Constitution
From Monarchy be changed to a Republic
Where nothing shall be done—save through the people
At my command let the unmeaning statues
Of those whom formerly we styled our kings[1]
Be dashed to earth and trailed along the streets ;
Let those of Damiens, Ravaillac and Clément
Replace the effigies of our Christian rulers,[2]
And let those Frenchmen who have quitted France
Pay with their goods my gallant huntsmen's guerdon.[3]
Next, we will rid ourselves of priests—proclaim[4]
No other paper money shall pass current[5]
Except our assignats—give all men license
To write and think and act as pleases them,
But if against us—let their doom be speedy.[6]
Grant the first posts in this our new-born State
To Gorsas, Noël, Marat—let there be[7]

[1] On August 11, 1792, the statues of Henry IV., Louis XIII., Louis XIV., and Louis XVI. were pulled down and dragged along the streets.

[2] The prediction of the *Sabbats-Jacobites* was in this case surpassed, busts of the divine Marat having replaced the effigies of the Blessed Virgin.

[3] The confiscation and sale of the property of the refugees was decreed by the Legislative Assembly on July 27, 1792.

[4] According to the terms of the decree of August 26, 1792, all the clergy who had not taken the oath were ordered to leave France within fourteen days. If found after that time, they were to be transported to French Guiana.

[5] The abuse of assignats was carried so far by the Government of the Republic that at one time the louis d'or was worth 18,000 francs, which would give 35 francs in assignats the value of a sou (Mercier, 'Le Nouveau Paris,' ch. cliv.). Marchant's prediction that *no other paper money than assignats should pass current* was realized to the letter. In November, 1795, Dubois-Crancé, a member of the Council of Five Hundred, was obliged to confess that the manufacture of assignats at the rate of 100,000,000 per day scarcely sufficed for half their needs, and that the Government had been on the brink of bankruptcy owing to the want of paper on which to print them (*Moniteur*, year IV., No. 162).

[6] 'The liberty of the press must be absolute. There is only one exception—the Convention reserves the right of passing sentence of death against those who by word or writing shall attack the indivisibility of the Republic or provoke the re-establishment of the Monarchy.'— Robespierre's speech on April 19, 1793, *Moniteur* of 1793, No. 111.

[7] Noël, the editor of the *Chronique de Paris*, was on the morrow of the Tenth of August appointed director of the Ministry of Foreign Affairs. Gorsas was appointed printer to the Department of Justice, and took possession of the printing-presses of *L'Ami du Roi ;* whilst Marat, by virtue of an order of the Municipal Vigilance Committee, made a raid upon the *ci-devant* Imprimerie Royale, and took four presses and an assortment of type.

A Club of Jacobins in every village,[1]
And let no charge of treason pass unheeded ;[2]
Then let the pick of that illustrious regiment,
The Royal Sans-Culottes, enforce our Edicts[3]
At the sword's point on everybody.   This
Is what the happiness of All requires—
This is the road, sirs, to Regeneration.

PETION.

Robespierre is right—in all he says, we catch
The spirit of the Club of Jacobins.'

The conspirators then indicate the means by which they may attain their ends—addresses from the departments and affiliated clubs demanding the dethronement and trial of the King ; motions from the Palais Royal ; caricatures of Louis XVI. and Marie Antoinette ; incitements to revolt to be daily spread amongst the people by the democratic journalists,

‘ Feydel[4] and Desmoulins,[5] Sonthonax[6] and Prudhomme ;'[7]

[1] In August, 1790, the Jacobin Club had 152 branches (Camille Desmoulins, *Révolutions de France et de Brabant*, tome vi., p. 112).   In April, 1791, the number of branches amounted to 2,000 (Dumouriez, ‘ Mémoires,’ tome ii., p. 104).   At the end of 1792 there was not a village but had its Jacobin Club.

[2] The Legislative Assembly and the National Convention issued a number of decrees inviting citizens to turn informers.   See the decrees of August 11, 1792 ; August 26, 1792 ; February 14, 1793 ; May 3, 1793 ; July 3, 1793 ; November 13, 1793 ; December 14, 1793, etc.

[3] On September 5, 1793, the National Convention, upon the report of Barère, resolved to establish a Revolutionary army, composed of 6,000 men and of 1,200 gunners, to be paid for out of the public funds, and intended to carry out, both in the provinces and in Paris, the programme that the Commune had dictated to the Convention in these words : *Terror must be the order of the day.*

[4] Feydel, editor of the *Observateur*, a paper which had commenced to appear on August 1, 1789, with this motto, borrowed from Bailly : ‘ Publicity is the safeguard of the people.'

[5] Camille Desmoulins, editor of the *Révolutions de France et de Brabant.*   The first number had appeared on November 28, 1789.

[6] Sonthonax, joint-editor of the *Révolutions de Paris.*   ‘ The celebrated Loustallot, who was editor of the *Révolutions de Paris* for some time, fell ill ; Sonthonax took his place, but only in editing the philosophical articles.'—‘ Memoirs or Reply of P. J. J. Bacon-Tacon to the Denunciations of Sonthonax Senior, Merchant, of Oyonnax, of Sonthonax Junior, ex-Commissioner of the Directory of Saint Domingo, and Consorts.' Sonthonax, born at Oyonnax, in the department of the Ain, died in 1813. See Philibert Le Duc's excellent work, ‘ Histoire de la Révolution dans l'Ain,' tome ii., p. 377, etc.

[7] Joint-editor of the *Révolutions de Paris.*   The first number appeared on July 17, 1789.

songs against the Royal Family to be each day repeated in all
the public squares :

> ' Insults now are ornaments of style ;
> But set in songs, their value is enhanced.'

But all such means are incomplete.   There is a more decisive
one which Danton does not hesitate to recommend to his colleagues :

> ' That it be more inured to war's alarms,
> And to the striking of great blows—
> This people, taught and led by us,
> Must try its 'prentice hand at slaughter
> In the Abbaye.'[1]

Poor Marchant was treated as a *visionary*, and his piece was
laughed at, but the scoffers little knew how near they were to
the truth.   The short play written in 1791 was indeed a *vision*
of 1792 !

---

[1] The September massacres, of which Danton was one of the principal
instigators, commenced with the prisoners in the Abbaye.   Concerning
Danton's share in the massacres, see Louis Blanc (tome vii., p. 120, etc.).
' Danton,' says Louis Blanc (p. 169), ' had led the Terror to such a pitch
in Paris that he was ready, as will be seen, to spread it over the whole of
France.'

CHAPTER XXV.

THE HOSTAGES OF LOUIS XVI.

Tuesday, December 18, 1792.

On December 16, M. Guelon-Marc, a respectable merchant of Troyes, sent the President of the Convention a letter, which was not read in the Assembly, and of which no mention has been made in the papers. Several copies have, however, been circulated amongst the public, and the following are a few of the principal passages that this document contains:

'Citizen President, whilst awaiting the issue of a decree which is to decide the fate of a beneficent Monarch, every Frenchman has the right to give free utterance to his opinions. Whoever contributes to the triumph of Louis is doing his country a service. . . . If his life is sacrificed, France, a prey to every evil influence, will soon offer a sad spectacle of ruin and desolation. . . . Has not too much blood been already shed around the tree of Liberty ? . . . Had I more eloquence I would, in humble imitation of Malesherbes, Tronchet, and Desèze, sacrifice myself for the King. Empty wishes form too feeble a homage for a soul full of love and fidelity. Less powerful interests have induced a Roman to give up his life to his country's good ; Regulus lost no time in hastening to the death that awaited him in Carthage. History, which places criminals in the pillory of public opinion, immortalized him. Never did France have greater interests to safeguard than at the moment when the whole world awaits in mournful suspense the issue of deliberations, the preliminaries of which give unmistakable indications of murderous designs. If the King's life be spared, the Powers will entertain such conditions as can alone lead to peace ; but if Louis . . . we shall be slaves, since liberty and wisdom can only dwell where justice reigns. I therefore conjure the Convention in the name of that eternal equity which is superior to all past and future laws, to weigh the inevitable results of a decision that would punish an innocent man in order to satisfy twenty of his accusers, who are both the witnesses and judges in this cause. Let the safety of the people, which the Convention looks upon as the supreme law, form the basis of a decree which will enable Louis and his august family to console themselves far from their native soil with the remembrance of the benefits they have bestowed. Do not steep a sensitive nation in ingratitude and bloodshed. If a decree of death was already passed at the electoral meetings; if at your elections you pledged yourselves to pass this vote, accept a victim proud to lay down his life; let the blood of one faithful subject alone be shed. I offer my life in place of that of the King. Let the friend of religion and of order, the guardian of the people, the self-denying King, the good husband and kind father, go free, so that 25,000,000 men may not be bereft of the happiness he assured them. Let the imaginary crime with which he is charged be atoned for by the death of a citizen whose last prayer will be: *Glory to God, fidelity to the King, prosperity to France, and peace to the world.*' [1]

Already, in August, 1791, M. Guelon-Marc had placed his name upon the list of the King's hostages; but since that date such terrible events have followed so closely upon each other that we have forgotten not only the names, but even the generous acts, of so many faithful Royalists, who offered their liberty, and even their life, to save the King. The mention of M. Guelon's letter recalls the episode of the King's hostages, fuller reference to which may not be inappropriate here.

On the morrow of the flight to Varennes the King was a prisoner in the Tuileries. A petition drawn up by Laclos and Brissot demanded his abdication and the organization of a fresh executive power. It was at this moment that the idea of the *King's hostages* took shape. De Rozoi, the editor of the *Gazette de Paris*,[2] submitted this idea to his readers in the following terms, on July 11, 1791:

---

[1] The complete text of the above letter will be found in 'Louis XVI. et ses Défenseurs,' tome i., p. 23, and in Michaud's 'Biographie Universelle': Supplement, tome lxvi. See also Albert Babeau, 'Histoire de Troyes pendant la Révolution,' tome ii., p. 20. Pierre Prosper Guelon-Marc was born at Troyes on September 5, 1752, and died in 1823. Imprisoned on December 2, 1793, and detained until December 7, 1794, he owed his escape from the scaffold to the fall of Robespierre.

[2] In all biographies, as well as in all histories, of the Revolution, the name of the editor of the *Gazette de Paris* is written Durosoy, Durozoy, or Du Rozoy. A poster preserved in the Archives de la Préfecture de

'The whole of Europe is filled with indignation at this attempt to drag the good King Louis from his throne. The presentation of Brissot's petition is a monstrous proceeding that must be effaced in a manner worthy of that French honour of which we were once so proud. Whenever a King is prisoner, hostages are accepted in his place. This is what I propose to the National Assembly :

'I. That all true Royalists shall offer themselves as hostages.

'II. That the officers of any regiments now in Paris shall be accepted.

'III. The National Assembly may be assured that the King will not leave the country, since he was unwilling both on October 6, 1789, and on June 20, 1791, to allow a single one of his subjects to expose his life in his defence ; he would therefore scarcely deliver up to death two or three hundred hostages who would have become doubly dear to him by the most evident proofs of their great affection.

'IV. We shall ask to have a special establishment, such as the old École Militaire, set aside for the incarceration of the hostages. . . . As soon as I have received 200 signatures I shall draw up a petition to the National Assembly ; no doubt some right-thinking deputy will consent to present it. I shall sign last, and if I am allowed to write in my prison, I will say to the band of faithful Royalists around me : Dictate, that my words may henceforth be yours, for in uniting you in this grand cause I have done the best day's work of my life.'

On July 14, on the very day when the federates of the Revolution assembled in the Champ de Mars, the *Gazette de Paris* published the pledges of the first hostages. ' I, the undersigned,' wrote the Marquis d'Espagne, ' am very proud to surrender myself as a hostage for the liberty of my King. I have three sons ; they would be sorry to appear wanting in senti-ments so dear to every Frenchman. I sign on their behalf as well as on my own, happy to give my Sovereign this proof of a devotion and fidelity which will last as long as life itself.'

In this first list, after the Marquis d'Espagne, come Guilbert de Montdejeu and De Thouzellier, two of the body-guards of *Monsieur*, the Chevalier d'Antibes, Baron de Pélissier-Viens, the

Police bears his autograph signature De Rozoi (Granier de Cassagnac, ' Histoire des Girondins et des Massacres de Septembre,' tome ii., p. 17). The *Gazette de Paris* appeared from October 1, 1789, until the Tenth of August, 1792.

Chevalier le Corgne de Launay, Bernard de Tachainville, De Balzac, and the Abbé de Monteil. 'I am ambitious,' said the latter, 'to be the chaplain of these Royalists who are ready to sacrifice all for their God, their King, and the honour of their country.'

Hostages offered themselves in crowds; each number of the *Gazette de Paris* contained fresh names, and the text of the petition to the National Assembly appeared on July 30.

'The King,' it ran, 'has been subjected to most outrageous insults; full reparation must therefore be made him. Love is always ready to pay the debts of hatred, and gratitude those of thanklessness.

'In whatever way you style the present condition of the King, the Monarch, even upon your own admission, is not free. A numerous guard watches over him day and night, whilst the captain of that guard is answerable with his life for the august—I had almost said *prisoner*, unacquainted as I am with any other French word expressing the same idea. No King of France has ever been in a similar position; for some time now we have been speaking a new language, but it is still incapable of describing the fresh things we see.

'One, two, three hundred hostages offer themselves as a guarantee for the King; a thousand will come forward if necessary. It has been suggested that the King might leave the country, but of this there need be no fear.

'On October 5, 1789, Louis XVI. forbade his faithful henchmen to cut down the Hydra of crime; I ask you to consider whether he would expose the lives of those who have given up their freedom for him.

'The École Militaire would be well suited for our incarceration.

'The weaker sex have asked to be allowed to share the honour of our devotion. The Lycée Royal de Saint-Cyr or the Val-de-Grâce have already been pointed out to me by some of the would-be hostages as a suitable retreat for women.

'It is necessary for the glory and peace of the State that the King be free—not in the manner in which he is now supposed to be so, but free in the eyes of the world.

'Whether the King agree to subscribe to the whole Constitution or not, he must be free if his refusal or consent is to be valid.

'Hasten, then, to give him his full liberty. As soon as you have decided to take this step, hostages will be found in plenty; I have received their signatures, and you may be assured that they are all honourable names. Mothers offer their children; old men send their sons and grandsons. The weakness of our language is unable to express the strength and ardour of their wishes, but their devotion speaks for itself. Fix the number of hostages you require; the more you ask, the more happiness will you create, and the sooner shall we be honourably acquitted before the tribunal of Europe.'

This petition was about to be presented to the National Assembly, and the *Gazette de Paris* was about to publish a fresh list containing 150 names, when De Rozoi learnt that at Auxerre six young men had been imprisoned for having addressed the following letter to him :

'To serve God, the King, and the country honourably and faithfully, is the duty of every Frenchman. We are discharging that sacred duty to-day in asking you to add our names to the list of those who have become hostages for the King, and who guarantee his residence in the kingdom with their life.'[1]

De Rozoi suspended the publication of his lists, but from all parts came letters to say that the writers were not intimidated by the example made of the six inhabitants of Auxerre. Their imprisonment, on the contrary, only served to redouble the ardour of the people; priests, soldiers, magistrates, merchants, and independent gentlemen, urged the editor of the *Gazette de Paris* not to abandon his undertaking. The approaching completion of the Constitution would render the intervention of the hostages more opportune than ever. De Rozoi therefore decided to continue his plan, and published a list which filled no less than sixteen columns.

On this roll of honour the most humble names stood side by side with the most illustrious in France. Here in the same column we find Comte de Miromenil, Brigadier-General, and M. Chometton, a poor inhabitant of Monistrol, who had served under Louis XV. as a private, and as a corporal under Louis XVI., and who 'offers himself as a hostage so that his twelve children

---

[1] This letter was signed Bonneville.; Jeannin, Procureur au Parlement de Paris ; Baudelot fils, élève à l'École-Royale-Militaire d'Auxerre ; Caverot fils, avocat ; Bourdeaux, avocat ; Boulage, avocat. M. Bonneville and his five associates were arrested on August 3, 1791.

may ever remember the lesson of their father's love for the
best of Kings ;' Comte de Blacas d'Aulps and Paul Méchin, an
agricultural labourer of Vass, near Château-du-Loir. 'I am
poor,' writes the latter, 'but my heart is French, and bleeds
for the King. If I am thought worthy of the honour, I will
wear the prison chains, and if I have not enough money to pay
for the journey, I will sell my buckles and my watch.' Here,
again, are the descendants of brave Arnauld d'Espagne, who,
at the battle of the Massoure, covered the Comte d'Artois with
his own body ; of that Sigognes de Beauxoncles who, at the
battle of Ivry, carried the *white cornet of France* ;[1] of Néret,
the Alderman, who with Langlois, another Alderman, and
Lhuillier, the Provost of the merchants, opened the gates of
Paris to Henry IV. ;[2] and here, too, are the descendants of
Malherbe, M. Louis de Malherbe, M. de Malherbe Longvilliers,
and his son, Henri de Malherbe. The names of M. Victor
Philippe de Cordey and that of his son are accompanied by the
following note : ' After having been tried four times by the
Revolutionary tribunals on account of the devotion and courage
with which he resisted the enterprises of the rebels, after having
miraculously escaped death on three occasions, this faithful
Royalist, the Seigneur de Cordey, Master of the Rivers and
Forests of Argentan, congratulates himself on having saved his
life in order that he may once more offer it to his King. His
son fully shares his sentiments.' The name of many a father
is accompanied in this list by those of his sons ; Comte de la
Boulaye, a Lieutenant-Colonel and a Knight of Saint Louis,
signs for himself and his ten children. I also note M. Royou,
avocat, and his five sons ; M. le Comte d'Espagne and his three
sons ; M. de Blessebois-Meslay and his three sons ; M. Bourbel-
Montpinçon and his three sons ; M. Dubuisson Dombret and
his two sons ; M. de la Martelière and his two sons ; while the
following twelve hostages sign the pledge for themselves and
one son each—MM. de Banville, De Clinchamp, Devaux, De
Polignac, Germain, Guyot, Leneuf de Sourdeval, De Marcenay
De Rabaudy, Tridon de Rey, De Valmenier, and De Violaines.

[1] Sully's 'Mémoires.'
[2] ' Histoire du Règne de Henri IV.,' by M. Auguste Poirson, tome i.,
book iv., ch. ii.

Whole families share the same love and a common devotion. In the columns of the *Gazette de Paris* I find the name of De Piédoue eleven times, that of Castillon six times, that of Baritault, De Flavigny, Le Harivel, De Saint-Project, De Serignac, De Tilly-Blaru, and Le Vaillant four times ; while Guilhand Ducluzeaux, Lhoste de Beaulieue, and Cautwel occur three times each, and Chappe, Duchesnoy, Hélie Legras, Mellemont, and Regnaud twice.[1]

Upon the publication of this fresh list, De Rozoi wrote to the President of the National Assembly :

' M. le Président, in the name of three or four hundred well-known and honourable citizens, I have the honour to ask you to lay the accompanying petition before the National Assembly.

' The Constitution Committee has been asked to determine under what conditions most compatible with independence and liberty the King will best be able to examine and accept the Constitutional Charter. In the petition which I ask you, M. le Président, to lay before the Assembly, will be found a suggestion worthy of the national honour, and best calculated to reconcile all opinions.'

The Chevalier d'Antibes undertook to present the petition, the list of hostages, and M. de Rozoi's letter to the President of the Assembly. No one was more worthy to discharge that honourable duty. On August 24, 1791, the day on which he proceeded to the National Assembly, he inserted in several newspapers a variation of Blondel's lines in ' Richard Cœur de Lion ':[2]

> ' O Louis, O my King,
> With love thy life is compassed !
> Fidelity to thee
> Is on our hearts engraved !'

[1] It has occurred to me that the following names, taken from the list of hostages, Du ville, not mentioned in the text, might be of interest   D'Allon-Coetlosquet, De Barruel-Beauvert, De Beaumont, De Belzunce, Du dorcet, D'Eprémesnil, De Bouillé, Boyer, De Coulaincourt, De Con-De Montalembert, D'Esgrigny, De Ferrières, Garnier-Dufougeraise, Musset de Pathay, De Puisaye, and De Rode.

[2] In 1792, the Chevalier d'Antibes published a pamphlet entitled ' Marie Antoinette, de France, à la Nation.' In 1793 he had already been arrested in the Vendée, and did not yes. Having managed to escape, he reached he was arrested for the te to Paris until 1797. Under the Consulate in the Temple. When he w ne, and underwent a long imprisonment under supervision, and was no rated, in 1805, he was sent to Orleans 1814 (' Biographie des Contemp ed to return until the Restoration in tome i.).

It was impossible for him to reach the President, who on that day was M. Dupont (of Nemours). But M. Malouet, the most honest, independent, and prudent Royalist member of the Assembly, was good enough to undertake to place the packet upon the table, and to watch over its safety.[1]

On August 25, the day after the petition had been deposited in the Assembly, the *Gazette de Paris* published a list of names of ladies who offered themselves as hostages for the Queen. The list was headed by Mme. Félicité de Montlezun[2] and Mme. de Paysac, Marquise de Fausse Lendry. I also note the name of the Marquise de Favras, the widow of the hero who laid down his life on February 19, 1790. Even young girls claimed the privilege of suffering and dying, if necessary, for the Queen and Royal Family. I will quote the name of one only—Mdlle. de la Rochejacquelein, a sister of a gentleman of Poitou who, after having served in the body-guard of the King, fought like a hero on the Tenth of August.[3]

Meanwhile time passed, and the petition was left unnoticed. In vain did De Rozoi, the Chevalier d'Antibes, and those of the hostages who were in Paris, ply the President and the members of the Constitution Committee with oft-repeated prayers and entreaties.

'Monsieur,' wrote De Rozoi to the President of the Committee at the beginning of September, 'I lay before you the entreaties of eight or nine hundred citizens, all of whom cry aloud for justice, and whose cause now attracts the attention of the whole of Europe.

'A decree has gone forth for the presentation of the Act of Constitution to the King, but the acceptance of an Act requires, as has been said, a free and independent examination. As long as the King is not in enjoyment of the most absolute liberty, liberty

---

[1] Malouet's 'Mémoires,' edited by his grandson, should rank among the most important documents concerning the history of the Revolution.

[2] 'Twenty-two Montlezuns fought at the Battle of Fontenoy.'—*Gazette de Paris*, August 25, 1791.

[3] Letter from Mdlle. de la Rochejacquelein to M. de Rozoi, editor of the *Gazette de Paris*, dated from the Château de la Durbelière, August 26, 1791: 'Too happy if, by giving up my liberty (and even my life), I could contribute to restore it to the Royal Family, from whom it has been so shamefully taken, in spite of the loyalty of so many good Frenchmen. (Signed) ANNE-LOUISE DU VERGIER DE LA ROCHEJAC-QUELEIN, aged seventeen.'—'Archives Nationales,' C. ii., 160.

recognised as such by the whole of Europe, His Majesty's accept
ance cannot be characterized as independent.

'Faithful subjects have offered to undergo imprisonment in the
place of their King. History affords a score of instances in which
liberty was granted to Sovereigns upon the guarantee of hostages
whose devotion served as a ransom.

'We are ready ; we ask for our chains.

'We ask that some reply shall at least be made. The hostages
who have taken this solemn pledge glory in the restriction of liberty
they have already imposed upon themselves, for whatever duty
might call them elsewhere they await your summons, feeling no
longer free.

'Be good enough, therefore, to bring our petition to the notice of
the Assembly to-day, or to-morrow at latest. . . . The hostages
count every hour ; the next may bring about a new order of things
destructive of our hopes. Can there be anything more sacred or
more urgent than the prayer of children asking to bear the chains of
the most revered and cherished of fathers ? . . . If it is a virtue to
ask, is it not a crime to refuse ?'

In publishing this letter in the *Gazette* of September 13, De
Rozoi added : 'Neither the Committee nor the President have
thought fit to reply. Meanwhile we are bound by our pledge.
The only thing that now remains to be done is for each of the
hostages residing in Paris to go to the Constitution Committee
and to demand a reply of some kind.' At the moment of the
publication of this appeal, the President of the National
Assembly received from the hands of the Keeper of the Seals a
letter from the King, in which he said :

'I have carefully examined the Act of Constitution laid
before me. I agree to it, and undertake its execution.'

The final scene of this episode of the hostages of Louis XVI.
took place before the tribunal of August 17 at the Abbaye, at
the Conciergerie, and at the Carmes.

De Rozoi, arrested at Auteuil a few days after the Tenth of
August, appeared on the 24th of the same month before the
tribunal presided over by Citizen Osselin. The letters which
he had received from the hostages became so many proofs of the
existence of a great conspiracy, and the courageous editor was
condemned to death. He heard his doom without betraying
the least emotion, and before leaving the court—on August 25

—he handed the President a letter containing only these words :
' It is fitting that a Royalist, like myself, should die on the day
of Saint Louis.'[1]   He was guillotined at half-past eight the
same evening in the Place du Carrousel.

Among the victims of the September massacres were many of
the hostages.   M. Marchand, Incumbent of Notre-Dame de
Niort, was massacred at the Carmes,[2] and the Chevalier de la
Bourdine at the Conciergerie.[3]   Mme. de Fausse-Lendy, a
prisoner at the Abbaye, only escaped being massacred by a
miracle.[4]   How many more will have to expiate with their
liberty, and perhaps with their life, the crime of fidelity to the
King and Royal Family ?[5]

[1] ' Bulletin du Tribunal Criminelle du 17 Août,' No. 3.

[2] ' Les Martyrs de la Foi pendant la Révolution Française,' by the
Abbé Guillon, tome iv., p. 14.

[3] ' Histoire des Girondins et des Massacres de Septembre,' by A. Garnier
de Cassagnac, tome ii., p. 346.

[4] See her curious book, entitled ' Quelques-uns des Fruits Amers de la
Révolution.'

[5] In the list of victims of the Revolutionary tribunals are to be found
some of the names inscribed on the list of the King's hostages, *e.g.*,
Boyer, the journalist of Nîmes, and young Louis de Malherbe, twenty
years old.   In vain did his defenders dwell upon the fact that he
was the great-grandson of the poet Malherbe (' Bulletin du Tribunal
Révolutionnaire 1ʳᵉ partie,' No. 74).   He was condemned on July 20,
1793, the execution of Charlotte Corday having taken place on the 17th.
The great-grandson of Malherbe mounted the scaffold three days after
the great-grand-daughter of Corneille.

CHAPTER XXVI.

Thursday, December 20, 1792.

THE hostages of Louis XVI. led me to mention the acceptance on September 13, 1791, of the Constitution by the King, and to recall the very words of his letter to the President of the National Assembly: 'I have carefully examined the Act of Constitution laid before me. I agree to it, and undertake its execution.'

Has Louis XVI. kept that promise?

The newspapers, the clubs, and the members of both the Brissot and Robespierre parties, answer this question by an immense shout: *Louis has betrayed the Constitution!*

But where are the proofs in support of this accusation? There is not a single one to be found, either in Gohier's report to the Legislative Assembly,[1] in those of Dufriche-Valazé and Mailhé, or in the indictment drawn up by the Commission of Twenty-One.

The truth is that from September 13, 1791, until the Tenth of August, 1792, Louis XVI. remained perfectly faithful to the Constitution, and I, for my part, know a good number of excellent citizens who reproach him with having been only too scrupulous. The Constitution of 1791 was calculated to bring France to anarchy and ruin, and this was fully foreseen by the Jacobins when they made such a show of the title of *Friends of the Constitution;* this was also felt by Robespierre when he called his paper the *Defender of the Constitution.* All true

---

[1] Report upon the papers found in the offices of the Civil List, laid before the Assembly on September 16, 1792, by Louis Jérôme Gohier.

friends of Liberty, on the contrary, thought the abolition of the Constitution and its re-establishment on a more Monarchical basis indispensable.   So thought M. de la Fayette himself ;[1] and who—except the factionists—could have made a crime out of the fact that the King had no greater respect for the Act of Constitution than the author of the *Declaration of Rights?*

Unfortunately for himself and his country, Louis never violated the Constitution ; of this there are abundant proofs, a few of which I will adduce.

Completed on September 3, 1791, the Constitution was presented to the King on the same day by a deputation of sixty members.   Malouet advised him not to accept it as it was ; the King, he thought, should point out to the Assembly and the nation the vices it contained, and the dangers to which its execution must necessarily give rise.   Malouet sincerely desired the maintenance of the Constitution, and for that reason he wished to rid it of conditions that would make its execution impracticable and ruinous.   Louis XVI. fully agreed with this far-thinking man, and, like him, wished a trial of the Constitution to be made in good faith, and under such conditions as might lead one to hope for success.   If he decided, contrary to Malouet's advice and his own wishes, to accept the Act of Constitution in its entirety, it was because all his Ministers, with the exception of M. de Montmorin, as well as Barnave and Adrien Duport, were in favour of his doing so.[2]

As soon as the Legislative Body had reassembled, M. Bertrand de Moleville, Minister of Marine, begged the King to make known his intentions with regard to the Constitution, and his wishes with regard to the course his Ministers were to pursue. 'That is but right,' replied the King.   'I do not look upon this Constitution as a masterpiece ; I believe that it has very great faults, and if I had been free to make a few observations to the Assembly, it might have been very advantageously amended, but it is now too late.   Having accepted it as it is, and sworn to have it observed, I must be true to my word, the more so

Letter from M. de Lally-Tollendal to the King, dated July 9, 1792.
Mme. Campan, ' Mémoires,' tome ii., p. 161 ; ' Mémoires de Malouet,' tome ii., p. 106, etc.

since I believe that a faithful observance of the Constitution is the surest means of demonstrating to the nation in what manner it requires amending. I have, and can have, no other intention but that ; I shall certainly not swerve from it, and trust that my Ministers will conform to my wishes.' M. Bertrand having asked whether the Queen's opinion in this matter coincided with the King's, Louis XVI. replied : ' Most decidedly ; but she shall tell you so herself.' The Minister then went down to the Queen's rooms. Marie Antoinette, after having thanked him with her usual kindness for the proof of devotion he had given the King by accepting office at such a critical moment, added ' The King has acquainted you with his intentions respecting the Constitution. There surely can be no better way than that of keeping one's oath.' ' Certainly not, madame.' ' Well, you may be sure that we shall not change our mind. Come, M. Bertrand, courage ! If we are but patient and firm, I think that all may yet be well.'[1]

Shortly before leaving the Ministry of War, M. de Narbonne[2] one day induced the King to inspect three battalions of the National Guard deeply devoted to His Majesty. Louis XVI. was on foot, and wore a silk coat with black breeches and white silk stockings. At the end of the review, one of the Guards— it was, I believe, M. Chaudot, a notary of the Rue Plâtrière— stepped out from the ranks and exclaimed : ' Sire, the National Guard would feel greatly honoured by seeing your Majesty wear its uniform !' ' Sire,' added M. de Narbonne, ' be good enough to accede to this request. Wearing that uniform at the head of these three battalions of heroes, you will utterly rout the Jacobins.' After a moment's reflection the King replied : ' I must ask my Council *whether I am permitted by the Constitution to wear the uniform of a National Guard.*'[3]

In March, 1792, the Brissot party imposed its Ministers upon Louis XVI.—Roland for the Interior, Servan for War, Clavière

[1] Bertrand de Moleville, 'Histoire de la Révolution de France,' tome vi., p. 22.

[2] M. de Narbonne was Minister of War from December 6, 1791, until March 10, 1792.

[3] 'Mémoires de M. de Vaublanc,' p. 174. The notary Chaudot was guillotined on February 13, 1794.

for Taxes.   The latter, who came into office immensely prejudiced against the King, was not long in recognising that he had been greatly mistaken. He had the courage to publicly give Louis XVI. credit for the purity of his intentions and the loyalty of his conduct. Étienne Dumont narrates an anecdote which is worth telling, concerning as it does Louis XVI., Clavière, Roland and his wife. Clavière and Roland were convinced that Louis XVI. had loyally accepted the Constitution, and that he relied for its amendment much more upon its fair trial than upon force or violent measures. One evening when several members of the Brissot party were assembled in Mme. Roland's salon, Clavière related how the King had found him ignorant on a certain point in the Constitution, and had laughingly taken a book from his pocket with the words : ' You see, M. Clavière, that I am better acquainted with it than you are.' Brissot hereupon displayed some anger and doubted the tale, and when Clavière appealed to Roland, the latter dared neither confirm nor deny it. Mme. Roland was seated at her desk, pale and trembling and pretending to write. Dumont crossed the room and asked her to interfere and calm the storm. ' Do you think I ought to ?' she asked. At last she decided to leave her seat, and a few moments later, thanks to her tact, the conversation had changed its course.[1]

More than once Roland himself had given Louis XVI. his due —when his wife was not there.   At one of the last meetings of the Jacobin Club, François Robert, a deputy for Paris, gave an account of a dinner at Petion's some time after Roland's entry upon office, at which the latter had spoken as follows : ' People do not know the King ; he means well, and those who charge him with harbouring guilty intentions calumniate him. He is much under-estimated ; he has great talent and knowledge, good judgment, and a wonderful memory. . . . As Minister of the Interior I see the King more often than my colleagues do, and visit him daily. He treats me as though I were one of his family, and always insists upon my sitting down.'[2]

[1] Étienne Dumont, ' Souvenirs,' pp. 395, 405.
[2] Meeting held at the Jacobin Club on December 17, 1792 ; *Journal des Débats et de la Correspondance des Jacobins*, 322. Against Louis XVI. and Marie Antoinette, Mme. Roland entertained a hatred that their blood itself could not assuage. Her testimony in this instance is therefore the

Roland was right in saying that the King meant well. In the beginning of August last, whilst the pretended friends of the Constitution were openly trying to upset it, and were arranging a plan to march upon the Tuileries and butcher the King, some of his most faithful servants, M. de Montmorin, M. Bertrand de Moleville, M. de Clermont-Tonnerre, M. de Lally-Tollendal and M. Malouet, agreed that the King must be got out of Paris at any cost. M. de Liancourt, who was in command of the troops at Rouen, and M. de la Fayette, had promised their support. All was ready. The King appeared to consent, and told M. de Montmorin to see M. de Sainte-Croix,[1] who, with M. Terrier de Montciel,[2] was also occupied with plans for saving the Royal Family. On the morrow M. de Lally-Tollendal and M. de Montmorin went to the palace to take their last instructions; Louis XVI. then told them that he would not go, and that he would rather brave any danger than commence a civil war.[3] Five days later the Tenth of August was upon us.

more valuable. In her 'Mémoires,' p. 350, she says: 'Louis XVI. was on very good terms with his new Ministers. . . . He had a good memory, and was very active, never allowing a moment to pass unoccupied. He was well acquainted with the different treaties that France had made with foreign Powers; he had a good knowledge of history, and was the best geographer in his kingdom. He not only remembered the names of all the persons he saw about him at Court, and the anecdotes relating to them, but had extended this art to all the more or less prominent personages of the Revolution; it was impossible to mention anyone to him about whom he had not some well-founded information. . . . When he had once chosen Patriots for Ministers, he took great pains to inspire them with confidence, and in this he succeeded so well that for a period of three weeks I have seen Roland and Clavière so enchanted with the manners of the King as to flatter themselves that the Revolution was finished, and that we had entered upon a new order of things. "Good God!" I would say to them, on seeing them set off for the Council in such good spirits, "you look as if you were going to make fools of yourselves." "I assure you," Clavière would reply, "that the King is perfectly well aware that it is to his interest to observe the laws just established; his arguments prove that he is convinced of that truth."'

[1] L. C. Bigot de Sainte-Croix, Minister of Foreign Affairs from August 1 to August 10, an author of an excellent 'Histoire de la Conspiration du 10 Août, 1792.'

[2] Minister of the Interior from June 18 to July 21, 1792.

[3] Letter from Lally-Tollendal to the King of Prussia in favour of M. de la Fayette. See also the note appended to the letter sent by Marie Antoinette to her brother, the Emperor Leopold II., on September 8, 1791. 'The King,' it says, 'has done all he can to avoid civil war, and he is still of opinion that such a war can do no good, and can only be destruc-

Louis has therefore not betrayed the Constitution; those who have violated it are the Jacobins and the members of the Brissot party. Brissot himself is never tired of boasting that he only swore fidelity to the Constitution, and pretended to defend it in order to deceive the Royalists, while he loudly proclaims on behalf of himself and his friends that the overthrow of the Constitution had been their constant aim, as the Revolution of the Tenth of August had been their work.[1]

And it is such men as these who summon Louis XVI. to appear before them! Were hypocrisy, falsehood and crime ever carried farther than this? The Tartuffe of the Revolution has killed the Constitution, and now we see him dragging the King to the scaffold after having hung upon his breast a label with these words: *Condemned to death for having killed the Constitution.*[2]

M. Taine ('La Révolution,' tome ii., p. 142) says: 'In accepting the Constitution Louis XVI. had an idea that by putting it into force he would lay bare its faults and bring about its reform. Meanwhile he scrupulously adhered to it, and kept his oath to the letter, both from interest and as a matter of conscience.' That the King remained faithful to the Constitution which his enemies violated daily is proved not only by the facts set forth

tive of everything. . . . The King must save his people from civil war, even at the risk of his crown and his life' (*Revue Rétrospective,* série ii., tome ii., pp. 7, 8). The original letter and the note are extant in the Austrian Imperial Archives ('Louis XVI., Marie-Antoinette et Mme. Elisabeth: Lettres et Documents inédits,' publiés par F. Feuillet de Conches, tome ii., p. 287, et suiv.).

[1] Beaulieu, 'Essais Historiques,' tome iv., p. 187.

[2] Camille Desmoulins, concerning whom M. Cuvillier Fleury ('Portraits Politiques et Révolutionnaires,' p. 319) has rightly said, 'Of the Revolutionary mob he is one of the worst among the bad,' proposed the following resolution: 'The National Convention declares that Louis Capet deserves to die. It decrees that the scaffold shall be erected in the Place du Carrousel, whither Louis shall be conducted, wearing on his breast a label with these words: *Perjurer and traitor to the nation,* and on his back another label, bearing the word *King,* in order to show the world that the degradation of nations cannot efface the crimes committed by Royalty, even after a lapse of fifteen centuries; it also decrees that the tomb of the Kings at Saint-Denis shall henceforth be the burial-place of thieves, murderers, and traitors.'

in the foregoing chapter, but also by the correspondence discovered in the Archives, and first published in 1835 in the *Revue
Rétrospective*, série ii., tome ii.   Had Louis XVI. had any ulterior
object in view in contradiction to his public declarations, he
would no doubt have alluded to it in this 'Correspondance
Secrète.'   On the contrary, we find there how loyal and sincere
his acquiescence in the Constitution really was.   All further
doubt is dispelled by a private letter written by the King on
September 25, 1791, to his brothers, the Comtes de Provence
and D'Artois, and by the note appended to that letter.   'I am
desirous,' says the King, 'of acquainting you with the motives
of my acceptance, in order that your behaviour may be in conformity with mine.   Your affection for me and your prudence
should make you renounce those dangerous ideas that I do not
share. . . .   I have received the letter which you have sent me.
I had seen it in print before receiving it, and it has had a wide
circulation.   You cannot think how deeply this matter has
grieved me ; I was already sorry enough to see the Comte
d'Artois take part in the conference of Pilnitz without my consent.   I cannot bring myself to reproach you ; I will only say
that while you are acting without me we shall be playing at
cross-purposes.   You tell me that public opinion has come round,
and of this you pretend to be a better judge than I.   I have
already told you that the people endured all kinds of privations
because they were always fed on the hope of having a Constitution.   They have now had one for two days, and you pretend
that they have already come round !   I have the courage to
accept this Constitution in order to give the nation time to see
what this pretty thing really is, and you want me to give up
making the experiment.   The factionists have prevented the
nation from judging their work by continually talking of the
obstacles that I place in the way of its execution ; instead of
taking from them this last resource, ought I to serve their cause
by laying myself open to the charge of having commenced a
civil war ?   You flatter yourselves that you will deceive them by
declaring that your action is contrary to my wishes ; but how
can you persuade them that this is so, since the proclamation of
the Emperor and of the King of Prussia was made at your in-

stance ?   Will it not be thought that my brothers are only carrying out my orders?   You will therefore hold me up to the nation as accepting the Constitution with one hand and making overtures to foreign Powers with the other.   What honest man could countenance such conduct, and do you think you are serving me by robbing me of the esteem of honest men ?   I hope that you will adopt wiser ideas ; you must remember that victory is useless unless you can go on governing, that it is impossible to govern a great kingdom in the face of a dominating faction.'

In December, 1791, Baron de Goguelat, who had shown great devotion to the Royal Family on the occasion of the flight to Varennes, was asked by Louis XVI. to deliver to the Counts of Provence and d'Artois a letter of a private nature undoubtedly containing the King's real thoughts.   This letter, published in the ' Mémoires de M. le Baron de Goguelat' (tome iii., ' Des Mémoires de tous' Paris, 1835), agrees in every respect with that which appeared in the *Revue Rétrospective*.   ' I wash my hands,' wrote the King, ' of any enterprise that may be formed against the Constitution which I have just accepted ; I shall oppose it with all my might from whatever quarter it may come, and I look upon the authors of all such plans as criminals. This, my brothers, is my unalterable opinion.'

CHAPTER XXVII.

Friday, December 21, 1792.

THE members of the Convention are getting ready to try, or rather, according to Danton's expression, to kill, the King. Can it be that these men, not one of whom believed in a Republic before the Tenth of August,[1] have since become convinced Republicans? By no means. Those who talk loudest of their principles, those who make the greatest parade of their *sans-culottisme,* cherish the hope of one day placing the Duc d'Orléans upon a re-established throne.

That such is the plan of the Cordeliers or 'Grey Friars,' who form the most advanced and violent section of the Revolutionaries, cannot be doubted for a moment, since Camille Desmoulins, that *enfant terrible,* has let the cat out of the bag.

It was at the end of July. Prudhomme, the author of the *Révolutions de Paris,* had been honoured by a visit from Danton, Camille, and Fabre d'Églantine.

'We have come,' said Danton, 'to consult you upon a matter of some importance: for although you are no longer in the swim, you are an old Patriot, and as you have often foreseen both events and their results, we wish to have your opinion upon a plan of insurrection.'

'How can you consult a man,' replied Prudhomme, 'who is, as you say, "no longer in the swim"? I do not understand you. I am perhaps more desirous of liberty than you yourselves, but in an equal measure and for all citizens. What more do you want to know?'

'We wish to turn out the tyrant.'

---

[1] See Chapters V. and VI.

' Which tyrant ?'

'The one in the Tuileries.   This damned Revolution has done the Patriots no good.'

'That is to say, gentlemen, that you wish to make your fortunes in the name of Liberty and Equality.   How do you expect to upset the Monarchy ?'

' By force.'

' What ! destroy the palace of the Tuileries ?   Be careful, for the stones might fall on your heads.   I advise you not to hurry yourselves.   Since the King has become a prisoner in the palace, there is no Sovereign.   The Government is a sham, and has no power.   The King's weakness is leading him on to ruin.   With the refugees up in arms, and the coalition of the German Princes, the fall of the Monarchy in France will be an accomplished fact before six months are over.   Then it will be time for you to see what is to be done.   Your plan is the work of a small section of the clubs of the Jacobins and Cordeliers.   You are unacquainted with the views of the inhabitants of Paris and the provinces.'

' We have,' said Fabre d'Églantine, ' the consent of a hundred Brissotin deputies, and of agents in all the political clubs in France.'

Prudhomme, however, still persisted in his opinion.

' You wish,' he said, ' to turn out Louis XVI.   Whom will you put in his place ?'

' The Duc d'Orléans,' said Camille Desmoulins.

' We shall see about that later,' interposed Danton, desiring, no doubt, to repair Camille's imprudence.   ' Revolutions are like battles—you cannot tell what will happen next.   I will be answerable for the mob of the Faubourgs Saint-Antoine and Saint-Morceau; they will be led by the Marseillais, who have not come to Paris for nothing.'

' I cannot help it,' said Prudhomme, ' but I am afraid.   There may be a great many victims. . . .'

' We cannot consider these things in a Revolution !' cried Fabre d'Églantine.   ' In politics pity and honesty are crimes.'[1]

---

[1] Prudhomme, ' Histoire Générale et Impartiale des Erreurs, des Fautes et de Crimes commis pendant la Révolution Française (1796-1797),' tome iii., pp. 189-191.

In the famous sitting of September 21, Danton and his friends were careful not to take the initiative in the abolition of the Monarchy. Couthon, having proposed that the members should take an oath to hold in execration monarchy, dictatorship, triumvirate, or any kind of individual power, Danton rose, not to support this motion, but to move as an amendment a formal declaration to the effect that the Constitution should be accepted as a whole by the majority of the primary assemblies. A few moments later, when the Assembly unanimously adopted by acclamation the resolution moved by Collot-d'Herbois and Grégoire concerning the abolition of the Monarchy, it was Basire,[1] one of Danton's lieutenants, who pointed out that a decree of such importance could not be passed in a moment of enthusiasm, and that it ought to be fully discussed and considered.[2]

On December 4 Buzot demanded that the death penalty should be pronounced against anyone proposing or attempting to re-establish in France either the Monarchy or any other power restricting the sovereignty of the people.

It was Basire again who rose to oppose this motion. Phillippeaux,[3] another friend, moved that the motion be set aside, and that Louis XVI. be tried forthwith.[4] 'The proposal made by Phillippeaux,' rejoined Basire, 'is the only one that can be adopted. Buzot's, on the contrary, would restrict the liberty of the people with regard to the sanction they are called upon to give to the Constitution.' These words having been received with loud murmurs, Basire cried : 'Is it with tumultuous shouts and with waving of hats that you should pronounce a decree of death? Do you wish it to be alleged that your Republic is established by the force of a faction—that it is based upon a law of blood, and not upon the free will of the people?' In the midst of the agitation that reigned in the

---

[1] Claude Basire, deputy for the Côte-d'Or, was executed, together with Danton, Camille Desmoulins, and Fabre d'Églantine, on April 5, 1794.

[2] *Moniteur* of 1792, No. 266.

[3] Pierre Phillippeaux, member for the Sarthe, included in the trial of the Dantonists, was condemned to death, and guillotined with them on April 5.

[4] *Moniteur* of 1792, No. 266.

Assembly, Rewbell wished to explain the motives for Buzot's proposal. 'There is simply a desire,' he said, 'to frame a penal law which does not yet exist against attempts to re-establish the Monarchy.' 'Well, in that case,' replied Merlin de Thionville, who sits on the same benches as Basire and Phillippeaux, 'let these words be added to Buzot's motion: *unless it be in the primary assemblies.*' 'Order!' 'To the Abbaye!' 'That is Royalism!' 'The secret is out!' were the cries that came from all sides. Under pretence of calming the storm, Guadet made light of the words that had escaped Merlin. 'Everyone here,' he said, 'must be allowed to give free expression to his sentiments, and the Convention ought not to be sorry to have heard an opinion which gives it the key of a plan, now formed, I think, some time, for replacing one despot by another—a despot under whose protection those who had helped him to his throne would be sure to enjoy immunity for their crimes, and permission to commit fresh ones.'[1]

Buzot was quite aware that this was the point towards which the attack should be directed, that this was a weak spot in his adversaries' armour. He therefore returned to the charge on December 16, and demanded that when Louis XVI. had been sacrificed to the public security, the whole of his family should be exiled. He showed very clearly that if any exception was to be made, it must not be in favour of the Orleans branch, and expressed himself as follows :

'The very fact of this branch being more beloved makes it more dangerous to liberty. From the very beginning of the Revolution, D'Orléans has been the cynosure of all eyes ; his effigy, borne through the streets of Paris on the day of insurrection, gave the people a new idol. Soon he was accused of harbouring plans of usurpation, and though this may have been untrue, such plans appear at least to have existed, and were covered by his name. The blood of Kings is therefore a pretext, even when it is no longer a cause for trouble and agitation ; let it not be added to the many disturbing influences that surround the formation of a Republic. An immense fortune and great hopes ; close relations with the nobility of England ; the name of Bourbon in the ears of foreign Powers eager to give us a master in order to have themselves an

[1] *Moniteur* of 1792, No. 341.

ally; the name of Égalité in the ears of the French, a nation easy to move, and whose singular choice only makes its object the more conspicuous by its attempts to hide him; children whose youthful and impetuous courage can easily be seduced by ambition, whose ambition may be cleverly excited by a close alliance with foreign Kings—all these are reasons too powerful to admit of Philippe's remaining in France without endangering liberty. . . . Ignorance has not been dispelled to such an extent but that it is still possible to use it as a weapon, and even were it simply a question of obviating slight disturbances and an unnecessary struggle, the public peace is too valuable for any measure to be neglected which may ensure it. The suspicion of Royalism is a continual source of trouble, and we are tormented by it even to-day; it is a cause of mutual fear and recrimination. By banishing the name and the blood of Kings, you will extinguish the hope of those who love them, and of such as would make use of them to divide you.'[1]

Everyone must acknowledge that in this matter Buzot was right, and that it was only those who had not given up the idea of re-establishing the Monarchy who could refuse to include Philippe d'Orléans and his sons in the measure which banished the Bourbons from France. This is, however, what the members of the Mountain did. 'If this decree passes,' cried Camille Desmoulins, 'France is lost!' All the members who sit at the extremity of the right side[2] protested most furiously against Buzot's motion; both Bourdon and Calon were three times called to order, and the President was obliged to declare the sitting suspended. After a long and uproarious scene, the Assembly adjourned the question relating to Philippe-Égalité, and passed the following decree:

'All the members of the family of the Bourbons-Capets now in France, excepting those detained in the Temple, and whose fate the Convention will shortly decide, are ordered to leave the department of Paris in three days, and French territory, as well as territory occupied by the Republican troops, in eight days.'

The question was discussed the same evening at the Jacobin Club. 'Citizens,' said Camille Desmoulins, 'since the Revolu-

---

[1] *Moniteur* of 1792, No. 353.

[2] As we have explained in Chapter II., the benches on the right of the hall were occupied by the members of the Left, and the extremity of the right side by the members of the Mountain (*Mercure Française*, December 28, 1792).

tion there has been no more stormy sitting of the Convention
than that of to-day.' And in a speech of unusual length for
him—for he is anything but an orator—he inveighed against
Buzot's proposal:

'To demand the banishment of Égalité, who has contributed so
greatly to the Revolution, to demand the banishment of such a
sincere friend of liberty, is to ask for his assassination at Coblentz. . . .
The Convention should not only be grateful, but just. Should it,
however, be more severe for Philippe Égalité than it was towards
the traitor Lafayette—should it give this Charles IX. and this
Médicis a life of pleasure instead of their due punishment—I fear
that it will bring everlasting ignominy upon itself.'[1]

Marat is also for leaving the Duc d'Orléans alone. 'Égalité
must stop!' he cried,[2] and his words are received with applause
by the Assembly and the galleries. Réal, the old Public
Prosecutor of the criminal tribunal of August 17, maintained
that even the most extreme principles did not call for Égalité's
exile.[3] A citizen wearing the uniform of a Lieutenant-Colonel
spoke in eulogistic and pompous terms of the virtue and
patriotism of Philippe Égalité, and ended his speech with the
following words: 'Égalité's party must show itself, and his
friends—all his friends—must rally to his defence. That party
exists, and will not desert the brave and virtuous defender of
Liberty.'[4]

On the morrow several members of the Mountain who are
also members of the Jacobin Club returned to the charge with
strangely suspicious persistence and ardour. One of the two

---

[1] 'Society of the Friends of Liberty and Equality: Speech of
Camille Desmoulins, one of the deputies for Paris, upon the decree for
banishing the family of Orleans, and upon the question of excluding
Philippe Égalité, a representative of the people, from the National
Assembly.' Printed by L. Potier, at Lille, 16 pp.

[2] 'I have seen a poster signed by Marat, in which he demands 15,000
francs from the Duc d'Orléans as a reward for what he has done for him.'
—BEAULIEU, 'Essais Historiques,' tome i., p. 445. See also the
'Memorial' by Governor Morris, tome i., p. 260.

[3] Réal, after the death of Danton, whose friend he was, was imprisoned in the Luxembourg, and kept there until the 9th of Thermidor.

[4] Meeting at the Jacobin Club, December 16, 1792: *Journal des Débats
et de la Correspondance de la Société des Jacobins; Courrier des Départements*, number of December 20.

Goupilleaus[1]—the one who sat in the Constituent Assembly—expressed himself as follows:

'I wish to make a few remarks upon what took place in the Legislature yesterday. You will remember that the minority in the Legislative Assembly once saved the country. It is now the duty of the minority in the Convention to again rescue the Commonwealth. . . . Neither the Constituent nor the Legislative Assembly ever had a more infernal set of officers than those whom we now have in the Convention. . . . Liberty will not perish; however bad the Convention may be, it will never exterminate Liberty, for the people will manage to take care of themselves. Had the Patriots been at their posts yesterday, there would never have been brought forward a decree against *Égalité,* which will send a thrill of indignation through the whole of France. Égalité has asked for permission to speak on the subject to-day. . . . We must rally more than ever round the Mountain, and die, if necessary, to save our liberty. . . . Let all true Patriots unite in the defence of Égalité.'[2]

Drouet, the man of Varennes, is also opposed to any interference with the Duc d'Orléans, that Prince and all his family being sacred to him. 'I raise my voice in protest,' he cried; ' for though the liberty of the people were exiled, it would

---

[1] Jean François Goupilleau, called de Fontenay, member for the Vendée in the Constituent Assembly and the Convention, was born at Apremont-sur-Vie on July 25, 1753, and died at Montaigu on October 11, 1823. He sat in the Convention amongst the Dantonists of the Mountain, near his cousin, Philippe Charles Aimé Goupilleau, called de Montaigu, member for the Vendée in the Legislative Assembly and the Convention, who was born at Montaigu on November 19, 1749, and died at the same place on July 1, 1823. The lives of these two Conventionalists are strangely confused in the ' Table Alphabétique et Chronologique du *Moniteur* de 1789 jusqu'à l'an VIII. de la République,' all the acts and speeches of Goupilleau de Fontenay being attributed to Goupilleau de Montaigu, and *vice-versâ.* This error was perpetuated in the ' Biographie Moderne ' (1806), in the ' Vie Politique de tous les Députés à la Convention Nationale,' by Robert (1814), in the ' Biographie des Hommes Vivants' (1818), in the ' Biographie des Contemporains ' (1830), and in Michaud's ' Biographie Universelle' (1838). The ' *Table du Moniteur* ' is, nevertheless, a great and carefully-written work, which the student of Revolutionary history should always have at hand. It was compiled by Alphonse de Beauchamp, the historian of the Vendean war; Caubrière, one of the authors of the ' Biographie Moderne '; and Joseph Giraud, who, after having edited an ultra-radical sheet called the *Républicain,* during the Revolution, was one of the first editors of the *Constitutionnel.*

[2] Meeting at the Jacobin Club on December 17, 1792: *Journal des Débats et de Décrets de la Société des Jacobins,* December 19.

find sanctuary here. . . . Shall the family of Égalité share the same fate as that of the . . . Where should it find a refuge ? Nowhere.   It would therefore be a terrible injustice to condemn it to banishment !'[1]

The Conseil-Général de la Commune, in which the members of the 'Grey Friars' predominate, has not confined itself to words, but passed the following resolution at its meeting of the 18th :

'The Conseil-Général de la Commune having received petitions from a large number of sections, inviting it to demand from the National Convention the repeal of the law of the 16th instant ;

'And considering that in all matters in which the rights of man are violated, or in which good citizens are threatened with unjust exile, all the citizens of the Commune should express their opinion and take energetic measures for the defence of liberty and equality, and for the safety of persons and property ;

'The Procureur de la Commune having spoken,

'The Conseil-Général hereby convokes the forty-eight sections for to-morrow, the 19th, at eight o'clock in the morning, to consider the petition of the Section of the Gardes-Françaises demanding the repeal of the Decree of December 16.[2]'

In reply to this proclamation the sections sent to the Conseil-Général delegates charged with drafting an address to the Convention upon the lines laid down by the Section of the Gardes-Françaises.[3]   Nearly all demanded the repeal of the Decree pure and simple ; some, however, limited themselves to a request for its suspension until the wishes of the people had been clearly expressed.   The majority being in favour of the former measure, it was adopted, and it was decided that the

---

[1] Meeting at the Jacobin Club on December 17, 1792 : *Journal des Débats et de Décrets de la Société des Jacobins*, December 19.

[2] *Mercure Française*, December 22, 1792.

[3] The Section of the Gardes-Françaises had at its meeting of December 18 passed the following resolution, which had immediately been communicated to the municipal body and to the forty-seven other sections : ' When the time for action has come, fine speeches are superfluous.   You have heard of the Decree banishing from France the whole family of the Bourbons.   This Decree alarms every good citizen.   It is impossible to describe to you feelings with which you are yourselves filled ; we will content ourselves with asking the municipality of Paris to appear before the National Convention to-morrow for the purpose of demanding the repeal of the Decree.'

address should immediately be taken to the Convention by
the 144 members of the Conseil-Général and the forty-eight
Commissioners of sections.   At one o'clock the procession,
headed by the Mayor,[1] proceeded to the Convention ; it was,
however, refused admission on the ground that this was not one
of the days set aside for the presentation of petitions.[2]   Cooped
up in the corridors,[3] the petitioners broke out into the most
insulting language against the Assembly ; their shouts and
those of the crowd who accompanied them could be heard in the
Convention itself, and the uproar was so great that the sitting
had to be suspended for a few moments.   Upon the return of
the members of the Conseil-Général and the delegates of the
sections to the Hôtel de Ville, Citizen Hébert was the first to
speak.   On the previous day he had published in his paper :
'THE GREAT ANGER OF PÈRE DUCHESNE *concerning the Decree
which sent Philippe Egalité and his wife to Coblentz ; his advice
to the deputies who are not yet " Brissotés " to put their heads
together and kick out all the jackanapes who howl to the same
tune as the wife of Coco Roland.*'[4]   Citizen Hébert is a strange
personage, as careful in his toilet as he is careless in his language.
The old check-taker of the Théâtre des Variétés bears very little
resemblance to the squalid figure that adorns the front page of
his newspaper, and under which is the device : *I am the real
Père Duchesne.*   He is almost a dandy—small, slim, and with
rather a good-looking face.[5]   He speaks with facility and in
very good style.

' Citizens,' he said, ' the voice of the sovereign people has been
drowned, your magistrates insulted, and the inalienable rights of
man trodden under foot.   The National Convention has refused to
hear us. . . .   I will not dwell long upon the measures that you
have to adopt.   Time presses ; carry your minds back to the Tenth

---

[1] Nicolas Chambon de Montaux, formerly head-physician at the
Salpêtrière, was elected Mayor of Paris on November 30, 1792, by 8,358
votes against 3,906 given to Lulier—not Lhuillier, as wrongly given by
Mortimer-Ternaux and the other historians of the Revolution.

[2] At its sitting of November 4, 1791, the Legislative Assembly had, on
the proposal of Quatremère de Quincy, decided that Sundays only were
to be devoted to the reading of petitions.   In this the Convention had
followed the example of the Legislative Assembly.

[3] *Révolutions de Paris*, No. 180.   [4] *Père Duchesne*, No. 202.

[5] Charles Brunet, ' Le Père Duchesne d'Hébert,' p. 38.

of August. It is in the splendid deeds of that celebrated day that we shall recognise our duties; our position is the same now as it then was; our oppressors, it is true, are others, but their tyranny is no less insupportable. I demand that the sections be specially convoked; that a report of the refusal we have just met with be drawn up, and immediately sent to them, as well as to each of the eighty-three departments, in order that the whole Republic may know how our just demands are treated by those whom we have returned to power.'[1]

This motion was received with much applause. A sectional commissioner went farther, asking that a list of all the members of the Convention who had betrayed the interests of the people should be added to the report which was to be sent to the departments. During the debate to which this motion gave rise the Mayor announced that the National Convention had sent an order summoning him to the bar. The whole assembly rose to follow him, and the procession started for the second time. Upon its return to the Hôtel de Ville, the Mayor gave an account of the manner in which he had been received by the representatives of the people. The President and several members having asked him if it was true that he had invited the sections to assemble and give their opinion upon the Decree of the 16th, he had replied that the petition had not been provoked by any one section in particular, but that all the citizens of Paris had simultaneously assembled in their respective sections to vote against the Decree. The General Assembly applauded Chambon's speech; several members reiterated the demand that the printed report suggested by Hébert should also include the petition of the sections, and the Mayor's account of his reception, whereupon the Conseil-Général made the following order:

'The Conseil-Général, wishing to give its constituents a proof of the zeal with which it executes all their orders, and wishing also to give all the citizens of Paris a proof of its Republican sentiments:

'Orders the report of the proceedings of December 19 to be printed, published, and sent to the forty-eight sections.'

[1] Minutes of the meeting of the Conseil-Général de la Commune of December 19, 1792. At that date Hébert was only a member of the Conseil-Général, having been elected on the Tenth of August by the section Bonne-Nouvelle. He was not appointed second deputy for the Procureur de la Commune until December 22, 1792. Citizen Réal—the Comte Réal of the Empire—was appointed first deputy on the same day.

Meanwhile the majority in the Convention, adding one more to the already long list of its cowardly acts, rescinded its vote and decided (on Petion's proposal) that 'the execution of the Decree of the 16th concerning the family of the Bourbons should be delayed, and that the consideration of the question should be adjourned until after the trial of the *ci-devant* King.'[1]

In the evening crowds gathered in many places; groups of workmen paraded the streets shouting, ' *Vive Égalité!* ' and swearing to shed their last drop of blood for D'Orléans.[2]

These disturbances were renewed yesterday, and assumed rather a serious character. General meetings were called in several sections in order to discuss the refusal of the Convention to hear the deputies who had presented themselves at the bar on the previous day. Several rumours of plots got afloat. Amongst other news calculated to excite the mob, a report was assiduously spread that five or six thousand sacks of corn had been burnt. In the streets a pamphlet entitled 'Adieux de la Citoyenne d'Orléans ' was being sold in large numbers.[3] In the evening, in spite of the rain, large crowds continued to form, the Terrasse des Feuillants in particular being, until a very late hour, the scene of much uproar and of noisy demonstrations in honour of Philippe-Égalité.

Beaulieu tells the following curious and significant anecdote, which has its proper place here.

In the month of October, 1792, when Dumouriez was in Paris, after the Battle of Valmy, the *ci-devant* Duc de Chartres, then General Égalité, was also in the capital. Danton met him somewhere, and reproved him in an amicable way for the freedom of his language respecting the September massacres and their organizers. 'Young man,' he said, ' you speak of what you know nothing about. It was I who arranged the Second of September, and what I did I was obliged to do. I fairly terrified the mob of Paris, ready to shout, "*Vivent les Prussiens!*" I exterminated or frightened the aristocrats, who would always have been the enemies of the Revolution, and who would always

---

[1] Sitting of December 19, 1792, *Moniteur*, No. 357.
[2] *Mercure Français*, December 21, 1792.
[3] *Courrier des Départements*, December 21, 1792.

have conspired against it. France owes me thanks, and you, perhaps, more than any one else.'

Upon the Duc de Chartres expressing his surprise at these words, Danton continued : ' One never knows what may happen. *This country is not fitted for a Republic.* Some day it will shout : " Vive le Roi !" That may be your opportunity, and what I have done will have helped to pave your way and rid it of obstacles. Therefore, young man, serve the Republic well and faithfully ; behave wisely, and be careful what you say.'[1]

Beaulieu—and no one knows the secrets of the Revolution better than he—thinks this language in Danton's mouth of immense importance. He does not, however, believe that the Duc d'Orléans ever seriously dreamt of ascending the throne, and thinks that cowardice alone, and not ambition, is the motive of his conduct. Beaulieu may be right. But though this question is, and perhaps always will be, shrouded in mystery, it is an undoubted fact that since 1789 the worst demagogues have looked upon the Duke as a willing instrument to further their plans ; and even to-day Danton, Marat, Camille Desmoulins, and a large number of the members of the Mountain, diffident concerning the duration of the Republic, are unwilling to let him go, and hold him in reserve until such time as they can seat him on the throne, place in his dishonoured hands a ridiculous sceptre, and satisfy under cover of his usurped rank and tarnished name their greed of power and of gold.

[1] M. de Barante, ' Histoire de la Convention Nationale,' tome ii., p. 447 ; Lamartine, ' Histoire des Girondins' ; N. Villiaumé, ' Histoire de la Révolution Française,' tome ii., p. 217.

CHAPTER XXVIII.

Tuesday, December 25, 1792.

THE celebration of the *fête* of Sainte-Geneviève has not been lost upon our municipality;[1] profiting by that lesson, it distributed copies of the law forbidding nocturnal assemblies, and issued an Order for the closing of all churches on Christmas Eve. This Order was made by the Conseil-Général de la Commune, at its sitting of December 23, after a speech by Chaumette, which deserves to be reported. General Santerre had just assured the Council that he had taken every precaution for the maintenance of public order during Christmas night, when Chaumette asked for permission to speak. 'It is not,' he said, 'at such a moment as this, when the *ci-devant* King, that crowned monster, is still described as the Lord's Anointed, that priests should be allowed to preside over midnight meetings. Besides, if on the day when the villain in the Temple is brought to the bar to appear before the Sovereign People,[2] the aristocrats should come and say, " We have a religion of which we wish to observe the ceremonies "—what could you answer if, on the previous day, you yourselves had allowed a midnight mass to be celebrated ? There is no doubt that the morality of Christ was a pure one ; Jesus loved neither the rich nor the money-lenders, and He told them that it would be easier for them to pass through the eye of a needle than to enter the kingdom of heaven. He hated priests and preached equality. " You are," He used to say to His disciples, " all children of one Father." In fact, we may say

[1] See Chapter XXII.
[2] Louis XVI. was to appear at the bar of the Convention on Wednesday, December 26.

that Jesus was the leader of the *sans-culottes* of Judæa, and I am certain that as such He would have mercilessly prohibited a midnight mass, that remnant of Egyptian orgies.' Dorat-Cubières, a municipal officer—a wretch who, to get himself elected to the Conseil-Général de la Commune, declared, in a sectional meeting, ' that his mother had committed a crime in making him a noble, for his father was not one'[1]—proposed an amendment suggesting that the midnight mass should be tolerated only on condition that whilst the sacred orgy was being held on one side of the church, the sections should hold a meeting on the other. The Conseil-Général took the advice of its Procureur-Syndic, and issued a decree ordering all churches to be closed from five o'clock on Monday afternoon, the 24th, until six o'clock on Tuesday morning, the 25th.[2] It was also decided that some municipal officers or members of the Council should visit the different parishes to see that the order was carried out. These measures were approved by a large number of sections, and in particular by those of the Rights of Man, of Gravilliers, and of the Pantheon, in which *all the priests' shops* were ordered to be closed.[3]

Protests were raised in a few sections only, notably in those of Mauconseil, the Maison Commune, the Louvre, and the Arsenal. That of the Louvre, in a petition drawn up by Marc Étienne Quatremère, requested the Commune to rescind its Decree ;[4] that of the Arsenal openly proclaimed that the men of the Tenth of August wished to attend mass.

[1] The Chevalier Michel de Cubières, known as Dorat-Cubières, was born at Roquemaure on September 27, 1752. Mme. Roland draws the following portrait of him in her ' Mémoires ' : ' Cubières, faithful to the double character of insolence and villainy, so plainly depicted upon his repulsive face, now preaches *sans-culottism* as he once sung of the Graces, composes such verses upon Marat as he used to dedicate to Iris, and humbly prostrates himself, though in a cold, bloodless way, before the idol of the hour, be this Tantalus or Venus. What matters it so long as he crawls and earns his bread ? Yesterday it was by writing a sonnet, to-day it is by copying a report or by signing a police order.' This wretch, who wrote the ' Éloge de Marat,' and who called himself ' the poet of the Revolution,' died in Paris on August 23, 1820.

[2] The *Courrier des Départements*, December 26, 1792.

[3] *Révolutions de Paris*, No. 181.

[4] Marc Étienne Quatremère, a cousin of Quatremère de Quincy, a member of the Right in the Legislative Assembly, and the most cele-

The greater part of the people, however, heedless of what had been decided in the Commune and the majority of the sections, flocked to the churches last night in every quarter, but principally in the poorer ones. Where the churches were closed, the armed force was surrounded by immense crowds, the women, who were present in great numbers, taunting the men with their cowardice and inciting them to break open the doors. In more than one case the members of the Commune were hooted and roughly handled. Before the church of Saint-Séverin, and in many other places, arrests were made. At Saint-Eustache mass was celebrated in great pomp before the *dames de la Halle*, who appeared nowise intimidated by the presence of the municipal officers. Citizen Bugniau, a master-mason, and a member of the Commune, got his face slightly damaged whilst attempting to execute the orders of the Conseil-Général, and was obliged to retire from the field.[1] Midnight mass was also celebrated at Saint-Jacques-de-la-Boucherie, Saint-Merry, Saint-Gervais, Saint-Laurent, Saint-Victor, Saint-Médard, and Saint-Marcel. In the Couvent des Anglaises the magistrates were also set at defiance. In more churches than one the priests were unwilling to contravene the municipal decree, and their less timorous parishioners were almost obliged to coerce them.[2]

At Saint-Laurent, at Saint-Merry and at Saint-Germain-l'Auxerrois the bells rang out merrily—this time it was not the tocsin, nor a call to revolt, nor the prelude to insurrection and massacre; it was a call to prayer, peace and the union of souls. The sacred sounds touched the purest and sweetest chords in our heart, awakening reminiscences of those beautiful Christmas

---

brated art critic of his day, was one of those simple citizens of Paris who so courageously proved their fidelity to the Royalist cause during the Revolution. Having in 1793 attracted the attention of the authorities by his excessive liberality to the poor, he was on these proofs denounced as an aristocrat and a Royalist, and executed on January 21, 1794, the first anniversary of the King's death.

[1] 'Quelques Souvenirs, ou Notes Fidèles sur mon Service au Temple, depuis le 8 Décembre, 1792, jusqu'au 26 Mars, 1793,' by M. Lepitre.

[2] *Le Patriote Français*, No. 1,233. In his paper Brissot is obliged to confess that in many parishes the priests were forced to perform the office by the masses of the people. After which he himself affirms that religion went for nothing in this rising, which he styles a Maratic-religious riot.

nights when with our parents we sat around the hearth, dressed in our best, waiting for the bells to summon us to the illumined church where the infant Jesus lay in His cradle lifting towards His smiling mother and the adoring crowd His little hands filled with forgiveness and peace.

I attended mass at Saint-Eustache. Whilst returning home I met some Jacobins shouting, ' *Death to the Calotins! Death to Capet!* ' And I remembered how it was formerly the custom at this same hour for good folks to go from door to door announcing the glad tidings, ' *Christ is born!* '

With the exception of Mortimer-Ternaux, Louis Blanc is the sole historian who has devoted a few lines to this curious episode of Christmas night, but brief as they are, they contain more than one error. ' At Saint-Germain,' he says (tome viii., p. 33), 'some women were on the point of lynching a passer-by whom they mistook for Manuel, because at the sitting of December 30 Manuel had proposed to abolish the *fête des Rois.*' It was, indeed, at the sitting of December 30, 1792, that Manuel made this proposal; it is therefore inexplicable how the women of the parish of Saint-Germain could have owed him a grudge for this on December 25—that is, five days before his motion was proposed. Louis Blanc might, it is true, have committed this error intentionally in order to prove that on the eve of the King's appearance at the bar of the Convention, Paris was threatened with a Royalist movement which it was necessary to stifle by sending Louis to the scaffold. Do not the lines written a little higher by Louis Blanc point to a desire to make his readers believe in the reality of this imaginary plot? 'The friends of the throne and of the altar assembled that night in garrets to chant hymns and burn candles and incense in honour of the King, the Queen and the Dauphin.' In support of his affirmation, he refers his readers to the *Révolutions de Paris*, No. 181.

In the *Révolutions de Paris* we read : ' There is not much harm in exhibiting dancing puppets, or in performing tricks in the public streets in broad daylight—the children and their nurses must be amused. But to assemble at night in obscure garrets to chant hymns and burn candles and incense in honour of Mary and her Son is a scandalous thing.' *Of the King, the Queen and the Dauphin* not a word is said. Louis Blanc is not sparing of references as foot-notes ; by these examples we may form an opinion of their value.

CHAPTER XXIX.

December 26, 1792.

Thursday, December 27, 1792.

Louis XVI. appeared at the bar of the Convention yesterday for the last time.

On the 25th Manuel had suggested that the Inspecteurs de la Salle should take measures to prevent the citizens in the galleries from staying there all night, as had happened on the occasion of Louis' first appearance at the bar. The Convention, however, passed no resolution on the subject, and the galleries were not evacuated during the night between the 25th and 26th.[1] Nevertheless I managed to get into the hall, thanks to an old acquaintance of mine, one François Poiret, an old servant of M. de Talleyrand and the Comtesse Diane de Polignac, and now one of the ten ushers of the National Convention.[2]

As early as seven in the morning many of the streets were paraded by patrols commanded by officers who forced all the citizens they came across to follow them, the corporals meanwhile entering the houses and private apartments, dragging citizens from their beds, and obliging them to fall in with the others.[3]

On the 25th the Section of the Quatre-Nations had issued the following decree :

'Captains of the armed forces are requested to send for such citizens as shall not appear under arms at head-quarters at the stated hour to-morrow, exception to be made only in the cases of public servants and of commissioners of the section.'[4]

---

[1] *Mercure Français*, December 27, 1792.
[2] Guillotined March 29, 1794.
[3] *Révolutions de Paris*, No. 181.   [4] *Ibid.*

In spite of these extreme measures, the double row of armed men which was to line the boulevard and the streets from the Temple to the Cour des Feuillants was not yet formed when Louis left the Temple at half-past nine; the troops had only then assembled at the different head-quarters with their standards and guns.[1]

As on December 11, Louis was seated in the Mayor's carriage with Chambon, the Mayor, Chaumette, the Procureur, and Coulombeau, the Secretary of the Commune. The escort was formed of a detachment of cavalry from the École Militaire. It rained heavily, and a high wind was blowing; the windows of the carriage, however, were left down, doubtless in order to satisfy the crowds who wished to see the prisoner. Though held up as a kind of show to his enemies, Louis preserved the most perfect calm during the whole of the journey, taking part with the utmost *sang-froid* in a conversation that turned upon literary topics, and especially upon a few Latin authors, such as Seneca, Livy and Tacitus.[2] His serenity was not even disturbed by an incident that occurred on the boulevards. As the carriage and the cavalry that accompanied it were dashing along, the men stationed at one of the guard-houses thought that the *ci-devant* King was being carried off, and the gunners made a movement as if to turn their pieces upon the party.[3]

The journey from the Temple to the Riding-School occupied a quarter of an hour. Louis was led through the cloister and the corridor of the Feuillants into the Conference Hall, where he found his counsel, MM. de Malesherbes, Tronchet, and Desèze,

[1] *Révolutions de Paris*, No. 181.

[2] 'Reports laid before the Commune upon the King's Second Journey to the Convention.' 'Whilst the carriage was rolling along between two long lines of armed men,' says Louis Blanc (tome viii., p. 5), 'the ex-Monarch conversed familiarly on literary and historical topics, *with one of his counsel seated beside him.*' Neither Malesherbes nor Tronchet nor Desèze was in the carriage which took the King to the Convention; he had beside him only enemies, which renders his *sang-froid* and his serenity still more extraordinary. Can Louis Blanc have wished to diminish the admiration which the ex-Monarch's behaviour at this juncture inspires by making Louis XVI. converse with one of his counsel? It is difficult to believe in an involuntary error respecting a fact so formally contradicted in official documents, with which Louis Blanc was better acquainted than anyone, and to which he himself frequently refers.

[3] *Le Courrier des Départements*, December 29, 1792.

awaiting him, and with whom he conversed for about twenty-three minutes. Citizen Treilhard, a member of the Convention, passing through the hall and hearing the King's defenders employ such words as 'Sire' and 'Majesty' in speaking to their august client, stopped before them, and said, in a threatening tone, 'What makes you so bold as to utter names which the Convention has proscribed?' 'Contempt for you and contempt for life!' replied M. de Malesherbes.[1]

A few minutes later Louis appeared at the bar, accompanied by his three defenders, as well as by the Mayor and the commander of the National Guard. The Convention was presided over by M. Defermon, member for Ille-et-Vilaine, who during the whole of the sitting displayed most courageous moderation and noble dignity.

M. Desèze read his speech, which lasted nearly three hours.

Louis was then taken back to the Conference Hall, whither he was followed by his defenders. Taking M. Desèze in his arms, he embraced him most affectionately; then, turning to the persons around him, he said: 'He is wet through; would it not be possible to get him a change of linen at once?' Balza, one of the ushers of the Convention, brought a shirt, which the King himself aired before the fire.[2]

Meanwhile tremendous excitement reigned outside the hall. On the Terrasse des Feuillants the crowd continued to gather in spite of the heavy rain, whilst wretched hags shouted '*Death to Louis!*' till they were hoarse.[3]

The crowd in the Place Vendôme was still greater. The National Guard was under arms, forming a double line on the right, opposite the Porte des Capucines, and a single line on the other side, where the guns were drawn up. Reliable emissaries mixed with the crowd, saying that if the Convention did not do its duty it would have to be taught it. As an Aide-

---

[1] 'Dernières Années de Louis XVI.,' by M. Hue, who had these details from Malesherbes himself. It appears that under the Empire Citizen Treilhard, as Councillor and Minister of State, Grand Officer of the Legion of Honour, etc., became reconciled to the use of such words as 'Sire' and 'Majesty.'

[2] *Ibid.*

[3] *Courrier des Départements*, December 29, 1792.

de-camp **rode across** the square, the civic **guard** stopped him, **and made energetic** representations that the return journey from the Convention to the Temple should be performed at a walking **pace.** The Aide-de-camp promised to transmit these wishes to Santerre.[1]

Meanwhile, the time was slipping **away, and** the crowd began to grow impatient. It was known **that Louis** had **left** the bar nearly an hour ago—why was he not taken back to the **Temple?** The strangest rumours began **to spread,** for the delay was inexplicable. It was caused, as was afterwards **known,** through compliance with a decree passed by the Assembly, and by the terms **of** which the *minutes of the defence* were to be signed by Louis and his **counsel.**

It was two o'clock when the King left the building; he walked with a firm step **and** head erect.[2] **He re-entered** the **carriage** with Chambon, Chaumette, **and** Coulombeau. This time **the** journey was performed at a walking **pace, in** conformity **with the** desire of the National Guard. During **the long** itinerary his calm, serene manner did not leave him **for a single moment.** To Coulombeau, **who** kept his hat **on,** he said with a smile: 'The last time you came you **had** forgotten your hat: **you have** been **more** careful to-day.'[3] **The** conversation having **turned** upon **the** hospitals of Paris, **he entered** into details of the expenses of these establishments, **and** of the different plans put forward with regard to them. **In the course of his** observations he expressed a wish that there might **be one in each** section.[4]

Five **o'clock** was striking **as** Louis **once more entered the** Temple. In the evening his defenders **came to see him. He** said to M. de Malesherbes: 'You **must** certainly be **convinced** now that I was not mistaken from the first, and that my sentence was pronounced before I had been heard.'[5]

[1] *Courrier des Départements, loc. cit.*

[2] 'He walked with a firm step . . . as if he were holding a review of his guards at the Palace of Versailles.'—*Révolutions de Paris,* No. 181.'

[3] 'Report laid before the Commune,' by Coulombeau, on December 27, 1792.

[4] *Ibid.*

[5] 'Anecdotes relatives à **la Mort de Louis XVI.**,' by M. de Vaines. The author has taken his narrative from the mouth of M. de Malesherbes, who was incarcerated in the same prison with him in 1794.

The strength of mind displayed by Louis XVI. during the whole of that day is therefore proved not to have proceeded from a false idea of the fate that awaited him. Whence came this strength, if not from the clearness of his conscience and his deep piety ?[1]

In the evening I went to the Palais Royal. Five or six *sans-culottes* entered the Café du Caveau, and after uttering threats of death against all deputies who hesitated to strike the *ex-tyrant*, bawled out a song with the refrain: '*A la guillotine, Louis !*' No one joined them in this brutal demonstration. They then adjourned to the Café des Chartres, where they resumed their abominable song. Two of the deputies from Brest who were present made them understand that such jests were not to their taste, and the singing gentlemen prudently made for the door.[2]

---

[1] In his report to the Commune on the morrow of that day, Coulombeau said : 'This man must be a fanatic, for it is impossible to otherwise explain how one can be so tranquil with so many reasons for fear.' Louis Blanc has, however, attempted to 'otherwise explain,' and has not hesitated to insinuate that the courage and serenity of Louis XVI. were due to his mad illusions. 'He so little felt,' he says, 'the gravity of his situation, or he so completely lost sight of it, that he spoke of his plans for the future, *and especially of his intention to make a tour through France in two years' time.*' Can Louis Blanc, who here quotes Mercier's 'Nouveau Paris,' written several years after the events, have believed for one moment that such words were really uttered by Louis XVI. at such a time ? Could he have believed this when he had before him the *Révolutions de Paris*, which relates the episode in these words : 'Capet inquires of Citizen Chambon from what part of the country he comes.—"From the Haute-Marne." The ex-King at once names the rivers, mountains, and other geographical details of this department. "And you, M. Chaumette, where do you come from ?"—"From the department of the Nièvre, near the banks of the Loire." "That is a charming country." "Have you ever been there ?" —"No," replied Capet, "but I intended to make a tour through France in two years' time, to learn all its beauties." ' And Louis Blanc on that same page (tome viii., p. 10) charges M. de Barante with deliberately perverting the truth ! *Deliberate perversion of the truth !* Louis Blanc has no scruples in lending others his qualities.

[2] *Courrier des Départements*, December 29, 1792.

CHAPTER XXX.

Friday, December 28, 1792.

I HAVE had the honour of shaking hands to-day with M. Desèze, whom I met at the house of our common friend, the Abbé Morellet, in the Faubourg Saint-Honoré, not far from the Place de la Révolution.[1]

From the Abbé I learnt many interesting particulars respecting the defender of Louis XVI.

On December 15 the Convention decided that Louis should be heard for the last time on Wednesday, the 26th; it also appointed a commission of four of its members to immediately proceed to the Temple, and to hand over to Louis and his counsel copies of the documents that had not yet been laid before him. The work of examining these papers was commenced at four o'clock, and was not concluded at midnight. Taken aback by the enormous mass of documents upon which the accusation was based, and fearing that there would be no time to study and answer them, MM. de Malesherbes and Tronchet urged upon their august client the necessity of calling in the aid of another counsel.

'Do so,' said Louis, with a smile; 'the greater the danger, the more doctors are required. You make me think that my case is desperate, but I will show you that I am a good patient.'

Before asking the Convention for leave to call in M. Desèze, they wished to make sure that he was willing to give his help, and confided this task to two of his friends, MM. Colin and de Merville. It was past midnight when these two gentlemen

---

[1] 'Mémoires de l'Abbé Morellet,' tome ii., p. 13.

called upon M. Desèze. His answer was as follows: 'A few days ago the Conseil-Général de la Commune passed a resolution ordering the counsel accorded to Louis by the National Convention to be most thoroughly searched, to undress, and to put on fresh garments under the supervision of the Commissioners. The resolution further adds that the counsel are not to leave the Tower until after the King's trial. The Convention has modified these measures, but the Commune is none the less all-powerful, and I look upon its resolution as an act of proscription against the defenders of the King. I will devote myself to the cause with all my heart.'

At the opening of the sitting on the 17th, the letter was read in which MM. de Malesherbes and Tronchet requested, in view of the brevity of the time at their disposal, that M. Desèze might be allowed to take part in the defence. This demand having been agreed to, M. Desèze went to the Temple the same day about five in the afternoon.

He has practised at the Paris bar for about ten years, and on his *début* immediately took a place in the front rank; his defence of M. de Besenval before the Châtelet in January, 1790, was a masterpiece. No advocate is more pathetic nor more persuasive. Those who have sworn that the King must die were therefore afraid that M. Desèze might succeed in moving the members of the Convention. In the *Révolutions de Paris* of December 22 we read:

'We fear the weakness of the Convention the more since Louis has called in fresh assistance in the person of an ornament of the Bar—an insidious orator who even when he proves nothing persuades you that you have been convinced. Desèze is the very man for Louis XVI. In hearing him the public has never been able to repress its enthusiasm. The first steps in his career were marked by great success—he moves even the most stubborn hearts. Frequently has he been carried from the court in triumph by a crowd of his hearers.[1] The physical defects under which he labours

---

[1] Louis Blanc (tome viii., p. 2): 'Desèze, a young barrister from Bordeaux, was charged with the defence.' 'Tronchet and Malesherbes,' says Mortimer-Ternaux (tome v., p. 281), 'had obtained permission to call in a young barrister from Bordeaux.' Born on September 26, 1748, Desèze in 1793 had already been at the Bar for twenty years. In Bachaumont's 'Mémoires,' we find him, in 1784, making a brilliant speech in the law-

he even turns to advantage.   It is a difficult thing for him to raise
his voice, and to this difficulty he lends the appearance of sentiment, pretending that his words come from the bottom of his heart.
Every shade of feeling is depicted on his face, and he carries away
his hearers by every means in his power.   It is certain that he will
neglect none of his gifts in a cause which has no parallel in the
history of our courts.   But if Desèze discharges his duty as a zealous
defender, the National Convention must not forget that it has taken
upon itself all the duties of a judge, and that it is obliged to be on
its guard against the surprises of eloquence. . . .   The orator,
whose cause does not furnish matter for much argument, and who
will be overwhelmed by the weight of facts, will no doubt apply
himself to moving his audience and his judges—to speak rather to
the heart than to the mind.   A large assembly is generally very
weak when once it has been moved ; when the first blow has
taken effect it is easily led, and itself forms the torrent which
carries it away.'

M. Desèze did not realize the fears of the King's enemies ; he
did not apply himself to move his audience and his judges, and
I now know why.

Obliged to help his two colleagues in the examination of an
immense number of documents, often spending many hours, and
sometimes whole days, in the different offices of the Convention,
he had not yet commenced to write his speech at nightfall on
Saturday, December 22.   He then composed the whole of it in
one day and two nights—from Saturday evening to Monday
morning—neither sitting nor sleeping in that time, and dictating
the sentences as they first occurred to him.[1]   On Monday, the
24th, at five in the afternoon, he read the whole to Louis XVI.
in the presence of MM. de Malesherbes and Tronchet, who could
not help being hopeful on hearing the most pathetic passages,
and especially the peroration, into which M. Desèze had put not
only all his eloquence, but all his heart and soul.   Taking his
advocate by the hand, Louis thanked him with much warmth ;

suit concerning the division of the Helvetius property.   An advocate in
the Parlement de Paris, where he had made his *début* under the auspices
of Target, who had in a measure retired to make way for him, he
was, in the words of the *Révolutions de Paris*, an ornament of the metropolitan Bar.   M. Louis Blanc and Mortimer-Ternaux are, therefore,
somewhat inaccurate when they speak of him as being a young barrister
of Bordeaux in December, 1793.

[1] 'Mémoires de Morellet,' tome i., p. 406.

he then added : ' I scarcely hope to persuade them, but I do not
wish to affect them,' and asked M. Desèze to sacrifice all those
sentences which appealed to the feelings of his judges.   M. Desèze
was obliged to give way, and the King with his own hand struck
out the most touching parts,[1] though MM. de Malesherbes and
Tronchet begged him to spare at least the peroration, which had
moved them to tears.[2]   Their prayers were in vain.   ' Cut out
your peroration, eloquent as it is,' said the King to M. Desèze ;
' it is beneath my dignity to bewail my lot.   I wish to awaken
no other interest but that which should spring from the simple
statement put forth in justification of my conduct.   What you
cut out, my dear Desèze, would injure you more than it would
benefit me.'   M. Desèze was therefore obliged to suppress the
greater part of his peroration also.   ' Does not this trait of
Louis XVI.,' asks Morellet, ' remind you of a passage in Cicero
perfectly applicable to this noble and unhappy monarch ?'   Cicero
speaks of P. Rutilius, who, accused before the people, did not
wish his defender to play upon the feelings of his judges.   ' *Nam
cum esset ille vir exemplum, ut scitis, innocentiæ, cumque illo nemo
neque integrior esset in civitate, neque sanctior ; non modo supplex
judicibus esse noluit, sed ne ornatius quidem aut liberius causam
dici suam, quam simplex ratio veritatis ferebat.*'[3]

Louis may sometimes have shown a want of energy and
strength at Versailles and at the Tuileries, but since he has been
in the Temple he has not ceased to give proofs of the most kingly
qualities and of a most noble and sustained heroism.   What
Voltaire wrote of Louis IX. history will say of Louis XVI. : ' It
is not given to mortal man to carry virtue farther.'[4]

In the pages which Lamartine has devoted to the trial and death
of Louis XVI., and which are amongst the finest of our historical

[1] Morellet, *loc. cit.*
[2] ' Anecdotes relatives à la Mort de Louis XVI.,' by M. de Vaines, who
had them from Malesherbes himself.
[3] ' De Oratore,' i. 53.   ' This man, who, as you all know, was a model of
virtue, and whom no citizen ever excelled in integrity or piety, was most
unwilling to appear as a supplicant before his judges, and would not allow
his defence to be embellished with aught else than the simple truth.'
—MORELLET, tome i., p. 407.
[4] Voltaire, ' Essai sur les Mœurs et l'Esprit des Nations.'   Genève,
1758.

literature, he says of the speech for the defence: 'His advocate, Desèze, spoke with dignity, but without brilliancy. He remained perfectly cool and argumentative before the heat of public passion. His speech only rose here and there to the solemnity of the occasion. He debated when it was necessary to strike a blow. He forgot that for a people there is nothing so convincing as emotion, that bold words in certain cases embody the height of prudence, and that in extreme cases it is only a desperate eloquence that can save all at the risk of total ruin. It was one of the fatalities in the life of Louis XVI. that he had not found to help him in his struggle with the people one of those voices that turn pity to advantage, and which are now and again heard amidst the fall of thrones, the crash of empires and the blows of revolutionary axes, uttering words as great, as grand, and as solemn as such events. If a Bossuet, a Mirabeau or a Vergniaud had found himself in the place of Desèze, Louis XVI. would not have been defended with more zeal, more prudence or more logic; but the words of such men, judicious if not judicial, would have echoed avengingly in the ears of the judges and remorsefully in the hearts of the people; and if the cause had not been gained before the tribunal, it would for ever have been illustrious before posterity. In these causes which are not of a day, it is a mistake to speak to the men of the time; we must speak to those of the future, for they are the real judges.'—'Histoire des Girondins,' book xxxiv. Eloquent as they are, the reproaches addressed by Lamartine to Desèze are not justified, as has been proved by the details contained in the foregoing chapter.

CHAPTER XXXI

A LETTER FROM THE KING.

Saturday, December 29, 1792.

I AGAIN called on the Abbé Morellet this morning, in whose enlightened judgment, well-balanced mind, and cool courage I have great faith in these troubled times. André de Chénier was with him. From January, 1788, until June, 1791, Chénier was secretary to M. de la Luzerne, the nephew of M. de Malesherbes and French Ambassador in London. This relationship brought the venerable defender of the King and the young and eloquent writer much together; they often met in the *salon* of the Trudaines,[1] and the articles published by Chénier in the *Journal de la Société de* 1789 and in the *Journal de Paris* had more than once won him the congratulations of his old friend. Of late M. de Malesherbes has frequently spoken to him of the sacred interests placed in his hands, and of the steps to be taken to save the King. Chénier has promised him his help and has already prepared matter to be laid either before the Convention or before the nation itself.[2]

In the course of our conversation I expressed my regret that the King had not followed the example of Charles I. and refused to recognise the jurisdiction of the revolutionary tribunal before which he was compelled to appear.[3] Impelled by the desire to

---

[1] 'Notice sur la Vie et les Ouvrages d'André de Chénier,' by Gabriel de Chénier, p. 97.

[2] See Chapter XXXVI.

[3] Macaulay speaks of the trial of Charles I. in the following terms : 'That the ancient Constitution and the public opinion of England were directly opposed to regicide made regicide seem strangely fascinating to a party bent on effecting a complete political and social revolution. In

free himself before France and posterity of the imputation of
having wished to shed the blood of his people, Louis XVI. has
consented to play the part of a defendant, the only one which
would enable him to refute this odious charge.[1]   I would rather
that he had left to posterity the task of defending him, and had
disdained to reply to those who had no right to be his judges.

'You may be right,' said Chénier, 'and the attitude which you
wish Louis XVI. to have taken up was in reality the one that
the King himself preferred.' After hesitating for a few moments,
he drew a paper from his pocket and handed it to me. It was
the copy of a letter written by the King to M. de Malesherbes,
which ran as follows :

'I am unable to express to you, my dear Malesherbes, how deeply
sensible I am of your sublime devotion.

'You have done more than I could have wished ; your venerable
hand has been put forth to save me from the scaffold, and if my
throne were still left me, it would be my duty to share it with you
in order that I might be worthy of the remainder. But I have only
those chains the weight of which you have helped to lessen. I trust
that Heaven and your own conscience may bring you your reward.

'I entertain no false hopes respecting my fate. Those who are
ungrateful enough to have dethroned me will not stop in the middle
of their work. It would be too irksome for them to see their victims
continually before them. I shall share the fate of Charles I., and
my blood will flow to punish me for not having shed that of others.
But would it not be possible to lay down my life with dignity ?
The National Assembly contains the destroyers of my Monarchy,
my accusers, my judges, and probably my executioners. Such men
are impervious to argument, justice is not in them, and to move
their hearts is still more hopeless. Would it not be better to take

order to accomplish their purpose, it was necessary that they should first
break in pieces every part of the machinery of the Government, and this
necessity was rather agreeable than painful to them. The Commons
passed a vote tending to accommodation with the King. The soldiers
excluded the majority by force. The Lords unanimously rejected the
proposition that the King should be brought to trial. Their House was
instantly closed. No Court known to the law would take on itself the
office of judging the fountain of justice. A revolutionary tribunal was
created. That tribunal pronounced Charles a tyrant, a traitor, a murderer,
and a public enemy.'—'History of England,' vol. i., ch. i.

[1] See the words spoken by Louis XVI. before the Convention on
December 26, 1792, after the speech for the defence (*Moniteur*, 1792,
No. 363).

up a bold attitude, since the weakness of my defence cannot save me? I suggest an address, not to the Convention, but to the whole of France, which would judge my judges, and give me back that place in the heart of my people which I never deserved to lose. In that case I should merely refuse to recognise the jurisdiction of that tribunal before which I was forced to appear. I should preserve a dignified silence, and in condemning me the men who call themselves my judges would be no less than assassins.

'But, my dear Malesherbes, both you and Tronchet, who shares your devotion, are wiser than I. Compare my suggestions with yours; I subscribe blindly to whatever you may do. If you save my life, I shall use it only to remind you of what you have done. If it be taken, we shall meet, I trust, in the abode of immortality.

'LOUIS.'

After having carefully considered this delicate question, MM. de Malesherbes and Tronchet decided to advise Louis XVI. not to dispute the jurisdiction of the tribunal, and the royal prisoner acted upon that advice.[1]

---

[1] The King's letter to M. de Malesherbes was published for the first time in 1803 in the 'Correspondance Politique et Confidentielle inédite de Louis XVI.,' edited by Maria Helena Williams. Many of the documents contained in this collection are apocryphal, and were fabricated by Sulpice de la Platière and Babié. See Beuchot, *Journal de la Librairie*, June 13, 1818; Eckart, 'Une Lettre sur l'Education du Dauphin, attribuée à Louis XVI., est-elle authentique?' or, 'Observations sur les "Recueils de Lettres" publiés en 1803 et 1817 sous le Nom de ce Prince,' 1819; Barbier, 1869; Vatel, 'Vergniaud,' i. 59. The authenticity of the King's letter to Malesherbes is, nevertheless, indisputable; it was published in 1867 by Tocqueville from a copy taken from the original at Lausanne by the Baronne de Montboissier, the daughter of Malesherbes ('Extraits des Souvenirs inédits de M. le Comte de Tocqueville, Ancien Pair de France,' in the *Contemporain*, tome xii.).

CHAPTER XXXII.

Thursday, January 3, 1793.

ALL Royalist newspapers were suppressed on the Tenth of August. Since that date a few have reappeared. Brave men have been found who have dared to throw themselves once more into the breach, heedless of the dangers that await them, exposing their fortune, their liberty, and their life, and well aware that if they are not massacred, like Suleau, they will be guillotined like De Rozoi.[1] But what of that? Terrible as is the risk, they did not hesitate. These valiant men account it no small satisfaction to ease their conscience, to show the contempt they feel for the miserable wretches who govern us, and to say to that unhappy people of Paris, which is being so terribly deceived : ' *Louis XVI. was your best friend ! Louis XVI. is an honest man !*'

On September 21, the day on which the Convention decreed the abolition of the Monarchy, Étienne Feuillant, the former editor of the *Journal du Soir sans Réflexions*, published the first number of the *Journal du Soir de Politique et de Littérature.*[2]

The *Véridique, ou l'Antidote des Journaux*, appeared on October 1. Its editor is Corentin Royou, formerly editor of the *Ami du Roi.*[3]

[1] François Suleau, the journalist, was killed on the Tenth of August, his head being carried in triumph through the streets of Paris for two days ('François Suleau,' by Auguste Vitu).

[2] 'Étienne Feuillant, born at Brassac, Auvergne, founded the *Journal Général de France*, was arrested during the Hundred Days, and elected member of the Chambre des Députés for the department of the Maine-et-Loire in 1815. He died in 1838.

[3] Corentin Royou, a brother of the famous Abbé Royou, was born at Quimper, and died in Paris in 1828. On the 18th of Fructidor he was

On November 15 the *Journal Français, ou Tableau Politique et Littéraire de Paris* made its appearance, and started with a violent attack upon the Jacobins. It is edited by Gabriel Henri Nicolle.[1]

The same day saw the birth of the *Nouvelles Politiques Nationales et Etrangères*, intended by its founders to be a continuation of the *Gazette Universelle*, the presses of which were broken on the Tenth of August, and the editor, Antoine Marie Cerisier, obliged to flee from Paris. The *Nouvelles Politiques* is edited by Suard, a member of the Académie Française.[2]

Pariseau's *Feuille du Jour* was suppressed on the Tenth of August. On November 24 the brave writer founded the *Feuille du Matin, ou le Bulletin de Paris.*[3]

These sheets do not conceal their Royalist sympathies, a fact which exposes them to incessant persecution on the part of our Republicans, partisans, as is well known, of the unbounded liberty of the Press. The *Feuille du Matin* was obliged to stop on December 30 last.[4] The *Véridique* has been so mercilessly tracked by the Jacobins that, since October 1, Corentin Royou has had the greatest trouble in publishing four or five numbers.[5]

We are living at a time when the list of subscribers to a

---

transported to the Ile de Ré. He wrote several excellent historical treatises, the tragedies of 'Phocion' and of 'La Mort de César, and 'Le Frondeur,' a comedy in verse.

[1] Gabriel Henri Nicolle, aided by his brother, the Abbé Nicolle, the friend of the Duc de Richelieu, founded the Collège de Sainte-Barbe, now the Collège Rollin, in the Rue des Postes, in 1821, and was the principal until his death, in 1829.

[2] Antoine Suard, born at Besançon on January 16, 1733, died at Paris on July 20, 1817. From February 20, 1803, he was permanent Secretary to the Académie.

[3] Pierre Germain Pariseau, dramatic author and journalist, was born in Paris in 1753. He was condemned to death by the Revolutionary tribunal on July 10, 1794, and went to the scaffold with the son of Buffon and forty-two other victims.

[4] The editors of the *Feuille du Matin* were not only brave and clever men, but possessed perseverance that under the circumstances may be termed heroic. Obliged to suspend the publication of their paper on December 30, 1792, they resumed it on January 28, 1793, and continued until March 29 following, when they were once more condemned to silence. On April 23, 1793, the *Feuille du Matin* reappeared for a few days only; on the 28th it definitely ceased to appear.

[5] Eugène Hatin, 'Bibliographie de la Presse Périodique Française,' p. 238. Only ten numbers of the *Véridique* appeared in all, between October, 1792, and March, 1793, when it stopped altogether.

paper may be suddenly turned into a list of proscribed, and
when consequently the sheets suspected of aristocratic or
moderate leanings cannot depend upon a large number of
readers. It is, no doubt, this fact that inspired M. Gautier,
the former editor of the *Journal Général de la Cour et de la
Ville*, and M. La Pie de Lafage, with the idea of starting a
newspaper to be placarded.[1] The *Bulletin de Paris*, by Gautier,
and the *Avertisseur*, by La Pie de Lafage, posted up on all the
walls of the capital, are naturally perused by all passers-by who
can read. At first sight they have the appearance of an ordinary
poster, but on closer examination the nature of the interesting
matter thus placed before the public is easily distinguishable
from the worthless rubbish around it. The number of the
Avertisseur posted up this morning quotes a long passage from
an ' Address presented by 150 Communes of Normandy to the
National Convention upon the trial of Louis XVI.' The following are the last lines :

' The reply that we require to this address is the person of our
King. After having had it printed to inform France of our resolution, after having invited all true Frenchmen to unite with us, and
to free themselves from the yoke of fearful regicides, we will go
and seek our Sovereign, tear him from the hands of his executioners,
and, if they have already committed their crime, avenge him with
their blood.'

Every day the agitation caused by the King's trial manifests
itself in energetic protests, pamphlets, and addresses ; in posters
and in newspaper articles, in petitions to the Convention, and
in demonstrations in the public streets.

Since the opening of the trial many brave citizens have
solicited the dangerous honour of defending the King. M. Huet
de Guerville, formerly a barrister in the *Parlement* of Normandy,
was the first to offer his services, on November 13. After him
came M. Sourdat, formerly Lieutenant-General of Police at
Troyes ; M. Gustave Graindorge, a former Adjutant-General ;
and M. Guillaume, an old member of the Constituent Assembly.

On the evening of the day when Target's strange desertion

[1] Gautier and **La Pie de Lafage** were arrested during the first days of
January, 1793 (*Journal des Débats et des Décrets de la Convention
Nationale*, sitting of January 9, 1793).

was known, M. Tronson du Coudray assembled the principal advocates who have during these last few months resumed the exercise of their profession. Bellart, Berryer, Delacrox-Frainville, Blacque, Chauveau Lagarde, Bareau du Colombier, Bitouzet des Linières, and several others, answered his call. They were unanimous in deciding that if the King's choice should fall upon one of them, all the others would assist him as counsel.[1]

To the list of honour given above it is only right to add the names of MM. Malouet, Mounier, Cazates, and Lally-Tolendal, old members of the Constituent Assembly;[2] of MM. Piet,[3] Christophe Lavaux,[4] and Ducancel,[5] members of the Paris Bar; of M. Bouvier, barrister in the former *Parlement* of Dijon;[6] of M. Louvel de Valroger, an advocate of Grandville;[7] of M. de Pastoret, formerly President of the Legislative Assembly;[8] of M. Chassaignon, of Lyons;[9] and of M. Former, of Soissons.[10]

As soon as Louis XVI. had definitely chosen for his counsel MM. de Malesherbes, Tronchet, and Desèze, there was no further excuse for applying to the Convention for permission to defend him there. There remained only the Press, and the number of those who adopted this means of writing on the King's behalf was considerable.

His former Ministers were not behindhand in their duty. M. Necker, who had been appointed Comptroller-General three times,[11] published, on October 30, 1792, 'Reflections upon the Approaching Trial of Louis XVI.' From M. de Narbonne, the old Minister of War,[12] and from his successor, the Chevalier de

---

[1] 'Souvenirs de M. Berryer, Doyen des Avocats de Paris, de 1774 à 1838,' tome i., p. 146.

[2] 'Mémoires de Malouet,' tome ii., p. 267.

[3] 'Correspondance de M. de Serre,' tome ii., p. 109.

[4] 'Les Campagnes d'un Avocat, ou Anecdotes pour servir à l'Histoire de la Révolution,' by Christophe Lavaux. 1815.

[5] 'Esquisses Historiques,' etc., by Ch. Ducancel. 1821.

[6] 'Biographie des Hommes Vivants' (1816), tome i.

[7] 'Revue des Questions Historiques,' January, 1877.

[8] 'Etudes Critiques sur les Girondins,' by A. Nettement, p. 132.

[9] 'Biographie Universelle,' by Michaud, tome lx.

[10] *Mercure Français*, December, 1792.

[11] He was in office from October 22, 1776, to May 19, 1781; from August 25, 1788, to July 11, 1789; and from July 29, 1789, to September 4, 1790.

[12] From December 7, 1791, to March 10, 1792.

Graves,[1] we have a 'Declaration '[2] and an ' Address to Citizens,'[3] in which they refute those accusations brought against the King referring to the period of their ministry. M. Bertrand de Moleville, formerly Minister of Marine, has written quite a number of pamphlets; the last, ' Denunciation to the National Convention of Prevarications committed in the Trial of Louis XVI.,' fully establishes the King's innocence and the baseness of his accusers.

Many of those who would have been glad to defend the King before the Convention have written and published their speeches. Amongst these are Malouet, Lally - Tolendal,[4] Guillaume, Sourdat, and Huet de Guerville.

Other brave-hearted men who published defences of Louis XVI. are J. B. Dalmas, member for the Ardèche in the Legislative Assembly; the Chevalier de Rougeville; M. le Grand; M. Myèvre, of Lyons; M. l'Abbé Corbin, tutor to the first Dauphin; M. Larocque, Queen's Chamberlain; M. Riston; M. Lacroix, Professor of Law at the Lycée; M. Drappeau, formerly Professor of Elocution at the University of Valence; M. Brochart de Saron, formerly President, and M. Gin, formerly Councillor, of the Parlement of Paris; M. Pichois; M. Louis Mazon; M. Barbier, of Nantes; M. Pulcherante; M. de Foulaines; M. Flécheux; M. Dugour; M. d'Yvrande d'Herville; M. l'Abbé de Salignac; M. Hubert-Parvillers, Judge of the Civil Tribunal of Saint-Quentin; and MM. Failly, Lauraguais, and Mazo d'Entraigues.

Some of these productions are of great length and importance. Such is, for instance, the ' Mémoire Justificatif pour Louis XVI.,' by A. J. Dugour, a work of no less than 250 pages. Longer still is the ' Défense Préliminaire de Louis XVI.,' by M. de Foulaines, which was published, in seven parts, during the

---

[1] From March 10 to May 8, 1792.
[2] 'Déclaration de M. Louis de Narbonne dans le Procès du Roi.'
[3] From December 7, 1791, to March 10, 1792.
[4] The ' Plaidoyer du Comte de Lally-Tolendal pour Louis XVI.' is full of deep feeling, and rises in parts to heights of eloquence. The author had taken for his epigraph these lines from Plutarch : ' Agistrate threw himself upon his son's body, and, kissing it tenderly, said, " O my son ! It is the excess of thy gentleness and goodness, it is thy great indulgence and mercy, which has ruined thee and undone us too." '

month of December. The manuscript of each part was submitted to M. de Malesherbes before being sent to the printer. The work contains the text of all the resolutions relating to Louis XVI. moved at the Jacobin Club by members of the Convention since the beginning of the trial, and which the *Journal des Débats* of the club itself has given in a very incomplete form. It was the Abbé Emery, formerly director of the seminary of Saint-Sulpice, who hit upon the idea of having these motions printed and published immediately after each sitting of the club, in order that the votes of the authors of such motions might be challenged in the Convention as those of persons prejudiced against the King.

As for pamphlets published anonymously, I have more than a hundred on my table. Their pages, composed in haste and written with a feverish hand, have been printed by men who risk their liberty, and perhaps their life. Will they save that of the King? Alas! that is scarcely to be hoped. Some of the matter has found its way into the Temple, and has afforded the martyr King great consolation. He will thus have heard, even in the retirement of his cell, mingled with the revolutionary cries of hatred, cries of love and loyalty from honest Christian France!

CHAPTER XXXIII.

Saturday, January 5, 1793.

At the sitting of January 2, the Girondist Carra, editor of the
Annales Patriotiques, attempted to reply to the speech delivered
by Desèze for the defence.   In this harangue, full of gross
invective and gratuitous insults, the deputy for Saône-et-Loire
was obliged to admit that proofs were wanting to establish the
principal count in the charge, that of treason.   'How,' he cried,
' does the defender of Louis Capet explain his client's innocence
with regard to the coalition of foreign despots?   By the
fictitious correspondence which Montmorin and Lessart took
care to leave in the pigeon-holes of the Foreign Office, they
having for a long time expected an invasion there, and prepared
a plan for making the people believe that neither Louis nor
his Ministers have taken part in that coalition; but the true
and secret correspondence has either been hidden in walls, burnt,
or buried.'[1]

According, therefore, to Carra's own confession, all the documents in the Foreign Office helped to establish the King's
innocence.   But for Carra and his colleagues these documents,
although lying before them, have no existence, the only documents they recognise being those which must have been hidden
in walls, burnt, or buried.   The iron cupboard has been discovered, the documents hidden in the walls of the Tuileries have
been found, and not a single one contradicts the correspondence
left behind by MM. de Montmorin and de Lessart.   Besides,

[1] *Journal des Débats et des Décrets,* No. 107.

are not the facts in this case more eloquent than all revealed or secret documents?

If Louis XVI. had had the intentions imputed to him, if he had wished to introduce foreign armies into France, he had simply to precipitate us into a war. War would have rendered inevitable such an alliance as, according to his accusers, was to his tastes and his interests; he would then have had the double advantage of preserving his popularity whilst entering into relations with foreign Powers, and of introducing into France the armies which would have enabled him to re-establish his rights and his authority. Is this what he did?

War was declared, it is true, but by whom? By the Legislative Assembly—by those who in that Assembly fought most fiercely against the King's authority and rights. It was Isnard who already on November 29, 1791, cried: 'War is the only recourse left you,' and who, on January 5, 1792, flung the following incendiary words at the excited Assembly: 'War is at our gates—a war which is indispensable to the consummation of the Revolution. The opportunity for embarking upon such a war is too valuable to be missed. A free France is about to enter into combat with an enslaved Europe. We must undertake this war.'[1] It was Vergniaud who, on December 27, 1791, proposed an *Address to the French*, in which he strongly advocated a war, declaring that it was the duty of France to propagate, sword in hand, the principles of the Revolution.[2] It was Brissot who, at the sitting of December 29, delivered a speech that created a sensation throughout the whole of Europe, and in which these words occurred: 'Therefore war is necessary; France must undertake it for its own honour. At the present moment war would be a national blessing, and the only calamity to be feared is that it may be averted.'[3] It was Gensonné who, at the sitting of January 14, 1792, cried: 'Tell the King that war is necessary, that public opinion desires it, and that the safety of the Empire demands it.'[4] It was a Diplomatic Committee, in which Brissot and his friends were predominant, that persuaded the Assembly to pass a decree on

[1] *Moniteur* for 1792, No. 6.
[2] *Ibid.*, January 11, 1792.
[3] *Ibid.* for 1791, Nos. 364 and 365.
[4] *Ibid.* for 1792, No. 15.

January 25, 1792, which made war inevitable. In this decree
it was said that if the Emperor of Germany had not given the
nation full and complete satisfaction before March 1 next his
silence or any evasive and dilatory reply would be looked upon
as a declaration of war.[1]   It was Dumouriez who, appointed to
the Ministry of Foreign Affairs by the Girondist party, proceeded to the Jacobin Club on March 14, the day before he
entered on his duties,[2] and, waving a red cap, announced, amidst
great applause, that war was not far off. Lastly, it was the
Legislative Assembly that at its sitting of April 20, 1792,
declared war against the Emperor of Germany.

It was therefore—and nothing is clearer—the Assembly and
the Brissot party who desired this war[3] to which the King was
so much opposed.[4]   When he was compelled to submit to it,
and when, before the deputies who had forced it upon him, he

---

[1] *Moniteur* for 1792, No. 26.

[2] General Dumouriez was Minister of Foreign Affairs from March 15
to June 13, 1792.

[3] See Taine's 'Révolution,' tome ii., p. 120, etc. ; Masson's 'Département des Affaires Étrangères pendant la Révolution,' ch. ii., iii., and iv. ;
and our 'Légende des Girondins,' ch. viii.

[4] Of this there is no possible doubt. See the 'Mémoires du Marquis
de Bouillé,' 'written,' according to M. Barrière, ' with a soldier's simplicity
and the veracity of an honest man.' On p. 309 he says : 'On September 12, 1791, I had been sent for by the Emperor Leopold . . . and I
then took the liberty of asking His Majesty whether he was informed of
the real intentions of the King. He said he was ; he knew that that
Monarch was averse to violent measures. . . . I was certain that after
the conference of Pilnitz the Emperor would not have agreed to this pacific
and extremely reasonable plan unless he had consulted Louis XVI., who
had always desired some arrangement and the employment of negotiations
rather than more violent measures.' He further says, on the same page
'The refugees were desirous of making an attack upon Strasburg, in
which city they relied upon friends who would have opened the gates.
The King, who was informed of the plan, commanded, and even begged,
them not to carry it out, and not to commit any act of violence. To this
effect he sent the Baron de Vioménil and the Chevalier de Coigny to the
Princes, his brothers, to express to them his disapproval of the arming of
the French nobility, to which the Emperor also strongly objected.'
And, further, on p. 312 : 'The Emperor, after the acceptance of the Constitution by the King, had again received the Ambassador of France,
whom he had previously forbidden to appear at his Court. He was even
the first to admit into his ports vessels flying the national colours. The
Courts of Madrid, St. Petersburg, and Stockholm were the only ones
which at that moment withdrew their Ambassadors from Paris. All these
details help to prove that the views of the Emperor Leopold were for
peace, and that they were formed under the influence of Louis XVI.'

uttered these words, 'According to the terms of the Convention it is my duty to formally propose a war against the King of Hungary and Bohemia,' his eyes filled with tears.[1]   It is a well-known fact that in a State Council held in the month of April last he expressed himself most strongly against any war.[2] He even demanded (what he had never done before at any Council meeting) that the separate and signed consent of each of his Ministers should be handed to him, so that he himself should be free of all responsibility before the nation and posterity.[3]   On this point, too, we have the admission of his bitterest foes, of Brissot himself, who on January 9, 1792, wrote in the *Patriote Français:* '" We do not want an offensive war," say some misled Patriots, " because the Court demands it."   The Court did indeed demand it, or appeared to do so for a moment ; but it has really never desired it, and desires it to-day less than ever.   Such is the sense of those cleverly-worded messages which have been sent to the National Assembly in order to prevent it from adopting a vigorous policy.'

Before April 20, the date of the declaration of war, there was no pretext for the pretended treason of Louis XVI. ; let us see whether such pretext was found between April 20 and the Tenth of August.

Mallet du Pan, the bravest and wisest of our journalists, having resolved at the end of April to give up the editorship of the *Mercure de France* and to leave the kingdom, Louis XVI., by Malouet's advice, took advantage of this to ask M. Mallet to go to Vienna, Berlin, and Coblentz in order to acquaint his brothers, as well as the Emperor and the King of Prussia, with his intentions and views respecting the war and its consequences. Mallet du Pan left Paris on May 21 with instructions drawn up by Malouet and corrected by the King, and bearing a ' Mémoire' which, though written by himself, had been revised by Louis XVI. and entirely approved by him.[4]   Although these

---

[1] ' Mémoires Tirés des Papiers d'un Homme d'État,' tome i., p. 333.

[2] ' Mémoires de Mme. Campan,' tome ii., p. 222.

[3] ' Lettre de Servan à Mallet du Pan,' in tome ii. of the ' Mémoires de Malouet,' second edition.   Servan was Minister of War from May 10 to September 25, 1792.

[4] ' Mémoires de Malouet,' tome ii., p. 210, and ' Mémoires et Correspondance du Mallet du Pan,' tome i., p. 208, etc.

documents were not seen by the friends of Mallet du Pan, they
have it from a reliable source that the ideas and wishes he was
about to lay before the Emperor Francis I.[1] and King Frederick
William in the name of Louis XVI. were in full conformity
with his own principles.   No one had a greater horror of war,
no one had made greater efforts to save France from such a
curse at home or abroad.[2]   No one, on the other hand, was
more alive to the necessity of giving France a constitutional
government ; a partisan of mixed governments and of limited
monarchies,[3] he was one of those who had always said with
Malouet : 'There can be no stability in any absolute government that succeeds the present Revolution.'[4]

The following is the substance of the instructions given to
the King's Envoy, particulars of which I received from the Abbé
Morellet, to whom M. de Malesherbes has frequently spoken
about them :

'To urge upon Monsieur, upon the Comte d'Artois, and the
French refugees the desirability of not allowing the present war
by any act of theirs to lose its character of a foreign war carried
on between one Power and another ; to intimate to them that
in any case the King would never allow them to enter France
with the hostile armies, either as auxiliaries or at the head of
separate forces.[5]

'To obtain from the Courts of Vienna and Berlin a formal
declaration that they had no intention of destroying the
integrity of the kingdom, that they were ready to conclude a

---

[1] The Emperor Leopold II., the brother of Marie Antoinette, had died
on March 2, 1792.   The eldest of his sixteen children succeeded him, by
the title of Francis I., and reigned for forty-three years, from 1792 to
1835.

[2] In the *Mercure de France*, December, 1791, No. 51, Mallet du Pan
wrote : 'I separate myself from the band of those who invoke war at
any price ; it is impossible for a true friend of the Monarchy to look forward to such war without apprehension.'   And in the first number of
January, 1792, we find : 'I have said, and I shall not cease to repeat what
facts will soon repeat more energetically still, that the war will complete the dissolution of the Monarchy.'

[3] See Sainte-Beuve's remarkable and judicious article on Mallet du Pan
in his 'Causeries du Lundi,' tome iv.

[4] 'Mémoires et Correspondance de Mallet du Pan,' tome i., p. 282.

[5] 'Mémoires de Malouet,' tome ii., p. 210.

peace, but that they could only treat with the King, and that
it was therefore necessary to restore him his full liberty.'[1]

When Louis XVI. gave these instructions to Mallet du Pan
in May last, he was certainly not inviting a foreign enemy into
France. Those who had already called them here in the month
of April were the King's enemies, the men who had involved us
in a war—in spite of Louis XVI., be it remembered—and who
had done so with the idea—nay, the hope—that our troops
might be beaten. Was it not their leader, was it not Brissot,
the Republican, who openly declared that when he had
advocated war it was with the conviction that the foreign troops
would invade our territory as conquerors, and that our defeat
would be the signal for the fall of the Monarchy?

'It was the abolition of the Monarchy that I had in view
when declaring war,' wrote Brissot on October 4 last in a letter
'To all the Republicans of France concerning the Jacobin Club
in Paris.' 'Men of sense understood me when on December 30,
1791, allaying Robespierre's fears of treason, I said : "*I have
only one fear, and that is that we shall not be betrayed.*" We
want to be betrayed—our safety lies in that—for there is still
a good deal of poison in the bosom of France, and strong
explosions are required to remove it.'

Brissot and his friends, to whom power did not seem too dearly
bought even at the price of blood and national defeat, were at
first admirably served. The opening of the campaign was
marked by two serious reverses at Mons and at Tournay.[2] It
was in the face of this situation, for which he was not responsible, that Louis XVI., interposing between the hostile
armies and his kingdom, asked the King of Prussia and the
Emperor to distinguish between the nation and the factionists,
and, whatever happened, to respect the integrity of our territory.
Every good Frenchman must be grateful to him for having used
the remnant of his influence for the good of his country.

Poor France! Her Patriots are men like Brissot and Carra—
Brissot, who wished to place the Duke of York upon the French

---

[1] 'Mémoires et Correspondance de Mallet du Pan,' tome i., p. 282, etc.
[2] April 28, 1792.

throne;[1] Carra, who both in his paper and at the Jacobin Club proposed to place the crown of France upon the head of the Duke of Brunswick.[2] The country's enemy is said to be Louis XVI.! Louis XVI., whose heart has never beaten except for the happiness of his people and the glory of his country! Is it not he who by great perseverance has raised our navy to its present state of efficiency and enabled it to carry the French flag victoriously through the seas of the world? Was it not by his orders that important works were carried out in the ports of Agde, Port-Vendres, Bayonne, la Rochelle, Rochefort, Lorient and Brest, and that at Cherbourg were commenced those magnificent works thrown out as a defiance to England?[3] On the eve of the Revolution had he not placed France at the head of European nations, and was it not he who in 1787 put a stop to the war between Russia and Turkey? Were not the following words uttered in the English House of Commons in January, 1787, by the illustrious Fox: 'From St. Petersburg to Lisbon the French Court rules all the Cabinets of Europe with the exception of that of Vienna'? And was it not the clever as well as energetic policy of the King which had even some years before caused Lord Chatham to say, not in the House of Commons, but in the Privy Council: 'England will never enjoy the supremacy of the sea and of commerce as long as the Bourbon dynasty exists'?[4] If the King's trial lasts for another fortnight, and if on January 20, 1793, Louis XVI. is still at the bar of the Convention, will he not be able to say to his judges: 'Ten years ago—on January 20, 1783—I signed the preliminaries of peace

---

[1] 'Mémoires de Barère,' edited by Carnot and David d'Angers, tome ii., pp. 43-45.

[2] Meeting of the Jacobin Club on January 4, 1792. See the explanations given by Carra himself in the *Annales Patriotiques* of January 9; see also *Révolutions de Paris*, No. 159.

[3] In his correspondence with Washington, Governor Morris tells us that in 1792 the French Patriots offered England, as a price for her neutrality in the war between France and the Emperor, the cession of Tabago, the extension of the treaty of commerce, and the destruction of the works at Cherbourg. 'Thus,' adds the translator of Morris, 'it was Louis XVI., who had built the port of Cherbourg, who was accused of connivance with the foreign foe, whilst those who claimed the exclusive right to be called Patriots proposed to England the destruction of that port.'

[4] 'Esprit de M. Pitt,' by Luneau de Boisgermain.

with England at Versailles, forcing the natural enemy of France to recognise the independence of the United States, to return the captured colonies to Holland, and Minorca and Florida to Spain. I further compelled her to strike out from the Treaty of Utrecht the clause relating to Dunkirk, and to cede to France the island of Tabago, the river Senegal and its dependencies, Forts Saint Louis, Podoc, Galam, Arquin and Portandick on the coast of Africa, and in India the districts of Valanour and Bahour and the territories bordering upon Karikal'?

'The Letter from Louis XVI. to his Brothers,' from which we have already had occasion to quote (see Chapter XXVI.), and the sincerity of which cannot be impugned, since it was intended to be kept secret, and was, as a matter of fact, not published until 1835, leaves no doubt concerning the King's feelings with regard to the intervention of foreign arms.   We submit the following passages

'Force can only be employed by foreign arms, and only introduced under pretence of war.   Can a King be allowed to carry war into his own States ?   Is not the remedy worse than the evil ?   I know that there is an idea of raising immense forces in order to render resistance impossible, and thus prevent bloodshed ; but has the state of the kingdom and the vested interests of those who are now in power been taken into consideration?   All the leaders, that is to say, those who are able to influence the people, will think they risk too much by surrender ; they will never believe that their crimes will be pardoned or forgotten, and the offer of an amnesty would scarcely reassure them.   On the contrary, they will think themselves able to make better terms sword in hand than in a bloodless surrender.   They will press into their service the National Guards and other armed bodies, and gain their attachment by calling upon them to defend the cause of the people and to resist its enemies.   They will even take the offensive by throwing themselves upon the aristocrats in order to make the parties more divided ; and when this example has first been given in Paris and by the Assembly, will it not be followed throughout the country ?   War would therefore be inevitable, since all those who are in authority are interested in bringing it about ; it would be horrible, because its principles would be violence and despair.   Can a King coolly face all these misfortunes and bring them upon his people ?

'I know that Kings have always made it a point of honour to regain by force what had been taken from them, and that fear of the evils of war is in such a case called weakness.   But I confess that these reproaches affect me less than the unhappiness of my people, and I am sick at heart when I think of the horrors which I should cause. I know how greatly the nobility and clergy have suffered by the Revolution, and that they have been rewarded for all the sacrifices that they had so generously proposed by the destruction of their property and the forfeiture of their lives. It would be impossible to be more unfortunate, and to have deserved it less, but is it right to punish a crime by committing others? I, too, have suffered, but I feel brave enough to suffer more rather than to inflict my misfortunes upon my people.

'. . . Many hopes are staked upon the success of the war. . . . But the foreign troops will not be able to stay in the kingdom, and when they are gone how will the country be governed in case of fresh insubordination? And how can that be avoided if the spirit of the nation has not changed? . . . If we were successful to-day in getting rid of the Constitution, the people would always have an idea that it would have been the true means of happiness, and when the troops, who had helped us to get rid of it, had left the kingdom, this chimera would be sufficient to agitate the people unceasingly, whilst the Government would find itself in a position opposed to the public spirit, yet without the means of restraining it. A nation can never be governed contrary to its accepted principles. . . . The accepted principles of this nation lie in the rights of man, mad as they are. An immense force could not govern it for long upon contrary principles; how, then, could it be done at all if that force were withdrawn?

'. . . I have thought it well over, and it is my opinion that war produces nothing but horrors, and always discord. In my opinion the idea must be discarded.

'. . . I have therefore preferred peace to war because it has appeared to me more virtuous as well as more useful; I have gone over to the people because it was the only means of winning them back; and of two systems I preferred that which was least obnoxious to my people and my conscience.'—*Revue Rétrospective*, serie ii., tome ii., pp. 50-57.

Amongst the judges of Louis XVI., Carnot stands forth as a type of the honest and proud Republican—Carnot, who, as a member of the Committee of Public Safety, was for several months one of the feeders of the guillotine, and of whom M. Lanfrey, whose testimony in this instance is of real value, said : 'He had become so accustomed to sign documents blindly that one day two of his clerks were arrested upon an order signed by him, on another day the innkeeper who served him with his meals, on a third day the lady in whose house he lodged, and all without his knowledge. On this being brought to his notice, he remained no less attached to the functions which imposed such horrible duties upon him—an impossible and abominable *rôle*, repulsive alike to conscience and honour. . . .' (' Portraits et Études Politiques,' p. 110). The Patriot Brissot would have given the throne to the Duke of York, while the Patriot Carra would have given it to the Duke of Brunswick. Several years later, in 1817, the Patriot Carnot, following their example, took part in a conspiracy which aimed at placing a foreign Prince upon the throne of France ; it is true that this Prince was, like the Duke of Brunswick and the Duke of York, a Protestant. Thanks to the information furnished by a Revolutionary historian, we are in possession of all the details of this plot.

An acting committee, composed of such tried Patriots as Generals de Lafayette, de Thiard, Corbineau and Merlin, Colonel Duchand, MM. de Voyer-d'Argenson, de Saint-Aignan, Combes-Sieyès and Chevallier, met at M. de Lafayette's house in Paris, and kept up a close correspondence with the French refugees in Brussels. Both refugees and members of the committee were determined to invoke the aid of foreign arms, and, supported by them, to place upon the throne of France the Prince of Orange, son of the King of the Netherlands, and brother-in-law of the Emperor of Russia.

' A plan was soon concocted,' says M. de Vaulabelle. ' This was in 1817. The 150,000 foreign troops forming the army of occupation that had remained in France were mostly encamped on the frontiers of Belgium, and included a certain number of Belgian regiments, as well as a large body of Russian troops under the command of General Woronzoff. It was with the help of this body and these regiments that the plan was to be carried out. The Comte de Woronzoff, however, required an order from Alexander before lending the support of his army to this attempt ; it was agreed that to obtain this authority a man should be sent whose name and character would command the Czar's confidence. General Max Lamarque, then in retirement in Amsterdam, was suggested ; two exiles, Commandant Brice and J. B. Teste, formerly Chief of the Police at Lyons,[1] went to him with a proposal of this mission, but he refused it on the grounds of the gratitude he owed the King of the Netherlands. Carnot, who had at first fled to Warsaw, was then living at Magdeburg ; to him MM. Teste and Brice betook themselves. "The accession of a Protestant Prince would be a good thing for France," replied Carnot ; " I am ready to go to Alexander." But there was no occasion for him to undertake the journey ; the

---

[1] J. B. Teste, the same who as a peer of France and President of the Cour de Cassation, figured in the trial of the Gouhenans Mines in 1847.

two envoys of the refugees of Brussels had scarcely left Magdeburg when Alexander, indirectly informed of the plans of his brother-in-law, despatched General Czernicheff to that Prince to intimate to him that he would do well to abstain from making any attempt against the royal Government of France.'[1]

Carnot, Brissot, and Carra, Republicans who ask for a King, but only on condition that he be doubly a stranger to France, both by nationality and religion—these are the men who sent Louis XVI. to the scaffold for having betrayed his country!

[1] Achille de Vaulabelle, 'Histoire des Deux Restorations,' tome iv., p. 444.

CHAPTER XXXIV.

Sunday, January 6, 1793.

It was Dante who said in his ' Inferno ': ' I know of no greater misery than that of recalling in days of trouble the happiness that is past.' To-day is Twelfth Day! What a glorious festival that used to be! Parents, children, and grand-children would all sit around the family table with the eldest of the company at the head. The cake was cut into equal parts, which the youngest of the children distributed blindfolded ; the guest who got the bean was proclaimed King, and what shouts there used to be when he chose his Queen! What cheers there were when he raised his glass to his lips! ' *The King drinks!* ' *The King drinks!* In this *fête*, which was held to commemorate the stable of Bethlehem, the poor were never forgotten ; their share was always carefully put aside. In the country it was the custom for one of the children to stand on the threshold and invite the first poor person who passed to enter ; he was made to sit down next to the head of the house, and hospitality was extended to him till the morrow, his presence at the table and under that roof being looked upon as a blessing from Heaven. With the poor man's share were always reserved two other portions no less sacred—the share of the absent one and the share of the Lord. Unhappy is he in whom the simple name ' Twelfth Night ' does not awaken tender recollections! Such a one has never known the delights of a home.

The King of the Bean has found no favour in the sight of the Revolution ; this humble Monarchy has also had its Fourteenth of July and its Tenth of August. I was just reading in Gorjy's work—in those little volumes that hide so many serious truths under a peculiar title and an airy form[1]—an account of Twelfth Night, or the *Fête* of the Kings, in the year of grace 1792.

The hero of that novel—if it may be called a novel—is well known. Jean Claude 'Ann'quin Bredouille is an excellent man—he is, in fact, no other than Jacques Bonhomme himself —who is more willing to follow the inspirations of a little toady called *Adule* (Vanity) than those of *Mme. Jer'nifle* (Reason, sometimes scolding and cross), or of the *Dame de Liesse*, the good old Gaiety of yore. This *Dame de Liesse* was, however, ' the friend of his father, of his grandfather, of his great-grand-father, and of all his family, and never failed to visit him, especially on high holy-days, such as Christmas, New Year's Day, Shrove Tuesday, Easter, April 1, and on the occasions of marriages and baptisms.'[2]

Circumvented and incited by Adule, who reproaches him with his too modest station in life, and with his too limited ambitions, and who is constantly repeating, 'Glory, my dear Bredouille—glory, glory!' Jean Claude leaves his native village, and arrives in the capital of the *Néomanes*. He has been putting up for some time at an inn of that great city, when his host invites him and the other guests to keep the 'Feast of the Kings' with him.

'Our landlord,' says the niece of 'Ann'quin Bredouille—for it is she who narrates her uncle's adventures—'our landlord had invited rather a large number of guests. As each one arrived, I hastened to look into his eyes to see whether he had been one of the friends of the *Dame de Liesse*, and whether he still remembered her All seemed as though they had never known her, or at least as if they had entirely forgotten her. Instead of the gaiety that I expected, instead of that flow of joy which was formerly never absent from this festival, they wrangled about trifles, and held discussions in bitter tones when pleasure and joy should alone have animated them.'

---

[1] ''Ann'quin Bredouille, ou le Petit-Cousin de Tristram Shandy,' six vols., 1791, 1792. The author of this very remarkable work, which would, indeed, not have disgraced Sterne, was Jean Claude Gorjy. He was born at Fontainebleau in 1753, and died at Pinceloup, near Rambouillet, in 1795. For Gorjy, see 'Les Originaux du Siècle Dernier,' by C. H. Monselet.

[2] ''Ann'quin Bredouille,' tome i., p. 53.

As Gorjy's book—this living picture of Paris and of France in 1792—has already become extremely rare, and will before long have entirely disappeared, I will continue to quote from it.

'We sit down to table. The cake is cut up ready for distribution. In my young days this task was given to the smallest child, so that it might be presented by Innocence. But, there! they have changed all that; it was Adule. . . .

'I am persuaded that it was sheer malice on his part to make the bean come to my uncle.

'"Hurrah!" cried the latter, as soon as he saw the bean—"hurrah! I am the King!"'

'"M. Bredouille," said the landlord, "are you still such a simpleton as to be really glad?"

'"Certainly. Although the *rôle* is not a long one, it is a fine one to play. I am rather a glutton; I shall have the best bits, and whenever I drink I shall hear a shout of joy, of which, by the way, you seem to be sadly in want."

'They looked at him with an air of pity. He went on:

'"But there is only true happiness when it is shared. I am in need of a Queen, and this is yours, mademoiselle," he added, throwing the bean into his neighbour's glass.

'My uncle was both a connoisseur and a gallant; he was on the point of formulating a compliment which since the existence of the family of Bredouille has never failed to make a hit upon similar occasions.

'But his fine compliment froze on his lips, and my poor uncle stood with mouth wide open as he saw his fair neighbour faint almost away. . . .

'After a moment's silence the new Queen exclaimed, amidst her sobs:

'"Ah, monsieur, what harm have I done you to play me such a wicked trick?"

'Those for whom I am writing this chapter are no doubt filled with astonishment at reading the maiden's words; but what will they say when I tell them that Sir 'Ann'quin Bredouille as well as his neighbour (who was unanimously condemned to share his fate) was obliged to take his place at a small side-table seated on a rickety stool, which it required all one's dexterity to balance? The large table, according to custom, sent a share of everything to the little one; but, contrary to custom, it did not send the best morsels, and the wine that was sent was largely diluted with water. We must explain that the new manner of celebrating this feast being in every way opposed to the old method, the old-fashioned honours were replaced by spiteful tricks that were perpetrated by the guests with much zest.

'It was thought great fun, for example, to rub the plates for the little table with bitter aloes, to serve them with fine empty dishes, or with pies made of a thin crust only, to give them candles containing crackers, and so on.

'As each fresh trick was played upon them, Adule called for general applause.

'If, on the other hand, anyone, from force of habit, cried: "The King drinks!" he was instantly made the butt of the whole company, and banished from the table.

'Mme. Jer'nifle wished to take the part of the first one who had yielded to this involuntary movement. She only succeeded in setting all the guests (to whom, by the way, she was already very distasteful) against her, and, thinking to punish her, they sent her to the small table. This was not all. When the time came for dessert, uproar took the place of the *Dame de Liesse*. She, too, had a large following, but instead of the chubby urchins of Gaiety, they were cross-grained churlish little devils, always wrangling. On entering they threw upon the table an apple of discord, on which was written *the burning question*.

'The apple had hardly left their hands, when a frightful din ensued. Noise led to blows. In vain did Mme. Jer'nifle, my uncle, and his partner do all they could to stop the fight. They ran the risk of getting cuffed themselves, and they were now thoroughly convinced that it was a great misfortune to have the bean, for according to one of the new customs my uncle had to pay the damage.'

How many houses were there more unlucky even than the inn at which 'Ann'quin Bredouille had put up, and in which, on January 6, 1792, no woman so reasonable as Mme. Jer'nifle would have been found! The majority of the Patriots made a point of closing their doors on that day to relatives, friends, cakes, and beans; the bean especially was mercilessly proscribed. This proscription, however, was not general, to the great grief of the austere editors of the *Révolutions de Paris*, who, in their number of January 14, wrote: 'This kind of pleasure has somewhat abated under the Revolution. The habit has, nevertheless, been kept up this year in a fairly large number of circles. All colleges and private schools have remained faithful to the custom, this despot of pedants and fools.' Besides, on January 6,

1792, the Patriots had other things to do than drawing the bean and putting aside the share of the poor, of the absent, and of the Lord. Had they not to be present at the second performance of the 'Gâteau des Rois' ('Twelfth Cake, or the Cake of the Kings'), an allegorical opera in one act by citizens Destival and Valcour?[1] In this piece Mars appears disguised as a National Guard, and Liberty distributes the cake amongst the nations, France obtaining the bean, or, rather, the red cap which now takes its place. The idea is a very poor one, and the authors have therefore been careful to bestrew their opera plentifully with incitements to vengeance and murder, the harmless Twelfth Cake having thus become a poisonous one in their hands.

Who would this year have thought of celebrating the *Fête des Rois* with Louis XVI. in the Temple awaiting sentence of death? Besides, has it not been abolished by the Commune? On the motion of Scipion Duroure,[2] the Conseil-Général, at its sitting of December 30, 1792, decreed that on and after January 6, 1793, the fête hitherto called the *Fête des Rois* should be called the *Fête des Sans-Culottes*.

And still Prudhomme's paper is not more satisfied than it was a year ago. Yesterday it pointed out, not without reason, that one can only destroy by replacing ; it therefore proposes to substitute the *Cake of Égalité* for the Cake of the Kings, and a *Fête of Good-fellowship* for that of Twelfth Night. The bean

---

[1] Performed for the first time at the Théâtre Patriotique on January 5, 1792 (not 1796, as wrongly given in Welschinger's 'Théâtre de la Révolution,' pp. 9, 206). The Théâtre Patriotique was situated on the Boulevard du Temple, and was known before 1791 as the Théâtre des Associés. The authors of the 'Gâteau des Rois' were both actors. The real name of Aristide Valcour, as he called himself, was Pierre Plancher. He also wrote some obscene stories and plays, in which he celebrated Marat and the guillotine ; he was accordingly made a Justice of the Peace of the Faubourg Saint-Martin ('Les Originaux du Siècle Dernier,' by C. Monselet).

[2] Count Louis Henry Scipion Grimourd Beauvoir Duroure was born at Marseilles in 1763, and died in London in 1822. He was the grandson, on his mother's side, of the Earl of Catherlong, an Irish peer, and the celebrated Lord Bolingbroke was his great-uncle. Elected to the Conseil-Général de la Commune on the Tenth of August, 1792, by the Section of the Faubourg Montmartre, he made himself conspicuous by his exalted ideas and the violence of his language.

would serve to determine in whose house the fraternal banquet would be held, and every guest would contribute his share. The future will tell us what we must think of the *Fête of Good-fellowship*. Prudhomme's paper appears to be much more practical when it adds:

'Whilst we are now engaged in effacing all vestiges of Royalty, how is it that the impure ashes of our Kings still repose intact in the vaults of the former Abbaye de Saint-Denis? We have overthrown the images of all our despots; not one has been spared, whether it be of stone, marble, or bronze. Statues, pedestrian or equestrian, busts, bas-reliefs, pictures, drawings, or engravings, every counterfeit presentment of Royalty has been taken out of our sight. Why, on December 22, 1792, on the morrow of the day when the Monarchy was abolished and the Republic established, did not the Patriots of the Tenth of August proceed to Saint-Denis and order the executioner to disinter the vile remains of all those proud Monarchs, who from their tombs seem even now to defy the laws of equality? Of the edifice that marks their place of sepulture not one stone should have been left standing. Let the tombs of our tyrants disappear and cease to longer pollute the soil of Liberty! Let their ashes be cast to the winds, and let a pyramid transmit to posterity the long-deferred sentence passed upon these crowned criminals!

'Their hearts, embalmed and deposited in the Val-de-Grâce, in Paris, have been taken from their gold and silver caskets, and are now strewn pell-mell upon the flags of the mortuary chapel which contained them. This is not enough; we must ask the authorities to have them taken in a tumbril to the Place de Grève, and burnt, after having been for three days placed in a pillory, with a placard recording the names of all the Kings, Princes, and Princesses.'[1]

The paper which publishes these infamous lines is the one which is most widely read. To-night these lines will form the only *fête* of thousands of families forgetful of that other festival for so many centuries consecrated to the most honourable sentiments, the most joyful gatherings, and the most simple mirth. Many things that die to-day will be born again to-morrow; the Monarchy will rise again—of that I feel convinced—the Monarchy of the Bourbons, and with it, perhaps before it, the royalty of the bean. But what will not come back again is the

---

[1] *Révolutions de Paris*, No. 182.

gaiety, that old Christian and Gallic gaiety, which our fathers called the *poor dear Dame de Liesse!* 'Poor dear Dame de Liesse,' says the witty Gorjy, somewhere in his book, 'have you, then, abandoned this people, your darling child, for ever—this nation of whom one could never think without adding your sweet image?'[1]   Alas, my poor Gorjy, yes, for ever! The old French gaiety is dead—the Revolution killed it.[2]

---

[1] ''Ann'quin Bredouille,' tome iii., ch. clvii.

[2] François Chéron, in his 'Mémoires,' published in 1882 by M. Hervé-Bazin, relates how he celebrated the *Fête des Rois* on January 6, 1793, with a few of his friends.   'It was the *Jour des Rois*, 1793, and the trial of the unhappy Louis XVI. was proceeding.   Mme. Filleul, who lived in the Château de la Muette, often invited a select company—all Royalists, as may be imagined.   It was there that we celebrated the *Fête des Rois* in secret, like the first Christians in their Catacombs.   One of the guests—it was, I think, M. de Trudaine—had the cake made at home, and brought it in a large bag.   We cut it up in one of the remotest rooms in the château, out of sight of the servants.   The dinner was sad and silent. Signs had been agreed upon with which to drink to the health of the august prisoners. . . .   My brother and I are the sole survivors of the fourteen guests who were present.   All perished as victims of the Terror.'   François Chéron (1764—1828) wrote, in collaboration with Picard, 'Duhautcours, ou le Contrat d'Union,' a comedy in five acts, and in prose, performed on August 6, 1801.   His brother, Louis Claude Chéron (1758—1807), a member of the Legislative Assembly, is the author of 'Le Tartufe de Mœurs,' a comedy in five acts, and in verse, performed at the Théâtre Français on April 4, 1805.

Thursday, January 10, 1793.

THAT the Girondists have a majority in the Convention, and that, consequently, the fate of Louis XVI. is in their hands, is an indisputable fact concerning which there could be no possible doubt after the sittings of yesterday and to-day.

Yesterday the Convention re-elected the members of the Committee of General Security. Of the fifteen members elected, fourteen belong to the Girondist party. Their names are Chambon, Grangeneuve, Duperret, Champeaux, Jarry, Lemaréchal, Gommaire, Dupont, Ruault, Rebecqui, Gorsas, Zangiacomi, Bordas, Estadens, and Jouenne-Longchamps. The last-mentioned is the only one who has a seat in the Mountain. Whilst, therefore, Manuel, one of the clerks, was reading over the names, Marat was seen to start up repeatedly from his seat, gnash his teeth, and shake his fist. When the 'Friend of the People' heard the names of Rebecqui and Gorsas, he could contain himself no longer, and sprang down from the summit of the Mountain, shouting, 'This is a horrible plot! This is a committee of conspirators!'[1]

This evening the Convention proceeded to the election of a President and three Secretaries. The voting was open. Vergniaud was elected to the Presidency, the three new Secretaries, who are all prominent members of the Girondist party, being Gorsas, Lesage, and Bancal, the intimate friend of Madame Roland.

Special importance attaches to Vergniaud's election, by reason of the present state of things. It is he who will preside over the deliberations of the Convention on January 11 and 24; it is he who will be called upon to pass the sentence with which the trial of Louis XVI. will conclude. He will do more than pass it, he will dictate it; for there is no doubt that, in the present

---

[1] *Courrier des Départements,* January 10, 1793.

divided state of the Assembly, his example, his words, and his vote, will exercise a decisive influence upon a certain number of members who are still wavering, and who will vote for or against the death of the King, according to what the President himself does.

What will Vergniaud do? He has already done more than anyone, more even than Robespierre, to hasten the fall of Louis XVI.[1]

An opportunity now presents itself by which he may repair in one day the evil he has done for the past year. Will he have the courage to seize it? Perhaps we may allow ourselves to hope so, if it be true, as it is affirmed, that for some time past he has manifested great horror for the cannibals who demand with yells the head of the *tyrant*. M. de Ségur, who was French Ambassador in Berlin before the Tenth of August, has had several interviews with him, and has received the most reassuring promises. The last time that M. de Ségur saw the eloquent deputy of the Gironde, the latter drew a rough picture of the present state of Europe, dwelling forcibly upon the dangers to which the death of the King would expose France. He demonstrated the frightful injustice of such a sentence, and concluded with these words: "*I* vote for the death of Louis XVI.? No, no! It is an insult to suppose me capable of such an infamous action!' I have these details from Morellet, the friend of M. de Ségur.[2]

---

[1] 'A fact which has never been properly recognised by any historian of the French Revolution is that Vergniaud was the *fatal man* of Louis XVI.' —' Histoire Parlementaire et Vie Intime de Vergniaud,' by G. Touchard-Lafosse, p. 24, etc. Touchard-Lafosse was an ardent admirer of Vergniaud ; his statement is therefore the more valuable.

[2] 'Histoire et Mémoires of the Comte de Ségur,' tome i., p. 13. Harmand, in his 'Anecdotes,' relates that Vergniaud dined with him on January 17, 1793, and swore not to vote for the death of the King. A few minutes later he registered his nefarious vote. M. Chauvot (*Barreau de Bordeaux*, f. 204) has refuted Harmand's story, and M. Vatel ('Vergniaud : Manuscrits, Lettres, et Papiers,' tome i., lx.) supports the refutation. Though not so worthless as Vatel pretends, Harmand's authority is indeed but poor. But that of M. de Ségur is not so by any means, and it seems impossible to contradict the fact that Vergniaud did, shortly before voting for the death of the King, resent as an insult the supposition that he could so vote. See also D'Allonville, 'Mémoires Secrets,' tome iii., p. 132, etc. The conclusion is evident. Since Vergniaud in sending Louis XVI. to the scaffold was not obeying convictions dictated by passion and fanaticism—since he had no desire to vote for death, and yet did vote so—the crime in his case was accompanied by cowardice.

CHAPTER XXXVI.

ANDRÉ CHÉNIER.

Friday, January 11, 1793.

I met André Chénier this morning in the garden of the Tuileries, and went home with him to his house in the Rue de Cléry,[1] where he showed me several things he had written in the King's interests.[2] They are meant to enlighten the nation if an appeal to the people is decided upon. I was much struck by one composition in particular, in which Chénier, addressing the *country-people*, tries to dispel that indifference and timidity which is a trump-card in the hands of the Republicans.

The following are the concluding paragraphs of this eloquent work :

' For the benefit of those who have no grudge against the lives of Louis and his family, I will add that it is in their ranks that we fear to find a large number of indifferent and timid men. Those who hold, or, at least, profess to hold, a contrary opinion ; those who carry death-warrants in their hearts or on their lips ; those— I speak from experience in the past—we have no doubt will vote as early and in as large numbers as possible. May the Assemblies be spared their influence, not only that which is insidious and secret, but that which is manifest and tyrannical ! For, to the shame of humanity be it said, passions of hatred and malevolence are more active and bold than the desire for good and the love of law.

' These are, fellow-men, the reflections that an obscure but loyal

---

[1] The entry in the gaol-book of Saint-Lazare runs : ' André Chénier, thirty-one years old, born in Constantinople, and living at No. 97, Rue de Cléry.'

[2] See ' Œuvres en Prose d'André Chénier,' edited by Becq de Fonquières, p. 270, etc.

citizen has thought it well to lay before you in a brotherly way. He trusts, less in the interests of the accused than for your own honour and peace of mind, that the few words he addresses to you may make a deeper impression than the furious tirades of those who do all they can to madden and to deceive the people. He hopes that you will easily see the difference between their language and his. Hitherto they have only spoken to you in the language of hatred ; he speaks to you in the name of humanity. They have spoken to you only of revenge ; he speaks to you only of justice. They have spoken to you only of your power ; he speaks to you of your conscience. They have employed only inflated and exaggerated expressions ; he employs only plain and simple language. To persuade you they appeal to your passions and your prejudices ; he appeals only to your hearts and your reason.'[1]

Grouber de Groubentall, formerly a barrister in the *Parlement* of Paris, has also prepared a memoir in favour of Louis XVI., which is to appear, like that of André Chénier, as soon as an appeal to the people has been decided upon. Chénier's address is very short, and its object is to get all loyal citizens to attend the primary assemblies. Groubentall's memoir is quite a book, and refutes *seriatim* all the charges brought against the King. The sheets are sent to the printer's as he writes them, and as soon as the proofs have been revised, the copies are immediately struck off, so that the work may be ready for distribution throughout the whole of France the moment the Convention decides upon making the appeal.[2]

André Chénier and Grouber de Groubentall are, however, not the only Royalists who have placed their services at the disposal of the King's defenders. Hyde de Neuville,[3] Charles de Lézar-

---

[1] 'Œuvres en Prose d'André Chénier,' p. 283.

[2] Groubentall's work was entitled 'Appel de Louis XVI. à la Nation,' and was printed by J. J. Rainville, Rue de Seine, Faubourg Saint-Germain, 1793. When the idea of an appeal to the people was rejected, the author had the whole edition of his work, then useless, destroyed, preserving only one copy, which was presented to Louis XVIII. in 1814. The printer had kept the proofs corrected by Groubentall, and from these this remarkable and valuable document was reprinted in the *Revue Rétrospective*, série ii., tome ix., and série iii., tome i.

[3] Hyde de Neuville was born at La Charité-sur-Loire on January 24, 1726, and died in Paris on May 28, 1857. Under the Restoration he was Minister of Marine in the Martignac Cabinet (1828—1829), and as such took an active part in the emancipation of Greece.

dière,[1] and Roux de Laborie,[2] formerly secretary to the Minister
Bigot de Sainte-Croix,[3] have, since the beginning of the trial,
attended every sitting of the Convention, and immediately
report all the proceedings to the King's counsel, who are thus
made acquainted with the deliberations of the Assembly more
rapidly than by means of the newspapers; their information is also
more complete and reliable, for the papers by no means record
all the incidents that occur. Of Charles de Lézardière's three
brothers, one was slaughtered in the massacres of September,
while the two others are being looked for by the police.[4] This,
however, does not deter him from rendering the services of which
he is so proud. What matters danger when honour and duty
point the way ?

A letter written by Mademoiselle de Lézardière, and never before
published, will not be without some interest here; the original
is in the collection of M. Gustav Bord :

[1] Charles de Lézardière, born at the Château de la Verie, in Poitou, left
Paris after the death of Louis XVI., and took part in the Vendean war
as Aide-de-camp to Charette. A member of the Chamber of Deputies
under the Restoration, he made himself as conspicuous by the moderation
of his ideas as by his talents. His sister, Marie Charlotte Pauline de
Lézardière, published, under the title of 'Théorie des Lois Politiques de
la Monarchie Française,' one of the most learned works that our history
has inspired. An excellent judge, M. Guizot, said of this work : ' Before
Mdlle. de Lézardière the history of France was a closed book ; she is the
first who opened it.'
[2] Roux de Laborie was born in 1769, and died in 1840. Marmontel
says of him in his 'Mémoires' : 'The intermediary between M. Desèze
and myself was a young man named Laborie, who already, in his nine-
teenth year, had attracted notice by writings which might easily have
been attributed to a man of more mature mind and taste . . . He has an
ingenuous mind and a warm heart . . . a lovable and happy disposition.'
In April, 1814, Roux de Laborie discharged the duties of an Assistant-
Secretary in the Provisional Government, and took a leading part in the
events of that time.
[3] Louis Claude Bigot de Sainte-Croix, Minister of Foreign Affairs from
the First to the Tenth of August, 1792, author of an admirable ' Histoire
de la Conspiration du 10 Août, 1792.'
[4] Charles de Lézardière's two brothers, one of whom was a naval
Lieutenant, and the other a naval cadet, only escaped the September
massacres to be guillotined on July 7, 1794. M. Émile Campardon, in
' Le Tribunal Révolutionnaire de Paris,' tome ii., and Henri Wallon, in his
' Histoire du Tribunal Révolutionnaire de Paris,' tome iii., speak of them
as Robert, called Désardières (Jacques Paul), and Robert, called Désardières
(Sylvestre Joachim). Their real surname is Robert de Lézardière.

'La Proutière, near Avrillé (Vendée),
January 20, 1815.

'In reading your number of January 14, I perceive that there is some doubt concerning the fate of the venerable divine who accompanied Louis XVI. to the scaffold. I consider it my duty to state the facts in order to show that such a man was never allowed to seek a refuge in cellars or in the woods.

'Baron de Lézardière, my father, obliged to leave his part of the country in 1791, had entered into intimate relations with the Abbé Edgeworth in Paris. After the massacres of September, 1792, they decided to go and live at Choisi-le-Roi. M. Edgeworth took some rooms in the name of Essex, in the house of one Boulachin, whilst we lived at the widow Achenay's. M. Edgeworth used to say Mass for us every morning, and we spent the days together.

'When our unhappy Monarch desired to have the confessor with him, he applied to my eldest brother, the Marquis de Lézardière, through the medium of M. de Malesherbes.

'Having seen the head of his King fall, M. Edgeworth passed through the midst of the regicides, who, seized with the terror of their crime, saw nothing. Lost in the midst of an infuriated mob, he got away unnoticed. The stains of blood that are supposed to have been on his clothes never existed ; he entered Madame de Senosan's house, saw M. de Malesherbes there, then walked to the offices of the Choisi stage-coach, and arrived at our house the same evening, never leaving us till the beginning of April, 1793.

'The armed forces of the Paris Commune then carried off my father and a portion of his family in so sudden a manner that M. Edgeworth must have escaped by a miracle. This is the only occasion on which he wandered in the woods, and in the evening he re-entered the deserted house, but we were fortunate enough to promptly procure him a safer refuge until the time of the amnesty, when those of us who had escaped rejoined him at Bayeux, in Normandy, to separate no more until he left France in 1796.

'M. Edgeworth then went to England, reaching that island by means which for a long time helped to snatch the faithful servants of the King from the sword of the Terror.

'Such are the facts which I beg you to lay before the public, well knowing that you will not for a moment hesitate to entertain such a request.

'I have the honour to be, etc.,
'Marie de Lézardière.'

CHAPTER XXXVII.

'PAUVRE JACQUES.'

Saturday, January 12, 1793.

THE nearer we draw to the day on which the King's fate is to be decided, the more are we inundated with threatening posters, homicidal motions, and cries of vengeance and death. Now it is a deputation from eighteen of the sections to the National Convention demanding the death of the tyrant. 'On the Tenth of August,' says the spokesman, 'you promised to avenge us— where are your promises? Does not the murder of thousands of our brethren demand its punishment? Louis is a traitor and an assassin, and he must die.'[1] Now it is the section of Gravilliers which, through the medium of a paper called *Le Petit Marat*, edited by a priest named Jacques Roux, demands the death of Louis XVI., not only in the name of the French, but in the name of humanity, of which Capet has always been the plague and greatest enemy. The members of the Luxembourg section swear to assassinate Louis Capet if the majority in the Convention does not send him to the scaffold. Sébastian Lacroix, charged by the Commune of Paris with the superintendence of the food-supply, lays before the Jacobin Club, in the name of a good Republican, an offer to present the country with a gun of the calibre of the King's head.[2] Bands of *sans-culottes* parade the streets singing the *Marseillaise*, and laying special stress upon the line:

'Qu'un sang impur arrose nos sillons !'[3]

---

[1] *Courrier des Départements*, January 1, 1793.

[2] *Moniteur* of 1792, No. 252.

[3] 'Let our fields be watered with impure blood !'—'Histoire de France,' by l'Abbé de Montgaillard, tome iii., p. 422.

Women and children nightly yell forth in the squares and promenades an abominable song that I first heard on December 26, at the doors of the National Convention, and the refrain of which is, ' *To the guillotine with Louis !*' Yet at the same time, and in this same city, this is what is taking place. In the Théâtre de la Nation the public eagerly seizes upon every allusion that affords it an opportunity of expressing its sympathy with the King and Queen. Four times since January 2 have immense audiences come to witness the ' Friend of the Law,' which is in reality from first to last an energetic protest against this odious trial in which every law is overridden and violated. At the end of each performance the author has been obliged to appear on the stage to receive the plaudits of an enthusiastic house.[1] ' Mithridates ' was performed at the Théâtre de la Nation the day before yesterday, when all the lines that could in any way be made to allude to the august prisoner in the Temple were vigorously applauded, and particularly the following :

In the First Act.

' This King, with whose great deeds the whole East rings—
Whom we may justly style that East's last monarch—
In his own kingdom cannot find a grave,
Or lies unnoticed in a nameless crowd,
Yet blames not Heaven which lets such outrage pass,
Nor his unworthy sons who dare not wreak it.'

In the Second Act.

' When my foe Fortune would have cast me lower,
Conquered, proscribed, unfriended, and uncrowned,
Naught left me save the name of Mithridates,
Know that so long as that great name I bear,
Where'er I go the whole world's eyes will follow.'

In the Fourth Act.

' Traitors ! I have too long delayed my vengeance !
But still I fear you not—despite their vauntings,
The mutineers would never dare to face me ;
I only ask to meet them.'

---

[1] Étienne and Martainville, ' Histoire du Théâtre Français pendant la Révolution,' tome iii., p. 49.

Loud applause also greeted the two lines with which the play closes :

' MONIMES.

' He dies.

' XIPHARES.

' Ah ! lady, let us join our sorrows,
And through the world we'll search him out avengers.'[1]

At the Théâtre Italien, where ' Raoul, Sire de Créqui ' is being performed, the liberation of a noble prisoner, in whom the audience is pleased to recognise Louis XVI., is received with transports of joy.[2] Prudhomme states despairingly that the people is still monarchical, and that the King is beloved even in the wine-shops. ' I have seen,' he says—' yes, I have seen the drinkers drop more than one tear into their wine as they spoke of Louis Capet. In some of these places, too, paid singers drawl out a silly but touching lament upon the fate of the tyrant. It is sung to the air of " Pauvre Jacques," and begins thus :

"Good people, how am I to blame ?"

Thousands of copies are being sold ; it is even replacing the *Marseillaise*.'[3]

I have bought this lament, which did not strike me as being so silly as Citizen Prudhomme says. It runs as follows :

' LOUIS XVI. TO THE FRENCH.

' *Romance.*

'" Popule meus, quid feci tibi ?"

' *Air:* " Pauvre Jacques."

' Good people, how am I to blame ?
Virtue and justice held I high ;
Your welfare was my only aim,
Yet now you hale me forth to die.

[1] ' Opinion de Sergent,' a member of the Convention, ' sur le Jugement de Louis Capet,' p. 14.
[2] *Les Révolutions de Paris*, No. 182.   [3] *Révolutions de Paris, loc. cit.*

' Frenchmen ! 'twas in your midst, I ween,
    That his first breath this Louis drew,
One well-loved clime our births has seen,
    My childhood was your childhood, too.

' What evil have I done to earn
    Such woes, good people, and such grief ?
I gave you freedom—in return
    You heap these fetters on your chief.

' While still in years a child, I found
    All France had fixed her hopes on me,
And ere as Monarch I was crowned,
    Your father I might claim to be.

' And when I reached this throne at last—
    This glorious throne my birth secures—
In the first Edict that I passed
    I sought your good, and only yours.

' Henry, whose name you've long held dear,
    Some grounds for scandal did afford,
But Louis, Virtue's friend sincere,
    Minions and light-o'-loves abhorred.

' Can you one subject's name recall
    Whose life my hand has signed away ?
One day now sees more Frenchmen fall
    Than doomed my fifteen years of sway.

' Could but his death ensure your weal,
    Your good King grants it at your call,
Bowing his neck beneath the steel,
    Dies guiltless and forgives you all.

' Hear my farewell before I go,
    Live happy—'tis not hard to die ;
But when you see my life-blood flow,
    Would all your hate be quenched thereby.'[1]

---

[1] These touching verses are by M. Hennet, who has written several pamphlets on financial matters and a work entitled ' Poétique Anglaise,' the third volume of which is devoted to translations of poems by the best English writers. The words and music of ' Pauvre Jacques ' were by the Marquise de Travanet, one of Mme. Elisabeth's ladies-in-waiting. See the ' Vie de Mme. Elisabeth,' by Beauchesne, tome i., p. 296.

A reply of the French nation to Louis XVI. is also being sold. It runs as follows:

'Good Louis, grant us pardon, pray,
    If we condemned you without cause
Whom many strove to lead astray
    By painting you the Foe of Laws.

'To check the wrongs, the right advance,
    Our noblest rulers' course you chose ;
E'en Henry laboured less for France.
    "Another Nero !" howl your foes.

'We know not what your fate will be,
    But if your punishment's decreed,
All honest Frenchmen such as we
    Will curse so infamous a deed.

'Shall Louis die?   Oh, dreadful thought !
    And shall this land his life-blood stain ?
Could kindly Louis have been brought
    To shed enough he yet might reign.

'Ye men of blood who swear his doom,
    By your hands let our blood be spilt,
Since to drop tears above his tomb
    Is in your eyes the cast of guilt.'

Another romance, written, like the two preceding ones, to the air of 'Pauvre Jacques,' has for its title

'THE DAUPHIN'S ADDRESS TO FRANCE.

'Frenchmen ! I'm but a child as yet,
    But do not lack the wit to know
Your monarch never would abet
    The schemes designed to work your woe.

'You charge him that, with traitor's art,
    He strove to reign a despot here.
How little do you know his heart !
    From earliest youth he held you dear.

'Oft by my mother I've been told
    That justice was to Louis dear ;
How for your laws he battled bold,
    And yet you say his doom is near.

' Recall how, in his proudest state,
    He held its pomp and glitter cheap,
And strove that King to imitate
    Whose mem'ry your affections keep.

' To the new styles your laws contrive
    I am too lowly to aspire ;
I'd rank as meanest wretch alive
    If only you would spare my Sire.

' Great God, whose eyes see everything,
    In mercy hear my piteous cry !
Nor let our good and noble King
    On scaffold like a felon die.'

On March 8, 1794, Louis Desacres de l'Aigle, *ci-devant* Comte, and formerly a Field-Marshal in the King's army, was arraigned before the Revolutionary Tribunal, mention being made in the indictment against him that the *romance* of ' Louis XVI. to the French' had been found amongst his papers. He was sent to the scaffold, together with his niece, Anne Alexandrine Rosalie de la Rochefoucauld, Comtesse de Durtal. This lady had received no notice of any charge preferred against her, nor had she even been formally summoned as a witness, but having been brought from the Conciergerie to furnish the tribunal with some particulars, she was forthwith hustled to a seat on the prisoners' bench, and sentenced to death on the Public Prosecutor's demand (' Histoire du Tribunal Révolutionnaire de Paris,' by H. Wallon, tome ii., p. 467).

CHAPTER XXXVIII.

THE 'FRIEND OF THE LAW.'

Tuesday, January 15, *1793.*

ON the 2nd of this month the 'Friend of the Law,' a comedy in five acts and in verse, by M. Laya, was performed for the first time at the Théâtre de la Nation. It is not a very interesting piece; the plot is incoherent, and the verses are harsh and prosy. Nevertheless, the 'Friend of the Law' was enthusiastically received.

The first four performances attracted immense audiences. Before three in the afternoon the approaches to the theatre were blocked by an impatient crowd. No masterpiece had ever excited such curiosity, or called forth such transports, but never had a French stage re-echoed with more honest sentiments. The author attacks the men who now rule Paris and France, and tearing the mask from these false patriots, lays bare all their ugliness. In *Nomophage* (the devourer of laws) we recognise Robespierre, in the cowardly *Filto* the virtuous Petion, and in *Duricrane*, the journalist, we see Marat. What all honest people have long thought M. Laya has dared to say openly, and hence all this excitement. Incredible to relate, the honest people have even dared to show their feelings. With an ardour and an energy to which we have long been unaccustomed, they have spat upon revolutionary maxims and practices, and have hailed the principles of moderation, justice and honour with acclamation. It is impossible to mistake the character of this demonstration and not to see in it a striking protest against the trial of Louis XVI., and against the men who, in contempt of all law, wish to send him to the scaffold. What proves, moreover, that this movement is a truly popular one, in the best sense of the word, is that during the four performances not a single spectator dared to show the least disapproval in the face of the enthusiasm that reigned in every part of the house. There is no doubt that in this vast audience there were friends of Robespierre or of Marat, but in spite of their insolence they were silent, their common-sense telling them that it were useless to resist sentiments so general and so pronounced.

Great was the fury of the Republican papers and their editors. These fiery friends of Liberty excitedly demanded the suppression of the play, the arrest of the author and actors, and a rising of the people against the audience itself. Hébert's sheet appears with the following heading: ' Père Duchesne's great anger at seeing that the aristocrats dared to lay aside their masks and seek the death of all good citizens. What he thinks of the mountebanks who perform the farces written in the boudoir of Queen Roland, and who are paid by the Minister Coco to throw mud at the brave fellows who have remained faithful to the people.'[1]

The clubs have not been behind the papers, and at the Jacobins the younger Robespierre has denounced this ' infamous play,' in which, he says, they have had the audacity to place his brother and the excellent citizen Marat on the stage. He concluded by exhorting true patriots to proceed to the theatre, and put an end to the scandal.[2]

These exhortations produced no results. There were no disturbances, and the Commune had therefore no reasons for interfering. Nevertheless, on the 11th, the Conseil-Général, on the motion of Citizen Hébert, issued an order suspending the performances of the ' Friend of the Law.' When the Order of the Commune was posted on the walls of the theatre, on the 12th, the public had already assembled to take their tickets. It was about half-past three when Dr. Chambon, the Mayor of Paris, he whom Père Duchesne calls a ' damned herb-seller,'[3]

---

[1] *Le Père Duchesne*, No. 208.   [2] *Mercure Français*, January 16, 1793.
[3] This is how Hébert, on November 30, 1792, welcomed the election of Chambon as Mayor of Paris ' Père Duchesne's great anger on hearing that Petion is replaced by a damned herb-seller, who will put us all on diet instead of giving us bread, who will feel the pulse of the drunkard Capet, and give him stuff to keep him alive and well, and who will bleed the *sans-culottes* after the manner of Bailly and Lafayette.'—*Père Duchesne*, No. 198.

arrived in the square in which the theatre stands ;[1] this square
and the adjoining streets were filled with a crowd numbering
about 30,000 people. The Mayor's carriage not being able to
proceed through the crowd, he was obliged to alight, and, after
a great deal of trouble, succeeded in getting inside the theatre.
There he wished to address the crowd from a window under the
peristyle, but he was unable to make himself heard.[2]   He thereupon decides to enter the house itself.   Hardly has he put foot
in his box when the cry of ' The " *Friend of the Law* " !' that met
him everywhere is thundered forth by the audience.   Chambon
tries to explain the motives that impelled the municipality to stop
the performance.   His voice is drowned by cries of ' The " *Friend
of the Law*" !   The play !   The play !   Curtain !' Fleury, the
principal actor of the Théâtre de la Nation, then steps forward,
and silence is immediately obtained.   'Citizens,' he says, ' the
ardour with which you have flocked to see the " Friend of the
Law " proves how desirous you are of obeying that law.   A
power set up by yourselves suspends the performance of the
piece, and I therefore beg you to be good enough to accept
" Le Conciliateur " in its place.'   This, however, the public
refuses to do.   Much against his will Chambon at last consents
to a deputation being sent to the National Convention to
demand that the liberty of the theatres shall be respected.   This
deputation, headed by Citizen Laya, leaves the house amidst
great applause.   Chambon now wishes to withdraw to the *foyer*,
but he is compelled to remain in his box.

Things are beginning to quiet down, when suddenly loud
cries of ' *Santerre !   Here comes Santerre !*' are heard.   It was
indeed the Commander of the Parisian National Guard, who,
accompanied by his staff, had come to place his services at the
disposal of the Mayor.   He tries to speak, but in vain.   Two
thousand voices drown his words.   'Down with the frothy
General !   Down with the 2nd of September !   Out with him !
We want the play !   The play or death !'[3]   Santerre then with-
draws amidst much hooting and whistling.

---

[1] Now the Place de l'Odéon.
[2] *Mercure Français*, January 14, 1793.
[3] *Mercure Français*, January 14, 1793 ; Étienne and Martainville,
tome iii., p. 51.

Santerre and his staff are succeeded by a band of more than a hundred and fifty Jacobins, who rush into the house armed with swords and pistols; a few wear the uniform of the National Guard and carry guns. They declare that the piece shall not be performed, and reply to the shouts of the audience by threatening to use their weapons.[1]

Meanwhile the deputation has returned, and Laya is said to be the bearer of an Order of the Convention; the uproar is stilled, and the Mayor leaves his box to read the Decree from the stage: 'The Convention acknowledges and proclaims that there is no law authorizing municipal bodies to censure stage plays.'

The curtain rises amidst shouts of joy, and the performance begins.

From that moment the most perfect order reigns.[2] The Jacobins had disappeared, with their pistols, guns, and swords, and the spectators were only eager to support the courage of the author and the actors with their applause. Fleury was perfect in the part of M. de Forlis, the friend of the law. When he came to the line,

'The shadow has gone by; black murder, get thee hence,'

the audience rose as one man; it was not enthusiasm, but delirium. A no less significant demonstration broke out when Nomophage, having uttered the axiom repeatedly laid down in the Convention during the King's trial, *The safety of the people is the supreme law*, Filto replied:

'No, no; though 'twere the people's right to kill,
To kill the innocent is murder ever.'

The applause this passage called forth was sufficient evidence of the sentiments of the whole house concerning the King's trial.

Duricrane is represented by Larochelle, whose dress and by-play recall the clothes and gestures of Marat.[3] He appears only for a moment, and says but a few words:

'I was born informer, spying is my lot.
When I cannot unearth a plot I make one.
. . . In fourteen days I have laid bare
No less than eight; 'tis four a week.'

---

[1] *Mercure Français, loc. cit.*   [2] *Ibid.*   [3] *Révolutions de Paris*, No. 184.

How the laughter shakes the house! How the people enjoy
seeing their friend thus held up to ridicule not two steps from
the den in which he writes his infamous charges![1]

'The true cit is your only honest man.'

With that line the piece concludes. As the curtain fell the
public again called for the author and the actors. M. Laya
came forward with Fleury on one side and Vanhove on the
other. They were received with an indescribable ovation. The
audience seemed animated by one heart and soul; people fell
into each other's arms and shed tears of joy. It was nearly one
o'clock in the morning when we left the theatre.[2] The square
was full of *honest men and true citizens*, who had remained outside the theatre all the evening, and who received us with shouts
of ' *Vive l'Ami des Lois! Vive la Liberté!*'

On the morrow of this performance, 'Semiramis' and the
'Matinée d'une Jolie Femme'[3] were performed. Between the
two pieces the audience demanded the 'Friend of the Law.'
Dazincourt appeared on the stage, and said that in view of the
calumnies that had been maliciously spread, both the author
and the actors were desirous of giving the calumniators time to
recover from their error, and to convince themselves, by a
perusal of the work itself, that the principles of the 'Friend of
the Law' were dictated by true and sincere patriotism. It was
therefore their intention to wait a few days before giving a
fresh performance of the play, convinced as they were that the
calumnies would fall of themselves, and that the whole public
would then do justice to the author and the interpreters. But
the house would hear of no adjournment, and to calm the storm
Dazincourt was obliged to promise in the name of his society
that the 'Friend of the Law' should be performed on the following Tuesday; that is, to-morrow.

[1] Marat lived at No. 20, Rue de l'École de Médicin.
[2] In 1793 the theatres opened their doors at four in the afternoon, and
the performances were over by ten. But on account of the Order of the
Commune, and the necessity of waiting for the decision of the Convention, the play could not begin on January 12 until some hours after the
opening of the doors.
[3] A play by Vigée (1750—1828), author of 'Les Aveux Difficiles,' 'La
Fausse Coquette,' 'La Belle-Mère, ou les Dangers d'un Second Mariage,'
etc., and a brother of Mme. Lebrun-Vigée, the celebrated painter.

But the actors and the public reckoned without their host, without that excellent Conseil de la Commune, which opposes the performance. Although the National Convention had at its sitting of the 12th admitted that there was no law authorizing municipal bodies to censure stage plays, and that the performances of the 'Friend of the Law' could not be stopped, the Conseil-Général yesterday issued a fresh Decree ' ordering General Santerre to take proper measures' to prevent the piece from being played.

The Directory of the department has also confirmed the Decree of the Conseil-Général, and ordered the play called the 'Friend of the Law' to be suspended.

It was therefore impossible for the actors of the Théâtre de la Nation to keep the promise that Dazincourt had made in their name, and this morning the bills announced 'L'Avare' and 'Le Médecin Malgré Lui' instead of 'L'Ami des Lois.'

Santerre was determined to have his revenge, and took care that this time he should be more fortunate than he had been three days ago. The square in front of the theatre resembled a military parade-ground.[1] The Luxembourg and its approaches were filled with soldiers and National Guards, whilst patrols were continually on the move in the neighbourhood of the theatre.[2] In spite of this military display, the audience persistently demanded the 'Friend of the Law.' The actors having refused to perform it, the uproar became so great that by closing one's eyes one might have imagined one's self to be in the Convention. Vigner, the Commissioner of Police, and one of his colleagues, attempted to gain a hearing. They were in the balcony; some of the spectators from the pit made their way up to them, and, amidst many threats, intimated to them that they would not be allowed to leave the house.[3] At that moment Santerre entered, accompanied by an armed force and a deputation from the Commune. They were received with cries of ' *Down with the murderers of September! Down with*

---

[1] Étienne and Martainville, tome iii., p. 60.
[2] Santerre's report to the Conseil-Général de la Commune at its sitting of January 15, 1793.
[3] Vigner's report to the Conseil-Général at its sitting on January 15.

the frothy General! Santerre, who appears to be accustomed to this kind of reception, bravely faced the storm, and, taking advantage of a temporary lull, said that he would defend those who were insulted ; that he would have the decisions of the municipality observed ; that the play of the 'Friend of the Law' not being on the bills, the public had no right to demand it, and that he would have the first man seized who made the slightest disturbance. His last words gave rise to tremendous uproar, a terrible *crescendo*, in which could only be heard two dominating notes : '*Cut-throats!*' '*Murderers!*'[1] Santerre then put his hat upon his head, and declared that in this mob he refused to recognise the people, and that the house was packed with aristocrats. Shouts were then raised that the play should be read from the stage. Heedless of the energetic protests of Santerre and the members of the Commune, a young man rushed upon the stage, holding in his hand a copy of the 'Friend of the Law.' Silence was restored, and some of the principal scenes were read out,[2] nearly every line being interrupted by frenzied applause. Three times did Santerre try to silence the reader, who, however, did not stop until he had read the last lines of the fifth act :

> ' The reign of tricksters now is o'er,
> In vain they seek to steal away our hearts ;
> The people, pitiless, when once deceived,
> With loyal cries has drowned their lying words.'

He then left the stage amidst the enthusiastic applause of the audience, who carried him in triumph through the house. It was ten o'clock when the theatre doors were closed.

M. Louis Moland, in the interesting introduction to his 'Théâtre de la Révolution,' has fallen into several errors concerning this performance of January 15. Like M. Théodore Muret (' L'Histoire par le Théâtre,' i. 74), he reproduces the mistake committed by Étienne and Martainville, and gives the date of the performance as the 14th ; it took place on the 15th, as is fully proved by the report laid before the National Convention at its sitting of the 16th, by

----

[1] Étienne and Martainville, *loc. cit.*
[2] *Mercure Français,* January 17, 1793.

Garat, the Minister of Justice, by the minutes of the Conseil-Général de la Commune of Tuesday, the 15th, and by Santerre's report, which commences: 'I lay before you a report of what took place at the Comédie to-day.' 'Since the piece cannot be performed,' says Moland, 'it shall at least be read. Some young men clamber on to the stage and read the different parts, amidst the applause of the vast audience.' These details, borrowed from Étienne and Martainville, have likewise been reproduced by Théodore Muret (i. 60), by Jauffret ('Théâtre Révolutionnaire,' p. 212), and by Welschinger ('Le Théâtre de la Révolution,' p. 405). But they are incorrect. Only one of the spectators got upon the stage and read, not the whole piece, but merely a few scenes. Santerre's report is very clear on this point, and is confirmed by the newspapers of the day. See, amongst others, the *Mercure Français* of January 17, 1793.

On September 3, 1793, within eight months of the first performance of the 'Friend of the Law,' all the actors who had performed in that play, as well as their comrades, were arrested. Fleury, Vanhove, Saint-Prix, Saint-Phal, Larochelle, Dazincourt, Dupont, Dunant, Bellemont, Florence, Naudet, Girard, Champville, Narsy, and Alexandre Duval, were sent to the Madelonnettes, whilst Mesdames Suin, Rancourt, La Chassaigne, Contat, Thénard, Joly, Devienne, Petit, Fleury, Mezeray, Montgautier, Ribou, and Lange, went to Sainte-Pelagie. 'The head of the Comédie Française will be guillotined, and the rest transported,' Collot-d'Herbois had said. Thanks to the devotion of Charles de Labussière, a former actor, employed in the offices of the Committee of Public Safety, and who, at the risk of his life, destroyed the documents relating to the actors of the Théâtre de la Nation, they escaped the Revolutionary Tribunal, and were liberated after the 9th of Thermidor ('Mémoires de Fleury,' tome ii., ch. xi.)

The author of the 'Friend of the Law' was also impeached by the Committee of Public Safety, but he succeeded in escaping, and hid himself in an abandoned quarry. 'One day whilst walking through the excavations he hears the sound of footsteps. Whilst trying to escape from the risk of an encounter, he finds himself face to face with a man, who rushes up to him with the words: "For Heaven's sake, sir, do not betray me!" Louis Laya was on the point of uttering those very words himself.' M. Dauban, who narrates this fact in his 'Étude sur Mme. Roland,' p. 176, gives as his authority M. Léon Laya, the son of the author of the 'Friend of the Law.'

CHAPTER XXXIX.

THE SIXTEENTH OF JANUARY.

Thursday, January 17, 1793.

YESTERDAY's sitting of the Convention lasted from ten in the morning until a quarter to eleven at night.[1]

It was entirely given up to taking the vote on the second question : '*Shall there be an appeal to the people—yes or no ?*'

On the motion of Biroteau, member for the Pyrénées Orientales and one of the Girondist party, each vote was given from the tribune.

As had been fully foreseen, the appeal to the people was rejected.

Voting on the third question—*What sentence shall be passed upon Louis ?*—had been adjourned until to-day. The sitting opened as usual at ten this morning, but the voting did not commence until eight o'clock this evening. It was impossible to find a seat in the galleries, and I had therefore to content my-self with gaining admission to the room set aside for refreshments. It was filled, already this morning, by the agents of the Jacobin Club, who are always to be found there when anything important is going on, apostrophizing the members who have come to get something to eat, and especially attacking such as by their words or manners show signs of wavering. To-day I noticed some of these members write down their votes, and then alter or erase them in compliance with the pressure brought to bear upon them by the King's enemies.[2] Ushers were continually hurrying to and fro, carrying ices, oranges and drinks into the hall in which the sittings are held, the centre of which is transformed for the nonce

---

[1] *Journal des Débats et des Décrets,* No. 120.
[2] Lacretelle, 'Convention Nationale,' i., p. 154.

into stalls, and occupied by ladies in the most charming undress.[1]
Two of these, decked out in tricolour ribbons, passed through
the refreshment-room. The 'Dowager Duchess,' the Amazon
queen of the Jacobite bands—she who, from the gallery, gives
the signal for the applause, also put in a short appearance; she
tossed off two or three glasses of brandy and then hastened back
to her post. 'You should see,' said an usher, who seemed to have
intense admiration for the 'Dowager'—'you should see how
excited she gets when any of the deputies seem reluctant to vote
for death.'[2]   Another usher, who is anything but a *sans-culotte*,
and whom I have to thank for frequently gaining me admission,
furnished me with some curious details respecting the appearance
of the Convention. The topmost galleries, usually given up to
the public, are filled with strangers and people of all classes who
are drinking and behaving as though they were in a wine-shop.
The reserved galleries are filled with women, nearly all wearing
long tricolour ribbons. These are the mistresses of the members,
who go there as they would go to a theatre to witness a fine
tragedy. 'It is the gentlemen of the Mountain,' said my usher,
'who bring us these fine ladies. We have to see them to their
seats and run on errands for them as though we were their
servants.' Instead of fans they hold in their hands the cards
upon which they mark off with pins each vote as it is given.[3]
As the deputies succeed each other in the tribune, the women
approve or criticise their bearing, their manners, their expression,
and even their tone of voice. Some of them pretend to faint
when they hear the word 'Death!' ring out; others exchange
greetings and smiles with deputies below, and the latter frequently
leave their seats to go and converse with their fair friends or to
get them refreshments.[4]

The members of the Haute Garonne were the first called upon
to vote. Next came those of the department of the Gers, and
then those of the Gironde. It was half-past eight when
Vergniaud, the first of the Girondist deputies, ascended the
tribune. Everyone was convinced, from all that he had said,

---

[1] Mercier, 'Le Nouveau Paris,' ch. ccxlvii.
[2] *Ibid.*   [3] *Ibid.*
[4] 'Histoire de France'; Montgaillard, tome iii., p. 349.

that he would vote for imprisonment, but he voted for *death*.
Out of the twelve members returned by Bordeaux, nine voted
for death, only three, Grangeneuve, Lacaze and Bergoeing, voting
for imprisonment until the conclusion of peace.

After waiting for some time, I decided upon going home. As
I left the building a deputy, whom I failed to recognise, was just
entering, pursued by a crowd who made the corridors re-echo
with their threatening cries of 'Death! Death! Either his
death or yours!'[1]

It is midnight. The voting is still going on. How will it
end? The Mountain will vote unanimously for death, and the
chiefs of the Girondist party—Vergniaud, Guadet, Gensonné,
Boyer-Fonfrède—have done the same. What will Paine do? Is
it to be expected that these weak and cowardly men will resist
the tremendous pressure brought to bear upon them for the past
two months by the press and a large section of the public?

To the numerous facts already quoted to prove the threatening
nature of this pressure, I will add a few others. At the sitting
of the day before yesterday, Korsaint was not contradicted by
any of the members of the Mountain when he described the
doings of the Jacobin Club in the following terms: 'On the very
doors of the Convention the Jacobin Club has stuck up posters
denouncing the members of the Assembly as conspirators. In
these posters that club invites all citizens who are of that opinion
to assemble this evening; that club has a president who only a
few days ago exclaimed: "I am a rebel, and mean to assassinate
all the Rolandists and Feuillandists."'[2]

The language of the president of the Jacobins is that of all
the members of the club. The orator, surnamed the Demos-
thenes of the Terrasse des Feuillants, has written a song with
the refrain '*Off with the heads of Rolandists, Brissotins and
Girondists.*' This song is distributed gratis, every evening, at
the door of the Jacobin Club and in the galleries, where the talk
is only of *shortening* the deputies who are not up to the mark.[3]

At yesterday's sitting, Gamon, a deputy for the Ardèche, re-

[1] Lacretelle, 'Convention Nationale,' i. 154; Montgaillard, iii. 348.
[2] *Journal des Débats et des Décrets*, No. 119.
[3] *Mercure Français*, January 16, 1793.

corded his vote in favour of an appeal to the people in these words : ' I say *yes* in spite of the daggers pointed at me, because such is the cry of my conscience.'

At the end of the same sitting, Dussaulx, a deputy for Paris, who had also voted in favour of the appeal to the people, was most violently abused by a man in the galleries, who turned out to be no other than the notorious Jourdeuil, one of the principal organizers of the September massacres.[1]

At to-day's sitting, Chambon, member for the Corrèze,[2] read a letter from the Minister of the Interior to the Committee of General Security, dated January 16, at eight in the morning. ' Two hours after midnight,' writes the Minister, ' I received the letter in which you inform me that many people are flying in terror from Paris, and that it would be best for the maintenance of public order if the barriers were closed. It is an undoubted fact that for the past month many citizens, especially those of independent means, have left a city in which we are constantly being promised a renewal of past horrors ; it is a fact that for a good many days past I myself have laid before you much information respecting the state of popular feeling, the rumours of plots and the threats of murder.

' It is an undoubted fact, I say, that the irregular proceedings of the authorities, the incendiary resolutions passed by the sections, the bloodthirsty doctrines preached in the clubs, and, lastly, the arrival of the guns from Saint-Denis, have naturally terrified peaceful citizens, who have not forgotten how millions of men stood looking on whilst a handful of murderers dishonoured the name of France in the early days of last September. Is it surprising that they should fly ? I know that the Commune and Santerre tell you that tranquillity reigns in Paris—I know that they gave you the same assurances on September 2. But I say that the same faction exists, and that the same misfortunes

---

[1] *Journal des Débats*, No. 121, January 15, 1793.

[2] Antoine Benoît Chambon, member for the Corrèze, must not be confounded with his namesake, Nicolas Chambon, who was then Mayor of Paris. Outlawed on May 31, 1793, Antoine was killed at Lubersac in the following November, whilst defending himself against his pursuers. Nicolas Chambon resigned his post of Mayor on February 1, 1793, and escaped the Revolutionary proscriptions.

threaten us.' A few moments later, one of the members makes the following declaration : ' Charles Villette begs me to inform the Convention that he was just now told at the doors that if he did not vote for the King's death he would be killed himself.'

Lehardy, a member for the Morbihan, rises in his place. ' I wish to state another fact. This morning I saw a man in the street selling a " List of the Royalists and Aristocrats who voted for the Appeal to the People." '

Finally, just before the voting was about to begin, Lanjuinais, a man who belongs to no party, but who rules them all by his courage, uttered the following words which will go down to posterity : ' You have cast aside every form which justice and honesty required ; full liberty of action can only be enjoyed where the vote is taken by ballot. This Assembly has the appearance of being a free Convention, but it is controlled by the daggers and the guns of the factionists.'

A few moments before, Marat, with a hideous grin, had said : ' They say that they are voting at the point of the dagger, but not one of them can show a scratch !'

Between the word of Marat and that of Lanjuinais, I am sure posterity will not hesitate.

A historian has been found who has not hesitated to take Marat's word in preference to that of Lanjuinais. This is Louis Blanc, who (tome viii., p. 47, etc.) asserts that the King's judges were perfectly free to give what verdict they wished, that they were not influenced in any way, and that Paris was never more tranquil. Never was there an assertion more false than this ; never was there a more audacious lie.

Let us compare the statements of those historians who were eyewitnesses of the facts, those of the Conventionalists themselves, with the statement of Louis Blanc.

Beaulieu (' Essais sur la Révolution ') : ' The Convention was surrounded by the scum of the earth.'

Lacretelle (' Histoire de la Convention ') : ' The men of September 2 were all there, armed with swords and bludgeons. Thirsting for the blood that had been promised them, they besieged all the approaches to the hall from an early hour, and waited for the deputies as they passed in and out. They cheered those who smiled upon them, and who carried death to Louis in their faces ;

but when they recognised such as had already spoken in his favour, they followed him with threats of violence and death.'

Lanjuinais ('Notice Historique sur la Vie du Comte Lanjuinais,' written by his son from the brave Conventionalist's reminiscences) : 'On the morning of the 16th the deputies proceed to the Assembly, and find all the approaches beset by a furious mob. Each representative is received with coarse compliments or insulting threats, according as he is believed to be favourable or not to the sentence of death.'

Carnot ('Mémoires,' edited by his son, tome i., p. 293): 'Louis XVI. would have been saved had not the Convention carried on its deliberations at the point of the sword.'

Louis Blanc finds it convenient to feign ignorance of this testimony, with which he was as familiar as we are, and bravely adds : 'Fear there was none.' And this is the reply he gets from men of the day, not Royalists, but ardent Revolutionaries beyond suspicion :

Grégoire ('Mémoires,' tome ii., p. 426) : 'And of what was this majority in the National Convention composed? Of brutes and mainly of cowards!'

Mme. Roland ('Lettre à Buzot,' published by M. Dauban, p. 54): 'The defenders of Liberty were proscribed by an assembly of *cowards* ruled by rogues.'

Levasseur ('Mémoires,' tome ii., p. 196): 'The fear that we inspired was as much felt upon the benches of the Mountain as in the mansions of the Faubourg Saint-Germain.'

Bandot ('Mémoires Inédits') : 'It is thought that we had a system, but that is a delusion. Our motto was, *Kill, that ye be not killed.*'

Cochon, the regicide (quoted by Fabre, of the Aude, in his 'Histoire Secrète du Directoire,' tome ii., p. 274): 'Fear, sir, yes —fear! We trembled not only for ourselves, but for our families and our friends!'

Merlin de Thionville (sitting of the Convention of March 9, 1795): 'If, when I one day present myself at the bar of the Assembly after our work is done, anyone should dare to say that I have been wanting in courage, I would cry, "Who dares accuse me? *Who is there that was not as much a coward as I?*"'

Never did the words of Tacitus have a more fit application, *pavebant terrebantque* (they terrified others, yet trembled). The 'Terror' was born of the union of Crime and Fear.

CHAPTER XL.

Friday evening, January 18, 1793.

CHARLES LACRETELLE was told the following by Daunou, member for the Pas-de-Calais, to-day :

' One of my neighbours in the Assembly is Lecointe-Puyraveau, member for the department of Deux-Sèvres. On Tuesday he voted for the appeal to the people. On Wednesday he came to the Convention determined, like me, to vote for the King's imprisonment until after the conclusion of peace. He spent the whole night in a fever of agitation, listening to the votes as they were given ; I saw him turn a shade paler each time a vote for death fell from the lips of our colleagues. He congratulated me upon being called to the honour of giving my vote before him, and as I returned to my seat he shook hands with me, saying, "I envy you." At last his turn came this morning about half-past nine, the voting having then been going on for over twelve hours. He again shook hands with me, and rushed to the tribune. Imbert, Opoix, Defranc, and Bernier, the four members who had preceded him, had voted for detention, and all four had been well hooted by the galleries. Silence being restored, Lecointe-Puyraveau utters the following words : " I do not stand here as a judge, but as a representative of the people, and as such I am about to give my vote. On Tuesday I voted for the appeal to the nation." At these words a storm of execration bursts from the galleries. Cries of " Death to the coward! down with the traitor !" re-echo on all sides. Agitation is depicted on the orator's face, and in a voice trembling with emotion he continues : " You have decided not to make that appeal, and I respect your decision." "That's right," shout the galleries. "Vive la Montagne! Death to appellants!" "I represent the people," continues Lecointe-Puyraveau. "No, no, you don't." The threatening yells increase his agitation. "The people," he says, "have been murdered by the tyrant; I vote for his death." Applause, laughter, and shouts of joy greet his last words. Lecointe-Puyraveau returns to his place with a bewildered, woe-begone look on his face. So he sits until the Assembly rises at seven o'clock, afraid to address or even to look at me."[1]

Daunou also gave Lacretelle many other interesting details of this terrible sitting that lasted thirty-six hours. He declares that Louis XVI. would have been saved if the Girondist members had been called upon to vote last.[2] In his opinion, and in that of all brave and honest members of the Convention, it is Vergniaud in the first instance, and after him his colleagues of the constituency of Bordeaux, who are mainly responsible for the death of Louis XVI.

---

[1] Sainte-Beuve, 'Portraits Contemporains,' ii. 374. The above facts were published while Daunou was still alive.
[2] Pouloulat, 'Histoire de la Révolution,' i. 397

CHAPTER XLI.

Saturday evening, January 19, 1793.

AT half-past nine on Thursday, January 17, Vergniaud, the President, announced to the Convention the result of the vote concerning the King's fate.

'The Assembly is composed of 749 members; 15 are absent on commissions, 7 through illness, 1 for no specified cause, and 5 have not voted—in all 28 non-voters. Out of the remainder of 721, 366 have voted for death unconditionally, 355 for imprisonment or conditional death.

'I declare in the name of the National Convention that it has passed sentence of death upon Louis Capet.'

Another vote will be taken this evening to settle the question which the Convention has been discussing all day—whether there is to be any respite to the sentence of death passed upon the King.

Since the beginning of the trial deputations formed of women of the lower classes have repeatedly attempted to lay before the Assembly petitions in favour of Louis XVI.[1] I witnessed one of these attempts this morning in the Salle des Conférences. A number of women demanded to be admitted to the bar to present a petition begging for the postponement of the execution until the conclusion of peace. They were refused admittance to the hall in which the sittings are held. They then made their way to the offices, and insisted that their petition should at least be read. Gaudet, who was presiding in the absence of Vergniaud, would not give the petitioners any satisfaction, and after having waited for several hours they at last withdrew.

---

[1] *La Feuille du Matin*, No. 91.

Louis, though dethroned, captive and condemned, has therefore some devoted friends left, after all.   In our old and noble
France, and even in my poor Paris, misfortune has still its
courtiers, misery has still its faithful ones, in spite of the
Revolution.   I have already given more than one proof of this,
and now wish to adduce a few more.   How and where can I
find better consolation and hope in these dark days?

Fresh pamphlets are continually appearing in defence of
Louis XVI.

M. Sourdat, who on December 26 published his ' Vues Générales
sur le Procès de Louis XVI.,' has just issued a second ' Mémoire,'
no less courageous than the first.[1]

M. le Grand, author of two pamphlets—' Au Peuple, sur le
Procès de Louis XVI.,' ' À la Nation, sur le Jugement de
Louis XVI.'—has to-day issued a third one—' Aux Représentants
de la Nation.'

To-day, too, there is published at Webert's bookshop in the
Palais-Égalité an ' Appel à la Postérité sur le Jugement du Roi.'
It is full of vigour and logic, and is from the pen of M. Gallais,
formerly a Benedictine monk.[2]

During the past few days a pamphlet entitled ' Light for the
People; being a Conversation with Mme. Saumon, a Fish-
wife, upon the King's Trial,' has been handed about a good
deal.   Mme. Saumon's interviewers are Père Dustyle, a public
writer of the Halles, and Mme. Doucet.   At first Mme. Saumon
is all against the King ; but gradually her prejudices melt away
before Mme. Doucet's excellent logic, vigorously supported by
Père Dustyle.   Her concluding words are :

' Well, I begin to see a bit clearer.   I don't know what to
say myself, but our good Henri IV. used to say that you must
hear both sides.'[3]

---

[1] M. Sourdat was obliged to leave France in order to escape the Revolutionary Tribunal and the scaffold.   His wife and two daughters were
imprisoned as suspects for eleven months.

[2] The work ran through three editions.   The publisher, Michel
Webert, was guillotined May 20, 1794.   Gallais was arrested, detained in
the Force for seven months, and owed his life to the 9th of Thermidor.

[3] The author was M. Bellanger, who under the Restoration was
Conseiller d'État.   M. Bellanger distributed his pamphlet with his own
hands.

Side by side with these writings invoking natural right, justice, and humanity, and appealing to the good sense and reason of the people, are to be found a heap of songs and laments appealing to the emotions. I have already given a fair specimen of one of these,[1] but cannot refrain from introducing the beginning and end of a 'Lament of Louis XVI. in his Prison,' which has caused many a tear to flow.

> ' Now 'tis midnight—all forsake me,
>   All except my woes deny me ;
> Terror strives in vain to shake me,
>   Sorrow sleepless watches by me.
> All night long, 'twixt wake and sleeping,
> Sounds as of my dear wife weeping
>   Torture me : my ears I strain,
> But 'twas fancy—naught I heard
> Save the cruel chain which stirred
>   As I called my babes in vain.
>
> *   *   *   *
>
> ' God above, whose scales unswerving
>   Kings and peoples justly weigh,
> If Thou count'st my woes deserving,
>   And my torments wouldst repay,
> Guard my people as their sire ;
> Let Thy bolts of vengeful ire
>   Elsewhere, God of pity, fly.
> Deign this victim to receive ;
> If my blood Thy grace achieve,
>   I shall be content to die.'

[1] Chapter XXXVII.

CHAPTER XLII.

Sunday, January 20, 1793.

VOTING on the question of the respite began at half-past eight last night, and finished a little before midnight.

The deputies of the Gers were the first to be called, and the Girondists came immediately after them. Vergniaud's vote was therefore again of exceptional importance. He voted against the respite, whilst Gaudet and Bergoeing voted for it; Lacaze was ill, and Grangeneuve refused to vote at all. All the other members for Bordeaux—Gensonné, Jay de Sainte-Croix, Ducos, Garreau, Boyer Fon-Frède, Duplantier, and Deleyre—followed Vergniaud's example.

Three hundred and ten members were in favour of the respite, and 380 against it. It was half-past twelve when Vergniaud declared the result of the vote.

The Convention thereupon decreed that 'the Executive Council should that day notify to Louis the sentence passed upon him, and have that sentence carried out within twenty-four hours of such notification.'

The Assembly adjourned at three in the morning.

      *   *   *   *   *

The following proclamation has just been issued :

'The Provisional Executive Council have decided upon the following measures for carrying out the Decree of the National Convention of the 15th, 17th, 19th, and 20th of January, 1793 :

' 1. The execution of Louis Capet will take place to-morrow, Monday, the 21st.

' 2. The place of execution will be the Place de la Révolution, formerly Place Louis XV., between the pedestal and the Champs Elysées.

'3. Louis Capet will leave the Temple at eight o'clock in the morning, so that the execution may take place at noon.

'4. Commissioners of the department of Paris, Commissioners of the municipality, and two members of the Criminal Tribunal, will be present at the execution. The clerk of that tribunal will draw up a report, which the above-mentioned Commissioners and members of the tribunal will, immediately after the execution, lay before the Council.

'The Provisional Executive Council: *Roland, Clavière, Monge, Lebrun, Garat, Pache.* By the Council: *Grouvelle.*'

It seems as if even the Jacobins and the Maratists felt the enormity of the crime about to be committed. The noisy agitation of the past few days has been succeeded by a mournful silence broken only by the hawkers selling last night's voting lists. In the public squares most of the talk is being carried on in undertones, the faces of the speakers being sad and sullen.[1]

6 p.m.

Lepeletier Saint-Fargeau, member for the Yonne, has just been assassinated in Février's restaurant in the Palais Royal. A man wearing a gray overcoat and a round hat came up to him and said : 'You voted for the King's death, M. Lepeletier ?' 'I voted according to my conscience. What has that to do with you ?' The man in the round hat drew a sword from under his coat and plunged it into the deputy's body. It was just five o'clock. The room was full of people, but there was no commotion, and no one attempted to seize the murderer. There was not the slightest outcry against him. He left as peacefully as possible, after having conversed for some time with several of those present.[2]

10 p.m.

On coming home, I found a paper under my door inviting the people to save *the best of Kings.* It is signed Cujut.[3]

Since yesterday the following pamphlet has been distributed in large numbers : 'Breviary of the Ladies of Paris for the

---

[1] *Le Diurnal de la Révolution de France,* by Beauleu, January 20, 1793.

[2] *Mercure Français,* January 22, 1793.   [3] *Ibid.*

Defence of Louis XVI.' It concludes with an appeal to the *dames de la halle*—the fishwives of the capital.

'*Dames de la halle*—citoyennes of Paris, you who used annually to bring bouquets to the Queen and to the Royal Family, and were always graciously received,—mend the error of your ways. Restore to his palace Louis XVI., the illustrious heir of Saint Louis, Charlemagne and Henri le Grand. Let Louis be saved on Monday next !'

The pamphlet is signed by the Abbé de Salignac, formerly Canon of the chapel royal of Péronne, chaplain to the late Queen of Poland, and governor of the children of Prince Xavier, the King's uncle. The Abbé was arrested yesterday in the Section of the Quatre-Nations, as he was distributing copies of his pamphlet, and taken to the Abbaye.[1]

It is no doubt to the distribution of such tracts as these that we must attribute the various rumours that were afloat to-day, and which have acquired more consistency to-night. It is asserted that a number of ladies are to disguise themselves as women of the people, and to mingle with the *dames de la halle*, after which an attempt is to be made to obtain pardon for the King.[2] These are mere baseless rumours showing both the credulity of the simple Royalists and the fear which the Republicans cannot shake off even at the moment of con-summating their crime.

[1] *Révolutions de Paris*, No. 185.   [2] *Ibid.*

CHAPTER XLIII.

1 a.m., Monday, January 21, 1793.

I HAD just finished writing the preceding lines, when Beaulieu and Marignié[1] entered. I had not seen the latter since the 16th, and was struck by his altered appearance and the feverish look in his eyes. 'We have just left the Assembly,' said Beaulieu. 'I thought you would like to know what has taken place, and I persuaded Marignié to come with me. He will tell you himself what he has done, and, like me, you will be proud to count such a man among your friends.' 'Beaulieu,' observed Marignié, in tones of profound grief, 'your praise is not acceptable at such a time; I beg you to spare me.' He then sat down, and, hiding his face in his hands, wept like a child. Relieved no doubt by these tears, and grateful, perhaps, to me for not plying him with questions, he at length decided to tell me his story, which I reproduce as nearly as possible in his words

'Last night I went home, leaving the Assembly discussing the question of a respite. It was impossible to hope for a favourable decision. Throwing myself upon my bed to snatch a few hours'

---

[1] Jean Étienne François de Marignié was born at Sére, in Languedoc, in 1755, and died in 1831. He wrote a tragedy, 'Zorai, ou les Insulaires de la Nouvelle Zélande,' and a comedy, 'Le Paresseux, ou l'Homme de Lettres par Paresse.' At the beginning of the King's trial he had written a tract called 'Procès de Louis XVI. en Quatre Mots.' Obliged to leave France in 1793, he joined Mallet du Pan in England, and contributed to the *Journal Général de l'Europe*. He returned to France in 1796, but all his property had been confiscated. He assisted Chateaubriand in editing the *Mercure*, and M. Suard in the *Publiciste*, and was appointed Inspector-General of the University by M. de Fontanes. During the Hundred Days he refused to take the oath, and lost his place. Louis XVIII. made him a Knight of the Legion of Honour.

rest, I was immediately seized with an idea that I could not shake from me. The feeling of having a duty to discharge forced itself upon my conscience, and after a few moments' hesitation, I was seated at my writing-table, remaining there the whole of the night and morning, drawing up a petition in which I asked the Convention for mercy for the King.'

Here Marignié handed me what he calls a *petition*. It is no less than a complete defence of the King, and a vindication of every principle of law, justice, and honour violated during the trial. Several of the divisions into which the work is cut up are developed at some length, and with much eloquence ; others are merely indicated, Marignié having intended to dwell more fully upon them at the bar of the Convention. He continued his story in the following words :

' Sunday being the day appointed for the presentation of petitions, I hastened to the Convention, arriving there about two o'clock. Heedless of rules and regulations, I walked right into the hall where the sittings are held, and took a seat amongst the members. The agitation that prevailed in the Assembly and the assurance of my behaviour were so far favourable to my enterprise. Calling one of the ushers, I handed him a note for the President, who opened and read it. The note ran as follows :

' " Citizen President,—I ask for permission to lay before the Assembly a petition in favour of the King, based upon weighty arguments. I beg that you will get the Convention to hear me."

' A discussion was then going on concerning Kersaint's dismissal. I allowed about an hour to pass, and then called another usher, telling him to ask the President for an answer to the note sent him by one Marignié. The usher soon returned, saying that I must wait until the hour for the presentation of petitions, but that the President did not think the Convention would hear me. A few moments later Barbaroux happened to pass where I was sitting, and, stopping him, I told him the reason for my being there. He looked at me as though he thought me mad. " What an idea !" he cried, with an oath. " You won't be heard." Upon my insisting, he replied, " Well, I hope you may," and hastened away.

' A third usher now approached me, and asked whether I was a member. I replied in the negative, but added that I was there waiting for a reply from the President. He thereupon conducted me to the seats reserved for distinguished strangers, and left me.

' Time dragged on, and at last Garat appeared in the tribune to report that notice had been given to the King of the sentence passed upon him. He also produced a paper handed to him by Louis XVI., in which the Monarch asks for three days in which to prepare himself for death, permission to have a priest of his own choosing, and the privilege of being alone with his family for the last time. The King further expresses a hope that the Convention will provide for the future of his wife and children, and allow them to live wherever they wish, and finally commends to the generosity of the nation all those who had served him. The Convention thereupon decreed that Louis was at liberty to send for any priest he might prefer, and to see his family alone; it promised that the nation would provide for his family, but it took no notice of the reference to his faithful servants, nor of the respite he demanded. The execution must, therefore, take place before mid-day to-morrow, January 21. From that moment I felt more keenly than ever the value of the minutes that were speeding by. Suddenly I heard the President mention the petitioners. Joy, mingled with terrible anxiety, seized hold of me. The President continued, but only to propose that the petitioners should be put off till to-morrow—a proposal which was immediately agreed to.

' I was just rising from my seat to protest, when the President remarked : " There is, however, one petition——" It was mine, there could be no doubt about it—the hour had come! Vain hope ! The petitioner whom the President proposed the Convention should hear to-day was a Belgian officer, who immediately stepped up.

' Beside myself with agitation, I left my seat and again mingled with the members of the Convention. Finding myself next to M. Rouyer, deputy for the Hérault, I made bold to tell him in broken phrases what I had come to do. Like Barbaroux, Rouyer at once replied that he did not think I would be heard, but, more generous than his colleague, he offered to go and tell the President that I insisted upon being heard before the Assembly broke up.   I watched him as he spoke to the President and left his desk. Meanwhile the Belgian officer had finished reading his petition, and the President replied.   A few seconds more and the sitting would be over.   There was not a moment to be lost.   I leave the benches and hasten to the Presidential chair.   "Are you M. Vergniaud?" I ask.   "Yes."   The Assembly had now risen, and the deputies were getting ready to go.   "My name is Marignié, sir; you have read my letter.   I beg you to ask the Convention to hear the petition that I wish to lay before it. Why have you not already done so?"   "Why?" he says; "because if I had only mentioned such a thing I should have been stoned."   The members' benches and the public galleries were already beginning to empty.   "Then," I cried, "you leave me no alternative but to publish what I was not allowed to say here.   Though it will come too late, I will do it, and I warn you that at the same time I will publish the words you have used, which clearly show by what spirit your Convention is animated!"   "What do you mean?" retorted Vergniaud, no doubt regretting the words he had used.   "I mean, sir, that I shall publish your words, 'If I had only mentioned such a thing, I should have been stoned.'"   "I don't know what you are talking about," he said, shrugging his shoulders; "I receive so many letters and petitions!   I am perfectly ignorant of what yours contains!"   "You know perfectly well what it contains, M. Vergniaud, and your reply proves it.   I repeat that it shall be made public."   "Do as you like, but I tell you that I shall disavow it."   "I shall publish that too," I cried as I left him.   Once more I heard him say "I shall disavow it" as I left the hall with the last of the members.   In one of the corridors I met Beaulieu, who brought me here.'

'I am much obliged to him for doing so, my dear Marignié, for your visit has given me more consolation than I have felt since the beginning of this abominable trial.'

Marignié rose.

'I must go home at once,' he said, 'for I must keep my promise of immediately publishing the petition I was not allowed to read, the efforts I put forth to do so, and the President's replies.'

Both seized with the same fear, Beaulieu and I cried out together:

'Will you put your own name to it?'

A smile lit up his face, pale with fever.

'My friends,' he replied, as he took our hands, 'I shall sign it with my own name—would that I might seal it with my blood!'[1]

      *   *   *   *   *

Marignié and Beaulieu have left some time. Four o'clock has just struck from the steeple of Saint-Roch. I have opened my window. It is raining. The drums are beating the call to arms.

6 o'clock.

The rain has not left off, and I can still hear the roll of the drums in the street. From the direction of the Rue Saint-Honoré comes the noise of the cannons as they are dragged over the stones. On the horizon faint streaks of light announce the dawn of another day—a day which shall bear that date, accursed throughout the centuries, of the Twenty-first of January, 1793!

[1] 'Pétition de Grace et de Clémence pour Louis XVI.,' by Marignié. Paris, January 21, 1793.

CHAPTER XLIV.

Thursday, January 24, 1793.

I ONCE more take up my diary to jot down all the details I have been able to gather concerning the sacrifice of the Twenty-first of January.

The night between the 20th and 21st had been a cold and rainy one. At daybreak it was still raining, but the snow, which had the night before covered Paris with an immense pall, had partially disappeared. Patrols marched slowly through the streets. From all quarters came the roll of the drum and the blare of the trumpet, calling citizens to arms. House-doors opened, and men, both young and old, hurried off to their various sections in obedience to the orders of the Conseil-Général of the department and the Order of the Day issued by Santerre on the 20th.

By seven o'clock more than 150,000 men were under arms at the various posts assigned them.

The third legion, comprising the citizens of the Gravilliers, Arcis, and Lombard sections, is drawn up in the Place de la Révolution.

The post of honour, opposite the scaffold, at the entrance to the Champs-Élysées, is occupied by the battalions of federates from Aix and Marseilles.

At eight o'clock the rain ceases, but a thick cold mist lies upon the city. Not a single shop or warehouse is open, and all the windows are hermetically closed. In several places the following notice, written by hand, has been posted up :

'To the People,

    'The Assembly can drag an innocent King to the scaffold, and by thus outraging the feelings of the world, bring unutterable misfortunes upon us. What has it to fear? Nothing. None but honest folk are opposed to it. Are its decrees those of a God, that they cannot be revoked? Let us save him—there is still time.'[1]

Santerre, accompanied by a formidable train of artillery, arrived at the Temple a little after eight o'clock, and went straight to the King's apartments, followed by seven or eight municipal officers and ten gendarmes. Louis received him with perfect tranquillity. 'Have you come for me?' he asked. 'Yes.' 'Very well. I want to be alone with my confessor for a few moments, and then I will be at your disposal.' Hereupon he entered an inner room, and returned almost immediately after, holding his testament in his hand. Addressing the municipal officers, he said: 'Is there some member of the Commune amongst you?' The priest Jacques Roux stepped forward. 'I beg you, sir, to place this document in the hands of the President of the Conseil-Général.' 'That's not my business,' replied Jacques Roux; 'I am here to take you to the scaffold.' 'You are right,' observed the King,[2] and thereupon handed his testament to Baudrais, a Commissioner on duty in the Temple, who promised to deliver it to the Commune. After having commended Cléry, his valet, and his former servants in the Tuileries and at Versailles, to the municipal officers, he looked at Santerre, and said in a firm voice: 'Let us go.'[3]

A start is made. At the top of the stairs the King's eyes fall upon Mathey, the *concierge* of the Tower. He stops and says: 'I was somewhat hasty a day or two ago; pray forgive me.' They go down. The King walks across the first courtyard between a double hedge of pikes and bayonets; twice does he turn round to look at the tower in which he leaves sister, children, and wife. On reaching the second court, he finds a carriage awaiting him, with two gendarmes stationed at the

---

[1] Convention Nationale, sitting of January 21; speech by Garreau.

[2] 'Report to the Commune,' by Jacques Roux, January 21.

[3] *Journal de ce qui s'est passé à la Tour du Temple*, by Cléry; 'Dernières Heures de Louis XVI.,' by the Abbé Edgeworth; 'Report to the Commune,' by Jacques Roux.

door.   The carriage is painted green,[1] and is that of the
Minister Clavière.[2] Louis gets in, his confessor taking a seat
beside him, whilst the front seat is occupied by a Lieutenant[3]
and a Quarter-Master of the gendarmerie.   The Abbé Edgeworth is not in clerical garb, but wears a plain black coat.[4]

As the carriage leaves the Temple, cries of ' *Mercy! Mercy!*'
are uttered by some women, followed by an ominous silence.[5]

From the Temple to the boulevard, the street was lined with
more than 10,000 armed men.

Along each side of the boulevard was a line of men four deep,
all carrying guns or pikes ; there could not have been less than
80,000.   A train of artillery headed the procession, which was
composed of 12,000 to 15,000 armed men.   Immediately before
the King's carriage, a large number of drummers and trumpeters
kept up an incessant din ; behind it came more artillery.

As the carriage passed the Port Saint-Denis, four men—one
of them, the eldest, flourishing a naked sword—dashed through
the quadruple line of soldiers, and repeatedly shouted : ' Help,
Frenchmen ! Help us to save the King !' To this heroic
appeal there was no response, and the four Royalists dashed
back through the broken line and amongst the astonished crowd.
The man with the sword and one of his companions succeeded
in escaping, but the two others were seized just as they were
entering a house in the Rue de Cléry, and were cut to pieces
on the threshold.[6]   Meanwhile the procession continued to

[1] *Le Républicain*, January 22, 1793.

[2] And not that of the Mayor, as erroneously stated in No. 185 of the
Révolutions de Paris. On the 20th, Sanson, the executioner, asked the
authorities what arrangements had been made for the execution. ' It is
absolutely necessary,' he wrote, ' for me to know how Louis will leave the
Temple. Will he have a carriage, or will he go in the ordinary tumbril ?'
By an order of the Executive Council, the Mayor's carriage was to take
Louis Capet from the Temple to the place of execution, but the Com-
mune was opposed to this, and it was Clavière, Minister of Public Taxes,
who lent his. ('Archives Nationales,' AF ii. 3 : Conseil Exécutif
Provisoire.)

[3] Jean Maurice François Lebrasse. He was guillotined April 13, 1794,
with Chaumette, Simon, the two Grammonts, and others.

[4] *Le Républicain*, January 22, 1793.

[5] *Journal de Perlet*, January 22, 1793.

[6] The names of the two butchered men perished with them. The other
two were the Baron de Batz and his friend Jean Louis Michel Devaux, an
official in the Treasury. Devaux was condemned to death on June 17,

move towards the Place de la Révolution. The journey from the Temple to the end of the Rue Royale had taken more than an hour. During all this time, Louis, his face half hidden by a round hat with a wide brim, was engaged in reading, from his confessor's breviary, the prayers for the dying and the psalms of David. When the carriage at length stopped, the King, raising his head, half closed the book, and said to the Abbé: 'Here we are, if I am not mistaken.' The Abbé bowed, and Louis turned once more to his breviary, and read the last verses of the psalm he had left unfinished. At that moment one of Sanson's assistants opened the carriage-door and let down the step. The King calmly finished his last prayer, returned the book to the Abbé, and, laying his hand on his confessor's knee, said to the Lieutenant and his comrade: 'Gentlemen, I recommend the Abbé to your protection.' Neither of the officers

---

1794, after having refused to disclose to Fouquier-Tinville the hiding-place of De Batz. See the cross-examination of Devaux before the Revolutionary Tribunal, June 17, 1794=29th of Prairial, year II. The Baron de Batz was a character so mysterious and so little known to his own contemporaries that he would seem almost mythical. For full information respecting him, see the romance of 'The Red Shirts,' by Paul Gaulot, translated by J. de Villiers (Chatto and Windus, London, 1894) —'an artistic rendering of a plot' in which he played the principal part, and from which we take the following document:

'NATIONAL CONVENTION.

'"Report made in the Name of the Joint Committees of Public Safety and General Security on the Batz Conspiracy, or that of the Foreign Foe, by Elie Lacoste, at the Sitting of the 22nd of Prairial, year II."

'. . . Batz, ci-devant Baron and ex-deputy of the Constituent Assembly, is the infamous outlaw who was to direct the vilest attempts of the Kings against humanity. . . . Batz, supported by English gold and the rebellious towns of France, directed the plans of conspiracy that had been concocted by our foreign enemies and the emigrants. The principal objects of these plans were the rescue of the widow Capet, the dissolution of the National Convention, and, finally, the counter-Revolution. . . . Batz gathered round him the ci-devant Marquis de Pons, Sombreuil, and his son, the ci-devant Marquis de la Guiche, and others. To these was added a courtisane named Grandmaison, the mistress of Batz and a consummate plotter. Her maid, Nicole, and her man-servant, Biret-Tissot, were also in all the secrets, and it was by their aid that the conspirators kept up a very active correspondence among themselves. A villa called the Hermitage, situated at Charonne, was the place in which their mysterious councils were held. It was there that they planned the execution of their vile plots, and it was from there that the correspondence was sent to all the conspirators.'

having replied, the King repeated in a somewhat louder tone:
' I charge you to see that no harm is done him after my death.'
' All right—all right,' replied the Lieutenant; ' we'll see to
that.'[1] The King then got out of the carriage without any
assistance; it was just twenty minutes past ten.[2] He was wearing a brown coat and white waistcoat, gray breeches, and white
stockings. His hair was neatly arranged, and his face betrayed
no signs of agitation.[3] He then advanced with a firm step to
the scaffold, which had been erected between the avenue of the
Champs-Élysées and the pedestal of Louis XV.'s statue, overturned after the Tenth of August.[4]

An immense space lined with cannons had been railed off
round the scaffold. Turning to the armed masses which surround
him, the King, in a tone of command, orders the drummers to
be silent. They obey; but Santerre, who is on horseback a
short distance off, comes hastening up, and by his orders the
drummers resume their task.[5] The headsman and his assistants
now crowd round the Monarch, and wish to help him to undress.
He pushes them away, and, taking off his cravat with his own
hands, proceeds to divest himself of his coat, under which he
was wearing a white swan's-down waistcoat with sleeves. He
then turns down his shirt to leave his neck free, and kneels at
the feet of the Abbé Edgeworth to receive the last benediction.
Rising once more, he places his foot on the first step of the
ladder that leads to the scaffold; but the assistants stop him,

---

[1] ' Dernières Heures de Louis XVI.,' by the Abbé Edgeworth; *Révolutions de Paris*, p. 185.

[2] ' Report of the Execution of Louis XVI.,' signed by Lefèvre, Momoro,
Sallais, Ysabeau, Bernard, and Roux, 'Archives Nationales,' CII. 103
(Ass. Pol. Convention).

[3] ' Histoire de la Révolution de France,' by Two Friends of Liberty,
ix. 370.

[4] ' The scaffold,' says Mortimer-Ternaux (v. 504), ' was erected between
the entrance to the Champs-Élysées and the pedestal which, after having
served as the base of Louis XV.'s statue, was then surmounted by
that of Liberty.' This last detail is incorrect. On January 21 the
pedestal was empty, as is proved by contemporary engravings, *i.e.*, that
which adorns p. 202 of vol. xv. of the *Révolutions de Paris*, and that in
the Hennin collection, published on p. 34 of Dauban's ' Démagogie en
1793.' The statue of Liberty was not placed upon the pedestal until the
month of August, 1793.

[5] An account of the last moments of Louis XVI. published in tome ii.
of the ' Procès des Bourbons,' 1798.

and try to seize his hands. 'What is it you want?' he asks.
'To bind your hands.' 'Bind my hands! Never! It's not
necessary; I am quite calm.' The executioners raise their voices,
and seem to call for assistance. 'Sire,' says the Abbé, 'in this
fresh insult I see but an additional trait of resemblance between
your Majesty and the God who is about to reward you.' The
King submits, and, holding out his hands, says to the executioners:
'Do what you will; I will drain the cup to the dregs.'[1] They
then tie his hands with his handkerchief, and cut off his hair.

All is now ready. Louis looks at the scaffold for a moment,
and receives the following words from his confessor as a last
encouragement: 'Go, son of Saint Louis; Heaven awaits you!'[2]
Bravely he mounts the steps of the scaffold,[3] but as they are
extremely steep and his hands are tied he leans his elbow on
the Abbé's arm.[4] Whilst the priest remains kneeling on the
topmost step Louis rapidly crosses the platform, and on reaching
the opposite side looks towards the Tuileries, and again imposes
silence upon the drummers by an imperious gesture. In a loud
voice that is heard as far as the Pont Tournant he utters
these words: 'Frenchmen, I die innocent of all the crimes with
which I am charged.'[5] Turning to the executioners, Santerre
shouts, 'Don't let him speak!' A few cries of ' Mercy! Mercy!'[6]
are heard, and the crowd shows signs of great agitation. Many
of the citizens want Louis to speak, but most of them are
opposed to this, and encourage the executioners to do their
duty.[7] Santerre issues an order to the drummers,[8] and the
interrupted roll of the drums is resumed with fresh vigour.
The headsman's assistants now seize the King, who unresistingly

---

[1] 'Dernières Heures de Louis XVI.'; letter from Sanson to the *Thermomètre du Jour*, February 21, 1793.

[2] 'An Authentic Narrative of all that took place during the Trial and Execution of Louis XVI.,' etc., by Citizen Rouy, senior, an eye-witness. See also next chapter.

[3] 'The King, who had bravely mounted the scaffold, leaning on the arm of his confessor. . . .' Santerre himself uses these very words in a note published by M. A. Carro, author of a ' Vie de Santerre ' that appeared in 1847.

[4] 'Dernières Heures de Louis XVI.,' by the Abbé Edgeworth.

[5] *Ibid.*   [6] Note by Santerre, *op. cit.*

[7] 'An Authentic Narrative,' etc., by Citizen Rouy.

[8] *Révolutions de Paris*, No. 185. See also next chapter.

allows himself to be led to the board.[1] Whilst he is being strapped down[2] he utters the following words in loud, distinct tones : ' I forgive all those who have sought my death ; I pray to God that the blood you are about to shed may not be avenged on France. And you, unhappy people——' He says no more. It is twenty-four minutes past ten,[3] and the knife has done its work. Whilst the men of the Republic were performing their hideous task, the man of God was on his knees on the steps of the scaffold,[4] reciting the prayers for the dying. He did not budge till the knife had fallen ; then, passing un-molested through the ranks of the soldiers, he became lost in the crowd.[5]

The crime was perpetrated. One of the executioners—the youngest, almost a boy—took up the King's head by the hair, and showed it to the people from the four sides of the scaffold.[6] At sight of this a few shouts of ' *Vive la République !* are raised. Soon these are multiplied, and are re-echoed back from all parts of the Place de la Révolution, and repeated along the quays—' *Vive la République !* ' *Vive la Liberté !* ' *Vive l'Égalité !* ' *May all tyrants perish so !* Hats are stuck on the ends of guns and pikes, the citizens embrace each other in wild delight, and joining hands, they form a ring and dance round the scaffold.[7] This example is followed in several other parts of the square, and dancing goes on as far as the Pont de la Liberté.[8] The boys of the Collège des Quatre-Nations, who witness this horrible spectacle from their schoolroom windows, wave their caps and shout ' *Vive la République !*[9]

Meanwhile the National Guards, federates, and gendarmes posted round the scaffold dip their pikes, bayonets, and swords in the warm blood that is trickling down. The officers of the

---

[1] Sanson's letter to the *Thermomètre du Jour*, **February** 21, 1793.
[2] *Révolutions de Paris*, No. 185.
[3] *Le Républician*, January 22, 1793.
[4] ' Cabinet des Estampes : Bibliothèque Nationale.'
[5] Bertrand de Moleville, ' Mémoires Secrets,' iii. 221.
[6] ' An Authentic Narrative,' etc., by Citizen Rouy
[7] *Ibid.* See also an account by Joseph Trémié, a volunteer in the 2nd battalion of Marseilles, published in the *Revue Rétrospective* on February 1, 1892.
[8] As the Pont Louis XVI. was then called.
[9] Mercier, ' Le Nouveau Paris,' ch. lxxxii.

Marseilles battalion dip their letters in it, and as they afterwards march through the streets of the city at the head of their
companies, they stick these letters on the points of their swords,
and, flourishing them, shout : ' This is the blood of a tyrant !'[1]

A man climbs on to the scaffold, and plunges his naked arm
into the *tyrant's* blood. He then takes a handful of it, and
besprinkles the crowd that surges round the foot of the platform,
eager to catch a drop or two. ' Brothers,' cries the man as he
performs this hideous rite—' brothers, they have told us that
the blood of Louis Capet will be on our heads. Well, let it be.
Louis Capet has so often washed his hands in ours. Republicans,
a King's blood brings luck !'[2]

And for this blood the crowd still hungers. People fight to
dip the tips of their fingers, a handkerchief,[3] a pen, or a scrap
of paper, in it. A *sans-culotte* tastes it, and says : ' It's d——d
salty !'[4] A young man who looked like an Englishman gave
a boy fifteen francs to dip a very fine linen handkerchief in the
few drops of blood that were left.[5] One of the executioner's
men, seated on the edge of the scaffold, sells small packets of
the King's hair ;[6] the ribbon with which it was tied back fetches
ten francs.[7] A *sans-culotte*, named Heuzé, also makes his way
on to the scaffold, and, seizing the King's coat, holds it up at the

---

[1] *Révolutions de Paris*, No. 185.   [2] *Ibid.*

[3] Report made to the Commune, by Jacques Roux.

[4] Mercier, 'Le Nouveau Paris,' ch. lxxxii.

[5] *Le Journal de Perlet*, January 22, 1793. Soulavie ('Mémoires
Historiques du Règne de Louis XVI.,' tome vi., p. 517) says : ' A good
many people having carefully mopped up the blood that flowed over the
scaffold, it was used for colouring engravings of Sacred Hearts and
Crucified Saviours ; I have several specimens in my collection.' On
January 1, 1794, less than a year later, Pierre Joachim Vancleemputte, a
priest of the church of Saint-Nicolas-des-Champs in Paris, was brought
before the Revolutionary Tribunal. Amongst other relics belonging to
him had been found a small sealed paper bearing the words 'Blood of
Louis XVI.' Fouquier-Tinville accused him ' of being the author of a
plot to deceive the people, by showing them some blood supposed to be
that of the *tyrant*, in order to work upon their feelings, and so provoke
the re-establishment of the Monarchy.' The Abbé Vancleemputte was
condemned to death ('Les Martyrs de la Foi pendant la Révolution
Française,' by the Abbé Guillon, tome iv., p. 691 ; ' Histoire du Tribunal
Révolutionnaire de Paris,' by H. Wallon, tome ii., p. 307).

[6] ' An Authentic Narrative,' etc., by Rouy.

[7] ' Derniers Moments de Louis XVI.,' p. 7, published on January 22,
1793.

end of a pike. The coat is immediately torn to shreds by the crowd, and everyone is anxious to secure a piece of it.[1] The King's hat, which was left lying on the bottom step of the scaffold, is also torn into fragments and distributed.[2]

The crowd gradually disperses. The fog that has been hanging over the city since morning has become more dense. Every shop, workshop, and warehouse is closed ; in the afternoon a few of them are opened, as on minor *fête* days.[3] Patrols continue to parade the deserted streets, the silence of which is only broken occasionally by the bloodthirsty cries and savage capers of a few abandoned wretches.[4]

*   *   *   *   *

In spite of this fiendish barbarity, in spite of the horrible scenes that took place in a number of *cafés* and wine-shops, Paris all day wore a dreary dismal air.[5] In the evening the theatres were open as usual, but they remained empty. In one that is generally well packed there were not thirty spectators.[6]

Night came at last to spread its dark veil over the city. What anguish and grief was hidden behind those drawn shutters, and in those darkened silent houses ! How many prayers were sent up in those terrible hours for the women and children who were weeping bitter tears in their lonely prison in the Temple tower ![7] A soldier, on whose breast hung the cross of Saint Louis, died of grief on hearing of the King's death. A woman threw herself in despair into the river. Vente, the bookseller,

---

[1] *Révolutions de Paris*, No. 185.

[2] Extract from the Minutes of the proceedings of the Conseil-Général de la Commune on April 29, 1793 : 'Acting upon the information given in the report drawn up at the Temple, and which led to these fresh inquiries, the police authorities summoned the executioner and Dulong, the hatter, to appear before them. The former declared that Louis, on reaching the place of execution, took off only his hat and coat ; that he was buried in all his other clothes ; that the hat and coat were torn into fragments immediately after the execution and distributed amongst the spectators.'—*Journal de Paris National*, May 1, 1793.

[3] *Révolutions de Paris*, No. 185.

[4] *Chronique de Paris*, January 22, 1793 ; 'Histoire de la Révolution de 1789,' by Two Friends of Liberty, tome ix.

[5] *Révolutions de Paris*, No. 185 ; 'Histoire de la Révolution,' by Two Friends of Liberty, tome ix., p. 372.

[6] *Le Courrier des Départements*, January 28, 1793.

[7] *Révolutions de Paris*, No. 185.

went raving mad.   A wig-maker of the Rue Culture-Sainte-Catherine, an ardent Royalist, cut his throat with a razor.[1]   The mother of Charles de Lézardière, living in retirement at Choisy-le-Roi, fell dead with fright on seeing her son come home with the terrible news written in his face.[2]

Though the mob gave full vent to its terrible passions, the middle classes and all respectable citizens showed, by their attitude, that they disapproved of the crime that the Convention had had the cowardice to commit.   But was this enough ? Was it not the duty of every honest man to have prevented this abominable execution ?   Ought we not all to have responded to the heroic cry that was heard at the Porte Saint Denis : 'Help, Frenchmen !   Help us to save the King !'   Let us at least piously cherish the memory of the two young heroes who were butchered on the stones of the Rue de Cléry—of the two nameless martyrs who have already found a place in Heaven by the side of the son of Saint Louis !

[1] *Révolutions de Paris*, No. 185.
[2] 'Notice sur Mdlle. de Lézardière,' by Merland, 'Biographies Vendéennes,' tome iv.

A MAKER OF HISTORY.

'A SEPARATE work would not suffice to correct all the errors committed by the different historians of the French Revolution.' These are the words of Louis Blanc (tome viii., p. 412), and he adds : 'Perhaps we may ourselves some day undertake this work of historical criticism—nothing would be more *curious* and instructive.' Nothing, indeed, would have been more *curious* than such a work, especially if the eminent historian had taken the trouble to correct his own mistakes. We will simply take a few of those which he has committed concerning the death of Louis XVI.

In tome viii., p. 71, Louis Blanc shows us Louis XVI. recommending his confessor to the care of the executioner on alighting from the carriage which took him to the place of execution ! It was not to the executioner that Louis recommended the Abbé Edgeworth, but to the two gendarmes who were with him in the carriage, to Lieutenant Lebrasse and his comrade. In the *Révolutions de Paris*, No. 186, we find : 'On reaching the Place de la Révolution, he repeatedly recommended his confessor to the care of the Lieutenant and left the coach.' The Abbé himself has given us the following account : 'Messieurs, I recommend this gentleman to your care ; see that no harm comes to him after my death.' Addressed to these two officers, these recommendations were but natural ; they would be meaningless if made to the executioner and his assistants.

This is, however, but a slight inadvertence ; the following is a more serious one.

---

[1] Being notes on Chapter XLIV., too important and too long to be placed at the foot of the page.

In an earlier chapter we have shown how Louis Blanc attempted to credit Louis XVI. on his appearance before the Convention on December 26, 1792, with pretended illusions and hopes, thus substituting a foolish credulity for that greatness of soul which the King displayed under such trying circumstances; we have shown that Louis Blanc refused Louis XVI. that justice which even the members of the Convention accorded him.

It is the same with January 21. Louis Blanc has not feared to insinuate what the Commissioners of the Commune dared not suggest. According to him, the King had hopes of being rescued until he stood on the scaffold. At the Temple he is alleged to have put off the moment of departure as long as possible, and under every conceivable pretext; on reaching the Place de la Révolution, he is said to have exclaimed, when he saw himself obliged to give up all hope: 'What treason! I am lost! I am lost!' Louis Blanc further says that he had to be dragged along the scaffold, and that he uttered terrible cries whilst being strapped down—cries which were only interrupted by the fall of the knife. Of all these assertions there is not one that is true.

'*The King had hopes of being rescued until he stood on the scaffold.*' No contemporary account authorizes such a supposition; there is no trace of it either in the *Révolutions de Paris*, the most hostile of all the newspapers, or in the reports laid before the Commune by its several Commissioners. On January 20, it is true, two young men came to inform the Abbé Edgeworth of a plot to rescue the King; the King's confessor, although not really believing the possibility of success, was unwilling to close his heart to this last hope. 'There is no doubt,' says Louis Blanc, 'that he imparted this hope to Louis XVI.' We find, on the contrary, from the Abbé Edgeworth's own narrative, that he took care to keep from the King the information he had received. This narrative, too long to be reproduced here, should be read; every detail it contains is absolutely irreconcilable with Louis Blanc's assertion.

This assertion is further damned by the facts themselves—by the following, for instance, which, amongst others, Louis Blanc has carefully passed over. A plot had indeed been formed (was there ever a more legitimate one?) to rescue Louis XVI. from his

executioners whilst proceeding from the Temple to the Place de
la Révolution.   Hyde de Neuville, one of the conspirators, had
let M. de Malesherbes into the secret, and Malesherbes had in
turn confided it to the King.   The imprisoned Monarch was still
certain of being obeyed by the brave men who had remained
faithful to him.   He therefore ordered Hyde de Neuville and his
friends, through Malesherbes, to renounce their project.   ' My
young friend,' said the defender of Louis XVI. to De Neuville,
' your efforts and those of your comrades would be useless.   Give
up your undertaking; it is the will and the order of your King,
whose only thought is of France, and who will allow no blood to
be shed for his sake.'   (' Histoire de la Révolution,' tome i.,
p. 405, by M. Poujoulat, who had these details from Hyde de
Neuville himself.)

Louis Blanc asserts that when Santerre and the Commissioners
of the Commune presented themselves at the Temple, the King's
courage failed for a moment; that even after entering the inner
room and emerging with the will in his hand he attempted to
create fresh delay; that Santerre was obliged to say, ' Sir, it is
time to go'; that he then made a second excuse for returning to
the inner room, where he stayed until Santerre again urged him
to depart; that when he himself saw the uselessness of further
resistance, he stamped upon the floor in anger, and cried, ' Come,
let us go!'   Upon what testimony does Louis Blanc base this assertion?   Upon an anonymous narrative published five years after
the events in a compilation entitled ' Le Procès des Bourbons.'

With this anonymous narrative let us compare that of the
eye-witnesses—of those who were in the Temple on the morning
of January 21.   Cléry, in his ' Journal,' p. 106, says : ' Santerre,
accompanied by seven or eight municipal officers, entered at the
head of ten gendarmes, whom he drew up in a double line.
Hereupon the King emerged from his cabinet.   " Have you
come to fetch me ?" he asked.   " Yes."   " I shall be with you in
a moment;" and he re-entered the cabinet.   His Majesty returned
almost immediately, his confessor following him ; the King had
his testament in his hand, and addressing a municipal officer
named Jacques Roux, an apostate priest who happened to be
nearest to him, he said : " I beg you to give this document to the

Queen—to my wife." "That is not my business," replied the priest, refusing to take the document; "I am here to take you to the scaffold." I was behind the King, near the grate; he turned to me, and I offered him his overcoat. "I do not require it," he said; "give me only my hat." I handed it to him. His hand met mine, which he pressed for the last time. "Gentlemen," he said, addressing the municipal officers, "I should like Cléry to stay with my son, who is accustomed to his care; I hope the Commune will grant my request." Then, looking at Santerre, he said: "Let us go."' The following is the account given by the Abbé Edgeworth: '. . . It was Santerre and his men. The King opened the door, and he was told (I do not know in what terms) that he was to go to his death. "I am busy for a moment," he said in authoritative tones; "wait for me there, I shall be with you immediately." With these words he closed the door and threw himself on his knees before me. "All is over," he said; "give me your last blessing, and pray to God that He may support me to the end." He rose immediately, and, leaving the room, went up to the group in the middle of his bed-chamber. The faces of the men wore a look that was anything but one of assurance, though all kept their hats upon their heads. This the King noticed, and immediately asked for his. Whilst Cléry, bathed in tears, went to fetch it, the King asked: "Is there any member of the Commune amongst you? I charge him with the care of this document." It was his will. "I also wish to recommend Cléry, my valet, to the care of the Commune; he has rendered me valuable services. Let him have my watch and all my personal property, both what is here and what has been deposited with the Commune. As a reward for the attachment he has shown me, I should like him to be retained in the service of the Queen—of my wife" (for the King used both words). No one replying, the King said in a firm voice, "Let us go."'

On January 21, Jacques Roux made a report to the Commune of the mission which he had that day discharged in conjunction with Jacques Claude Bernard: 'We betook ourselves to the Temple, and there we announced to the tyrant that the hour of execution had come. He asked to be left alone for a few moments with his confessor. He desired to entrust us with a packet for you, but we told him that our duty consisted only in taking him to the scaffold. To this he replied : "That is true." He then gave the packet to one of our colleagues. He asked that his family might be cared for, and that Cléry, his valet, should pass into the service of the Queen—hurriedly substituting the words "*my wife*." He also requested that his old servants might not be forgotten, and then, turning to Santerre, he said : "Let us go."'

The want of courage and the anger of Louis XVI. are thus absent not only from the narratives of Cléry and the Abbé Edgeworth, but also from that of Jacques Roux. These three accounts, which agree so thoroughly, prove conclusively that the King, after having come out of his cabinet with his will, did not return and have to be invited to come out by Santerre.

Can we be certain that at the foot of the scaffold, when the drums drowned his voice for the first time, Louis XVI. uttered the words, 'What treason ! I am lost ! I am lost !' Here, again, Louis Blanc invokes the account published in the ' Procès des Bourbons '; but this time he has been careful, in order to lend this anonymous document some authority, to refer his readers to chapter lxxxii. of Mercier's ' Nouveau Paris.' Now, firstly, this work, like the ' Procès des Bourbons,' did not appear until 1798 ; and, secondly, it makes not the slightest mention of the above exclamation put into the King's mouth.

Instead of adducing these unreliable documents, published some years after the events, and which, moreover, do not contain the words that Louis Blanc pretends they do, why did not that historian quote from a contemporary document, from an article that appeared on February 13 in the *Thermomètre du Jour*, under the following heading, ' Anecdote très exacte sur l'Exécution de Louis Capet '? In this we find, ' A look of despair came into Louis's face as the roll of the drums interrupted his speech ; thrice he hurriedly cried, "I am lost !"' Can Louis Blanc perchance have been ignorant of the existence of this article ? Or can it be that he did not care to remember that his theory of the King's pretended illusions of deliverance had been supported by an infamous article in that very paper, the *Thermomètre*, and that the theory had been refuted by an eye-witness who was certainly no Royalist—by the executioner Sanson himself? (Letter from Sanson to the editor of the *Thermomètre du Jour*, February 20, 1793.)

If Louis XVI. did not pronounce the words imputed to him, did he, then, engage in a struggle with his executioners? Was it necessary to drag him along the scaffold by force? Louis Blanc does not hesitate to say so, and besides Mercier's 'Nouveau Paris,' he invoked the authority of the unpublished 'Mémoires' of François Mercier du Rocher, a member of the departmental Directory of the Vendée. In chapter lxxxii. of the 'Nouveau Paris' we do indeed read: 'It appears that Louis XVI. cherished some hopes until the last moment, for it is certain that he lost his temper and engaged in a kind of struggle with the six executioners.' If the struggle had indeed taken place, how is it that the newspapers of the day made no mention of it, and that even the most hostile as well as the most moderate passed over a fact like that in silence? To destroy the argument, invincible in our opinion, afforded by the silence of such newspapers as the *Révolutions de Paris* or the *Ami du Peuple*, something more than the story told to François Mercier du Rocher by Santerre would be required. Between the accounts given by Santerre and the Abbé Edgeworth we cannot hesitate in our choice, and if Louis Blanc is unwilling to accept the words of the King's confessor, let him at least hear those of his executioner. 'He ascended the scaffold,' wrote Sanson in his letter to the *Thermomètre du Jour* of February 20, 1793, ' and strode up to the balustrade as if he wished to speak. We told him that this could not be allowed, and he then let us lead him to the plank. . . . A few words passed at the foot of the scaffold, because he did not think it necessary to take off his coat or to have his hands tied. He also proposed that he should be allowed to cut his hair off himself. For the sake of truth, I must say that in all this he was remarkably calm, and gave proofs of a firmness that astonished us all. I am convinced that he owed that firmness to those religious principles with which he seemed so thoroughly imbued.' This letter also serves to destroy Louis Blanc's assertion concerning the terrible cries that Louis XVI. is said to have uttered, but which no one heard.

It is now time to turn to another error of this eminent historian. According to him, it was the actor Dugazon who ordered the drummers to drown the voice of Louis XVI., and the authority he invokes is again that of Mercier in the 'Nouveau Paris.' Louis Blanc gives us a little too much of Mercier. The latter, moreover, is far from being very affirmative. '*It is said*,' he writes, 'that it was the actor Dugazon. . . .' Now, the papers of the day and all contemporary historians are unanimous in declaring that it was Santerre who ordered the drums to beat. The account in the *Révolutions de Paris* is very precise on this point. In the 'Authentic Narrative of the Trial and Execution of Louis XVI.,' by Rouy senior, an eye-witness, we find : 'He wished to speak, and made a sign to the drummers to cease beating so that he might make himself heard ; there were at least sixty, and a good many of them obeyed him ; but Santerre wisely ordered them to continue beating, and the executioners to do their duty.' The author of the account of the last moments of Louis XVI. published in the 'Procès des Bourbons' says : 'The drums suddenly ceased. Santerre was some distance off, but hurried up and ordered the drummers to continue beating.' And a little farther we have : 'Santerre interrupted him, and said : "I have not brought you here to speak, but to die." The drums immediately drowned their voices.' The 'Two Friends of Liberty' (' Histoire de la Révolution de France,' ix. 370), Soulavie (' Mémoires Historiques du Règne de Louis XVI.,' vi. 518), Peltier (' Dernier Tableau de Paris,' ii. 29), Lacretelle (' Histoire de la Convention Nationale,' i. 168), and Beaulieu (' Essais sur la Révolution de France,' iv. 353), all declare that it was Santerre who ordered the roll of the drums to drown the King's voice. Beaulieu, whose book appeared in 1803, added in a note : 'As for the roll of the drums, I know that Santerre has claimed the honour only a very short time ago, saying that he had ordered it only to avoid more shedding of blood.' Santerre, who was then still living—for he did not die till 1808—did not deny Beaulieu's note. How could he have denied it after what passed at the

Commune on January 21, 1793? On that day Jacques Roux, one of the Commissioners ordered to be present at the King's execution, rendered an account of his mission to the Conseil-Général. ' We had our eyes on Capet,' he said, ' until he reached the guillotine. . . . He wished to speak to the people, but Santerre stopped him. . . .' Santerre, who was present, spoke immediately after Jacques Roux, and in the following terms : ' You have just heard an exact account of what took place, and I only rise to speak in praise of the implicit obedience of the forces under my command. Louis Capet wished to appeal to the pity of the people, but I prevented him ' (' Details of what took place before and after the Execution of Louis XVI.,' printed by the *Feuille de Paris*, January 22, 1793).

When we see Louis Blanc rejecting well-established historical facts merely because they contradict his theory, we must not be surprised if he disdainfully treats as a fable the words, ' Son of Saint Louis, Heaven awaits you !' In the ' Dernières Heures de Louis XVI.,' the Abbé Edgeworth has not mentioned this phrase, and one can understand what capital Louis Blanc has made out of this silence. ' This phrase,' he says, ' must now rank amongst the number of historical fictions.' I must say that more recent historians of the Revolution, such as De Barante, Michelet, and Mortimer-Ternaux, have, like Louis Blanc, looked upon the Abbé's silence as a proof that the words were not spoken. We can, however, not conform to this opinion.

If this phrase is, indeed, but a sublime fiction, how can we explain the fact of its having found a place in the accounts given by those who were themselves present at the execution ? The following is the statement made by Rouy in his ' Authentic Narrative ': ' The executioner then thrice asked him whether he had anything further to say to his confessor. The King having persistently replied in the negative, the Abbé embraced him, and said as he left him : " Go, son of Saint Louis ; Heaven awaits you !"' The *Révolutions de Paris*, which certainly had no disguised Royalists on its editorial staff, published in its number 185 an engraving representing Louis on the scaffold, and the Abbé Edgeworth standing on the top step of the ladder, with these words underneath :

'Louis Capet having reached the scaffold, his hands tied behind his back, gazed for a few moments at the objects around. His confessor then said: " Go, eldest son of Saint Louis ; Heaven awaits you !" '

Number 188 (February 9 to 16, 1793) of the *Révolutions de Paris* contains the following : ' The Abbé Edgeworth, who said to Louis XVI. as he led him to the scaffold, " Go, son of Saint Louis ; Heaven awaits you !" is in London, and receives many visits.' Thus, for the Revolutionaries themselves, the Abbé Edgeworth is the man who uttered these famous words.

Let us add that, of all the historians of the Revolution who wrote only what they had themselves heard, there is not one— either Republican or Royalist—who doubted that the Abbé Edgeworth had really used those words. Beaulieu (iv. 352) and Peltier (ii. 28) are in accord with the ' Two Friends of Liberty' (ix. 370), and with Soulavie (vi. 517). ' Louis XVI.,' says Soulavie, ' then kneels to receive from his confessor the absolution *in articulo mortis.* After helping him to mount the scaffold, his confessor kneels on the topmost step, and, as if by inspiration, cries : " Go, son of Saint Louis ; Heaven awaits you !" ' Since, however, Louis Blanc is always so eager to fall back on Mercier and the ' Nouveau Paris,' let us remind him of a sentence in that famous chapter lxxxii., from which he has so frequently borrowed. ' Religion seems to have lent Louis XVI. a strong support in that terrible journey from the throne to the scaffold, and the words of his confessor were sublime : " Go, son of Saint Louis ; Heaven awaits you !" '

Concerning the appearance of Paris after the execution and on the afternoon of January 21, Louis Blanc is not less incorrect than in the first part of his narrative. As a matter of fact, he appropriates this passage from Mercier's ' Nouveau Paris ' : ' I have been watching the people trooping by arm-in-arm, laughing and talking as though they were returning from a *fête*. It is an untruth to say that silence had fallen upon the city. . . . There was nothing to indicate that it was the day of the execution ; the theatres were opened as usual ; drinking was going on in the wine-shops around the Place de la Révolution, and cakes and pies were being sold at the very foot of the scaffold.' It is unfortunately true that dancing did go on in the square itself, and that on January 21 wretches were found to rejoice at the death of the King, as on September 2 they had rejoiced at the massacres in the prisons. But these wretches were not all Paris, and Paris was that day most undeniably plunged in grief. If Mercier denies this fact, Beaulieu and Lacretelle, as well as the 'Two Friends of Liberty,' support it, and their testimony is worth quite as much as that of the author of the 'Nouveau Paris,' who is more of a playwriter and a novelist than a historian.

'Grief,' says Beaulieu on January 21 in 'Le Diurnal de la Révolution de France'—'grief alone seemed to inhabit Paris.' 'As soon as Louis had ceased to live,' says Lacretelle (i. 168), 'the public grief, though it dared not break out, made itself profoundly felt. The people returned from the execution sad and distressed, and even the rabble, either from pity or from resentment at having had its curiosity balked, heaped curses upon Santerre for having drowned the King's last words. All day Paris was silent, almost deserted; people remained at home to weep in private; now and again the streets were paraded by troops of abandoned wretches, whose wild songs and dances expressed fury though they wished to imitate joy.' The 'Two Friends of Liberty' ('Histoire de la Révolution,' ix.) say: 'We hardly dared look into the streets. Grief was depicted in every face, and a deep restlessness seemed to have hold of every soul.' The volume from which this last quotation is taken appeared in 1797; Beaulieu's 'Diurnal' had appeared in the preceding year, his 'Essais sur la Révolution' having been published in 1801—1803; Lacretelle's 'Précis Historique' appeared in 1801—1806. The testimony of all these books is in complete accord with the memoirs of contemporaries (see especially the Comte d'Allonville's 'Mémoires,' iii. 161, and those of Marmontel, xviii. 462 and xix. 464) and the newspapers of the day.

Henri Nicolle, in the *Journal Français* of January 22, 1793, says: 'It is useless to conceal the fact—Paris is plunged in grief. Dumb grief stalks through her streets, and terror, which clogs all feelings, is engraved on the faces of her citizens.'

Claude Fouchet, a Girondist member of the Convention, writes in the *Journal des Amis:* ' It is not the death of the tyrant that grieves me.   The sorrow that will follow me to the tomb arises from the fact that these bloodthirsty wretches have succeeded in getting the people to sanction a legal murder ; that Paris, the city of Liberty, has endured, in mournful silence, the fury of a few unscrupulous villains who threatened with death the legislators of France !'

CHAPTER XLVI.

Saturday, January 26, 1793.

If the good people of Paris love sights, they get them to their hearts' content under the Republic. We have just had, in one week, the spectacle of a King ascending the scaffold, and that of a representative of the people being carried to the Pantheon.

In the sitting of the National Assembly of August 24, 1789, a deputy read an address he proposed to present to the King on the *fête* of Saint Louis, and which ran as follows:

'Sire, the Sovereign whose revered name Your Majesty bears, and whose virtues religion celebrates to-day, was, like yourself, the friend of his people.

'Like you, Sire, he desired the liberty of the French. He protected it by laws which adorn our annals, but he could do nothing to revive it.

'That glory, reserved for Your Majesty, will give you an immortal right to the gratitude and the tender veneration of the French.

'Thus will for ever be united the names of two Kings, who, with centuries between them, vied in performing the most signal acts of justice in favour of their people.

'Sire, the National Assembly has suspended its labours for a few moments in order to fulfil a duty that it holds dear, and one which is not beyond the scope of its mission, since in assuring its King of the love and fidelity of the French it is promoting the best interests of the nation and gratifying its most fervent wish.'[1]

The author of this ardent Royalist address was Louis Michel Lepeletier de Saint-Fargeau, a representative of the nobility of the city of Paris.[2]

---

[1] 'Archives Parlementaires de 1789 à 1800,' i. 485.

[2] On taking his seat in the National Convention as a deputy for the Yonne, the former representative of the nobility of the city of Paris modified his signature as follows   L. M. Lepeletier (Saint-Fargeau).

Although his Royalist zeal did not survive the fall of the Monarchy, he was still unable to connive at the King's death but a few weeks ago. In the Committee of Legislation, before more than twenty members, he stoutly advocated the idea of an appeal to the nation, adding that if the appeal were unsuccessful he would still advise incarceration instead of death.[1]

A few days later, moved by the threats levelled at him, he consulted Lanjuinais, and upon the latter urging him, with all the energy he could command, to vote for the King's imprisonment until the end of the war, and for banishment afterwards, he cried: 'But they will kill me.'[2]

Had he not already replied to one of his old friends who expressed his astonishment at the change which his nature and his opinions had undergone in a few months: '*Mon ami!* when one has sat in the *Parlement* of Paris, and one has a large fortune, there is a choice of only two courses; one must be either at Coblentz or at the top of the Mountain?'[3]

Such is the man of whom the Convention has made a hero and a martyr.[4] The truth is that Lepeletier de Saint-Fargeau, ex-President of the *Parlement* of Paris, and one of the wealthiest men in France, had only one care—to save his immense fortune. He tried to make people forget it as much as possible, and had adopted an eminently democratic mode of life. He took his meals in the most modest restaurants, and most frequently at Février's, in the former Palais-Royal, in a low, dimly-lighted cellar to which entrance was gained by a small flight of steps. It was there that he had dined on Sunday, January 20, when, as he stood at the desk to pay his bill, he found himself next to a young man wearing a gray overcoat and a round hat, who said to him: 'You voted for the death of the King, M.

---

[1] 'Brissot à ses Commettants,' May 22, 1793.

[2] 'Notice Historique sur le Comte Lanjuinais,' by Victor Lanjuinais, p. 22.

[3] 'Essais Historiques sur les Causes et les Effets de la Révolution,' Beaulieu, iv. 293.

[4] 'The Mountain,' says Mme. Roland in her 'Mémoires' (Dauban edition), p. 464, 'made a kind of saint of Lepeletier, who certainly expected no such honour. He was a weak and a rich man, who, like Hérault de Séchelles and a few others of the old nobility, had joined the party out of fear. The only advantage he brought it was by dying in the way he did.'

Lepeletier?' 'Yes, sir, and I voted according to my conscience. But what has that to do with you?' The man with the round hat—who was, they say, one Deparis,[1] formerly in the King's body-guard—hereupon dealt him a violent blow that sent him spinning against the wall.[2] Lepeletier seized a table-knife, but Deparis, who had already drawn a sabre from beneath his coat, plunged it into the other's side, crying : 'You wretch! you will never vote again!'

It was then five o'clock in the afternoon. The room was full of people, but no one attempted to secure the murderer, nor was any cry raised against him. He left in the most peaceful manner, after having spoken for some time with several of the persons present. It was this fact that especially incensed Lepeletier's colleagues, and induced them to issue the proclamation with which the walls of Paris are just now covered. It commences thus :

'THE COMMITTEE OF GENERAL SECURITY OF THE NATIONAL CONVENTION.

'Citizens,

'On Sunday, January 20, Michel Lepeletier, one of the representatives of the French people, was assassinated in broad daylight, at a restaurant in what is known as the House of Equality, at an hour when establishments of that kind are generally most frequented. According to the reports drawn up concerning this deplorable event, not the least cry was raised against the assassin, nor did the keeper of the establishment, or any of his numerous aids and guests, make any attempt to secure the murderer, whom they must all have seen, to whom several of them spoke for some time after the blow was struck, and who escaped entirely unopposed. . . .'

This poster is signed by Bernard, President ; C. Basire, Vice-President ; Tallien and Rovère, Secretaries ; Ruamps, Montaut, Lamarque, Legendre, Lasource, Chabot, and Ingrand, members of the Committee.[3]

---

[1] Not *de Paris*, as nearly all historians write it.

[2] 'Histoire des Montagnards,' Alphonse Esquiros, ii. 296.

[3] 'Committee of General Security of the National Convention,' printed by order of the Convention. In 8vo., 3 pp. The Committee of General Security, from which sprang the Committee of Public Safety, was the work of the Girondists. Already, on July 9, 1792, Brissot, their chief, asked the Legislative Assembly ' to form in its midst a small Commission

The Committee of General Security merely sums up what is within the ken of all Paris — the abetting of Lepeletier's murderer, the complicity in the crime of all those present, the lack of any feeling of horror against the assassin because the victim is one of the King's judges, and, lastly, the fact that Deparis was not afraid to show himself at the Café de Foy three hours after the murder.[1] Does not all this clearly prove what is the real feeling of the population of Paris, and that with the exception of the fanatics of the clubs and sections, all classes viewed with deep grief and indignation the sentence and death of Louis XVI. ?[2]

The Convention has offered a reward of 10,000 francs for the capture of Deparis. His description has been sent to all parts of the country, and runs as follows:

'DESCRIPTION OF DEPARIS.

'Height, five feet five inches; iron-gray beard; black hair; swarthy complexion; good teeth. Was wearing a gray overcoat with green lapels, and a round hat.'[3]

Pending the arrest of the murderer, the Convention has determined to make good use of the body in its possession. What better opportunity could be found of gaining a hold upon the imagination of the masses than by spectacular obsequies? What better means of winning heart and head than by pointing to the fate reserved for the judges of Louis XVI., the true friends, the founders, of the Republic? Was it not a clever stroke of policy to make of Lepeletier's funeral a renewal and a confirmation of the regicide vote of January 16?

It was Marie-Joseph Chénier who had the honour of bringing up the report and the resolutions relating to the funeral cere-

of security—a committee chosen from amongst the most active, most vigilant, most intrepid and most inflexible of its members, and the duties of which would be to examine all charges of treason' (the Moniteur of July 10, 1792).

[1] 'Arrêté du Comité de Sûreté Générale,' quoted in the Révolutions de Paris, tome xv., p. 245.

[2] The remarkable and significant facts that accompanied the murder of Lepeletier de Saint-Fargeau have not, we believe, been mentioned by any historian.

[3] Circular issued by the Minister of Justice, and dated January 26, 1793.

mony in the name of the Committees of Public Instruction and of Inspectors. He traced the programme of the spectacle, and asked before all else that religion should have no part in it.

'Let superstition,' he cried, 'make way for the religion of Liberty; let really sacred, really solemn, emblems appeal to sorrowing hearts. All eyes shall look upon the body of our virtuous colleague, and see the fatal wound it received for the cause of nations. The *parricidal* blade, sanctified by a Patriot's blood, shall glitter before us, a witness to the fury of tyranny and its vile adorers; the blood-stained garments of the victim shall strike our citizens with horror, and pronounce sentence of death upon the assassin. We shall see pass before us the genius of Liberty, the sole object of Republican homage, and the banner of the Declaration of Rights, the sacred basis of the people's constitution. The genius of a David will give life to this feeble sketch, whilst Gossec will lead the strains of that lugubrious but touching harmony that marks a triumphant death.'[1]

After the reading of the report, the Convention at its sitting of the 22nd resolved that it would attend the obsequies of Michel Lepeletier in a body; that the remains were to be deposited in the Pantheon, and that the martyr's last words were to be engraved upon his tomb, as follows: '*I am content to shed my blood for my country; I trust that it may serve to consolidate liberty and equality, and to bring our enemies to light.*'

These words have not only been inscribed on his tomb; they have been posted all over the walls by order of the Convention. Now, everyone knows that Lepeletier did not utter them, and that their real author is Citizen Maure, representative of the Yonne and a colleague of the dead man. In falling, Lepeletier said only these four words: '*I am very cold.*'[2]

The funeral ceremony took place on Thursday, the 24th. Lepeletier died at his brother's house in the Place des Piques,

---

[1] *Journal des Débats et des Décrets*, sitting of Tuesday, January 22, 1793.

[2] Beaulieu, 'Essais Historiques,' etc., iv. 348; 'Mémoires de Lombard de Langres,' i. 164; 'Mémoires du Comte d'Allonville,' iii. 147. 'I have it,' says the Comte d'Allonville, 'from Dufouard, formerly Surgeon-Major in the Gardes-Françaises, and who, called to the assistance of Saint-Fargeau, did not leave him, that he had heard him utter only these words: *I am very cold.*'

formerly the Place Vendôme. The crowd had invaded the square at daybreak, and stood packed around the base of the statue of Louis XIV.,[1] the pedestal being covered with a white drapery and festooned with garlands of oak and cypress. On two sides steps had been erected to allow of the platform being reached; on the two other sides were the famous words: ' *I am satisfied*,' etc.[2]

Between nine and ten o'clock, the bed upon which Lepeletier had breathed his last was placed upon the pedestal, amid a roll of the muffled drums. Whilst the body and all the accessories were being arranged, the four cressets that stood at the corners were filled with perfumes and lighted.[3]

The foundation of the bed of state was of black, studded with tears of silver. The sheets were blood-stained, and on these lay the body, stripped to the waist, and displaying the gaping wound on the left side all clotted with blood.[4] One of the arms hung out of the bed; the head, crowned with cypress and flowers, rested upon a pillow. By the side of the victim's clothes lay the murderer's blade, besmeared with fresh blood.[5]

David had taken up his position upon the pedestal with an easel and canvas before him, and the mob could gaze upon the spectacle of the painter copying this bloody model.[6]

Two hours passed, during which a choir sang plaintive songs, accompanied by the muffled roll of the covered drums. The sky was gray and threatening, and on all sides were seen cypress branches and funeral torches.

At half-past twelve the Convention left the hall of the Riding-School, and, marching four abreast, proceeded in silence to the

---

[1] The statue of Louis XIV. had been thrown down by the mob on August 11, 1792.

[2] *Le Courrier des Départements*, by A. J. Gorsas, member of the National Convention, January 26, 1793.

[3] *Ibid.*   [4] *Ibid.*   [5] *Ibid.*

[6] On March 29, 1793, David presented his picture of the death of Lepeletier to the National Convention, who had it placed over the President's chair in the hall of assembly. After one of the numerous invasions to which this hall was subjected, the Convention, fearing that David's painting might be destroyed, begged the painter to take it back, and it was still in possession of the latter at his death, which took place at Brussels in 1825. In 1826 Mme. de Mortefontaine, Lepeletier's only daughter, bought it for 100,000 francs. Being a very ardent Royalist, she wished to prevent the picture from being placed in a public gallery, and from thus immortalizing her father's regicide vote.

Place des Piques, headed by the Gendarmerie Nationale. Vergniaud, the President, then mounted the pedestal, and placed a crown of oak-leaves interwoven with immortelles upon the dead man's brow.

A roll of the drum now announced a speech by a municipal officer, Citizen Jullien. Delivered in sonorous accents, this speech gave rise to a singular incident, which added greatly to the strangeness of the scene. The Place des Piques is well known to possess a remarkably clear echo, and this echo repeated each of Jullien's words so distinctly that every phrase as it was uttered was half drowned by the repetition of the preceding one.[1]

After this discourse, and whilst the bed of state was being removed, a choir of a thousand voices sang a 'Hymn to the Divinity of Nations,' words by Marie-Joseph Chénier, music by Gossec.[2]

Just as the procession was about to start, the Patriot Palloy presented the family of Lepeletier de Saint-Fargeau with a stone taken from the cells of the Bastille, upon which was inscribed the letter from the President of the Convention to Lepeletier's mother. The inscription ran as follows :

'THIS STONE COMES FROM THE CELLS OF THE BASTILLE.

Citoyenne,
      The National Convention was filled with deepest indignation upon hearing of the horrible outrage committed upon him whom you mourn.
      It has accorded to his memory the honours of the Pantheon. Desirous of depositing its tribute of tears and flowers upon his tomb, it will follow his remains to their resting-place.
      May these marks of national gratitude help to assuage your grief and that of your family.
            The President of the National Convention,
                        (*Signed*)   VERGNIAUD.

---

[1] *Courrier des Départements.*
[2] *Ibid.* Charles Labitte, in his very conscientious study on the life and writings of Marie-Joseph Chénier, does not mention this hymn, and seems to be unaware of its existence (' Etudes Littéraires,' by Ch. Labitte, 2 vols. in 8vo., 1846). See the remarkable study on the composer Gossec by Augustin Bernard, in ' La Musique et les Musiciens Français pendant la Révolution' (*Revue de la Révolution*, September and October, 1887).

' This remnant of despotism contains the honourable titles of the family of Citizen Michel Lepeletier, member of the National Convention, who was assassinated by the villain Paris, for having voted for the death of the last chief of the tyrants.   Given as a mark of gratitude and esteem, on the day of his apotheosis, January 24, 1793, in the Second Year of the French Republic, by the Patriot Palloy, who escaped the blade of the same assassin on January 8, 1793.'

At about one o'clock the procession started for the Pantheon, in the following order :

A detachment of gendarmerie, headed by trumpeters.

A body of sappers.

Artillerymen without their guns.

A squad of twenty drummers with muffled drums.

The banner of the Declaration of the Rights of Man.

Volunteers from the six legions of the Garde Nationale and twenty-four standards.

Muffled drums.

A banner inscribed with the Decree of the Convention concerning Lepeletier's burial in the Pantheon.

Pupils from the national schools.

The Commissioners of Police.

The Bureau of Conciliation, the Judges, the Presidents and Commissioners of the forty-eight sections, the Tribunal of Commerce, the Provisional Criminal Tribunal, the six departmental tribunals, the municipality of Paris, the authorities of the districts of Saint-Denis and of the Bourg-de-l'Égalité,[1] those of the department, and the Tribunal of Appeal.

The figure of Liberty, borne by citizens.

Muffled drums.

The fasces of the eighty-four departments, borne by federates.

The Provisional Executive Council.

A detachment of the Convention guard.

The vest, breeches and shirt of Lepeletier, all dripping with blood, and borne aloft on a pike with wreaths of oak and cypress leaves.

The members of the Convention in two columns, one on each side of the street, and walking in double file, preceded by their

[1] Formerly the Bourg-la-Reine.

President; in the midst of the members, a banner inscribed with the words : '*I am satisfied*,' etc.

Lepeletier's body on its bed of state, borne by citizens. A bladder filled with blood had been placed in the gaping wound, and at each jolt a few drops of blood spurted out. Roused by this sight, the fury of the mob found vent in terrible imprecations against the Royalists.[1]

Around the body a band of artillerymen, with drawn swords, and a number of veterans.

The band of the Garde Nationale.

Lepeletier's family.

A group of mothers leading their children.

A detachment of the Convention guard.

Muffled drums.

Armed federates.

The Jacobin Club and other societies.

Cavalry and trumpeters.[2]

Escorted by an immense crowd, the men carrying wreaths of immortelles, the women branches of cypress, the procession passed along the Rues Saint-Honoré and du Roule, the Pont Neuf, the Rues de Thionville (formerly Dauphine), des Fossés-Saint-Germain and de la Liberté (formerly Fossés-Monsieur-le-Prince), the Place Saint-Michel, the Rues d'Enfer, Saint-Thomas, Saint-Jacques and du Panthéon.[3]

The first halt was made before the Jacobin Club,[4] of which Lepeletier had been a member since the end of September, 1792, and which had elected him its president on November 17 last.[5] The procession also stopped for a few moments before the Palais

---

[1] 'Souvenirs inédits de M. le Comte de Tocqueville' : *Le Contemporain*, tome xii., p. 106.

[2] *Les Révolutions de Paris*, tome xv., p. 225, etc. ; *Le Courrier des Départements*.

[3] 'Report drawn up by Order of the National Convention upon the Funeral of Michel Lepeletier, Member of the National Convention, assassinated January 20, 1793, in the Year II. of the Republic, for having voted for the Death of the Tyrant.'

[4] The Jacobin Club was situated in the Rue Saint-Honoré. It met in the old church of the Jacobin convent, which occupied a part of the space between the Rue Saint-Honoré and the Rue Neuve-des-Petits-Champs, between the Rue de la Sourdière and the Place Vendôme.

[5] *Les Révolutions de Paris*, tome xv., p. 258.

de l'Égalité, and again before the Oratory, the entrance to which was draped with black.   Here a second oration was delivered, and another wreath placed upon the pillow of the state bed.   A fourth halt was made upon the Pont Neuf, opposite to La Samaritaine, amidst a salvo of artillery.   A fifth, and a much longer one, was also made before the hall in which the Friends of the Rights of Man hold their sittings.[1]   The façade of the Grey Friars Club was covered with garlands of cypress; one of the members delivered a harangue, which was followed by the singing of a funeral hymn.   After two more halts—one at the crossing of the Rue de la Liberté and another at the Place Saint-Michel, the procession at length arrived before the doors of the Pantheon.   It was now four o'clock.   The confusion at this point became tremendous, and it was only with a great deal of trouble that Lepeletier's body could be borne into the temple, already invaded by the multitude.   The different representative authorities at length succeeded in finding places, whilst the musicians mounted to the topmost galleries, and took up once more the funeral chant that had marked the departure.

Lepeletier's two brothers stood bare-headed upon the pedestal that supported the bed of state.   The elder, wearing the uniform of the Garde Nationale, delivered a speech, in which his memory failed two or three times—a speech full of apostrophe, oaths, and imprecations.   'Tyrants, your reign is over!   Shades of the Gracchi, I invoke you!   My country, he has laid down his life for you, yet, like my brother, I vote for the death of tyrants!'   Having said this with much declamatory gesture, he threw himself upon his brother's body; but when he rose, the bystanders remarked that this last embrace had not cost him a single tear.[2]

[1] The Society of the Friends of the Rights of Man, better known as the Club des Cordeliers (Grey Friars), met in the refectory of the old convent of the Grey Friars.   This hall has escaped destruction, and is now occupied by the Musée Dupuytren.

[2] Félix Lepeletier Saint-Fargeau, having become the friend of Antonelle, the two Duplays, Didier, and other demagogues of the worst kind, was charged, under the Directory, with being the accomplice of Babœuf, and after the death of the latter he adopted one of his children.   Elected a member of the Chamber of Representatives in 1815, he pronounced a pompous eulogy upon Napoleon, whom he called the Saviour of his country, and spoke most violently against the return of the Bourbons.   He died in Paris, January 3, 1827.

A Marseillais, wearing a red cap adorned with crape, then took the place of Lepeletier's brother upon the platform. His marked accent and the hoarseness of his voice prevented me from understanding his words.

Another volunteer—this one wearing a helmet, and not a red cap—then took the sword hanging by the bed of state, and swung it about his head for some moments.[1]

This pantomime, in very doubtful taste, was followed by a harangue from Barère. The President Vergniaud was the last to speak. 'Citizens,' he cried, 'Brutus is immortal for having killed Cæsar. Michel Lepeletier voted for the death of the tyrant of the French; such an act is worth an entire life!' By using such language Vergniaud was voting a second time for the death of Louis XVI.; beneath the dome of the Pantheon he again committed the cowardice of which he was guilty on the night of January 16 in the hall of the Riding-School.

Vergniaud returned to his seat amidst a glacial silence. The spectators began to look at each other, and the ceremony was evidently dragging a bit, when the musicians again brought a little life into it. The chorus with which the proceedings terminated was not without a grandeur of its own.

If I may judge from the impression made upon those around me, the Convention has failed in its aims. The exhibition of the corpse and the display of the blood-stained garments have inspired all sensible people with a feeling of horror and disgust. More than one said, not without reason: 'This ceremony really looks more like a call to a massacre than a funeral.'[2]

The Convention also undertook to draw its own moral from this sorry business.

Chénier, in his report, had said: 'Michel Lepeletier, accompanied by his virtues, surrounded by his mourning family and in the midst of the National Convention, will be borne to the French Pantheon, where a nation's gratitude has marked his place. It is there that we shall deposit the remains of our beloved colleague. *It is there, too, citizens, that we shall bury the fatal prejudices that divide us.* Michel Lepeletier will hear

---

[1] *Les Révolutions de Paris*, tome xv., p. 228.
[2] Beaulieu, 'Essais,' etc., tome v., p. 19.

our oath from the depths of his tomb, and with whatever honours you may repay his services, *the union of all citizens will be the grandest reward of his life and death.*[1]

A few moments before proceeding to the funeral ceremony, the Convention adopted an 'Address to the French,' drawn up by Barère. It contained the following sentences: 'In attending the funeral of Michel Lepeletier, we are all about to swear upon the tomb of this martyr of Republican thought to save our country. *There we shall lay aside, in an equitable and necessary reconciliation, all rivalry and all mutual distrust.*[2] At the Pantheon, a few hours later, Vergniaud spoke the following words: 'There is a means of honouring his memory which will be more worthy of us and of him than the outpourings of our grief; it is by sacrificing to the love of our country all our individual passions.' Barère had expressed himself in similar terms over Lepeletier's body: 'O my colleague! May your death put an end to all our private feuds! Let us swear over Lepeletier's grave to harbour no other design than that of saving our country.' And all the members of the Convention held up their hands and took part in the oath proffered by the speaker.[3]

The same evening the Convention again met to nominate a

---

[1] 'Report drawn up by Order of the National Convention upon the Funeral of Michel Lepeletier.'

[2] This address of Barère was adopted at the sitting held by the Convention on the morning of January 24. *Le Moniteur* does not mention this sitting, and Buchez and Roux (tome xxiii., p. 373), deceived by this silence, say: 'There was no morning sitting, on account of Lepeletier's funeral.' There is, however, an account of this morning sitting in *Les Révolutions de Paris*, tome xv., p. 239: '*Thursday, 24th.*—Before proceeding to the obsequies of Lepeletier Saint-Fargeau, the Convention heard a few letters read; Barère then read the "Address to the French," with the drawing up of which he had been entrusted.' 'The Report drawn up by Order of the National Convention upon the Funeral of Michel Lepeletier,' printed and sent to the eighty-four departments by order of the Convention, commences thus: 'On Thursday, January 24, 1793, in the year II. of the Republic, the National Convention, having met at nine o'clock, was informed at half-past twelve that the procession which was to accompany Michel Lepeletier to the French Pantheon had assembled in the Place des Piques, formerly called Place Vendôme. The President thereupon adjourned the sitting.' The *Journal des Débats et des Décrets*, No. 129, also gives an account of this morning sitting.

[3] 'Report drawn up by Order of the National Convention upon the Funeral of Michel Lepeletier.'

President in place of Vergniaud, whose term of office had expired. Julien, a member for the Haute-Garonne, asks for permission to speak upon the minutes, and demands a report upon the Decree ordering Roland's letter to be sent to the departments.[1] Guadet, who is in the chair, points out that Julien has permission to speak upon the minutes, but not to demand a report upon a decree. Energetic protests are made from the benches of the Mountain, whilst the Right calls loudly for the Order of the Day. Julien, Thuriot, and several of their colleagues, insist upon speaking. The tumult increases; insults and threats are exchanged, and hurled from one side of the hall to the other. The chairman is obliged to suspend the sitting. When quiet is at length restored, the election of a President is proceeded with. Rabaut Saint-Étienne obtains 179 votes, and Danton 150. As soon as the result is declared, the Mountain gives vent to its anger, pouring forth a volley of abuse upon the acting Secretaries and the newly-elected President. Young Robespierre, Collot-d'Herbois, and Lecointre of Versailles ask for permission to speak upon the result of the ballot. This being withheld, they cling to the tribune, and refuse to budge until they are successively removed, one after another, by three special resolutions, each of which is passed amidst curses from one side and applause from the other. At length we come to the election of Secretaries, and this time the Mountain gets its own way, Bréard, Cambacérès, and Thuriot being appointed. The sitting closes at half-past twelve amidst a scene of indescribable excitement and mutual recrimination. This is the manner in which the National Convention has buried in Lepeletier's grave the fatal prejudices that divide them, and laid aside all rivalry and mutual distrust![2]

[1] The letter in question was that in which Roland resigned his post as Minister of the Interior. It had been read in the sitting of January 23.

[2] For an account of the sitting of Thursday, January 24, 1793, which began at seven o'clock in the evening, after the return from Lepeletier's funeral, see *Le Journal des Debats et des Décrets*, No. 129, and *Le Mercure Français* for January, 1793.

CHAPTER XLVII.

Tuesday, January 29, 1793.

On Tuesday, December 25, the eve of the final appearance of Louis XVI. before the Convention, the King wrote his will, and handed a copy of it to M. de Malesherbes, who succeeded in despatching it to its destination abroad.[1]

M. de Malesherbes had had several copies of the document taken, and one of these appeared in print on the morning of January 22, bearing the following title: 'The Will of Louis XVI.; together with all the Details of what took place before and after the Execution.'[2] On the same day Étienne Feuillant, the courageous editor of the *Journal du Soir*, who was also in possession of one of the copies, published it in his paper.[3] The Commune of Paris, the depositary of the original, seeing that it could no longer keep it secret, at length submitted to have it printed as *a proof of the fanaticism and crimes of the tyrant.*

---

[1] This copy forms part of the collection of Baron Feuillet de Conches. The original is deposited in the Archives Nationales.

[2] Eight pages, in 8vo. Published by the *Feuille de Paris*, Rue Grange-Batelière.

[3] *Journal du Soir de Politique et de Littérature*, edited by Ét. Feuillant, January 22, 1793. Étienne Feuillant, born at Brassac (Auvergne), had established the *Journal du Soir* in 1789, and the paper enjoyed a considerable success. Faithful to his Royalist principles, he founded the *Journal Général de France* in 1814. Information being lodged against him during the Hundred Days, he was arrested and detained in La Force. In 1815 he was elected to the Chamber of Deputies for the department of Maine-et-Loire, and in 1818 published a work entitled 'Les Lois Fondamentales.' He died in Anjou in 1840. One of his best friends was Michaud, the historian of the Crusades, and Berryer. See the 'Notice Nécrologique sur Étienne Feuillant in the *Gazette de France* for July 26, 1840.

This morning I have again read those sublime pages from which the virtue of the best of Kings shines forth with immortal splendour. I afterwards went out in search of news, and bought an armful of papers. Nearly all speak of the King's will.

Feeling, no doubt, that this proof of a merciful and Christian soul, this benevolence, this love, this superhuman power of forgiveness, will rest for ever upon the regicides as the most terrible and indelible curse, the Republican sheets, with redoubled fury, heap insults upon the King's memory. The Brissotin journals are not a whit less violent than those of the Mountain. I take the following extracts from the former:

' It is useless,' says the *Moniteur*, ' to dwell any further upon this will, in which may be found all the hypocrisy of a fanatic, all the superstition of a weak mind, all the incorrigibility of a King.'[1]

' This document,' says Carra, deputy for Seine-et-Oise, in his *Annales Patriotiques*, ' is a masterpiece of hypocrisy and superstition ; it recalls the kisses that Louis XI. showered upon his little leaden Virgin, and we know that, though a fanatic, he was none the less a tyrant. Godliness, especially in Kings, is quite compatible with any crime.'[2]

' Posterity,' says the *Bulletin des Amis de la Vérité*, ' will see from this document to what point an ill-ordered education and fanatic priests had impaired the mind of Louis Capet.'[3]

In the *Patriote Français* Brissot writes as follows : ' This is an authentic document, and was handed to the Commune by the Commissaries of the Temple. The anti-Revolutionary style in which it is couched is a formal recantation by Louis himself of all his pretended constitutional proceedings. Should his followers appeal to the tribunal of Europe or to that of posterity, we ask that this testament rank as the principal document in the trial.'

Whilst I was reading these papers in the garden of l'Égalité, a child was shouting and selling ' Les Crimes de Louis XVI.'[4]

I left the garden with my brain in a whirl and despair in my

---

[1] *Moniteur* of January 28, 1793.
[2] *Annales Patriotiques*, 1793, No. 22.   [3] *Ibid.* No. 25.
[4] *Le Républicain Français*, February 3, 1793.

heart, asking myself whether France, the true France, the France of Saint Louis, were dead. I cannot, I will not, believe it. Brissot and Marat may scrawl and scribble, Robespierre and Vergniaud may pour forth their harangues; but God will not permit France to perish as long as there are in the depths of the country, and even in the streets of Paris, such devoted souls as the one I found in a lowly woman of the people this evening. On entering my dwelling I was stopped by the poor fruit-seller who occupies a small shop on the ground-floor, and who, taking from her pocket a roughly-printed sheet, held it out to me, saying: 'Here, sir, this is the will of Saint Louis XVI.!'[1]

[1] 'Mémoires de Mme. Elliott sur la Révolution Française.'

CHAPTER XLVIII.

Thursday, January 31, 1793.

On January 21 Louis XVI. met his doom, and many of those who were present in the Place de la Révolution were probably cowardly enough to say : ' It is undoubtedly a great crime, but, after all, what business is it of mine ? An unoffending and humble citizen, am I not beyond the reach of the thunder-bolts that fall only on the high and mighty?' At the moment when the crime was being perpetrated, the Convention, on the motion of Bréard, supported by Osselin and Bourbotte, resolved that domiciliary visits should be re-established in Paris.[1] The most humble and obscure individuals immediately felt that they, in their turn, were being threatened ; not one but recalled that night of August 29, 1792, when the cut-throats of September held their vigil. That never-to-be-forgotten night forms an episode so characteristic of the Revolution that I cannot omit giving the details of it here.

On August 28 the Legislative Assembly — in which the Mountain scarcely numbered thirty members, in which the Constitutionnels no longer sat, and in which the majority undoubtedly belonged to the Girondist party—had, upon Danton's proposal and the formal motion of Merlin de Thionville, resolved that the forty-eight sections of Paris should each appoint thirty Commissaries charged with the duty of making domiciliary visits. On the morning of the 29th—it was a Wednesday— the Commune had bills posted prohibiting anyone from appearing in the streets under any pretence whatever. No vehicle of

[1] *Journal des Débats*, No. 126.

any kind was to be taken out, and any person living in Paris who should be found in any house but his own would, by that reason alone, be considered a suspect, and arrested accordingly.

At two in the afternoon the barriers were closed. At four the drums were beaten, and the citizens were warned not to be out after six. . . .

It is six o'clock. Who is there that has forgotten what Paris used to be at six o'clock on a summer evening in the reign of *Louis the Tyrant?* It is just the time when the sun, before disappearing below the horizon, throws over the city a mantle of purple and gold that hides its wretchedness and only displays its splendour. All is bustle, movement, and gaiety; it seems as if the great city contained no more poverty or misery, so filled are the streets with carriages, promenaders, and idlers! There is no city in Europe, no city in the whole universe, that offers such a scene of life, animation, and brilliancy as the streets of Paris on a fine summer evening.

At six o'clock on August 29, 1792, all the shutters are up and all the doors closed. Not a pedestrian nor a vehicle to be seen. At the corner of every street stands a body of improvised guards, the shouts of the sentries alone breaking the deathly stillness that hangs over the city. Here and there on the Seine are boats filled with armed men; even the washerwomen's barges are guarded. All the quays, and more especially the steps leading down to the river, are lined with soldiers ready to fire. The Marseillais have been placed in charge of the barriers.

Night has fallen, but no one thinks of taking refuge in sleep. Even the bravest tremble for those around them. The 20,000 who signed the petition against the excesses of June 20, 1792,[1] are quite aware that their life and liberty are in danger. Every one of them has his family and his friends, who know that he

---

[1] The petition, known as that of the Twenty Thousand, had been drawn up by Dupont and Guillaume, two former members of the Constituent Assembly, published in the *Journal de Paris*, and deposited with all the notaries of Paris. Out of 113 notaries, only 14 had refused to receive signatures, which within a few days numbered several thousands. During the whole of the Terror it was considered an almost irremissible crime to have signed or induced anyone to sign this petition.

is threatened, and who share his fears. The pain and anguish of these 20,000 signatories is multiplied by the pain and anguish of all who are dear to them. It is the scoundrels alone who are able to breathe freely to-day; they alone can lie down with that tranquillity that is assured them in these times by the conscience of crime and evil deeds.

Ten o'clock has struck, and the heavy tread of the patrol re-echoes along the street. The sentries order the windows to be lit up, and the order is executed throughout the city in the twinkling of an eye. These streets so bright and yet so dreary, these brilliantly-illuminated houses upon which an invisible hand seems to have cast a blight, present a weird, uncanny spectacle; under the starry vault of heaven the city looks like an immense funeral pile surrounded by a million torches.

It is midnight. The domiciliary visits have not yet commenced. Behind the blinds sits many an unfortunate wretch peering out into the night, and anxiously listening to the threatening words of the soldiers, whilst in some inner room a father, a husband, or a brother, a covered hammer in his hand, is completing a hiding-place with slow and muffled blows.'[1]

I had left my window half open. In the house opposite mine lived M. Séron, an official under the old *régime*, and there all the windows were closed. Suddenly one of the sashes was opened, and M. Séron appeared partially undressed, and commenced to play the flute. The house was immediately surrounded by a band of men wearing red caps and carrying pikes, but in spite of their threats the player quietly continued his air, which was Grétry's celebrated ' *O Richard, ô mon Roi !* '

The house-to-house visitation commenced at one o'clock in the morning. The silence that hung over Paris since the commencement of the evening was succeeded by a tremendous noise and confusion, from which distinct and terrible cries occasionally arose. Each street was occupied by a patrol of sixty pikemen. Whilst these mounted guard, a squad of *sans-culottes*, headed by two Commissaries, entered each house. If a door was somewhat slow in opening, the knocks were soon redoubled, and where the occupier was absent from home, the door was broken open.

' Dernier Tableau de Paris,' by J. Peltier, tome ii., p. 220.

Care had been taken to place locksmiths and masons in each squad; the former sounded the walls and wrenched the plates from before the chimneys, whilst the latter rummaged the cellars and raised the stones that cover the cesspools. Whenever a hiding-place was discovered, there were shouts of laughter, and the men who formed the patrols in the street answered with cries of joy and threats of death. Through the open windows might be heard the voices of the Commissaries questioning their victims, mingled with the prayers of women and the clamour of children. At length the squad made its appearance in the street, nearly always dragging one or two prisoners out with it. These were received by the *sans-culottes* with shouts of derision and the song of ' *Ça ira, ça ira, les aristocrates à la lanterne!*' They were then placed in a conveyance, and taken to the section or to the Hôtel de Ville. Now it is the turn of the next house, and everyone anxiously calculates how many minutes still separate him from the moment when the Commissaries and their band will break into his home. From time to time the report of firearms rang out. The cafés and wine-shops having remained open, the men who formed the patrols were nearly all in a state of complete intoxication, and they frequently discharged their guns in a spirit of mere wantonness, though it is true that they had received orders to fire on anyone attempting to escape. Citizen Lemeunier, a member of the Conseil-Général de la Commune, was seated on a very fine horse that he had taken from the royal stables on the Tenth of August, and was superintending the visitation of his section with great zeal. Suddenly his horse gets the bit between its teeth, and Lemeunier is carried, in the twinkling of an eye, from the Pont-Neuf to the Pont-au-Change. The guard at the Châtelet, taking him for an aristocrat, bids him stop, but as he continues his headlong course, the sentry brings him down with a bullet in his back.[1]

It was about three o'clock in the morning when the Commissaries entered my room. They had just arrested M. Séron,[2] and it was either the satisfaction they felt at having laid hands upon that honest fellow, or the knowledge that they could drag

---

[1] Peltier, tome ii., p. 224.
[2] Séron was murdered in the Abbaye on September 3, 1792.

many a man from his wife and children at any moment, that caused them to turn up their noses at a poor devil of a bachelor whose arrest would have cost no one a tear. Whatever the reason may have been, they went away and left me free, after having treated me to a few insults.

The arrests made during the night of August 30 and on the following day numbered 3,000, and the September massacres could now begin.

Such are the terrible souvenirs that the Decree of January 21, authorizing fresh domiciliary visits, recalled in the minds of the Parisians. To these souvenirs will now be added those of the night of January 27, 1793.

I had gone to read the papers in the Café Corazza. The cafés, the galleries, the gardens, the Flemish grottos, the Lyric Cradle, all were filled with an immense crowd. The number of citizens accompanied by their wives and children who had come to spend their Sunday evening in the Palais Royal—now called the Palais de l'Égalité—could not have been less than six or seven thousand. At eight o'clock a strange rumour suddenly spreads through the garden. It is said that the palace is blockaded by an armed force, and people speak of a train of artillery and loaded cannon. The strange rumour is only too true.

The Committee of General Security had ordered the Commandant of the National Guard to surround the House of the Revolution (this is one of the numerous names given to the former Palais Royal) with a force sufficient to ensure the arrest of all suspected persons.[1] Santerre had accepted the mission with enthusiasm, and had immediately ordered out 3,500 infantry and a troop of 200 horsemen. From the grass-plots of the Louvre, where the gallant General had drawn them up, these 3,700 men bravely charged the promenaders, the women and children who filled the Garden of the Revolution. Cries of anger and fear rose from the terror-stricken crowd. Flight was impossible; artillery had been stationed at every exit, and four loaded cannon stood in reserve in the outer court of the palace.[2]

[1] For this order of the Committee, see the *Révolutions de Paris*, tome xv., p. 245. It is signed by Bernard, Basire, Legendre, Duhem, Montaut, Ruamps, Ingrand, Lasource, and Chabot.

[2] *Mercure Français*, January 31, 1793.

Within a few minutes all the promenaders in the garden were surrounded and all the houses besieged. Restaurants, cafés, news-rooms, shops and private dwellings were invaded and searched without the slightest discrimination.

We soon found ourselves driven back into the centre of the garden, and several thousands of men, women and children were obliged to pass the night out in the open and exposed to the inclemency of the weather.[1] Each of us was questioned by the police-officers who accompanied Santerre's soldiers, and these thousands of interrogatories lasted until four o'clock in the morning.[2] Those only were set at liberty who had taken the precaution to carry their card of citizenship in their pocket. All the rest were detained and taken in groups by the police-officers to the different sections to which they belonged. As each group was formed, the officers shouted ' Is there anyone else for such-and-such a section ?'[3] and it then filed off between two rows of guards through the crowded streets.[4] I was marched off to my section in this manner, and had then to submit to a fresh examination ; it was not till six o'clock that I reached home. All whose replies were not considered satisfactory, or who could not find anyone to become surety for them, were taken to prison.[5]

The following is the official report of the siege of the Garden of the Revolution, and of General Santerre's great victory :

' By order of the Committee of General Security, the justices of the peace with the Commissaries and officers of police yesterday (Sunday) proceeded to the Palais de l'Égalité in order to arrest all persons who either possessed no card of citizenship or were without a home, and the factionists who openly threaten the members of the Convention and Liberty. General Santerre having been required by the same order to furnish an armed force, he commanded 3,700 men, cavalry as well as infantry, to meet on the grass-plots of the Louvre at a quarter to seven, so that from there they might proceed *incognito* to the Palais de

---

[1] *Les Révolutions de Paris*, tome xv., p. 247.
[2] *Le Courrier des Départements*, January 30, 1793.
[3] *Les Révolutions de Paris*, tome xv., p. 248.
[4] *Le Courrier des Départements*, January 31, 1793.   [5] *Ibid.*

l'Égalité at seven o'clock precisely. Several detachments came up late, and the movement was not carried out until eight o'clock. In less than three minutes all the houses were blockaded, the police taking part in the work. Many of the men seemed very anxious to carry out the orders given them satisfactorily, but others dawdled about and showed less zeal. About 600[1] men were found without a card of citizenship, and conducted to their several sections, so that it might be seen who these people were that went about neglecting their safety at a time when the Patriots were waging war against the aristocrats.'[2]

I had occasion to pass the Palais de l'Égalité to-day, and I could not help starting as my eyes fell upon the first word of the inscription that now adorns it :

' LIBERTY . . .'

[1] Not 6,000, as Barante ('Histoire de la Convention,' tome ii., p. 332) and Mortimer-Ternaux ('Histoire de la Terreur,' tome vi., p. 22) erroneously state.

[2] Santerre's report to the Commune of Paris ; *Mercure Français*, January 31, 1793.

CHAPTER XLIX.

A CAB-DRIVER.

YESTERDAY being Sunday, I spent the day with Mme. Pourrat, and her two daughters, Mme. Hocquart and Mme. Laurent Lecoulteux, at Luciennes,[1] and came home at night in a cab. On reaching what used to be called the Place Louis XV., the vehicle suddenly stopped. Believing that some accident had happened, I put my head out to see what it was. The driver had got down from his box, and as it was not quite dark, I could see him kneeling about ten yards off, bare-headed, and in the attitude of a man engaged in fervent prayer. Greatly puzzled, I got out of the cab and quietly approached him. The faint rays of the moon lit up the square, and as I recognised the spot on which the scaffold of January 21 had been erected, I distinctly heard these words in the silence of the night : 'No, you are not dead to me; you will live eternally in the hearts of all good Frenchmen.' Having spoken these words half aloud, my driver rose, and, as he turned round, found himself face to face with me. I could not refrain from shaking hands with him, and a few moments later the cab was again rattling through the deserted streets. It was half-past ten when I reached home, and I did not close my door until my hand and that of the cab-driver had once more met in a cordial grasp.

Strange coincidence ! In Mme. Pourrat's *salon*, a few hours earlier, André de Chénier had told us the following story : From

[1] For information concerning Mme. Pourrat and her two daughters, see Lacretelle ('Testament Philosophique et Littéraire,' tome i., p. 355), and L. Becq de Fouquières ('Étude sur la Vie d'André Chénier,' heading the 'Œuvres en Prose d'André Chénier ').

December 14 to January 20 M. de Malesherbes had not allowed
a day to pass without going to the Temple.[1] It was a long drive,
and the winter was a severe one. M. de Malesherbes was seventy-
two years old, and therefore obliged to take a cab. He had
struck a bargain with a driver who took him to the Temple
every day and brought him home again to the Rue des Martyrs.[2]
The interviews between the King and his defenders commenced
at mid-day, and sometimes lasted until six o'clock. One evening,
when he had remained longer than usual with the King, M. de
Malesherbes said to his driver, as he handed him his *pourboire*,
'I am very sorry, my good man, that you have had to wait so
long.' 'Never mind about that, citizen.' 'But with the ther-
mometer at zero it is a bit rough.' 'Bah! in such a cause I
would suffer a good deal more.' 'That's very well for you, my
friend, but how about your horses?' 'My horses, sir—my horses
share my opinions!'[3]

[1] M. de Malesherbes saw Louis XVI. for the last time on January 17.
On the 18th, 19th, and 20th he presented himself at the Temple, but was
not admitted.

[2] 'How joyfully,' says Lacretelle, 'I used to walk up to his house, in
the Rue des Martyrs, every morning! How often have I since pondered
upon the prophetic name of that street!'—'Testament Philosophique et
Littéraire,' tome i., p. 341.

[3] Alissa de Chazet, 'Mémoires, Souvenirs, et Portraits,' tome iii.,
p. 22. Arnail François, Comte, and afterwards Marquis, de Jaucourt
(1757—1852), a member of the Provisional Government in 1814, used to
tell how, having left the country after the Tenth of August, he ventured
to return in February, 1793, in the company of Joseph de Broglie. They
had scarcely trodden French soil when they met a young fisherwoman.
'What news?' was their first question. 'They have killed the King,'
replied the woman; 'they have opened the gates of Paradise for him,
and closed them for us.'

CHAPTER L.

Thursday, February 7, 1793.

ON January 5 there was played at the Vaudeville Theatre[1] a comedy in two acts by Barré, Radet, and Desfontaines. This piece, in which three clever men, long known for their adherence to the Revolutionary cause, have turned the Scriptures into couplets and travestied a scene from the Old Testament in a very disrespectful manner, could not have been very displeasing to the Jacobins, and yet they have stopped the performance.

On January 26 the Society of Defenders of the Republic One and Indivisible, which meets at the Jacobin Club, requested the Conseil-Général de la Commune to stop the performance of 'that aristocratic piece.' It based its request upon 'the insolence with which the beggarly supporters of the old *régime* had the night before applauded the criminal allusions it contains.'

I was not present at that performance, but two friends who were there gave me an account of it. Accaron and Barzabas, the two elders who have denounced Susanna, take their seats among the judges. Azarias, the chief of the tribunal, rises and says: '*You are her accusers ; you cannot be her judges.*' It was the very phrase that Desèze had flung at the members of the Convention: 'I look for judges amongst you, and find only

---

[1] The Vaudeville Theatre, opened in 1792, stood near the Palais Royal, between the Rue de Chartres and the Rue Saint-Thomas-du-Louvre. It had been built by the architect Lenoir on the site of a dancing-saloon, called Vauxhall, or Petit Panthéon. The theatre was destroyed by fire in 1838, and the Vaudeville was then transplanted to the Place de la Bourse.

accusers.' Azarias' words were received with prolonged applause that was evidently directed against the Accarons and Barzabas of the National Convention. Susanna is condemned to death, and the trumpets sound the signal for departure. As the guards approach to lead her to execution, young Daniel steps out of the crowd, and, addressing the chief of the tribunal, says : '*Judge Azarias, I am innocent of the death of this woman.*'[1] Here again the audience broke out into frantic applause, the significance of which it was impossible to mistake. It most clearly meant: 'Oh, judges! we are innocent of the death of our King.'

The Conseil-Général de la Commune referred the denunciation of the Society of Defenders of the Republic to the police. The next day—Sunday, January 27—a number of members of the Society presented themselves at the theatre, and tried to obtain admission without payment. Finding this impossible, they took tickets, and seated themselves in different parts of the house. A little later about a dozen of their comrades arrive, and, saying that they represent the Society of Friends of Liberty and Equality, force their way in without paying. They then ask to see the manager, and complain of the performance of the 'Chaste Susanna.' Barré[2] prevails upon them to see the play before condemning it, and puts them into good seats. The first act goes off very peaceably ; the second, too, is heard in silence, and there now only remain the two verses of the final air. The first, sung by Mdlle. Lejeune, who took the part of Daniel, passes without mishap ; but the second, in which there is some mention of suffering the tortures of death to preserve one's glory, is received with applause by a large portion of the audience, and encored. The Society men rose and protested furiously, some of them getting out of the boxes into the orchestra, and calling the audience, the authors, and the actors all ruffians. They then invaded the stage in their endeavours to get at the manager. They were, however, baffled in this,

---

[1] Act II., scene 3, of 'La Chaste Suzanne,' a play in two acts. Published by Maret, bookseller, Maison Egalité, Cour des Fontaines.

[2] Barré, the founder of the Vaudeville, undertook the management of the theatre, together with Piis, and did not give up his share of the work until 1815, when he was succeeded by Désaugiers, the famous singer.

and at length left the theatre, while threatening to turn it into a hospital.

Citizen Delpêche, who played the part of Azarias, and had sung the famous final couplet, had the courage to present the Conseil-Général with a petition, in which he complained of the right of censorship assumed by the Society of Defenders of the Republic. The manner in which this petition was received may easily be imagined. In its sitting of January 29 the Conseil-Général made the following Order:

'The Conseil-Général requests the Committee of Police to watch the performances of the "Chaste Susanna" in order to avoid any disturbance, and to prevent the play from perverting public opinion. The Conseil ignores the contemptible petition of Citizen Delpêche, and passes to the next business.'

Whilst Citizen Delpêche was at the Commune, the members of the Society were in Barré's room, and the harassed manager, yielding to their threats, consented to withdraw the piece from the bills. On January 31 the following note appeared in all the Patriotic papers:

'The authors of the "Chaste Susanna" and the manager of the Vaudeville Theatre have consented to withdraw the above-mentioned piece, in consideration of the troubles to which it might give rise. We beg, citizen journalist, that you will insert this note. Signed: Manins, President; Lebrasse, Secretary; Fillirel, Assistant-Secretary, of the Society of Defenders of the Republic One and Indivisible of the eighty-four departments.'

But the exploits of the Defenders of the Republic did not stop there. On the morning of Saturday, February 2, a hawker named Baptiste was selling copies of the 'Chaste Susanna' in the galleries of the Maison-Égalité, when some members of the Society tore the books from him and murdered him on the spot.[1] No steps were taken to arrest the assassins, who are still at large.

[1] *Révolutions de Paris*, tome xv., p. 302.

CHAPTER LI.

Wednesday, February 13, 1793.

On Friday last we had the pleasure of listening to a speech from Grangeneuve, one of the members for Bordeaux, which provoked violent protests from the members of the Left. Chabot, Fabre d'Églantine, and Duhem made a rush towards the speaker, whilst Ruamps[1] shouted at him in great excitement. 'Ruamps,' cried Grangeneuve, 'you are a villain!'[2] Such epithets as 'villain,' 'scoundrel,' 'pig,' 'murderer,' and 'rogue' are now quite common in the Assembly. Yesterday I saw Marat leave his seat, and run along the hall from bench to bench, foaming at the mouth, and yelling: 'Silence, you wretches! let the Patriots speak. . . . You are rogues, scoundrels, and aristocrats!' Turning to the right, he would shout: 'Hold your noise, you thief!' and again to the left: 'Silence, you plotter!' whilst Dufriche-Valazé, who happened to come in his way, was honoured with the title of 'Treasurer of France!'

From words they pass to deeds. Many of the members come to the sittings armed, one with a sword, another with a pistol, the greater part with sword-sticks. Louvet declares that he will not go to the Convention again without a blunderbuss. Merlin de Thionville, who has already worn pistols for some time, has now added a long sword, so as to resemble Marat in everything.[3] Granet, of the Bouches-du-Rhône, carries a

---

[1] Member for Charente-Inférieure.
[2] Sitting of the National Convention, February 8, 1793.
[3] 'Mémoires' of Buzot, p. 340.

bludgeon with which he is fond of threatening those who do not vote with him.[1] On one occasion it is Bourdon (of the Oise) who raises his hand against Chambon, and challenges him to a duel.[2] On another, Chambon, supported by five or six of his colleagues, rushes forward like a madman, and, in spite of the intervention of the ushers, threatens Robespierre with his sword-stick. Now it is Rebecqui, one of the deputies from Marseilles, who takes a colleague by the throat: now another member of the Right, who rushes upon Duquesnoy, and tries to run him through.[3]

Witnesses of these excesses, many of them deputies, try to keep aloof from them—much less for the sake of their dignity than from motives of prudence. They make no profession of belonging to either party, never speak, and never even risk making an interruption. Unable to render themselves invisible, which is evidently the height of their ambition,[4] they change their seat every day, and often change it several times during the same sitting—wandering shadows that will become fixed only when successful.

To the right of the President's desk sit the members of the Mountain,[5] the Maratists, and Robespierrots. To the left, in that part of the Convention that has been called

---

[1] Michaud, 'Biographie Universelle': 'Granet.'

[2] Sitting of January 7, 1793.

[3] 'Second Speech of Armand Benoit Joseph Guffroy, Member for the Pas-de-Calais, upon the Punishment of Louis Capet and the Plots to oppose the Supreme Will of the Nation, which condemned the Tyrant,' 38 pp. This speech not having been delivered in the tribune, there is no trace of it in the newspapers of the time, and the historians of the Revolution appear to have been entirely ignorant of it. It is, however, an important document, and one that contains perhaps more information than any other concerning the interior of the Convention.

[4] 'I determined to remain hidden under my veil of silence and obscurity. I could not render myself invisible.'—'Mémoires de Durand de Maillane,' a member of the National Convention, p. 38.

[5] In its sitting of December 27, 1791, the Legislative Assembly ordered a rearrangement of the hall, which resulted in the transposition of the Right and Left. The change was effected during the first days of 1792, and on January 6, 1792, Le Patriote Français announced that 'the Patriots would henceforth sit on the right of the President.' L'Ami du Roi of January 7 also states: 'By turning the hall upside down, the Right has gone to the left, and the Left to the right.' This state of things was never altered in the Legislative Assembly, nor in the Convention, as long as it sat in the Riding-School.

the *Swamp* (*Marais*),[1] sit the Girondists and Buzot, their leader.[2]

In the provinces Vergniaud and Brissot are still looked upon as the leaders of the Gironde, but that is a mistake.

Vergniaud is undoubtedly the most eloquent man of his party, and of the whole Assembly; but whether from unconcern or from laziness, he allows men and matters to go their own way, and takes no trouble to direct them. The sitting opens at ten each morning, but Vergniaud is rarely seen before noon, and he frequently stays away for several days together. For him pleasure goes before duty and business. Brissot, on the contrary, gives himself up entirely to politics, but though his influence is great in the press, it is not of much account in the tribune.

Endowed with rare energy and real oratorical power, always ready to throw himself into the breach either for attack or defence, Buzot has many of the qualities of a party leader. It is said that the ardour which animates him is fed not only by his hatred of Robespierre and Marat, but also by his love for Mme. Roland. However that may be, his colleague Guffroy was quite right in alluding to him as the commander-in-chief of the Girondist party.[3]

Buzot and his lieutenants have two head-quarters. They often hold a council on the upper benches of the Right, which are generally deserted. There, when any important matter is under discussion, will be found Buzot, Barbaroux, Salle, Estadens, Lahaye, Chambon, Deperret, Birotteau, Louvet, Gorsas, Couppé,

---

[1] Guffroy, p. 26. All historians give the name of the *Swamp* to the centre of the hall and to those deputies who belong neither to the Mountain nor to the Gironde. Guffroy's speech, on the contrary, shows that the Right, or the benches on which sat the Brissotins, was known as the *Swamp*. In his second speech he again says : 'Buzot is placed at one of the posts, whence he directs the movements of the Right, called the *Swamp*.' In the trial of the Girondins ('Bulletin du Tribunal Révolutionnaire,' No. 63), the President says to Antiboul, one of the accused : 'Was it not your intimacy with Rebecqui and Barbaroux that led you to sit in that part of the Convention known as the *Swamp*?'

[2] The name of Girondins, unknown in the Legislative Assembly, begins to appear in January, 1793 ; but in February it is still very little used, and does not really make its way into political parlance until much later.

[3] Guffroy, p. 28.

Rouyer and Larivière.   At other times Buzot and the men I
have just mentioned form a group round the stairs that lead to
the tribune.   The leader then gets upon the usher's stool that
stands close by, and distributes his instructions, which his aides-
de-camp carry from bench to bench.[1]   The most active of these
lieutenants is Barbaroux—Michel Morin Barbaroux, as Marat
calls him[2]—who spends all his time in giving the watchword to
the soldiers under him.

The members of the Buzot party also meet outside the
Assembly, in order to agree upon their plan of action.   These
meetings have taken place both at No. 148, Rue Richelieu,[3] and
at Vimca's eating-house in the Passage des Ecuries.   During one
of these gatherings at Vimca's, Birotteau, who was acting as
secretary, took down the names of the members present, and
there were found to be about a hundred.[4]   Other meetings,
attended only by the chiefs of the Girondist faction, are held in
Mme. Roland's *salon* in the Rue de la Harpe, at Citizen Talma's
in the Rue Chantereine,[5] and in the house of Dufriche-Valazé,
deputy for the Orne, who lives at No. 10, Rue d'Orléans.[6]   This
last gathering is by far the most important of all.   It is composed of about forty members,[7] who meet pretty regularly every
evening.   Among those who rarely fail to put in an appearance,
and who take the most active part in the discussions, are Buzot,
Lacaze, Gensonné, Brissot, Guadet, Boilleau, Duprat, Salle,
Lidon, Deperret, Barbaroux, Chambon, Bergoeing, Mollevaut
and Lesage (of the Eure-et-Loir).

---

[1] Guffroy, p. 29.

[2] *Journal de la République Française*, No. 20.   'The National Convention,' says Marat, 'allows itself to be wholly influenced by the cabal of
the Constituent and Legislative Assemblies, headed by the clique from
the Gironde and the Bouches-du-Rhône.   The soul of that clique is
formed of the pedantic Buzot, the irascible Guadet, the perfidious
Brissot, the double-faced Gensonné, and the hypocritical Rabaut. . . .   I
will say nothing of Brother Gorsas, nor of *Michel Morin Barbaroux*, who
carries about the resolutions of the Council, and passes round the watch-
words.'

[3] Sitting of the Convention of December 31, 1793.

[4] Guffroy, p. 30.

[5] *Le Publiciste de la République Française*, No. 159.

[6] Sitting of the Convention of May 23, 1793 ; 'Mémoires de Meillan,'
p. 16 ; 'Mémoires de Louvet.'

[7] Speech by Valazé, sitting of May 23, 1793.

Thus organized, and having at their command the services of orators and journalists, and on grand occasions the eloquence of Vergniaud, it would seem as if the members of the Gironde should triumph over their adversaries. They would, perhaps, if the Convention sat at Versailles. But at Paris—never ! Vergniaud, Guadet, Gensonné, and Isnard speak better than Robespierre, it is true. But what of that ? Of what avail is their eloquence in the face of these deputations of sectionaries and federates who march past the Assembly every week and impose upon it the *will of the* PEOPLE—of that PEOPLE whose justice, greatness and sovereign infallibility they have themselves so long and so slavishly extolled ? What is their power in the face of that applause, those shouts, and those threats which they themselves called the *voice of the* NATION, when the applause was for them and the threats for their adversaries ? On the day when Manuel, converted to reason, moved, (1) That the inspectors of the hall should send an equal number of gallery tickets to six successive sections of Paris daily for distribution amongst the citizens of such sections ; (2) That the same number of tickets should be sent to six departments in alphabetical order —on that day the Mountain rose as one man to protest. The uproar was so great that the President was obliged to leave the chair. Thuriot cried : ' If you adopt Manuel's proposal, we shall see in the galleries none but *cowardly apostles of moderation*, at a moment, too, when we need the support of men of tried patriotism.' What a monstrous thing it would indeed be were the galleries filled with honest, temperate spectators, who listened in silence, and made no attempt to influence the deliberations !

The discussions concerning the King's trial were then at their height, for Manuel brought forward his motion on December 14, 1792. Everyone saw that the aim of the mover was to save the head of Louis XVI. The Girondists joined the Mountain in opposing it, and it was rejected almost unanimously. The galleries, which are really the levers of the Convention, therefore remained in the hands of the Commune and of the worst demagogues. The men who preside over the debates with more power than the President, and who watch the Assembly with more care than the *inspecteurs de la salle*, hold their court in two cafés adjoining the Convention—the Café Beauquene and the Café Hottot. The latter establishment has a back-door communicating directly with the Riding-School,[1] and its *habitués* are in constant receipt of reports, either from spectators present at the sitting of the Convention and from deputies themselves, or from the Commune and the sections. Here they arrange their batteries, give the watchword and transmit the signal for applause or dissent, ordering at will the men and women who fill the galleries and corridors or crowd around the entrances.

France, with throbbing pulses and an aching heart, looks on in anguish at the great drama that is being played in the Riding-School, where Vergniaud bandies words with Danton, and Buzot with Robespierre. Her gaze is fixed upon the actors who play their parts so brilliantly, expecting them to work out the *dénouement* of this horrible tragedy. She little knows that this *dénouement* will be brought about by some thirty obscure and unaccredited men who direct the play from their table in the Café Hottot or the Café Beauquene behind the scenes.

---

[1] Adolphe Schmidt, 'Paris pendant la Révolution,' according to the reports of the secret police, tome i., p. 118.

CHAPTER LII.

Tuesday, February 19, 1793.

THE 'Chaste Susanna,' the performances of which had been stopped on January 31 by order of the *Defenders of the Republic One and Indivisible*, has just made its reappearance in the bills at the Vaudeville. The negotiations that led to this revival are sufficiently curious to be noted.

Barré, Radet and Desfontaines, who are excellent Patriots, and who certainly did not write their comedy with a view to injuring the Republic, lost no time in correcting it and in suppressing whatever might be construed into an unpleasant allusion. Thus altered, they submitted it in its new dress to the judgment of the Jacobin Club, humbly soliciting permission to have it performed. The Jacobins were no doubt in a bad temper that evening, for they sent the unhappy authors to the Commune, which seemed little better disposed. Without giving them a hearing, it passed to the next business, characterizing their request as merely a fresh trap.[1] Not yet discouraged, Barré applied to the Defenders of the Republic, begging them to be his censors, and after having submitted with great docility to all the observations of these experienced critics, he obtained from them permission to have his piece performed.

The play was therefore again placed before the public yesterday evening. I was very anxious to be present, and I do not regret having gone. Of course I did not hear either the line of Azarias, '*You are her accusers, you cannot be her judges,*' or Daniel's words, '*Judge Azarias, I am innocent of the death of this*

---

[1] *Le Courrier des Départements,* February 19, 1793.

woman,' or the last couplet so well sung by Delpêche.   All these passages have disappeared, and others, too, have been struck out, such as, ' *Base informers, you who have lied to the people, tremble! The Destroying Angel approaches.*'

It mattered but little, however, what the actors said or did not say.   The interest of the evening, according to my mind, was centred in the first row of the balcony, where sat four grave and reverend Jacobins, acquitting themselves, with incomparable dignity, of the official mission with which they were charged— that of judging whether the corrections made by the authors were sufficient to permit a continuation of the performances.[1] The papers this morning tell us that the gentlemen were quite satisfied.[2]

La Harpe, who was present at the performance, and who had been much tickled by the sight of the four Commissioners, said to me as we left the theatre : ' Ye gods! what strides we are making !   Under the Tyrant we got our censors from the Academy ; under the Republic, we get them from the Jacobin Club !'

---

[1] La Harpe, quoted by E. Jauffret in 'Le Théâtre Révolutionnaire,' p. 217.

[2] The alacrity with which Barré, Radet, and Desfontaines submitted to the injunctions of the *Defenders of the Republic* did not save them from being arrested a few weeks later.   They remained in prison for several months, and to regain their liberty, and perhaps save their life, they wrote a vaudeville entitled ' The Return,' burning with patriotism.

CHAPTER LIII.

Friday, February 22, 1793.

GENERAL SANTERRE—General *Hops,* as the *Feuille du Matin*[1] calls him—has just started on a campaign. 'Against the Austrians and the Prussians?' Not at all. Leaving to others the care of fighting the enemies without, he has taken upon himself to destroy the enemies within: for are they not most to be feared? 'I understand; you mean those incorrigible aristocrats, those mad *moderates,* who conspire in secret against the Republic.' You have not guessed it yet. Must you, then, be told that the real enemies within, the more dangerous, too, since they find a refuge in the very houses of the Patriots, are . . . the dogs and the cats? Fortunately, Santerre was on the watch. To him will fall the honour of having counteracted their plots against Liberty and of having preached the crusade against these domestic enemies.

This is the Order of the Day which he has just had posted upon the walls of the capital :

'The Republic has gained many friends since the death of Louis, but the high price of food may possibly serve the aims of

---

[1] Santerre, the commanding officer of the National Guard of Paris, was a brewer of the Faubourg Saint-Antoine. Hence the nicknames of the *frothy General* and of *General Hops* that had been given him. 'We are told,' says the *Feuille du Matin* (No. 43, February 6, 1793), 'that General Hops is shortly to be elected as the permanent President of the National Convention, in consideration of the talent he has shown in silencing those who speak contrary to the interests of the Republic.' In a preceding chapter of this work I have shown that it was indeed Santerre—and not Dugazon, the actor, as Louis Blanc asserts—who ordered the roll of the drums that drowned the voice of Louis XVI. on January 21. To the numerous and, I believe, decisive proofs given there must be added that set forth in the above quotation from the *Feuille du Matin.*

our enemies. Our armies on the frontiers, the belief held by the farmers that Paris is given up to fire and the sword, and the depreciation in the assignats brought about by the tactics of the aristocracy, are the chief causes of these high prices. I have two remedies to propose : the first is that all well-to-do citizens who have the common weal at heart should substitute rice and potatoes for bread on two days in the week. I believe that this would economize half the consumption of Paris, and produce fifteen hundred sacks of flour in two days. The second remedy is that all citizens should at once rid themselves of useless pets. Paris contains sufficient cats and dogs to absorb the nourishment of fifteen hundred men, which means ten sacks of flour wasted every day.

'SANTERRE.'[1]

General Santerre had shown the way, and others followed in his wake. The editor of the *Révolutions de Paris*, who pokes a little fun at the 'brave Santerre,' and who remarks that there never was so much noise at the mill for ten sacks of flour, has his own plan, and this is the remedy proposed by him for coping with the famine :

'Every Sunday there is at least one loaf used for religious purposes in every parish throughout the eighty-five or eighty-six departments. This loaf, which was formerly made of the finest flour, is now, it is true, only common household bread ; but it is bread none the less, and generally weighs about four pounds. Now, there are at present at least 50,000 municipalities in France ; given that there are, on an average, two parishes in each, this means that there is a weekly waste of 100,000 loaves of four pounds each, or a monthly loss of 1,600,000 pounds of bread. The loaves are cut up into small pieces in the sacristy, and though presented by the beadle to the congregants, these morsels are rarely swallowed. There is, consequently, a dead loss of 35,200,000 pounds of bread annually—let us say, in round figures, 30,000,000.

'Can the God of Nature be angry if we take from His altars an offering that is useless to Him, and which is a pure loss, not only to us, but to our clergy ? To suppress the bread of the Sacrifice in order to economize 30,000,000 pounds of bread is, therefore, a meritorious and patriotic action.'[2]

Prudhomme is a great journalist, but a poor arithmetician. A child could teach him that 1,600,000, multiplied by 12, makes, not 35,200,000, but 19,200,000. He makes a mistake

---

[1] *Chronique de Paris*, February 5, 1793.
[2] *Révolutions de Paris*, tome xv., p. 306.

of only *sixteen millions!* But this deficit of 16,000,000 pounds
of bread will not embarrass him much. For, as a set-off, he has
an expedient no less ingenious than the first, and, it may be said,
ejusdem farinæ. 'A custom,' he says, 'which consumes still more
flour is that of powdering the hair. Do not let us waste our
food-stuffs in this way. Rather let the citizens and their wives
give up powder, and deserve the gifts of Nature by the uses to
which they put them. The women will not be less beautiful,
and the men will appear only more manly.'[1]

But all these fine ideas are poor compared to the patriotic
scheme of Citizen Jeauffre. The *Chronique de Paris* has opened
its columns to it, and I cannot refrain from reproducing it here :

'Sparrows are pretty and pleasing little creatures. They cheer
me up in the morning, when I hear them through the pipe of my
chimney ; they enliven me still more in the spring. But I place
the love of my country far above all other considerations. Now,
everyone knows that there is nothing more voracious than a
sparrow ; that is why the English had proposed to drive them all
out of their happy island. I do not think that they have carried
their idea into execution ; it would even seem as if the Government were opposed to it, since it drives out French patriots, who
are certainly not little sparrows. However that may be, we must
not allow a good idea to be lost (even when it proceeds from our
enemies). I therefore move that all the sparrows in Paris be killed,
and I adopt the amendment which is proposed to kill all in France.
The harm these creatures do the nation by making corn dearer is
too evident. It is easy to convince one's self of the extent of their
depredations, by calculating how much corn a sparrow can eat per
day or per year. A sparrow eats at least from twelve to fifteen
grains of corn per day. A pound of sixteen ounces containing
4,072 grains, a single sparrow eats one pound of corn per year.
This does not seem very alarming, but the number of sparrows is
enormous. There are 260,000 houses in France, and ten persons
to a house. Supposing that there are only four chimneys to each
house, that makes 1,040,000 chimneys. Supposing that there are
only ten sparrows to a chimney (which is very few, for in some farms
they are seen by hundreds), this would make 10,400,000 sparrows,
and consequently a loss of as many pounds of corn. Nothing is to
be despised in politics, and everyone may convince himself that
this saving would feed 100,000 men for seventy days. Our Generals

[1] *Les Révolutions de Paris*, edited by L. Prudhomme, tome xv., p. 306.

and our soldiers would have had no occasion to murmur so loudly if our providers had made this calculation.

'Let it not be said that I am wasting my powder on the sparrows, and that one of these birds is not worth a shot. We must remember that by killing one sparrow we kill a thousand, since we also destroy its posterity ; but I must warn my fellow-citizens not to eat this kind of game, for its consumption brings on epilepsy. I might have given them advice that would have effected a real saving, and been profitable to the Republic, that of giving the birds to their cats ; but the Decree that has gone forth against the latter renders this advice useless. I, however, believe that there is more in my idea than in that of killing the cats. The death of the sparrows will only be hailed with delight by the flies, caterpillars, and wasps (creatures which increase most abundantly, it is true, but die in winter), whilst if, according to the advice of the Commander of Paris, the cats be killed, we shall be inundated by a multitude of rats, of which it will be impossible to rid ourselves. If our brave General had remembered the fables of one La Fontaine, he would have thought of the rats who got at the flour in the kneading-trough, and he would have reflected that thirty of these animals can do more damage in a night than an Angora can consume in a year. But we cannot think of everything when we have everything to do. As for me, who have not forty-eight battalions, and the rest, to look after, I have had the leisure to go into my subject thoroughly, and I persist in my motion.'[1]

Citizen Jeauffre, you have a great deal of wit for a Patriot, and I am very much afraid that your patriotic motion is aimed more at General Santerre than at the 10,400,000 sparrows in France. Are you not, perchance, one of those terrible journalists against whom our irritable General inveighed the other evening, at a public sitting of the Commune ? Citizen Jacques Roux— another hero of January 21—had just declared that ' at that moment there were 40,000 families in Paris living in the most horrible distress,' and he had mildly insinuated that the war upon cats and dogs was scarcely an efficient remedy for this lamentable state of things. Then Santerre rose. ' Citizens,' he said, ' the last speaker has almost reproached me for having suggested that all superfluous cats and dogs should be killed. I must ask you to believe that in doing so I had in view only the

welfare of the poor.   I took into consideration the fact that a
bushel of corn is worth more than millions in gold or in notes.
There are madwomen in Paris who keep sixty cats and as many
dogs ; I shall always think it my duty to protest against abuses.
The journalists who have found fault with my suggestion are
wrong in their calculations ; they have taken for a petty remedy
what is really of the greatest interest.'[1]

The journalists are not alone in making a laughing-stock of
General Santerre.   I have a caricature before me in which the
General is represented receiving two deputations, one of cats,
the other of dogs.   Before the spokesmen have time to open
their mouths, Santerre quickly draws a small guillotine from his
pocket, and ' cuts them short.'   At the foot of the print are the
words :

' The art of silencing the talkative.'[2]

Ye gods ! for whom, then, are we to have respect, if not for
Citizen Santerre himself ?   I am afraid that Mirabeau was right
when he sighed, a few days before his death, ' Oh, frivolous and
thrice frivolous nation !'

---

[1] Commune of Paris, evening sitting of February 18, 1793 ; *Chronique de Paris*, **February 21, 1793.**

[2] *La Feuille du Matin*, **February 9, 1793.**

CHAPTER LIV.

THE RIOTS OF FEBRUARY 25, 1793.

Wednesday, February 27, 1793.

THE riots which were foreseen and announced some days ago broke out on Monday.

The general destitution is so great that, if there is any surprise at all, it is that they did not break out before.

The scarcity of food goes on increasing, and the supply of bread may fail at any moment. Every evening this question of bread is discussed in the sections amidst terrible uproar ; every night great crowds gather around the doors of the bakers' shops —the women standing there bare-footed in the snow and rain, frozen and worn out with fatigue, waiting until nine in the morning for the small portion of bread that frequently they do not even obtain.[1] Hunger is an evil counsellor. How can these crowds help lending an ear to dark rumours, gross lies and guilty exhortations ? How can these unhappy women help listening to those who tell them that all the evil is due to monopoly ?

On Monday, February 11, a deputation from the forty-eight sections of Paris laid before the Convention a petition relating to the supply of food, and demanding that ' no farmer or merchant should be allowed to charge more than 25 livres for a sack of wheat weighing 250 pounds under pain of six years' imprisonment for the first offence, and death for the second.'[2] ' The people must have bread,' said the spokesman of the deputation ; ' for where there is no bread, there is neither law, nor

---

[1] Les Souvenirs de l'Histoire, ou le Diurnal de la Révolution,' by Beaulieu, Year 1793, February 11.

[2] Buchez and Roux, 'Histoire Parlementaire de la Révolution Française,' tome xxiv., p. 265.

liberty, nor Republic.'   Someone proposing to refer the petitioners to the Committee on Agriculture, they replied:
'*Hunger cannot be adjourned.*'

Since then the state of things has only grown worse.   The
price of bread has gone up alarmingly, and soap, which could
be bought a month ago at 14 to 15 sous a pound, has now
risen to 32 sous.[1]   The people are in an extraordinary state of
fermentation.   Last Friday, Saturday and Sunday, threatening
crowds assembled outside the bakers' and grocers' shops.   On
all sides—in the streets, at the Jacobin Club, in the municipality
and in the Convention—everywhere is heard the cry of '*Down
with monopoly!*'

On Friday the washerwomen went to the Conseil-Général de
la Commune to complain of the high price of soap.   Chaumette,
the Procureur-Syndic, supported their demands in the following
terms: 'We have destroyed the nobles and the Capets; there
still remains an aristocracy to overthrow—that of the rich and
of the shopkeepers, who make a monopoly of the food of the
people in order to bring the latter to their knees.   We must
fight them, and I say so openly, though I know well enough that
I shall be guillotined if they win.   I propose that we go in a
body to the Convention in order to obtain a sentence of death
against the monopolizers.'   Hébert spoke to the same effect, and
Jacques Roux expressed himself in most violent terms.   'If,' he
cried, 'we have faithless representatives, the guillotine is there
to punish them; and if they will not—if they cannot—save the
people, let us tell the people to save itself, and to revenge itself
upon its enemies.'[2]

Such incitement could not remain without effect.   On Sunday
the washerwomen marched in a body to the quay, where several
boats lay laden with soap, and compelled the wares to be given
up to them at a price fixed by themselves—that is, almost for
nothing.   When the operation was nearly concluded, and all
the women were abundantly stocked, some municipal officers
came up; they had some planks laid in order that the ladies
might leave the barges without the danger of getting a wetting,

---

[1] *Révolutions de Paris*, tome xv., p. 390.
[2] *Le Républicain Français*, February 23, 1793.

and then politely invited them to be off.   Everything was done, on both sides, with the greatest civility.[1]

Whilst the washerwomen, having concluded their little expedition, were directing their steps towards the Convention, the groups of women and children who had gathered round the bakers' shops, more numerous and noisy than usual, went first to the new Mayor, and, receiving no satisfaction from him, proceeded in their turn to the Convention.

The Assembly first received the deputation of washerwomen, whose petition concluded with these words: 'The head of the Tyrant has fallen under the sword of justice; let the sword of justice now fall upon the heads of the public leeches.   We demand the death of all monopolizers and jobbers.'[2]

Immediately afterwards, another deputation was admitted to the bar—that of the *citoyennes révolutionnaires*, who hold their meetings in the library of the former Jacobin Club.

The President Dubois-Crancé accorded the petitioners the honours of the sitting, and informed them that the Convention would consider their demands on the following Tuesday.

On the Terrace a tumultuous crowd of several thousands of people, yelling '*Bread and soap!*' awaited the return of the deputations, which finally made their appearance.   'They have put us off till Tuesday,' cried the petitioners; 'but we will only put ourselves off till to-morrow.   When our children ask us for milk, we do not put them off for two days.'[3]   The crowd then went off, shouting: '*Till to-morrow!   Till to-morrow!*'

From that moment the evidences of an inevitable riot became more abundant, but neither the Committee of General Security, nor the municipal authorities, nor the Minister of the Interior,[4] seemed to trouble themselves about it.   No precautions of any kind were taken, and General Santerre, the commanding officer of the National Guard of Paris, went to Versailles to review a troop of dragoons.[5]

---

[1] Beaulieu, 'Essais,' tome v., p. 53.
[2] Buchez and Roux, tome xxiv., p. 332.
[3] *Révolutions de Paris*, tome xv., p. 390.
[4] In February, 1793, the Minister of the Interior was Garat, one of the most cowardly men of the Revolutionary epoch.
[5] *Révolutions de Paris*, tome xv., p. 394.

On Monday morning Marat published an article in which he
incited the mob to plunder and bloodshed. The following is an
extract from it :

'When the cowardly mandatories of the people encourage
crime by allowing it to go unpunished, it cannot be wondered
at if the people in despair should take the law into their own
hands. Let us abandon the usual repressive measures. It is
only too evident that they always have been, and always will
be, ineffectual ; in every country in which the rights of the
people are something more than empty phrases pompously
strung together in a Declaration, *the pillage of a few shops and
the hanging of a few monopolizers would soon put an end to the
malpractices.*'[1]

This article is read, commented upon, and applauded. Cries
of '*Death to monopolizers!*' are heard on every side, coupled
with that of '*Down with the grocers!*' It is eight o'clock in the
morning when the mob begins work in the Rue des Lombards.
A few men go on in front, and say to the grocers : 'Have you
any sugar, coffee, or soap? Agree to let us have your stock at
the prices we fix, or—look out for the rope!' A few moments
later, all the shops in the quarter are besieged and invaded.
Some of the women wear pistols in their belts, and many of the
men are disguised as women, though in most cases they have
not troubled to shave off their beards. White sugar is valued
at 20 to 25 sous per pound ; moist sugar at 8 to 10 sous ; soap
and candles at 12 sous ; Mocha coffee at 10 sous ; cloves and
tea at 20 sous ; indigo—which is worth about 30 francs—at 20
sous ; cinnamon and vanilla—worth 120 francs—at 30 sous.[2]
Some paid, others simply gave the little money they had about
them ; the majority carried the things off without parting with
a farthing. Soon, too, the weak and miserable pretence of
order that had at first been kept up gave way to the most un-
restrained violence, and each one took by force what suited him
best. Butter, honey and wax were spilt and trodden under foot
in large quantities, whilst brandy, spirits of wine, and other
liquids ran down the gutters. By ten o'clock all the grocers'

[1] *Journal de la République Française*, February 25, 1793.
[2] *Révolutions de Paris*, tome xv., pp. 391, 392.

and chandlers' shops in the Rue des Lombards, the Rue des Cinq-Diamants, the Rue Marivaux, and the Rue des Trois-Mores were completely sacked.

The same scenes occurred in all the other quarters of the city. In the Rue de Saint-Jacques a grocer armed himself with a knife, and attempted to defend his stock;[1] he would have paid for his resistance dearly enough had his wife and two children not been there to plead for mercy. As it was, he got off with his life, but lost his goods. A grocer of the Ile Saint-Louis parleyed with his assailants, and agreed to distribute all his wares without payment, on condition that he should give each comer not more than one pound of sugar or of some other article. Even then he was accused of giving short weight![2] About mid-day the mob began to invade the street in which I live. The shop of our grocer, honest Gillet, was broken open, in spite of my efforts and those of a few sympathetic neighbours. Indignant at such lawlessness, we proceeded to the Hôtel de Ville to acquaint the Conseil-Général of the scenes we had just witnessed. The galleries received our report with shouts of laughter and cries of '*So much the better!*' 'Yes; so much the better,' re-echoed Jacques Roux, entering at the moment; 'for the grocers have only given back to the people what they have robbed them of for a long time.'[3]

We left the Council, under the very eyes of which, right opposite the Hôtel de Ville, a shop was being pillaged. Along the Quai Pelletier, in the Rue des Arcis and in the Rue Saint-Merri, crowds of men, women, and children were hurrying along, all laden with loaves of sugar, packets of candles, or bars of soap. At the door of a grocer's shop in the Rue de Venise, a barrel of brandy had been staved in, and some miserable wretches, lying flat on the pavement, were lapping up the liquor in the gutter. At the entrance to the Rue Saint-Denis a picket of cavalry was stationed, but the soldiers did not seem to trouble themselves about what was going on around them as they sat motionless in their saddles, only smiling occasionally at the shouts and songs of the drunken mob. At last—about three

[1] *Révolutions de Paris*, tome xv., p. 392.   [2] *Ibid.*
[3] *Le Courrier des Départements*, February 28, 1793.

o'clock—Pache, our new Mayor, makes his appearance. He is assisted by Chaumette, the orator of February 22. He harangues the rioters in a quiet, good-natured way, for are they not his electors?

At five o'clock the first roll of the drum is heard,[1] and the military patrol the city in every direction. They are everywhere and nowhere, for the pillage continues. In a few places the officers attempt to do their duty in getting the crowds dispersed, but they are abandoned by their men, and left exposed to the rough treatment of the mob. Several of them are wounded.

Night had long fallen, but the pillage still went on, thanks to the connivance of the patrols.[2] Were not the men who composed them the husbands and fathers of the women and children who were sacking the shops? Whilst returning home, a little before midnight, we frequently came across some prudent citizens selling for hard cash the stock they had laid in during the day.

At four o'clock on Tuesday morning Paris was again awakened by the roll of the drum. Santerre, having returned from Versailles, rode through the streets, accompanied by his staff, while all the military again turned out. Notwithstanding this grand display, several wholesale warehouses were visited by the mob. Things went on, I must admit, less impudently than on the preceding day. Here, some buyers hand over in payment folded pieces of paper, purporting to be notes, but which turn out to be valueless. There, men take out their money as if to pay for their purchases, and, in the hurry of leaving, put it into their

---

[1] *Le Patriote Français*, February 26, 1793.

[2] *La Chronique de Paris*, March 1, 1793 : 'The patrols that passed said not a word. . . . The guards, after having, as a matter of form, begged the women to stop plundering, finished by lending them their protection. . . . The neighbours of the grocers remained sitting at their doors very calmly, as if they approved of it all.' See also Lacretelle, who was an eye-witness. 'Plunder was so amusing that the rioters did not think of murder. The aspect of Paris during that day showed to what depths a great city can fall when it resigns itself to obey the most immoral wretches it contains. One neighbour would come to gaze upon the ruin of another, and if the first was not a grocer, he would cry out upon the selfishness of grocers ; many of those who were ruined hid their grief. The distribution of the booty proceeded with a certain amount of order, and those who would have blushed to steal were most eager to profit by a bargain obtained by violence and threats.'—'Histoire de la Convention Nationale,' tome i., p. 230.

pockets again.[1]   If Monday was a day especially devoted to
grocers, Tuesday was the day for the tallow-chandlers.   At the
Croix-Rouge an enormous crowd had gathered, and the patrol
stationed at this point, being composed of volunteers from
Brest, did its duty in maintaining order.   The women in the
mob, having come prepared with little pocket syringes, filled
them from the gutter and squirted the contents into the soldiers'
eyes.[2]   Thus ended, amidst a good deal of rough fun, this riot
that had lasted two days.

Friday, March 1, 1793.

The Brissotins have been uttering loud complaints in the
Convention against the rioters of February 25.   They denounced Marat, and proposed, some to charge him with incitement, others to temporarily exclude him, others again to
have him examined as to his sanity.   This fine indignation is all
very well, but it comes somewhat late in the day.   There was a
time, and it is not so long ago, when the very men who now
inveigh against Marat were ready to make every allowance for
him, when the very deputies who now take sides against the
brigands were their warmest defenders.

The riots of February 25 and 26, 1793, are only a repetition
of the riots of January 20 and 23, 1792.

On January 20 of last year the *people*, whom Marat and his
journalistic colleagues were already then inciting against the
monopolizers and *jobbers*, sacked a shop in the Rue Saint-Antoine,
and compelled a merchant in the Faubourg Saint-Marcel to sell
at 25 sous per pound sugar that was worth 3 francs.   On
January 23 a large number of shops were broken open and
sacked in the Rue Saint-Denis, Rue Saint-Martin, Rue du
Cimitière-Saint-Nicolas, Rue Chapon and Rue des Gravilliers.

In the Legislative Assembly, the members of the Right demanded that these outrages should be energetically repressed.
The Brissotin deputies, on the contrary, maintained that the
really guilty parties were not the plunderers, but those who had
been plundered.   Fauchet, one of the chief orators of the party,

---

[1] *Révolutions de Paris*, tome xv., p. 396.   [2] *Ibid.*

denounced the avarice of the merchants and the tactics of the monopolizers.[1]

M. Ducos, one of the members for Bordeaux, could not find a word to say against the *popular tax* and the honest people who had levied it; but he enlarged upon 'the infamous tricks of monopolizers who band together to cheat the public.' 'As for those,' he added, ' who, for some months past, gamble in corn and enrich themselves out of the people's want, you will, I trust, not accord them even a look of pity. I, who have watched their shameful trade and their infamous dealings, in despair at not being able to stamp them physically with a mark of ignominy, shall not, at least, quit this tribune without having paid them the tribute of indignation that every good citizen owes them.'[2]

Petion, now one of the leaders of the Gironde, was then Mayor of Paris. On January 24 he submitted to the Assembly a report upon the state of the capital and upon the disturbances caused by the high price of sugar and other commodities. After having ingenuously admitted that *for several days past he had perceived suspicious movements that made him fear a rising*—in the face of which he had, however, taken no precautionary measures whatever—he added that on January 20 he had gone to the Faubourg Saint-Marcel, and that he had there seen none but honest citizens *who had sworn, with righteous indignation, that they had not the slightest desire to plunder the shops, and who, in conformity with his advice, that they should petition the Assembly to regulate the price of sugar, had then peaceably withdrawn*—that is to say, after having laid in a stock at 25 sous per pound. Monday, January 23, had not, it is true, afforded the first magistrate of the city such great satisfaction. In many quarters he had been pained to see windows smashed, shops broken into, the guards insulted and heads threatened. But of what use was it to mention these things? Was it not better to bury these regrettable scenes in oblivion? He promised that the municipal body should hold a sitting on the spot *in order to prevent the spread of those exaggerated reports which are so subversive of the public peace.*[3]

[1] *L'Ami du Roi*, January 23, 1792.
[2] *Journal de l'Assemblée Nationale*, tome ix., p. 98.
[3] *L'Ami du Roi*, January 26, 1792.

Brissot, Vergniaud, Guadet, Gensonné, and the other members of the Gironde, warmly applauded the report of the worthy Petion. What troubled them more than these riotous scenes themselves were the 'exaggerated reports' that might be made of them.

A moment ago I said that the Girondists, who are now so bitter against Marat since he has become their enemy and their constant denunciator, criticised him less severely when he contented himself with demanding the heads of their antagonists. All those who frequented Mme. Roland's *salon* before the Tenth of August know that they were not startled by the *exaggerations* of the Friend of the People as long as Louis XVI., Marie Antoinette, and their defenders were the objects of his vile denunciations. Some of them can perhaps still remember the cries of indignation that escaped their hostess when they one day brought her the news that Marat's papers had been torn up by Lafayette's satellites.[1]

The hatred felt by the Girondists against Marat is also directed against Hébert; but here, again, it was not until they were themselves attacked that they saw what a filthy paper Hébert's was. As long as the wretch attacked only Royalists and aristocrats, they pardoned him all his iniquities. How often, in the Legislative Assembly, have I not seen the members of the Gironde cross the hall holding a copy of *Le Père Duchesne* in their hand, and smiling at its obscenities![2]

And they did not confine themselves to smiling. At the time when they had the majority of the Legislature entirely in their hands, it was decided that seats in the hall should be given to Hébert and his two assistants, so that they might take their notes without undergoing discomfort.[3]

Threatened by the rioters, attacked by Marat and by Hébert, the Girondists have a right to defend themselves, but they have no right to complain.

[1] 'Étude sur Mme. Roland et son Temps,' by C. A. Dauban, p. 101.

[2] 'Essai Historique et Critique sur la Révolution Française,' by Paganel, a former member of the Convention, tome iii., p. 95.

[3] 'Histoire Politique et Littéraire de la Presse en France,' by Eugène Hatin, tome vi., p. 513.

CHAPTER LV.

Friday, March 8, 1793.

THE National Convention has just changed its officers. Gensonné has been elected President; Isnard, Grangeneuve, and Guyton - Morveau have been appointed Secretaries.[1] The Girondists, therefore, still continue to lead the majority in the Assembly, Gensonné, Isnard, and Grangeneuve being some of their principal orators.

After the sitting a number of deputies went to finish their evening in the *salons* of the *ci-devant* Marquis de Villette, amongst them being Isnard and Delaunay.[2] As the two latter entered the room, they were immediately surrounded by a crowd of people all eager to congratulate Isnard upon his election. La Harpe, who was present, jumped about upon his little legs, and swung his little arms, crying; 'Well, well, M. Isnard, so you are a Secretary! All good citizens will rejoice at your success, because they will recognise in it the pledge of a more energetic policy. It is time, high time, that deeds should take the place of words, and that the representatives of the nation

---

[1] Sitting of March 7, 1793.

[2] Delaunay the Younger, deputy for Maine-et-Loire. At the trial of Louis XVI. he had voted for the King's banishment, and later for his respite. He was appointed President of the Court of Angers under the Empire, and died June 10, 1814. His brother, Delaunay the Elder, also sat in the Convention. He voted for the King's death, took his seat in the Mountain, and, being brought before the Revolutionary Tribunal with Danton, Camille Desmoulins, Chabot, Basire, Hérault de Séchelles, Fabre d'Église, Lacroix, and Philippeaux, was guillotined on the 16th of Germinal, year II. (April 5, 1794). For the two Delaunays, see the remarkable work by M. Bougler, 'Mouvement Provincial en 1789 et Biographie des Députés de l'Anjou.' 1865.

should at last suppress the Jacobins and the Commune. Do not say that this is impossible, for the majority of the Convention is with you; you are four or five hundred strong.' 'True,' replied Isnard; 'but we cannot rely upon more than two hundred.' 'That is more than you want,' rejoined La Harpe; 'the rest are closer to you than to the Mountain, and they will follow you, but only on condition that you make a forward movement. Your orators think they have done quite enough when they prove the Mountain to be in the wrong—as if that were the only issue in question. Do you not see that this is a battle to the death?' 'We do, indeed, since they are continually threatening to knife us.' 'Bah! they will not kill you in the street, nor in the Convention—neither they nor the rogues who surround you in the galleries and the lobbies. But when your majority has passed a resolution, fifty ferocious brutes rush to the table, yelling out their demand to have the members' names. The galleries threaten you with their fists, and you end by giving in—that is the manner in which they will crush you.' 'You have described the evil to perfection, M. La Harpe, but what is the remedy? There is no necessity to remind you, sir, of that line, the first half of which you have so gloriously belied, but of which the second part is eternally true:

'"Criticism is easy, but art is difficult."

You ask me what is to be done. I will tell you. Each day your enemies appeal to force. Well, you, in your turn, must use force in the service of the law. Let forty-eight out of your two hundred members proceed to the forty-eight sections of Paris on the same day and at the same hour; let them speak as only the representatives of the people can speak; let them boldly expose that long tissue of crimes, the proofs of which you have in hand. In the meantime, let the rest of your colleagues, even though they be but a hundred and fifty, march through the streets with the tricolour standard, calling upon all honest men, all those who desire neither massacre nor pillage, to follow them. Have you any doubt that all good citizens will crowd around you, and that the greater part of every section will follow you in arms? Then, masters of the city, masters of the galleries, from which you will drive the vile mob that now holds them, you will submit a Decree which you will have ready, and which will contain the details of the crimes brought home to your enemies. Put your impeachment to the vote on the instant, and it will be carried by an enormous majority. You know what cowards all these rogues are as soon as their satellites are no longer by them. Either they will not speak at all, or they will utter their usual absurdities. Let the President firmly pronounce the order for their arrest, and in eight days' time they will be led to execution. In an undertaking of this kind you must not be deterred by a stray pistol-shot or a chance sword-cut any more than by the occasional fall of a few tiles, and I will answer for your success.' The little man spoke with extraordinary animation, and the majority of his hearers were tempted to applaud him, when Isnard, not without great hesitation, said : ' What you suggest, M. La Harpe, is impossible.' ' Impossible ?   In that case, sir, we are all lost.'

A long silence, that had something lugubrious about it, fell upon the company, and was only broken by the charming Mme. de Villette[1] reminding La Harpe of the days long past when Voltaire, whose guest he was at Ferney, would encourage and lead him on by saying, ' *Macte animo, puer.*' ' You have as much courage, M. de La Harpe,' added the charming Marquise, with a smile, ' as you have wit, talent, and eloquence.'[2]

[1] **Reine** Philiberte Rouph de Varicourt, Marquise de Villette, had been brought up by Voltaire and Mme. Denis, his niece, at Ferney.

[2] See the curious pamphlet published in the year III. by La Harpe, entitled ' Le Salut Public, ou la Vérité dite à la Convention par un Homme Libre.' This treatise, which has not been incorporated in the works of the author of the ' Lycée,' is now nowhere to be found. ' I spoke in this fashion,' says La Harpe, ' to several of your colleagues who have since been proscribed, and whose testimony I could invoke—amongst others, Isnard and Launay d'Angers, whom I met at Mme. de Villette's a few days before March 10.'

CHAPTER LVI.

Monday, March 11, 1793.

HAVING always most assiduously attended the sittings of the Constituent and Legislative Assemblies and of the Convention, I have heard their greatest orators, Cazalès and Barnave, Vergniaud and Danton, the astonishing Mirabeau and the no less astonishing and ever-ready Maury. But not one of their speeches ever made upon me the deep and tragic impression called forth last night by one word, one single word, hurled by a member in Danton's face.

The Convention was discussing the desirability of establishing a special criminal court for the trial of conspirators and counter-Revolutionaries—a court from which there should be no appeal.

We had already heard Robespierre, Buzot, Vergniaud, Barère and Danton—Danton, who had cried, ' What care I for my reputation ? Let France be free, and my name tarnished for ever ! I have allowed myself to be called a bloodthirsty wretch ; well, let me drink the blood of my country's enemies !'[1]

The sitting had lasted eight hours, and it was beginning to get dark. Gensonné, the President, declares the sitting closed, but Danton rushes to the tribune for the second time. ' I call upon all good citizens not to leave their post,' he shouts in stentorian tones, and every member resumes his seat. A few lamps only had been lit, and there was but a feeble glimmer in the hall. The tribune was plunged in semi-darkness, and Danton's voice, issuing from this *visible gloom*, struck the audience with a kind of terror. ' It is most important that

---

[1] *Moniteur* of 1793, No. 72.

justice should be meted out to the counter-Revolutionaries, and this proposed court will serve as the Supreme Court of the nation's vengeance. The enemies of Liberty carry their heads high ; baffled on all sides, they continue to weave their plots ; and though they see the honest citizen in his peaceful home and the artisan in his workshop, they are foolish enough to believe themselves in a majority. Well, snatch these wretches from the people's vengeance, for humanity itself orders you to do so.'[1]

At that moment a powerful voice slowly uttered the one word, 'SEPTEMBER!!!'

That was all. An indescribable thrill ran through the Assembly, and the darkness in which the tribune was plunged was not deep enough to hide Danton's emotion. No protest came either from the Mountain or from the public galleries. They remained dumb before this avenging word, that came from the darkest corner of the hall, but straight from the heart of an honest man, like a lightning-flash that breaks through the darkest clouds.

We learnt not long after that the man who had recalled, with such terrible opportuneness, the massacres of September was Lanjuinais.[2]

In the same gallery with me were Beaulieu and Paul Royer,[3] a young man who has the honour to be a friend of the courageous deputy for Rennes. We left the hall together. M. Royer made his *début* at the bar of Paris in 1787, under the auspices of Gerbier. He is endowed with grave, calm, almost austere eloquence. All who know him speak of him in terms of great admiration, and, in spite of his twenty-nine years, with respect ; they say that he has something more than talent, and that is, character. Before the Tenth of August he sat in the Conseil de la Commune, to which he had been elected by the section of the Ile Saint-Louis. He was soon remarked for his moderation

[1] *Moniteur* of 1793, No. 72.
[2] 'Notice Historique sur la Vie et les Ouvrages du Comte Lanjuinais,' by Victor Lanjuinais, p. 23.
[3] Pierre Paul Royer-Collard (1736—1845), member of the Council of Five Hundred, of the Chamber of Deputies, and of the Academy. See the 'Vie Politique de Royer-Collard, ses Discours et ses Écrits,' by M. de Barante, two vols. 1861.

and his energy. Danton, who comes from his part of the country—they are both natives of Champagne[1]—and who knew him, sat near him at the Hôtel de Ville ; Royer has therefore a good deal to tell about him. In concise and peculiar language, which it is unfortunately impossible for me to reproduce, he showed us Danton indolent and bold, desirous of glory but still more of pleasure and wealth ; less envious than Robespierre, less sanguinary than Marat ; as indifferent to crime as to virtue ; possessing neither convictions, shame nor culture ; not devoid of natural talent, and having this at least in his favour, that in the midst of this hypocritical herd of cruel and cowardly dema- gogues, steeped in vice and crime, he claims to be called neither *virtuous* nor *incorruptible*.

We accompanied M. Royer as far as his house on the Quai d'Orléans, and on the way he told us a large number of anecdotes that give one a true idea of the famous deputy for Paris.

On the evening of June 20, 1792, when he heard that the rioters had left the Tuileries without having murdered Louis XVI., Danton cried : ' The fools ! Don't they know that crime has also its propitious hour ?'

On the morning of September 2 word was brought to him before about twenty people that the prisons seemed to be threatened, and that the prisoners were in a state of great terror. Shrugging his shoulders, he bellowed : ' I don't care a d—n for the prisoners ! Let them take their chance !'[2]

On September 3 he sent special Commissioners to the depart- ments, who were for the most part absolute thieves. Some time afterwards a deputy was simple enough to complain of the conduct of some of these rogues. ' D—n it all !' replied Danton, ' did you think we were going to send you young ladies?'[3]

M. Royer learnt from M. de Ségur, ex-Ambassador of France at the Court of St. Petersburg, the details of a very curious conversation that passed between the latter and Danton, a few weeks after the massacres in the prisons. Having met each other casually in the street, Danton stopped M. de Ségur and talked

---

[1] Royer-Collard was born at Sompuis, a village near Vitry, June 21, 1763. Danton was born at Arcis-sur-Aube, October 28, 1759.
[2] 'Mémoires de Mme. Roland,' p. 265.   [3] 'Mémoires de Louvet.'

about one thing and another until the former Ambassador could not refrain from mentioning the horrors that Paris had witnessed for several days. 'I cannot,' he said, 'grasp the motive. I cannot understand why you, as Minister of Justice, were unable to prevent, or at least to stop them.' They were at that moment walking side by side. Danton stopped, looked M. de Ségur full in the face, and replied : 'Sir, you forget to whom you are speaking. You forget that we are only the scum, that we come from the gutter; that with your principles we should soon find ourselves back there, and that we can only govern by terrorizing !'[1]

'M. Danton is a philosopher,' added M. Royer, 'and one day he did me the honour of explaining to me the main principle of his philosophy. It is as follows : " Whoever hates vice must hate mankind."[2] On another occasion—I was then assistant secretary to the Corporation—Danton, who was deputy to the Procureur de la Commune, said to me as we were leaving the town-hall : " Young man, come and brawl with us. When you have made your fortune you may then choose the party you prefer." '[3]

I asked both Beaulieu and Royer whether they shared the commonly accepted belief that Danton had taken money from the King.

Beaulieu, who, as a journalist, has frequently been brought into contact with M. de Lessart, Minister for Foreign Affairs,[4] was told by the latter that he had himself handed Danton 24,500 francs to get a resolution passed at the Grey Friars Club. 'To this testimony of M. de Lessart,' rejoined Royer, 'you may add that of M. de la Fayette. I was speaking to him about Danton while he was in Paris shortly before the Tenth of August, and these are his very words: " Danton sold himself on condition that he should receive 100,000 francs as compensation for the abolition of his post of Avocat au Conseil instead of the 10,000 francs agreed upon; the King's present was therefore 90,000 francs. I met Danton at M. de Montmorin's house

---

[1] 'Histoire et Mémoires,' by the Comte de Ségur, tome i., p. 12.
[2] Edgar Quinet, ' La Révolution,' tome i., p. 319.
[3] Beaulieu, ' Essais,' tome iii., p. 192.
[4] From November, 1791, to March 10, 1792.

on the very evening when the bargain was concluded.   He
received a good deal more money later on, but I have only
personal knowledge of the 100,000 francs.   Danton himself
spoke to me about it at the Hôtel de Ville, and tried to justify
himself by saying, ' General, I am more Royalist than you !'"'

'Never mind,' replied Beaulieu, who will have his joke ;
' M. Danton is a very honest man.   He has received the King's
money from M. de Lessart and from M. de Montmorin, it is true.
But did he not pay his debt to the King on January 21 ?   And
did he not cry quits with M. de Montmorin at the Abbaye on
September 2, and with M. de Lessart at Versailles on the 9th ?'[1]

[1] The Comte de Montmorin, Minister of Foreign Affairs from
February 14, 1787, to November 20, 1791, was murdered at the Abbaye
on September 2, 1792, and M. de Lessart, his successor in office, was
massacred at Versailles on September 9.   See the remarkable work by
Frédéric Masson, ' Le Département des Affaires Etrangères pendant la
Révolution, 1787—1804.'

CHAPTER LVII.

A TRIBUNAL CRIMINEL EXTRAORDINAIRE.

Wednesday, March 13, 1793.

Two days ago I spoke of the debate that had been opened in the National Convention concerning the establishment of a special criminal court. The debate was brought to a close to-day. Its importance is so great, and its consequences so serious, that I cannot refrain from giving the following details.

On Friday, March 8, Lacroix (of Eure-et-Loir), one of the Commissaries with our army in Belgium, ascended the tribune at the opening of the sitting, and announced that the Austrians had broken through our lines, and that our troops had been forced to evacuate Aix-la-Chapelle and Liège. While still under the influence of the excitement caused by this news, the Assembly appointed Commissioners to go that very evening into the forty-eight sections of Paris and remind all citizens who are capable of bearing arms of the oath they took to lay down their lives in the defence of Liberty and Equality, calling upon them, in the name of their country, to fly to the aid of their brethren in Belgium.

At the sitting of the 9th, the deputies who had undertaken the mission on the previous evening successively ascend the tribune, and congratulate the Assembly upon the patriotism and devotion with which they had everywhere been received. 'David and I,' said Jean Bon-Saint-André, 'proceeded to the section of the Louvre. We were struck with the determination, the courage, and the good feeling of the citizens. They all swore to fly to the defence of the country; but after having taken this sacred pledge, they submitted to us their fears concerning the dangers that threatened the provinces. They asked that whilst they were gone to fight our enemies abroad the Convention should punish traitors, and exterminate our enemies at home. Finally, they made a demand for the establishment of a court to punish the counter-Revolutionaries and the disturbers of the public peace.' Making this demand his own, Jean Bon-Saint-André added : 'I will put as a motion the petition laid before you by the sections,[1] and accordingly propose that the Convention should order the creation of a Revolutionary Tribunal, and request the Committee on Legislation to bring up a report to-morrow on the manner in which such a court should be organized.'

Carrier, one of the most obscure members of the Assembly, seconded this motion.

Guadet is now about to speak, but is forced to resume his seat in deference to the murmurs that come from all parts of the hall, and the storm that breaks out in the galleries. The courageous Lanjuinais—who is not a Girondist—is the only one to protest against a decree 'violating every principle of the rights of man, and of abominable injustice in suppressing appeal in criminal matters.'

To this the Assembly pays no heed, and accepts the following wording, proposed by Levasseur :

'The Convention decrees the establishment of an extra-ordinary criminal tribunal, from which there shall be no appeal, for the trial of all traitors, conspirators, and counter-Revolutionaries.'

On the 10th the Committee on Legislation brought up its report. The members of the Gironde are in a majority on this committee ; if therefore they are opposed to the creation of a new court, they will try and make the Convention rescind its vote of the day before. They have not cared to adopt this course, and Lesage, who is one of the leaders of the party,

---

[1] 'Histoire du Tribunal Révolutionnaire de Paris,' by H. Wallon, tome i., p. 45. Jean Bon-Saint-André, after having been a member of the Committee of Public Safety, and one of the most ardent spirits of the Mountain, became Baron de Saint-André under the Empire. Prefect of the Department of Mont-Tonnerre, he died at Mayence on December 10, 1813.

submitted a scheme based upon the following lines : 'The tribunal shall sit in Paris, and shall try all who are indicted to appear before it. The four Judges of which it is to be composed shall pronounce sentences from which there shall be no appeal. They shall be appointed by the Convention from amongst the Judges of the departmental criminal courts. The jurymen who shall serve in this court will be those appointed by the departments after the Revolution of the Tenth of August.'

Robert Lindet, a member of the Mountain, succeeds Lesage in the tribune, and presents an amendment to leave out the jurymen, and to substitute the following : 'An official shall sit in permanence in this court to receive denunciations.' Lindet had scarcely finished reading his amendment, when Vergniaud cried : 'We will rather die than consent to the establishment of an inquisition a thousand times more terrible than that of Venice !'

It was a fine phrase, but it was only a phrase, after all. What made the orator of the Gironde and his friends so indignant was not the creation of a Revolutionary Tribunal— they had supported that only the day before—but the suppression of the jurymen appointed by the departments. The Brissotins think that they may safely rely on the departments and on the juries they will send. If the Assembly lets them have their juries, they will raise no further objections. The proof of this was not long in coming. The officious Barère having declared that trial by jury was the right of every free man, Billaud-Varenne, one of the foremost members of the Mountain, supported the declaration, and amplified it in the following terms :

'I think, with Cambon, that a tribunal of nine might become formidable, even to the friends of Liberty. I propose the insertion of a clause stipulating that the juries for this tribunal be elected by every section of the Republic.'

This was all that the Gironde wanted. Lidon, one of the party, moves that Billaud-Varenne's words be entered on the minutes. To this neither Billaud nor any of his colleagues of the Mountain offer any opposition, thus affording the excellent

Barère the sweet satisfaction of knowing that all are agreed. The Assembly thereupon unanimously decrees that there shall be a jury, and, by a very large majority, that the jurymen shall be selected by the Assembly itself, and taken from all the departments.[1]

At the evening sitting, Duhem, one of the deputies of the Left, moves that the decree giving a jury to the new tribunal be rescinded. But Thuriot, one of the Mountain, proposes an amendment of a nature to conciliate all parties, and by the terms of which the jury is to deliberate in open court—a middle course that is finally adopted. The Convention then goes on to pass, almost without debate, the other articles of the scheme.[2]

Upon the minutes of the proceedings of the previous day being read over on the 11th, Robespierre points out the importance of defining what the Convention, in the first article of its Decree, means by *conspirators*, and proposes to word that article in this way : ' The law forbids, under pain of death, any attack upon the general security of the State, or upon the liberty, equality, unity, and indivisibility of the Republic.' Isnard proposes the following as an alternative :

' There shall be established in Paris an extraordinary criminal tribunal, which shall take cognizance of every anti-Revolutionary enterprise, of every attack upon the liberty, equality, unity, and indivisibility of the Republic, or upon the internal and external security of the State, and of all conspiracies aiming at a re-establishment of the Monarchy, or of any other authority antagonistic to the liberty, equality, and sovereignty of the people, be the accused either civil or military officers or private citizens.'

Isnard's wording was adopted in preference to that of Robespierre.

According to the terms of Article 7, framed with the object of getting the court into immediate working order, the Convention was at an early date to appoint twelve citizens of Paris to act as jurymen until May 1, when they would be replaced by others chosen from all the departments. On the 11th it was

---

[1] *Moniteur* of March 13, 1793, morning sitting of March 10.
[2] *Ibid.*

moved by **Rabaut Saint-Étienne**, seconded by another Girondist deputy, and **agreed, that** the first jurymen should be taken from the capital and the four neighbouring departments.

A member, whose name I could not learn,[1] then proposed to rescind Article 12, which provides ' that the jury shall vote and deliberate in open court.' On the day before this article had been passed without the slightest protest from any part of the Assembly. Guadet now energetically supports the proposal to rescind it, but is it not already too late ? And how can **Guadet** and his friends answer this pertinent remark made by Prieur : ' You yourself openly voted against the Tyrant, and were not afraid of being accused of intimidation ; why do you not believe the jurymen to be equally courageous ?' The article was allowed to stand.

On the whole, the members of the Gironde did not oppose the principle of a special criminal court ; they accepted without the least hesitation the suppression of appeal characterized by Lanjuinais as ' an abominable injustice ' ;[2] they required no other guarantee for the accused than that afforded by the existence of juries taken from the departments and appointed by the Convention—a perfectly illusory guarantee, since the choice of these jurymen will be subject to the fluctuations of an Assembly which is itself the slave of popular passion and the plaything of circumstance ; they passed without a word the article providing for the public deliberations of the jury, and only on the morrow of the vote did one of their number raise tardy and, as it proved, ineffective objections ; they took a very active part in determining the wording of the Decree, and it was Isnard,

---

[1] According to Buchez and Roux (' Histoire Parlementaire de la Révolution,' tome xxv., p. 68), the author of this proposal is said to have been one Burat. There was, however, no deputy of that name in the Convention.

[2] The **Girondins** had already voted for this ' abominable injustice ' when the Criminal Tribunal was established, on August 17, 1792. Brissot, in the name of the Special Commission of Twenty-one, upon which Vergniaud, Guadet, Gensonné, Lasource, and Condorcet also sat, had undertaken to prove the ' advantages of the suppression of the right of appeal.' In his report there occurred these words—words which would alone suffice to disgrace the Girondist party, and in which cynicism vies with cowardice : ' Nothing has been left undone to ensure either justice or despatch ' (*Moniteur* for 1792, No. 231).

one of their leaders, who proposed the accepted wording of the first article, the most important of all—a wording more comprehensive and more dangerous than that submitted by Robespierre, and well calculated to send to the scaffold anyone suspected by the ruling faction.

One last remark. The Decree referring to the organization of the special court necessitated the taking of a good many different votes, and the debate occupied several sittings, those of March 9, 10 and 11. It was therefore not passed by a snatch vote, and was really the work of the majority of the Convention. Now, at the election of a President on March 7 it was seen that the majority belongs to the Girondists, for Gensonné, one of their leaders, received the largest number of votes. On the same day Isnard and Grangeneuve, two other members of the party, were appointed Secretaries.

It appears, moreover, that the creation of the new court has filled them with joy. They rely upon it for ridding them of the Royalists; at the same time, thanks to the majority they have in the Assembly, thanks also to the influence which they intend to exercise upon the departmental jurymen, they hope to be able to send to the tribunal, and from the tribunal to the scaffold, their most formidable adversaries—the leaders of the Mountain and of the Commune. M. d'Allonville[1] tells a very curious anecdote about this. On the evening of the 11th he called at Mme. Ollivier's, a sister-in-law of General Montesquiou, whose *salon* is frequented by some of the leading members of the Gironde. At the time of the King's trial, M. d'Allonville had one day remarked to Barbaroux: 'Take care! If you make Louis XVI. lose his head, you may very likely lose your own some day.' As he entered Mme. Ollivier's *salon*, Barbaroux came forward to greet him, saying with a laugh: 'Well, you see, it is still on my shoulders.' 'Yes—still!' 'Yes, and it will stay there,' replied Barbaroux; 'no power was ever more firmly established than ours. This tribunal, which the Mountain has been foolish enough to demand, and which Lanjuinais more foolishly still wanted to hinder us from giving them, is in

---

[1] 'Mémoires Secrets de 1770 à 1830,' by the Comte d'Allonville, tome iii.

our hands, and through it we shall bring the Dantons, the Robespierres, and the Marats to justice.' Barbaroux spoke very loudly, and a small crowd, composed of Vergniaud, Rebecqui, and eight or ten of their colleagues, had gathered round him ; all applauded the words of the member for the Bouches-du-Rhône, and, like him, manifested entire confidence in the new tribunal.[1]

I should not be surprised if, at the same time that this conversation was going on in Mme Ollivier's *salon*, Robespierre had been using exactly similar language in Mme. Duplay's *salon* at No. 366 in the Rue Saint-Honoré, only a few yards off. He, too, sees the scaffold looming on the horizon, and his enemies ascending it ; this dream *makes him weep with sadness !* Who knows ? Perhaps they are both right ! The *tribunal criminel extraordinaire* will certainly not spare us Royalists, but it may possibly also ' bring the Robespierres and the Vergniauds, the Rebecquis and the Barbaroux, to justice !'[2]

---

[1] 'Mémoires Secrets de 1770 à 1830,' tome iii.

[2] Vergniaud was condemned by the Revolutionary Tribunal on October 30, 1793, and Robespierre on July 28, 1794 (10th of Thermidor, year II.). Barbaroux was executed at Bordeaux on June 25, 1794, whilst Rebecqui, to escape the scaffold, drowned himself at Marseilles on May 3 of the same year.

CHAPTER LVIII.

Friday, March 15, 1793.

EVENTS are following close upon each other, and party strife is daily becoming more fierce and embittered. The special court established by the Decree of March 10 is destined to become not an instrument of justice, but a weapon of hatred and revenge in the hands of factions. Each side flatters itself to have the handle of that weapon in its own hands, and to be able to direct the point against its enemies. The deputies of the Gironde, in particular, regard the establishment of the new court as a pledge of their victory. It is my opinion, on the contrary, especially after what passed at last Wednesday's sitting, that their defeat is certain and close at hand. I am aware that some honest people put their last hopes in them, and I see Royalists who, in their hatred for Robespierre and Marat, side with Brissot and the Rolandists; supporters of what they call the policy of the *lesser evil*, they desire to draw a veil over the crimes and cowardice of the Girondists. We are asked to forget that in the National Assembly the latter vied with the most ardent Jacobins; that they claimed the honour of having organized the Tenth of August; that, masters of the Assembly, of the Executive Council, and of the municipality of Paris during the interregnum between the Tenth of August and September 20, they instituted the criminal court of August 17, and allowed the massacres in the prisons to take place under their very eyes. Nor must we remember that in the Convention they constituted themselves the judges of Louis XVI., and dragged him to the guillotine; that, threatened in their turn by pitiless antagonists, they sought to save themselves from the latter by passing a decree of death each day against some common enemy ; that only yesterday they abolished the right of appeal, and all other guarantee of defence in criminal matters ; that they sided with Danton in instituting a tribunal of blood.

Well, since they wish it, let us forget all these things ; but how can we rely upon being defended by men who have no courage to defend themselves, as the events of the last few days have once more proved ?

In the night between March 8 and 9 the Vigilance Committee of the Defenders of the Republic, sitting at the Jacobin Club, passed a resolution inviting all the sections of Paris to declare themselves in a state of insurrection, to have the tocsin rung, to destroy the printing-presses of the Brissotin and kindred newspapers, and to march to the Convention and drive out the 'factious deputies.' At daybreak the mob invaded the approaches to the Riding School, took possession of all the exits, and gave orders to the sentries to refuse admission to women in view of ' the blow ' that might have to be struck. When the sitting opened, the galleries were thronged with spectators, mostly armed, but who, however, refrained from any act of violence. They, no doubt, considered that the Convention in deliberating, as it was then doing, upon the establishment of a Revolutionary Tribunal was performing good work, and that it was not meet to disturb it.

Though the principal item on the programme was not put into execution that day, such was not the fate of that relating to the destruction of the printing-offices. On the evening of the 9th the offices of the *Courrier des Départements* in the Rue Tiquetonne, and those of the *Chronique de Paris* in the Rue Serpente, were sacked by a band of two or three hundred men, armed with pistols, swords, and hammers, and led by Lazowski, one of the *heroes* of the Tenth of August.

It was nine o'clock when the rioters reached the Rue Tiquetonne. They broke open the doors, smashed the cases and presses, and then set fire to the house. Gorsas owed his life to his presence of mind. Without betraying the least emotion and without being recognised, he passed through a band of about fifty brigands who were threatening to blow his brains out. On reaching the bottom of the stairs, he finds the door guarded by some armed men who allow no one to pass. He then proceeds to the yard, scales a trellised wall, and passes into a neighbouring house, whence he rushes off to his section.[1]

Having finished their job in the Rue Tiquetonne, our worthies proceed to the printing-office of Garnery and Fiévée in the Rue Serpente. Garnery was away, but his sister was found in the office. She is threatened with the muzzles of two pistols, and told that if she utters a cry she is a dead woman.[2] At that moment Fiévée[3] enters ; he, too, is threatened with death. He tries to parley with the invaders, and addresses Lazowski as follows : ' A printer is no more responsible for what he prints than the child that picks up the rags that make the paper. You wish to be revenged upon the writers—well, you have missed your aim, for I have nothing in common with them. You are ruining me, and that makes no difference to them, for to-morrow they can get their printing done elsewhere. Very often I do not read what is printed here, and personally I have written nothing, for or against, since the beginning of the Revolution.' No doubt Fiévée's arguments were considered reasonable ones, for his auditors ceased smashing as soon as he ceased speaking. It is true that they had finished their work, and that it had only taken a few minutes to destroy the fruit of several years of work, care, and privation.[4]

---

[1] *Le Patriote Français*, No. 1,307.

[2] *Les Révolutions de Paris*, tome xv., p. 474.

[3] Joseph Fiévée was born in Paris in 1767, and died there in May, 1839. Imprisoned under the Terror, and proscribed after the 13th of Vendémiaire and the 18th of Fructidor, he wrote in exile two romances, 'La Dot de Suzette' (1798) and 'Frédéric' (1799). Again imprisoned in 1799 for corresponding with Louis XVIII., he was liberated after the 18th of Brumaire, and entered into personal relations with Bonaparte. Censor and director of the *Journal de l'Empire* in 1805, he was appointed Prefect of the Nièvre in 1813. Under the Restoration he made himself conspicuous by his ardent Royalism, and became a contributor to the *Conservateur* and the *Quotidienne*. After the Revolution of 1830 he took sides in the new Constitutional party, and wrote for the *Temps*, and afterwards for the *National*. His articles were signed T. L. or L., and sometimes with his name. His three curious volumes, 'Correspondances et Relations de J. Fiévée avec Bonaparte' published in 1837, contain an autobiography which would alone save the name of this witty and remarkable writer from oblivion.

[4] A letter from Fiévée in the *Chronique de Paris*, March 14.

On leaving Fiévée, the rioters proceeded to another printer's in the Rue Guénégaud, and in the excess of their fury dangerously wounded two women living in the house.[1]

Sunday, March 10, was a still more agitated and threatening day than the Saturday. To hang the Generals, arrest the members of the Executive Council and the leading deputies of the Right, give them a *popular* trial and send their heads to the departments—such was the Order of the Day that circulated among the groups that had gathered in the squares and in the principal thoroughfares. The streets re-echoed with statements and prophecies of every kind, mingled with narratives of the military disasters and the treason of the Generals. Woe to whosoever dared to contradict the absurd rumours of the loss of the whole of Belgium, of the siege of Givet and of Valenciennes, or of the loss of Verdun !

By nightfall the excitement had increased, and an uproarious mob fills the Jacobin Club, where Varlet, Desfieux, Lazowski, Fournier, the American, and other ringleaders, had made arrangements to meet. Above the din are heard the most incendiary harangues, accompanied by the clang of arms.[2] Desfieux denounces the treason of Brissot, of Petion, and of the other plotters who sit on the Right. ' As long as we have such men as these amongst us we shall do nothing. It is time we got rid of them. We must place them under arrest in their own houses, and have other men chosen in their place. Then all obstacles will disappear and the country will be saved.'[3] A soldier seconds this motion in strong language. Another succeeds him in the tribune, and opens his speech with the thrice-repeated cry of ' *Revenge !* ' ' Citizens,' he says, ' the satellites of the crowned ruffians murdered us at Liège in the persons of our comrades. We must be avenged ! What means the inviolability of the representatives ? Is it a shield for crime ? I will tread this inviolability under foot—we must strike ! Republicans recognise but one sovereign—that is, Liberty and Equality. We must

---

[1] *Révolutions de Paris,* tome xv., p. 475.
[2] ' Mémoires de Louvet,' p. 251.
[3] *Journal des Débats et de la Correspondance de la Société des Jacobins,* No. 370.

strike such blows as will for ever cripple those who wished to injure us. I ask you what the tyrants who are now making war upon us would do if they were masters of the Jacobins? Death is the last argument of free men; those who argue differently are not free.'[1] Amid the tumult that followed this speech, several citizens vainly tried to obtain a hearing. An orator at length succeeds in making the following proposal during a lull in the uproar: ' Let the Patriots assembled in this room divide themselves into two bands, one of which shall go to the Convention to avenge the people by punishing the traitorous deputies, whilst the other shall proceed to the Ministry of Foreign Affairs[2] and make a clean sweep of the members of the Executive Council assembled there.' This proposal is received with cheers, groans and cries of every kind; whilst the confusion is at its height, the lights are put out, and the rioters separate—some to go to the Convention, others to the Grey Friars Club.[3] To the latter go Varlet, Fournier and Lazowski. After having heard them, the members of the club ' over the water' pass the following resolution:

' The department of Paris, being an integral part of the sovereign power, is invited to exercise the rights of sovereignty. The electoral body of Paris is authorized to appoint fresh members in the place of those who have betrayed the people. Delegates are also to be sent to the Committee of Insurrection.'[4]

This resolution is immediately transmitted by trusty messengers to the forty-eight sections. That of the Four Nations responds in energetic terms, and draws up an address, from which we take the following passages:

' The defenders of the country rise up in arms; but their first care shall be to crush the conspiracies in their midst. . . . The establishment of a new Revolutionary Tribunal and the dismissal of the Ministers are inadequate palliatives and false measures, since they attack but indirectly the assassins who find a rallying-point in the very heart of the Convention. The defenders of

---

[1] *Journal des Débats*, etc., *loc. cit.*

[2] In March, 1793, the Ministry of Foreign Affairs was established at No. 4, Rue Cérutti, formerly Rue d'Artois.

[3] *Journal des Débats . . . de la Société des Jacobins*, No. 370.

[4] ' Histoire Parlementaire,' by Buchez and Roux, tomo xxv., p. 93.

the country demand, as the sole efficacious remedy, that the department of Paris should immediately exercise the sovereignty which is its right; that, to this end, all the sections and cantons should be convoked in order to authorize the electoral Assembly of Paris to recall the faithless mandatories unworthy of being legislators of a Republic. . . . The General Assembly of the section, having heard the energetic address of the Grey Friars Club, unanimously declares its adherence to the principles it contains, and has at once appointed Commissioners to communicate their sentiments to the forty-seven other sections, as well as to the Grey Friars and Jacobin Clubs, and *also to form the now indispensable Committee of Insurrection, the head-quarters of which should be at the Jacobins.*[1]

At that late hour of the night—it was already two o'clock—there were but very few members left in the sections, and only three of the latter followed the example of that of the Four Nations.

The adhesion of four sections out of forty-eight was a rather poor result; but the success of Fournier and Varlet in the Commune was poorer still. They had themselves undertaken to make known to that body the resolution of the Grey Friars Club, and to demand the closing of the barriers and the ringing of the tocsin. The Mayor and the Conseil-Général either thought the means at the disposal of the conspirators too slender to ensure success, or saw in the ringleaders competitors for the posts they themselves held; in any case they refused to support the movement.[2]

The *coup* had failed.

At the Convention, which met on Sunday evening at nine o'clock, and did not adjourn until half-past three in the morning, the galleries were filled with rioters who were only awaiting the signal to invade the Assembly and attack the members of the

---

[1] 'Literal Copy of the Address sent to the Sections by the Section of the Four Nations on Sunday Night' (*Le Patriote Français*, No. 1,303).

[2] 'Gorsas says that the real motive of the decision of the Commune in this matter is to be found in the following words of Chaumette : "There are some dangerous creatures bent on murdering good citizens in order to take their places, fill their pockets, and pander to foreign Courts." '—*Le Courrier des Départements*, March 21, 1793.

Right. But this signal did not come. The mob outside, on whom they depended, had been driven from the Terrace by the rain that came down in torrents. When Beurnonville, the Minister of War, and Kervélegan, the member for Finistère, escorted by the battalion of Brest volunteers, reached the Assembly at one o'clock, they found all the approaches quite deserted.

Although the conspiracy of March 10 was unsuccessful, it was nevertheless accompanied by particularly threatening symptoms. It affirmed its existence by the boldest acts, and made no attempt to conceal its aims. The Girondist deputies were its avowed victims; but what attitude did they take up in the face of danger? How did they attempt to ward it off? By hiding themselves. Being warned that a large and hostile mob surrounded the Convention, they decided not to go there. Instead of boldly taking their seats, they only left their homes, where they did not think themselves sufficiently safe, in order to meet in a place where the conspirators would never think of looking for them.[1] There were scarcely forty members of the Right present that evening.[2] It is possible that the absence of the principal Girondist members may have baffled Varlet's and Fournier's plans, but in addition to the fact of there being nothing heroic in this fashion of running away, I consider that it is not without its dangers. To have a chance of conquering, one must at least remain on the field of battle. Flight has never led to victory.[3]

---

[1] 'Mémoires de Louvet,' p. 252.   [2] 'Mémoires de Meillan,' p. 22.

[3] Mortimer-Ternaux has devoted a whole chapter (xxix., pp. 171-244), in the sixth volume of his excellent 'Histoire de la Terreur,' to the conspiracy of March 10, which he everywhere calls the conspiracy of *March 9*, giving the events which took place during the night between the 10th and 11th as having happened on the previous night. Contemporary documents, and more especially the newspapers of the day, leave no doubt as to the error into which Mortimer-Ternaux, following M. de Barante, has fallen ('Histoire de la Convention Nationale,' tome ii., pp. 420-424). Louis Blanc has not made this mistake, but he has thought fit, in view of the failure of the conspiracy, to impute the whole plot to the tactics of the aristocracy and the Royalists (tome viii., l. ix., ch. ii., 'Les Faux-Tribuns'). It is difficult to say what to admire most in Louis Blanc—his talents, his credulity, or his audacity.

Saturday, March 16, 1793.

The authors of the plot directed against Brissot, Petion, Gensonné, Isnard, and the other deputies of the Right, are now known to be Fournier, Desfieux, Lazowski, and Varlet, whose names I have already given. All the ringleaders and their supporters are demagogues of the worst type; there is not the slightest doubt or uncertainty about this. What, then, but the cowardice to which we have so long been accustomed on the part of the Girondists can explain their desire to make the conspiracy of March 10 appear to be the work of the aristocrats and Royalists?

It was Vergniaud who, on the 13th, was deputed to speak on behalf of his party.[1] His speech was one of the most eloquent he ever delivered, and I am ready to admit that it contained some very fine passages, and was, on the whole, remarkable for its brilliancy. These are a few sentences I remember:

' If your principles are so slow of propagation, it must undoubtedly be the fault of the blood-stained veil that envelops them. Do you think that when our forefathers first fell on their knees before the sun it was obscured by clouds that foretold a coming storm? Nay; it shone forth resplendent and with undimmed glory to receive the first homage of man.'

' There was once a tyrant who had all the victims of his fury laid upon an iron bed, and who by screwing up the tall ones and stretching the short ones brought them all to the length of this terrible couch.'

' My friends, this tyrant was also a lover of equality, and it is such equality as this which is too often imposed upon us.'

In the following passage, too, there is a very striking simile, destined, perhaps, to become a prophecy:

' Therefore, citizens, there is reason to fear that the Revolution, devouring all its children like Saturn, may end by giving birth to despots!'

But though this magnificent harangue showed the orator in all the brilliancy of his eloquence, it also brought to light once more the irremediable weakness and the deplorable incapacity

---

[1] 'Mémoires de Louvet,' p. 253.

of the politician. Is it credible that after a plot woven by avowed demagogues has been unmasked—a plot that aimed at violating the sanctity of the National Convention, and at butchering Vergniaud and his friends—Vergniaud himself should, in speaking against the conspirators, denounce—the *aristocracy!*

'I crave the permission of all my colleagues,' he cries, 'to dwell upon the means employed by the aristocracy in their attempts to fetter the liberty of the public.' Most certainly has he the permission of his colleagues, especially of his colleagues of the Mountain.

'Such was,' continued the orator of the Gironde, 'the nature of the movements undertaken by the *aristocracy,* that for some time past it has been impossible to speak of law, justice, or humanity without being treated as a Royalist, a counter-Revolutionary, or a conspirator. . . . Disturbances provoked by the *aristocracy* arose in the provinces. . . . The *aristocracy,* setting no limits to their hopes, conceived the infernal idea of putting an end to the Convention. . . . It is essential that the manner in which the *aristocracy* intended to disorganize the Army, and at the same time organize the Bench and the Ministry, should be laid bare.' And he went on to show how these poor Jacobins were wickedly compromised by the *agents of England.* 'It is well known that agents from England have for some time past made their way into the political clubs of the capital. Foreigners have lately been attempting to pervert the tone of these clubs. . . . On the 9th of this month, at a meeting of the Society of Friends of Liberty, a few agents of the aristocracy, abusing the privilege that the Assembly had been weak enough to grant them, issued a formal invitation for all to take part in an armed expedition to the Convention on the morrow. . . . On the evening of the 10th numerous groups of armed men assembled in the neighbourhood of the Convention, and *Pitt's agents* were busily at work agitating among them.'

Either Vergniaud is convinced that the conspiracy of March 10 is the work of the aristocracy—and in that case he is the most blind and foolish of men, or he does not believe it—in which case, why lie? Why flee before his adversaries in this way? Is he the only man who cannot see that by sparing them in this manner, by fearing to make an open and resolute attack upon them, he is simply increasing their audacity—that audacity which is their only strength?

However, Vergniaud's speech is sufficiently damned by the applause of the Mountain. The Convention was almost unanimous in agreeing that it should be printed, and a few moments later decided that the same should be done with Marat's reply. Ashamed of sharing an honour with Monsieur Marat, the member for Bordeaux declared that his speech was an improvised one, and that it would be impossible for him to write it out from memory. This the Assembly could not contradict, although it was well aware that Vergniaud invariably prepares his speeches with great care ; he does not improvise.[1]

After the sitting, Louvet, exasperated that Vergniaud had turned his own party to ridicule by attributing the movement of March 10 to the aristocracy, to Pitt, and to England, instead of frankly and vigorously denouncing the Gray Friars and the Jacobin Clubs, its true authors, could not refrain from asking him the motive of such strange behaviour. 'I thought it best,' replied the great but weak-minded orator, 'to denounce the conspiracy without naming the true conspirators, for fear of incensing such as are already too prone to indulge in every kind of excess.'[2] It is not by such means as these that the Gironde will get the better of its enemies ; on the contrary, it will lose all, even its honour, by employing them.

*   *   *   *   *

Beaulieu came into my room just now, and read what I had written. 'Ah!' he cried ; ' you will always be the same. You are still simple enough to be surprised that Vergniaud should impute to the aristocrats the crimes of the Jacobins. That is an old dodge of his. Do you remember the pillage that went on in Paris in September after the massacres in the prisons ? Thieves adorned with the municipal sash entered private houses

---

[1] 'Vergniaud was, perhaps, the most eloquent speaker in the Assembly. He did not improvise like Guadet, but his prepared speeches, strong in logic, full of warmth and colour, brilliant in their rhetorical beauty, and strengthened by the orator's noble delivery, gave much pleasure, even when afterwards read.'—Mme. Roland, ' Mémoires,' p. 317.

[2] ' Mémoires de Louvet,' p. 253.

under the pretext of affixing seals, and laid their hands upon whatever they could get. Others stopped the passers-by in the streets and squares in broad daylight, relieving men of their buckles, their watches and chains, and women of their ear-rings, necklaces, rings, and other jewellery. The prisons, emptied in the manner that you remember, were again filled by the issue of innumerable warrants. The meetings of the Commune and the electoral body re-echoed with threats against the rich and denunciations against the deputies. Marat's journal, posted up all over the walls, held up Dumouriez, Roland, Petion and all the Brissotin members to popular execration.

'That was the moment when Cambon—who was not yet of the Mountain—said in the Legislative Assembly: "It is printed, published and proclaimed to-day that 400 deputies are traitors." The Conseil-Général of the commune of Amiens informed the Assembly that it had received a circular bearing the signature of Danton, Minister of Justice, and emanating from the Vigi-lance Committee of the Commune, inviting the departments to massacre all prisoners and traitors. The prisoners of Sainte-Pélagie addressed a petition to the Legislative Assembly, begging it to watch over their safety and to prevent them from being butchered.

'This was the state of things when Vergniaud, speaking in the name of the Special Commission, as, three days ago, he spoke in the name of his whole party, declared that the excesses com-plained of were committed, not by the satellites of the Commune, but by the satellites of Coblentz. I still remember this passage in his speech: "If the people only were to be feared, we could hope for better things, for the people is just and abhors crime. But we have satellites from Coblentz here—ruffians who are paid to sow discord, spread terror, and precipitate us into anarchy." [1]

'Do you know,' continued Beaulieu, 'that if this Revolution were not so horrible it would be highly amusing. What an end-less and varied succession of dramatic scenes we have witnessed since the opening of the States-General at Versailles, on May 5, 1789! What royal tragedies following upon civic dramas!

---

[1] 'Histoire de la Révolution,' by 'Two Friends of Liberty,' tome ix., p. 373.

And what comedies interlarded between drama and tragedy! In this new theatre the actors have not an hour's rest; they pace the stage night and day, and the spectators—when neither imprisoned nor robbed nor killed—have really no time to feel bored. What, too, can be more interesting than to compare March 10, 1793, when Brissot, Vergniaud, Isnard, and their colleagues of the Right, had such a narrow escape, with that other March 10 last year, when Brissot, Vergniaud, Isnard, and their colleagues of the Left, were looked upon as heroes?'

With these words, Beaulieu took from one of the shelves of my library a volume of the *Journal Logographique*, and whilst turning over the leaves, went on :

'You surely remember that sitting of the Legislative Assembly. Brissot demands the impeachment of M. de Lessart, Minister for Foreign Affairs. In vain do Becquey, Boulanger and Jaucourt urge that Lessart should not be condemned without having been heard, or even summoned to defend himself. Isnard, Guadet and Gensonné are for passing an immediate sentence, fearing that their prey may escape them. Vergniaud is the most eager of all; in his speech, as eloquent as ever, but even more impassioned than eloquent, he passes from the Minister to the King, and holds up Louis XVI. to the blind fury of the mob. Listen to this passage :

'"From this tribune I can see the windows of the palace in which the counter-Revolution is being prepared, in which schemes are being concocted to plunge us once more into the horrors of slavery. . . . The day has come when you can at length put an end to such audacity and insolence, and confound the conspirators. Terror has often issued, in the name of despotism, from that ancient palace ; let it return thither to-day in the name of the law. Let it penetrate to the heart of every dweller there, making them feel that the law knows no distinction, and that not a single head convicted of crime will escape its avenging arm."[1]

'Exactly a year has passed, and now it is Brissot's turn to be impeached, whilst Isnard, Guadet and Gensonné are accused of

---

[1] *Journal Logographique*, edited by Le Hodey ; 'Première Législature,' tome xiii., p. 94, sitting of March 10, 1792.

treason; it is Vergniaud's turn to hear these words hurled at him by Varlet from the tribune of the Jacobin Club:

'"From this tribune I can see the windows of the hall in which the counter - Revolution is being prepared, in which schemes are being concocted to plunge us once more into the horrors of slavery. . . . Let those who sit there be told that the people knows no distinction, and that not a single head convicted of crime will escape its avenging arm."

'The *Man of the* 10*th of March* is, as you are aware, the name given to Brissot by François de Pange. You have not forgotten his eloquent article in the *Journal de Paris*, which ended with these words: "I no longer hold you back, Man of the 10th of March—take your place in the tribune."[1] Like Brissot, Vergniaud, too, has deserved the appellation of the Man of the 10th of March. This date was that of their crime; it will also be that of their punishment. On Sunday last Varlet, Fournier, Desfieux and the ruffians who follow them, only tried their strength. In a few weeks' time the blow will be successfully struck. June 20 was the prelude to the Tenth of August; March 10 will be followed, sooner perhaps than people think, by another date that will bring with it the fall of the Girondists, as the Tenth of August brought the fall of the Monarchy.'

[1] *Journal de Paris*, seventy-fifth supplement, May 25, 1792. The article is entitled 'A. J. P. Brissot ascending the Tribune to denounce the Austrian Committee' ('Œuvres de François de Pange,' collected and edited by L. Becq de Fouquières, 1872, p. 201).

CHAPTER LIX.

Monday, March 18, 1793.

THE *Feuille du Matin* made its reappearance a few weeks ago, and I cannot help admiring the courage, or rather the heroism, with which the editor of this little paper attacks the Revolutionaries and defends the prisoners in the Temple. He, however, knows from experience that the liberty of the Press was abrogated on the Tenth of August; that is to say, immediately upon the fall of the *Tyrant.* The *Feuille du Jour,* founded by him on January 1, 1791, was suppressed on the evening of the Tenth of August, its offices being sacked and its presses broken, to the great satisfaction of the *Chronique de Paris* and the *Courrier des Départements*—which have since, in their turn, received the visit of the *people*.[1] As soon as he was able to do so, the editor of the *Feuille du Jour* started another paper, calling it the *Feuille du Matin,* or *Bulletin de Paris.*

The first number appeared on November 24, 1792, but at the end of a month the paper was obliged to stop on account of the incessant persecution to which it was subjected by the Commune. This forced suspension lasted from December 30, 1792, till January 27, 1793. On the 28th the brave little sheet resumed with fresh ardour its battle with the victors of the day.

---

[1] In the three days from the Tenth of August to August 13, 1792, the Patriots sacked the printing-offices of all the Royalist and Constitutional papers, *L'Ami du Roi, La Gazette Universelle, Le Mercure de France, Le Journal de la Cour et de la Ville, La Feuille du Jour, La Gazette de Paris, Les Annales Monarchiques, Le Journal de Paris,* etc. These expeditions met with the warm approval of the Girondists, and of Brissot in particular, who for three years had not ceased to declare that the liberty of the Press was inviolable and sacred.

A few quotations will give an idea of the courage shown by the editor of the *Feuille du Matin* on the occasion of the King's trial, from November 24 to December 29.

On December 13 the paper gave the following account of the appearance of Louis XVI. at the bar of the Convention :

'Louis XVI. appeared at the bar of the Convention clothed in all the dignity, nobility, and we may say majesty, of the rank he once occupied. . . . His replies were firm and touching, and made a deep impression upon the hearts of all present, while many an eye was dimmed with tears.'

On December 24 the *Feuille du Matin* published the following letter, addressed to the Convention :

'Citizen representatives, remember that Louis belongs to the whole of France. . . . If you wish to avoid a crime, and yet get a part of the nation's debt acquitted, accept the following proposal : Send this unhappy family in safety to a foreign country. You will not stain your hands in blood ; Frenchmen will not be ashamed of their country, and strangers will not blush to have relations with you. A good deed shall not remain without its reward. The nation owes me, and a hundred thousand others, 20,000 francs each ; we will all bring our receipts to the offices of the Convention, and consider ourselves happy to pay this ransom, for although you may be persuaded that the existence of the prisoners in the Temple may harm the Republic, it is still more certain that thousands of avengers will rise from their ashes.'[1]

The *Feuille du Matin* never failed to notice, in each of its numbers, the appearance of any publication favourable to the King. On December 22 we find a statement to the effect that 'the publications favourable to the cause of Louis XVI. are becoming more abundant, and are being sold on all sides. That entitled "Suite des Réflexions de M. Necker" is very well written and full of the most vigorous logic. Another, having for its title "Louis XVI. at the Bar of the Sans-Culottes," is very powerful in its affected simplicity, and well calculated to convince the class of readers to which it appeals.'

---

[1] This letter, addressed to the Convention on December 9, 1792, was dated from Chartres, and signed 'BUDAUT, *a friend of humanity.*' It was distributed gratis in Paris on Sunday, December 23.

Whilst thus boldly taking up the cause of Louis XVI., the editor of the *Feuille du Matin* did not neglect to show his contempt for the heroes of the Revolution. On December 28, for instance, he reminded his readers of the thefts committed by Citizen Westermann, one of the leaders of the rising of the Tenth of August, and a friend of Danton's, who made him an Adjutant-General. 'Westermann was accused, by the Section of the Lombards, with having stolen a lot of table silver from the restaurants where he used to dine. Rumours of this affair got about, and Westermann became quite well known for this kind of larceny. In fact, whenever any silver was missed from a restaurant, it was charged to Westermann, who generally paid up without demur. At length the matter came to a head, and when it was carried to the Assembly, Chabot declared that this peccadillo was entirely effaced by Westermann's well-known patriotism.'[1]

Of Danton himself, the *Feuille du Matin* of December 6 told the following bold but witty story :

' " What has *not* been said of me ?" asked Danton one day in speaking of the heap of matter published about him since the Revolution. "That you are an honest man," coldly replied Mme. C——, well known for her smart and anti-Republican repartees.'

---

[1] Chabot, an ex-Capuchin monk, was member for Loir-et-Cher in the Legislative Assembly and in the Convention. He was guillotined on April 5, 1794, with Westermann, Danton, and Camille Desmoulins. It was on December 23, 1792, that a deputation from the Section of the Lombards visited the Convention and denounced Westermann as a thief, accusing him of having, in 1789, stolen table silver from a restaurant. This action on the part of the Lombard section was not due to a desire to bring a thief to justice, but arose from the necessity of answering in some way the accusation of cowardice brought by Westermann against the Lombard battalion of volunteers. Jules Claretie ('Étude sur Camille Desmoulins et les Dantonistes,' 1875) is therefore mistaken in saying 'that Danton and his friends were ignorant of Westermann's antecedents.' Claretie is obliged to admit that theft had become a habit with Danton's friend. Arrested a first time in March, 1775, for stealing clothes and silver, and again in January, 1776, Westermann was taken up for the third time in September, 1786, for having stolen some table silver from a restaurant in the Rue des Poulies. The papers relating to these charges all exist in the Archives Nationales. This thief was successively appointed a municipal officer, an Adjutant-General, a Commissioner of the Executive Power, and a Général de Brigade.

By the side of this story I find another concerning the Girondists, equally well worth quoting. After having roused the
people to rebellion, and aided it in perpetrating its worst
excesses, Brissot and the Girondists, seeing themselves threatened
in their turn, attempted to stop the movement to which they
had themselves given the impetus. Their tardy and useless
efforts inspired the *Feuille du Matin* with the following reflection :

'The Brissots, Petions and Guadets struggling with the
Jacobins resemble the Egyptian magicians who could turn their
rods into serpents, but were unable to turn the serpents back
into rods.'[1]

A few extracts from the numbers that have appeared since
January 28 will prove that the persecution to which the *Feuille
du Matin* has been subjected has not succeeded in intimidating
the brave man who edits it :

February 1, 1793.—'Epitaph for the tomb of a Great Personage who died in January :

> ' "Here lie Virtue, Honour and Innocence,
>   And all the Happiness of France." '

February 5.—' A young National Guard, named Delrive, who
was on duty at the execution of Louis XVI., died on Friday
(February 1) in fearful convulsions, brought on by the shock
that the terrible spectacle had given him.'

February 8.—' A lady begs to publish the following epitaph,
which we believe to be that of Charles I. :

> ' "Here lies one who, in spite of his good deeds,
>   Was sacrificed by his own subjects,
>   And who by his unparalleled courage
>   Turned his scaffold into a throne of glory.' "

February 9.—' Epitaph to be applied by our readers :

> ' "Here lies one who gave life to Liberty, and whom Liberty gave
> up to death.' "

Same date.—' Lines to be written beneath a portrait :

> " ' Faithful to virtue and the honour of my throne, I desired naught
> but the happiness of the people I loved ; but they, basely yielding
> to a wicked faction, gave up my life to the headsman's blade.' "

---

[1] *La Feuille du Matin*, December 18, 1792.

On February 13 the *Feuille du Matin* published the King's will, put into verse. On the same day the Girondist Dulaure, member for Puy-de-Dôme, and one of those who condemned Louis XVI., wrote in his paper, the *Thermomètre du Jour*, a few details concerning the King's execution, which he mendaciously and impudently puts into the mouth of the executioner himself. According to Dulaure, who is not above insulting those he murders, the remarkable coolness shown by Louis XVI. was due only to the *copious* breakfast he had made, and to his firm belief that he was to be reprieved at the last moment. Sanson, however, told the real truth in a letter of peculiar eloquence, almost echoing those immortal words of the Roman centurion: '*Vere hic homo erat justus !*' It ends with the following lines :

'To be faithful to truth, he bore it all with a coolness and firmness that astonished us. I am convinced that he owed this firmness to his religious principles, with which no one was more thoroughly imbued than he. You may rest assured, citizen, that this is the strict truth.'[1]

Can it be possible that honesty, truth and justice, driven from the Convention and banished from the Republic, have sought refuge in the executioner's breast? They are also still to be found, thank God! in the hearts of a few honest men, foremost amongst whom I place the editor of the *Feuille du Matin*. He has prefaced Sanson's letter with the following lines: 'No creature with any feeling will read this document without a shudder or a tear ; it has, however, been necessary to publish it in order to silence those calumniators who attempt to blacken, even after his death, this unfortunate Monarch.'

Here, again, are two further extracts :

February 26.—'At the moment of writing, bread is very scarce in Paris, and there is none to be had at the bakers'. We should be very sorry to frighten the people, and still more to accuse anyone living of having brought about this real or apparent famine, but can we not at least charge the *dead* with it ?'

[1] Sanson's letter was reproduced *in extenso* by M. de Beauchesne in his splendid work on Louis XVII., tome i., p. 514. The original of this letter was handed by Dulaure to M. Tastu, the printer, and came into the possession of M. Aimé-Martin. It is now to be found in the Bibliothèque Nationale.

After having related how, in Egypt, the actions of a dead King used to be very carefully examined in the presence of certain judges, so that it might be equitably determined what was due to his memory, the *Feuille du Matin*, in its number of March 8, adds:

'O thou too compliant King! Thou couldst with impunity have sat upon the throne of Sesostris and of Seti. Thy adored memory would have had naught to fear from the severity with which the Kings were judged after death. The austere Necrologer of Memphis could only have reproached you with your excessive kindness!'

The Patriots who sacked the printing-offices of the *Feuille du Jour* on the Tenth of August know very well that the *Feuille du Matin* has exactly the same editor, and that this editor is Germain Parisau, who made a name before the Revolution by several pieces performed with success at the Italiens and the Comédie Française.[1] He is therefore one of those, I am afraid, who some day or other will be dragged before the criminal court which the Convention has just established. His wit being only equalled by his courage, he is likely to go on writing verses upon his executioners until he reaches the scaffold stair. His collaborators in editing the *Feuille du Jour* were Desprès[2] and the Vicomte de Ségur.[3] It was Desprès, with his delicate wit and ready pen, who furnished the reports of the sittings of the

---

[1] Pierre Germain Parisau was born at Besançon in 1753. His principal pieces are 'Julien et Colette,' 'Le Ruban,' and 'La Veuve de Cancale,' performed at the Théâtre des Italiens; while 'Le Prix Académique,' a comedy in one act and in verse, was performed at the Comédie Française on August 28, 1787.

[2] Desprès (1752—1832), invited by Fontanes to take a seat on the Conseil de l'Université, was a writer of most varied knowledge and of correct, and even elegant, taste. He published a translation of Horace, together with M. Campenon, and also one of 'Velleius Paterculus.' See the notice which M. Royer, of the Académie Française, wrote of him in the *Gazette de France* on March 17, 1832.

[3] The Viscomte de Ségur (1756—1805), Maréchal de Camp in 1788, had already retired from the army at the beginning of the Revolution. He was successful in writing novels, comedies, and songs. When his brother, who had been the French Ambassador to Russia under Louis XVI., became Napoleon's Master of the Ceremonies, the Viscount would frequently sign himself *Ségur sans cérémonies*.

National Assembly and of the Jacobin Club. I believe that both Desprès and Ségur help him in the *Feuille du Matin*.[1]

On March 30, 1793, Parisau was once more obliged to interrupt the publication of his paper until April 23, when it again appeared, but only to come to a definite cessation six days later. Parisau, brought before the Revolutionary Tribunal, was guillotined on July 10, 1794. Desprès and Ségur were both arrested in October, 1793. The former remained for nine months in the prison of Saint-Lazare, where he occupied the same room as André Chénier. The Viscount published an account of his captivity under the following title : 'My Prison, from the 22nd of Vendémiaire to the 10th of Thermidor. By Citizen Alexandre Ségur, the Younger.' 30 pp.

[1] Allissan de Chazet, tome iii.

CHAPTER LX

'LES NOCES DE FIGARO.'

Saturday, March 23, 1793.

YESTERDAY evening, on our way to hear Mozart's opera performed at the Académie Nationale de Musique, Suard,[1] a licenser of plays under the old *régime*, and now director of the *Nouvelles Politiques*, said to me, 'At that time—I am speaking of 1778—there were two parties, as at the present day—two burning, irreconcilable parties, pushing their passions even to fanaticism. On the one side were the Piccinists, headed by Marmontel, D'Alembert, Diderot, the Chevalier de Chastellux, Baron Grimm, Ginguené, La Harpe, the Abbé de Canaie and our excellent friend the Abbé Morellet; on the other side were the Gluckists, commanded by the Abbé Arnaud and the Bailli du Rollet. I was one of Gluck's partisans, and you may perhaps have read the "Lettres de l'Anonyme de Vaugirard," in which I defended the author of "Armide" and "Iphigénie." What fine quarrels and what warm evenings we had! I still remember our humiliation and despair when, on adding up the receipts of the first twelve performances of "Roland"[2] in order to compare the total

---

[1] Jean Baptiste Antoine Suard, born at Besançon on January 16, 1733, was received into the Académie Française in 1774; whilst a licenser of plays, he had opposed the performance of the 'Mariage de Figaro.' In 1791 he was on the staff of the Royalist paper *Les Indépendants*, and became the chief editor of the *Nouvelles Politiques* in 1792. Proscribed on the 18th of Fructidor (November 4, 1797), he was obliged to leave France under the Consulate, but returned to take part in editing the *Publiciste*, and was appointed permanent Secretary to the Académie on February 20, 1803. At the Restoration he received the title of Honorary Censor, and died on January 20, 1817. His wife, a sister of Panckoucke, the printer, wrote several works. Her *salon*, one of the most frequented in Paris, was in the eighteenth century the rendezvous of the Encyclopædists. See Garat, 'Mémoires Historiques sur Suard,' 1820, 2 vols.

[2] Music by Piccini, words by Marmontel; first performed on January 27, 1798.

with that of the first twelve of "Iphigénie en Aulide," the
Piccinists found a balance of 87 francs in favour of "Roland."[1]
On that day, alas! my friends and I hung our heads, and more
than one of us gloomily repeated:

> '"Eurydice has gone from me,
> My unhappiness is great."[2]

'Alas! my dear friend, there are no more Gluckists nor
Piccinists; there are Rolandists and Robespierrists. The field
of battle has been transferred from the Opera to the Riding-
School. The leaders are no longer called Marmontel, Chastellux,
Arnaud and Rollet, but Brissot, Danton, Buzot, Marat and
Robespierre. Let us try to forget for a few hours, if possible, the
struggle that is going on; let us close our ears to their cries of
vengeance and death; let us seek in the divine art of Gluck and
Piccini oblivion of our present evils and the shadow of our lost
happiness.'

We had now reached the theatre,[3] and at once took our seats.
Suard, whom the sight alone of the house, associated in his mind
with so many happy reminiscences, had made at least ten years
younger, turned to me with a smile, saying: 'I am longing for
the curtain to go up, for I am impatient to hear whether
Mozart's opera can really, as has been asserted, compete with the
masterpieces of Gluck, not only in grandeur of conception, but
also in the charm and beauty of its melodies. The first performance was certainly not very successful,[4] but that does not

---

[1] 'L'Académie Impériale de Musique,' by Castil-Blaze, tome i., p. 373.

[2] These were the most famous lines in Gluck's opera of 'Orpheus,'
first performed on August 2, 1774.

[3] In 1793 the Opera was located in a building in the Boulevard Saint-
Martin, erected, under the direction of Alexandre Lenoir, in sixty-five
days after the fire of June 8, 1781, when the theatre in the Palais Royal,
occupied by the actors of the Académie Royale since 1770, had been
destroyed. On July 26, 1794, the Opera left the Boulevard Saint-Martin,
and the building, after an existence of ninety years, disappeared during
the conflagrations of May, 1871.

[4] The first performance of the 'Noces de Figaro' took place at the
Académie de Musique on March 20, 1793. The bills announced the
'Mariage de Figaro,' OPÉRA-COMIQUE, in five acts. It was no doubt this
appellation of opéra-comique that led De Loménie into the strange error
to be found in tome ii. of his 'Beaumarchais,' p. 457. 'In 1793,' he says,
'the "Mariage de Figaro" was produced in the form of a comic opera,

count for much. The Germans have always been pretty good judges of music. What would my good friend Marmontel say if he heard me give utterance to such a heresy? But he is in the heart of Normandy, and cannot hear me.[1] Well, when the " Noces de Figaro " were first performed at Vienna in 1786, the success was immense. Six of the airs had to be repeated, and one of the duets received a triple encore. At Prague, Mozart enjoyed a still greater triumph, all the airs, with the exception of one or two, having to be repeated amidst intense enthusiasm.'

Suard spoke with great ardour, his looks and gestures betraying his extraordinary excitement. ' The house is far from full,' he went on, shaking his head, ' and the audience does not seem to be a very select one. And yet it is Friday to-day. Formerly, you know, it was considered the proper thing to go to the Opera on Fridays only ;[2] the whole Court used to come from Versailles in order to be present at the performances of the Académie, whilst it was strict etiquette for newly-married couples to make their first appearance in public at the Opera on the first Friday after their marriage. Friday is now like any other day ; it is no more than Sunday or Tuesday—such is equality.'

Suard's face grew darker, as with a melancholy air he glanced round the house, and pointed out to me the boxes that had belonged to the notabilities under the old *régime*. There was the Queen's box, the box let to the Princesse de Lamballe for 3,600 francs a year, and that for which the Duc d'Orléans, the Duc de Choiseul and Necker had paid 3,200 francs between them. There also was the stage-box, for which the Duc d'Orléans gave 7,000 francs as sole lessee. Suddenly taking me by the arm,

---

with a wretched libretto by Beaumarchais. I do not know who wrote the music.' The composer of the music was no other than Mozart !

[1] Marmontel had left Paris on August 4, 1792, and taken refuge with Gaillon in the department of the Eure (' Mémoires ' of the Abbé Morellet, tome ii., p. 401).

[2] ' "Callirhoé " is being played at the Opera, and is not a success, although it is interesting and pretty ; but it is now considered the proper thing to go to the Opera on Fridays only.'—Mdlle. Aïssé, ' Lettres.' The days set apart for operatic performances were Tuesday, Friday, and Sunday ; in winter, Thursdays only. This rule, established in 1671, was changed in 1817, when performances were given every Monday, Wednesday, and Friday (Castil-Blaze, tome ii., p. 150).

Suard exclaimed, 'Look! there is Beaumarchais.'[1] It was indeed he, and I was able to take a good look at him. He is a man about sixty years old; his hair is thin, and not yet gray; he has a large mouth, a full face and a double chin.[2] He is big and fat;[3] Figaro has put on flesh. 'I am pleased to see,' said Suard, 'that his misfortunes have not made him thin. And who is there that has lost more by the Revolution than he? How far off he is now from that April day in 1784 when the "Mariage de Figaro" was first performed! What a mad day it was! The crowd was so great that the police and the attendants were swept aside, the gates forced by the tremendous pressure upon them, and the doors broken open.[4] Three people were suffocated.[5] Starting from the lowest rung, Beaumarchais had reached the top of the ladder; both fame and riches were his, and his society was courted by the finest lords and ladies in the land. But these lords and ladies, while lionizing the watch-maker's son, did not fail to remind him occasionally that they did not consider him their equal. 'Then let there be a Revolution which shall teach everyone his place—the front rank for men of wit and talent; the backmost one for those who have nothing but their birth to boast of.' The wish was realized; the Revolution came and swept away the Princes, Dukes and Counts who looked askance upon the author of the "Mariage de Figaro." But after that, with incontestable logic, the Revolution recognised a new aristocracy in the artist's talent, and saw in his fortune an outrage upon equality. Beaumarchais had held up the Comte Almaviva to the people's hatred and contempt; he is now denounced in his turn by Basilio. Arrested and taken to

---

[1] 'I went on the quiet to hear the second performance of the "Mariage."' The above occurs in a letter from Beaumarchais to the actors of the opera, published in 'Beaumarchais et son Temps,' by Louis de Loménie, tome ii., p. 585.

[2] This description is taken from a passport dated September 18, 1792, and reproduced in the sixth and last epoch of the work entitled 'Beaumarchais à Lecointre, son Dénonciateur.'

[3] In some verses written in 1796 Beaumarchais described himself as

'An old man, big, fat, and gray.'

[4] Bachaumont, 'Mémoires Secrets.'

[5] La Harpe, 'Correspondance Littéraire adressée au Grand-Duc de Russie,' tome iv.

the Abbaye, he manages to escape four days before the September massacres; but three months later a fresh charge is brought against him, and for the second or the third time the seals are placed upon his fine house on the Boulevard, the Maison d'Albe. He is forced to write some more "Memoirs." Have you read those which he has published under this title, "Beaumarchais to Lecointre, his Denouncer"? They are divided into six periods, and make a pretty big volume.[1] It seems as if Citizen Lecointre[2] does not furnish so much material for wit as Councillor Goezman, and that it is easier to make jokes about the Maupeon Assembly than about the National Convention. This much is certain, that in the whole of the six periods and 300 pages of Beaumarchais's book there is not a single word that is funny. On the other hand, there is more than one page that is really courageous. You remember this sentence from the famous monologue in "Figaro": "I have had to expend more wit and ingenuity in getting a bare subsistence than has been expended during the last hundred years in governing the whole of Spain." Well, Beaumarchais has had to expend more wit and ingenuity in saving his life and his fortune during the past two years than it once cost him to earn his millions and to write the "Mariage de Figaro." But here am I, too, indulging in a monologue as long as that of the famous barber—though a deal less witty. You will excuse me, will you not?' asked Suard, adding, as the first notes of the overture were heard, 'Mozart will make you forget my prosiness.'

When the curtain rose, and the opera commenced with a scene entirely spoken, the audience seemed somewhat disconcerted. It had come to hear Mozart's music, and was treated to the prose of Beaumarchais. It was the first time that a comic opera, that is, an opera both spoken and sung, had been performed at this

[1] The 'Mémoire' written by Beaumarchais in reply to Lecointre's denunciation appeared in March, 1793. It is signed and dated as follows:

'The ever-persecuted citizen,
'CARON-BEAUMARCHAIS.

'Written for my judges in Paris this 6th day of March, 1793, the second year of the Republic.'

[2] Laurent Lecointre, member for Seine-et-Oise.

theatre. The innovation does not seem to have been a very happy one, and I doubt whether it will be a success. In any case, the 'Mariage de Figaro' is a very bad choice for an experiment of that kind. A shorter piece should have been chosen ; Beaumarchais' five acts are extremely long ones, and what must they be when we add Mozart's music ? There is no doubt that the length of the opera was the real cause of its failure when first performed ; and it met with no better success last night. The artists, too, not being accustomed to *speak* in prose, performed their task in a very unsatisfactory manner, and suffered by the comparison that everyone in the audience was involuntarily making between them and the actors who had played the same parts at the Comédie Française. How could poor Laijs, for instance, who makes such a heavy Figaro, compare with Dazincourt ? Adrien takes the part of Almaviva ; he acts with warmth and intelligence, but however good he may be, what a difference there is between him and the incomparable Molé ! Neither can Mme. Ponthieu, in the *rôle* of the Countess, make us forget Mdlle. Sainval. It is the same with all the others. Mdlle. Gavaudan, who plays the part of Suzanne so charmingly, is perhaps the only one who is equal to her task. She had brought Beaumarchais luck once before. It was she who created the part of Spinette in 'Tarare,'[1] and in that character she gave proofs of so much grace, talent and wit, that the name of Spinette has stuck to her. But now, after the prose of Beaumarchais, we get the singing. Mozart's music is written on the Italian libretto by Lorenzo da Ponte, translated into French verse by Notaris. The verse is ridiculous, but the composer has hidden its ugliness under a veil of gold.

By the time that the curtain had fallen on the first act, I was quite enchanted.

'There is certainly some original phrasing,' said Suard, ' and some exquisite melodies of a very easy flow. But it is not my old " Mariage de Figaro." The wand of the musician—of the magician, if you like—in touching the castle of Aguas-Frescas, has completely changed all the inhabitants. Into this bright

---

[1] 'Tarare,' words by Beaumarchais, music by Salieri, was performed for the first time by the Académie Royale de Musique on June 8, 1787.

and simple dwelling, the abode of light-heartedness and mirth, he introduces love, passion and melancholy. Beaumarchais had given Cherubino senses only; Mozart gives him a soul. When the little page sings, you can hear his heart beat, and you feel that his love is deep and sincere. Mozart, too, presents Figaro's jealousy in quite a different light. In the comedy, Figaro loves Suzanne—for the moment. In the opera, he loves her for good. And what a change we see in our friend Bartholo! What a contrast between the pleasantries of the *immortal doctor* and these proud tones, quivering with hatred and revenge! As for the air beginning "*Mon enfant, plus de tendres fleurettes*," I admit that it is fully in keeping with the sense of the original lines, and in its irresistible effect we see that Mozart, when he chooses, can put as much wit and gaiety into his music as Beaumarchais puts into his words.'

The second act strengthened M. Suard in his opinion. Cherubino's song, '*Mon cœur soupire*,' is full of delicate charms, and instead of the somewhat harsh piping of Beaumarchais, we seem to hear the magic flute of Racine under the chestnuts in the park. This act is a good deal too long, and the fault is aggravated by the drawling delivery of the artists. It is the same with the airs; they are all sung *rallentando* instead of in their proper time. The *finale*, however, compensated us with its simple but charming vigour. It is, indeed, a master-piece in itself, and made Suard feel quite uncomfortable. ' No doubt about it!' he cried; 'that leaves Nicolo Piccini far behind! You will find nothing in "Atys" or "Roland" equal to that! Piccini does not reach up to Mozart's ankle!' ' And Gluck?' I asked, with a smile. 'Gluck, sir, has written "Alceste," "Orpheus" and "Iphigénie in Aulis." . . . But here comes the third act.'

In this act, Comte Almaviva is almost constantly on the stage, but I think Beaumarchais must have had some trouble in recognising him. In the play, his love is but a fancy; in the opera it is a passion, full of proud disdain and bitter sadness.

In the fourth and fifth acts, Beaumarchais has been almost entirely set aside, and Mozart reigns supreme. In fact, in the whole of this beautiful production, the musician has proved himself superior to the comic author. Mozart has managed to be as spiritual, as bright and as witty, as Beaumarchais, but he has set this wit and gaiety in a magnificent framework produced by his genius. 'Figaro'—Mozart's 'Figaro'—is henceforth immortal!

All was over, and the audience dispersed. I was still under the influence of the charm, when Suard's voice recalled me to reality. 'Well,' he said, 'if there are any Gluckists and Piccinists left, the best thing they can do is to shake hands and to admit that the god of harmony is neither Piccini nor, alas! Gluck, but Mozart!'

We returned by the boulevards. The evening papers were being sold, and I bought the *Gazette Nationale*. On reaching home, I commenced to read the report of the proceedings in the Convention, and came upon a speech by one Marat. . . . Unhappy me! In listening to the melodies of the divine Mozart, I had forgotten him whom Camille Desmoulins calls the *divine* Marat!

END OF VOL. I.

BILLING AND SONS, PRINTERS, GUILDFORD.